Jesus Was Not
a Trinitarian

Jesus Was Not a Trinitarian

A Call to Return to the Creed of Jesus

Sir Anthony F. Buzzard

Restoration Fellowship
Morrow, GA

ISBN 978-09673249-7-5

To Barbara my wife whose zeal for a biblical creed is an inspiration. She sees the point of sounding like Jesus when talking about God, the God of Israel.

Contents

Foreword

Christianity is often touted as one of the world's three great monotheistic religions, on a par with Judaism and Islam. This is not a correct assessment. And neither Judaism nor Islam will concede to Christianity the right to the title of monotheistic religion. For Christianity's more than two billion members believe in the doctrine of the Trinity, which says that God is three. And this is a creed which neither Judaism nor Islam consider monotheistic. As the author of this book argues, Trinitarianism is a belief which is not solidly grounded in either the Hebrew Bible or the New Testament. It became official doctrine only in the fourth century after the councils of Nicea (325 AD) and Constantinople (381 AD) in Asia Minor or modern-day Turkey.

This is a rare book. There are not many, in fact hardly any, like it in the religious marketplace. Why? Because it tackles the doctrine of the Trinity from a non-Trinitarian perspective, a perspective which is condemned by Christianity's four major divisions — Roman Catholicism, Greek Orthodoxy, Oriental Orthodoxy and Protestantism.

This is a bold book. In another day the author would have been anathematized and burned at the stake or hanged for this book. Michael Servetus paid with his life for his *De Erroribus Trinitatis* under John Calvin in the Reformation. And even in today's freer atmosphere which allows publication of such a work, a declaration of non-belief in the Trinity leads to instant ostracization and to immediate classification of heresy and heretic. The author has shown himself willing to pay this price.

This is a learned book. Written by a master spirit (so John Milton calls authors), it is an invaluable resource for those who have escaped the trap of Trinitarianism with its concomitant doctrines of the preexistence of Christ, the "eternal generation" of the Son, the Incarnation and the hypostatic union. Its wide range of both scriptural and scholarly quotations solidly buttresses and confirms the unitarian viewpoint. This is a cry for a return to the teaching of Jesus.

This book is a sequel to an earlier work, *The Doctrine of the Trinity: Christianity's Self-Inflicted Wound*, co-authored with Charles Hunting in 1998. In *Jesus Was Not a Trinitarian*, the author returns to the topic with renewed vigor and greater insight, the fruit of much study and debates with opponents around the country. The author has also written a monthly newsletter, *Focus on the Kingdom*, since 1998, which has kept the issue ever fresh before his mind. Both books are marked by an irenic tone, in which the author has refrained from hurling thunderbolts in the manner of the Reformationists.

One measure of the success of a book is its circulation. I wish this much-needed book a wide one. There are over two billion Christians alone who need to be evangelized and to be taught the Shema of Israel (Mark 12:29), to which Jesus himself subscribed, and John 17:3 ("This is eternal life, that they may know you, the only true God..."), which Jesus prayed.

Clifford Durousseau
M.A.Th., Ph.D. (Cand.)
Istanbul, Turkey

Acknowledgments

My sincerest thanks go to so many who have offered constantly wise advice and constructive criticism. Their enthusiasm for the great truths of Scripture and for the life, death and teaching of Messiah Jesus carries them forward on a wave of excitement about that very Jewish Jesus who recited Israel's non-Trinitarian creed. I remember with special gratitude Helen, Delroy, Alex, Ray, Dan, Charles, Greg, Jack, Clifford, Steven, Martha, and Sarah, my daughter and editor without whose skills and patience none of my books would have seen the light of day.

Introduction

"We must remind ourselves that Christian theology does not believe God to be a person. It believes Him to be such that in Him a trinity of persons is consistent with a unity of Deity."[1]

"Interpreters of Christian persuasion have ordinarily not been especially interested in what Jesus intended and did in his own lifetime."[2]

"To Jesus, as to His people through many centuries, God was one. *He did not modify this ancient belief.*"[3]

This book is about defining who the God of the Bible is. Such a project might seem to be a rather grandiose undertaking. But my goal is narrowly defined. I intend to search out the meaning of "the one God" as the object of our Christian worship. What does the Bible mean by "one God"? What is meant by biblical monotheism? Different, disagreeing groups of Christian believers all claim to be monotheists. Muslims claim to be monotheists. Jews also make that fundamental claim. The great and pressing issue is: *How does Jesus and how does the Bible define the idea of "one God"?*

My investigation involves a comparison between the creed of the historical Jesus and the New Testament writers, and the creed[4] as it has come to be almost universally understood by mainstream churchgoers, assembling with the claim to be followers of Jesus. In these chapters I return often to the central creed of Jesus, the Shema

---

[1]C.S. Lewis, *Christian Reflections*, Eerdmans, 1995, 79.
[2]Richard Hiers, *Jesus and the Future*, John Knox Press, 1981, 1.
[3]"God," *A Dictionary of Christ and the Gospels,* Charles Scribner's Sons, 1906, 1:650, emphasis added.
[4]The creed known to many churchgoers is the one decided on at the Council of Nicea in 325 AD, some three hundred years after the ministry of Jesus.

(Deut. 6:4; Mark 12:29). I carry on a running dialogue with many distinguished scholars who have commented on Jesus and his strict monotheism. I propose that a vast amount of Christian literature confirms my thesis that Jesus insisted on this unitarian creed. In that sense, current practice and belief in churches is adversely judged by its own literature and would be criticized likewise by Jesus. I propose also that replacing the creed of Jesus with a Trinitarian definition of God is not a valid "transition within biblical monotheism."[5] I am not persuaded, and neither are millions of others,[6] that Trinitarianism is biblical monotheism at all.

In later chapters I have tried to expose the fallacious arguments often called upon by "orthodox" apologists to support the mistaken notion that Jesus and the Apostles believed that God was three in one. I think that the public has been severely misled because it has not had the critical ability to see through such arguments.

I do not think that the New Testament ever reports Jesus as claiming to *be* the God of Israel, the one true God. Why then should Jesus' followers adhere to a belief which Jesus gave no indication of holding? If being a Christian means following Jesus Christ, then a Christian's first aim would be to share the same view of God as expressed by Jesus. The creed of Jesus would automatically be the creed of his followers. Jesus, as the scriptural records reveal, made it perfectly clear who he believed God to be. But churches have done much to make Jesus' perception of the identity of God at least bewildering if not incomprehensible.

I believe that Christians ought to be deeply concerned that their definition of God lines up with the definition of God given us by Jesus. I am not speaking here about the *qualities* or attributes of God, that He is love and so on. I am investigating this one question: How many is God? I am inquiring of the New Testament whether Jesus ever gave his approval to the idea that God is three Persons[7]

---

[5]Harold O.J. Brown, *Heresies: Heresy and Orthodoxy in the History of the Church*, Hendrickson, 1998, 431.
[6]I am thinking here especially of Jews and Muslims, in addition to a large number of Christian "dissidents" over the centuries. Jews are convinced that their Hebrew Bible excludes the Trinity and the Muslim Koran warns its adherents against compromising the oneness of God in any way.
[7]It is well known that expert Trinitarians do not like the word "Person," because it does not reflect the ancient Greek term used in the formation of

(Trinitarianism). Or did he teach that God is one Person (unitarianism)?[8] There is a profound difference between a one-Person God and a tri-Personal God.

Our decision as to which of these "Gods" is the God of the Bible will dramatically affect also our understanding of who Jesus is. We need to know first how Jesus defined God. If God is one Person, then the next issue is obviously, Who is Jesus? These are central questions about how the universe is now ordered. We need clear and solid scriptural answers. These are profoundly practical questions. We need clarity on these issues so that we can approach God "in spirit and truth," as Jesus said we must (John 4:24).

Bible readers instinctively gravitate to the opening words of John's gospel to provide them with a concept of a second Person in a divine Trinity. My thesis is that they misread John in that passage, and that John is being mishandled and made to contradict the Hebrew Bible and the strictly unitarian view of Jesus provided by the other gospel writers. The imposition of the Trinity on the New Testament thus interferes with the intrinsic and unified view of God provided by Scripture.

Creeds provide the foundational constitution of Christian churches. I propose that Jesus' creed, as recorded in the New Testament, is not that of the churches which now claim his name. The New Testament read within its own context never departed one iota from the creed propounded by Jesus as part of the greatest of all the commandments. Followers of Christ surely want to be assured that they are following Jesus at the very heart and core of faith — belief in God. But are they informed about how the creed of the church they attend came into existence, and have they made every effort to ensure that the church's creed is one which Jesus would recognize? Was Jesus a Trinitarian?

---

the creeds. However, their alternatives are very vague and indeterminate and convey no meaning at all to most churchgoers. Churchgoers hearing the word "Person" commit themselves to belief in three Persons, each of whom is God. The Hebrew *nephesh* is equivalent to "person, individual." Even God is described as being a *nephesh*, i.e, a single Individual. God speaks of "My soul" — "Myself" (Isa. 42:1). He is a single "self."

[8]The term unitarianism means simply belief that God is a single Divine Person. My use of the term should not be confused with contemporary Unitarian Universalist beliefs.

I very much doubt whether most churchgoers have given this fundamental question much thought. The traditional definition of God as "three in one" dominates the church scene as unquestioned dogma. Open discussion of the traditional creed is unusual. If however it is challenged, strenuous attempts are made by church authorities to insist on its truth. Churchgoers seem to be cowed into submission to a dogma about God. But church members have typically heard no sermons on the origin or meaning of the proposition "God is three in one." In most cases they cannot defend this concept against opposing points of view. They have simply been told to write off as "cult" anyone who questions the received definition of God. They are mostly entirely unaware of the steady stream of opposition from expert historians and Bible scholars who have objected to belief in God as one, yet inexplicably three at the same time.

I am convinced that "false belief holds the minds of men and women in bondage. Truth liberates them."[9] We cannot afford to hold mistaken beliefs, especially on such central questions about the God of the Bible and the God of Jesus. Above all, we need to be clear and confident about who God is. We all need to be sure that when we speak of God we are speaking of the same God whom Jesus called God. Above all we need as Christians to have the assurance of Jesus' approval for our creed. If we are followers of Jesus we will want to begin by assuring ourselves that we are following the creed of Jesus, confessing his definition of God. As ambassadors of Christ we need full confidence that we are taking the true God of the Bible to those many who recognize no God at all.

True views of God and Jesus are all-important for the following good reason. I quote R. Alan Cole: "To worship Christ with the wrong beliefs about Him is to worship a false Christ, by whatever name we call Him; for we, in so doing, falsely imagine Him to be other than He is, and other than He is revealed in Scripture to be."[10]

The Church as many know it has an ugly history of persecuting and even killing any who dare to question its cherished dogmas. It was precisely at the time when the Church began to identify itself with a military power, under Constantine, that it was busy setting in stone its conciliar decisions about God and Jesus and their

---

[9]F.F. Bruce, *The Gospel and Epistles of John*, Eerdmans, 1994, 196.
[10]*Mark (Tyndale New Testament Commentaries)*, Eerdmans, 1983, 199.

relationship. The institution of violence as a valid means of dealing with enemies and "heretics" seemed to go hand in hand with a policy to persecute and banish any who refused to agree with the extraordinary definition of God called the Trinity. Could there be lurking behind that very non-Jewish definition of God a loveless power by which the Church sold out to the world and lost its "resident alien" status so precious to the New Testament? Did the Church in fact ban Jesus from its midst as it insisted on a fearfully complex Greek philosophical theology which Jesus would not have recognized? Is there a lurking, latent anti-Semitic tendency in the Church's avoidance of Jesus' Jewish creed?

I am no innovator. One has only to consult the widely-read account of *The Reformation* to see that our subject has a rich history:

> Some of the radicals in the early 1530s posed even more profound questions about the Church after Constantine: they said it had radically misunderstood the nature of God...The problem lay at the heart of Christianity. It centered on the paradox that the Church in its earliest days identified the crucified man Jesus not merely as the Messiah or Christ expected by the Jews, but as God himself...So a religion which inherited a strong conviction that God was one, also talked about Him in three aspects, Father, Son and Holy Spirit. The Church spent its first four centuries arguing about how this could be. It needed to reconcile its story of a triune God made human with its Jewish heritage of monotheism and with its Greek heritage from Plato...These theological arguments, which were bitter, intricate and increasingly mixed up in power politics, culminated in decisions made during the fourth and fifth centuries at a series of councils of the Church from Nicea (325 CE) to Chalcedon (451 CE).[11]

These facts speak for themselves. The question is whether the Jewish Jesus, hero founder of apostolic Christianity, suffered an eclipse during those regrettable centuries of bitter argumentation about who God and Jesus are. Might it not be better for believers to distance themselves from that formative and quarrelsome period of history and go back to the Christian documents themselves?

---

[11]Diarmaid MacCulloch, *The Reformation*, Penguin, 2003, 184, 185.

Does the Church today simply reinforce blindly its sense of social coherence and identity, based on a definition of God which has become cherished and honored by centuries-long repetition? These questions are worthy of careful investigation by everyone claiming to love God and Jesus with all their heart and mind. To that investigation the following chapters are dedicated.

Chapter 1

Foundations for Belief in God and His Son

"Early Christianity consciously adopts from Judaism the monotheistic formula 'God is one.' According to Mark 12:29, 32, Jesus explicitly approves the Jewish monotheistic formula."[1]

"The Church cannot indefinitely continue to believe about Jesus what he did not know to be true about himself! The question of his Messianic consciousness is the most vital one the Christian faith has to face."[2]

Jesus defined God for us frequently. He defined God deliberately and simply in a famous creedal statement. Jesus habitually addressed the One God of biblical monotheism as "Father" (John 17:1 and many other texts). But are churches really listening to Jesus' definition of God, or have they abandoned his view for a traditional idea of God which Jesus would not have accepted?

Kenneth Richard Samples writes:

Specific statements in Scripture were used as creedal statements even in biblical times. For example, in the Old Testament the ancient Israelites used the Shema as a creed emphasizing their uncompromising commitment to monotheism, even though they lived surrounded by a pagan, polytheistic world. The Shema, which Jews continue to use today, consists of the prayerful reciting of Deuteronomy 6:4-

---

[1] *"Eis*, one," *Exegetical Dictionary of the New Testament,* Eerdmans, 1990, 399.
[2] J.W. Bowman, *The Intention of Jesus*, SCM Press, 1945, 108.

9. *Shema* is Hebrew for "hear," and verse four appropriately begins as follows: "Hear, O Israel: The Lord our God, the Lord is one."[3]

Jesus as the founding teacher of the Christian religion was no less insistent on the Shema as the guide to true theology and faith (Mark 12:28-34).

As a Christian I accept the foundational truths of our faith as revealed in the Scriptures, the Hebrew Bible and the Greek New Testament. I believe the Bible provides solid divine authority for the truth-claims made for the Christian faith. It is clear to me that Jesus and the Apostles viewed the Bible as divine revelation, a perennial guide to human beings struggling in an obviously fallen world. Jesus was the ultimate "Biblicist," asserting that "the Scripture cannot be broken" (John 10:35), and conducting a full-length Bible study about himself, his true identity, from the "law, prophets and writings" (Luke 24:44). My object is to follow Jesus in his description of who God is and who he, Jesus, is. After all, this is the foundation of our approach to God and worship of Him.

Paul of course was equally solid in his conviction about the inspiration of the canon of Scripture. For him God had "breathed out" the sacred writings, which consequently represented the mind or spirit of God (2 Tim. 3:16). Scripture was a divine library designed to instruct us in the will of God. Paul, as an Apostle of Jesus, claimed to be speaking under inspiration.[4] He was certainly aware of the Jewish creed of Jesus, and spoke of his own Jewishness. The God whom he,

---

[3]Kenneth Samples ("Apologetic Lessons from the Past: The Ancient Christian Creeds," www.augustinefellowship.org) reminds us of the value of creeds. But we need to be certain that they go back to Jesus himself: "The American philosopher George Santayana once proclaimed, 'Those who do not remember the past are doomed to repeat it.' Christians should especially be attentive to the important lessons from the past. For the truth-claims of Christianity (which center upon the life, death, and resurrection of Jesus Christ) stand rooted in the facts of history. Contemporary Christians can be enriched greatly by the careful study of Christendom's creeds and of the events that surrounded their formulation. The appropriate use of the creeds can and do enhance Christian education, worship, and evangelism. However, an exploration of the ancient creeds can also reveal some important apologetic lessons for twenty-first century Christians." Ibid.

[4]2 Pet. 3:16 designates the writings of Paul as Scripture.

and all the Apostles served, was the God of Israel, "the God of his and Israel's fathers" (see Acts 3:13; 5:30; 22:14; 24:14).

There is not a hint that Paul or Peter ever questioned this creed, much less abandoned it. Belief in God, as the Father of Jesus and the One God of the Bible, is part of the fixed datum of Paul's theology. For him to have altered the creed of his and Jesus' heritage would have required extensive treatment in the New Testament records, rather like the shattering new truth that Gentiles could become fully part of God's people without circumcision in the flesh, as discussed in detail at the first council of the Church in Acts 15 and in the book of Galatians.

There is not a word in the New Testament about any such revolutionary changes in the definition of God. There is nothing in the recorded ministry of Paul which points to a new definition of who the God of Israel and thus of Christians is.

I am alarmed at the hostility encountered by anyone questioning the dogma of the triune God. Instead of the Protestant principle of free and independent inquiry, there reigns a frightening atmosphere of anger and indignation that anyone might suggest that Jesus was not a Trinitarian. Have we forgotten that our Savior was a Jew? Have we taken seriously Jesus' lesson that violence is unthinkable? That reasoned persuasion is the apostolic method for teaching truth? That the use of force to compel conformity in matters of doctrine is a rejection of Christianity at its heart?

A recent experience involved me in a conversation with a Calvinist pastor. His approach to me on the question of defining God was fierce and condemning. The awful word "heretic" was used freely and the accusation was that I and my family were not Christian in any sense. We were worshipping a strange God. The discussion was a frightening reminder of the dreadful events of the sixteenth century when Protestant leader John Calvin set his heart on the destruction of a young biblical scholar, Michael Servetus, simply because the latter could not accept that God was a Trinity and objected to infant baptism. He paid with his life for these beliefs at the hands of one of the most influential of all Protestant reformers. The story is a shocking testimony to a brutal murder by burning at the stake in the name of Jesus. And Calvin died unrepentant for his part in the death of Servetus. This event ought to provoke a widespread discussion amongst churchgoers, especially those who align themselves with the name of Calvin. It is a fearful thing to be associated sympathetically with those whose absence of Christian love is so marked that they consider it right to kill theological opponents.[5]

Church history is replete with accounts of the Church venting its wrath and even exacting the death penalty from any who would question the creeds established by church councils. This appalling fact should be a matter of urgent concern amongst students of the saving teaching of Jesus. Brutality in support of a traditional doctrine is unthinkable if the mind of Jesus is to be taken as our guide.

On another occasion an organization keen to keep "heresy" at bay announced that a unitarian Bible college was a theological cult, to be avoided at all costs. I will never forget the gasps of some 400 people when the spokesman for "orthodoxy" told them that though Anthony believed Jesus was the Messiah and Son of God, and in the

---

[5]Well did the dean of Canterbury, F.W Farrar, write in 1897: "Renée, Duchess of Ferrara, daughter of Louis XII, was a thoughtful and pious princess and a warm admirer of Calvin. In a letter to the great reformer of Geneva she made the wise remark that 'David's example in hating his enemies is not applicable to us.' It might have been supposed that Calvin would at once have endorsed a sentiment which only echoed the teaching of Christ...'I say to you, love your enemies, bless those who curse you and pray for those who despitefully use you and persecute you.' But Calvin was shocked by the remark of the Duchess! He curtly and sternly answered her that 'such a gloss would upset all Scripture;' that even in his hatred David *is* an example to us, and a type of Christ; and 'should we presume to set ourselves up as superior to Christ in sweetness and humanity?' The Princess was wholly right and the theologian disastrously in the wrong. It would have been better for Calvin had he more truly understood the teaching of Christ...Had he done so, he would have been saved from the worst errors of his life — the burning of Servetus, the recommendation of persecution to the Protector Somerset and the omission to raise his voice in aid of the miserable and exiled congregation of John à Lasco. But as Grotius truly said, the Calvinists were for the most part as severe to all who differed from them as they imagined God to be severe to the greater part of the human race. And unhappily the Pilgrim Fathers and their earliest descendants imbibed these perilous errors and though they were themselves fugitives from kingly despotism and priestly intolerance, they tortured harmless old women whom they called witches and treated saintly, if misguided, Quakers with remorseless fury" (*The Bible: Its Meaning and Supremacy*, Longmans, Green and Co., 1897, 92, 93).

resurrection and future return of Jesus, he did not believe that he was actually God. Many of the ladies in the audience rushed up to me and my wife at the end of the session, begging us to be saved from an eternal hellfire. I noted that their zeal far outran their knowledge of this subject. They seemed unaware that the Apostle of our faith, Jesus (Heb. 3:1) had plainly declared his belief in the unitarian creed of his Jewish heritage. But those simple facts seemed not to matter. Supporting the traditions of their church was the driving force behind this obvious zeal to save us from our catastrophic "heresy." Any knowledge of the historical development of their Trinitarian creed was absent from these enthusiasts.

I am thoroughly persuaded that the New Testament writers spoke the truth when they report, with one voice, that Jesus proclaimed the saving Gospel of the Kingdom, and invited all who came to him to prepare as royal family for royal office in the coming Messianic rule on earth. He died for the sins of the world and to ratify the New Covenant, and three days later came back to life. I am convinced that he left his tomb, and was visibly and tangibly present with those who had known him before his crucifixion. I am pledged to belief in the non-negotiable historical fact of Jesus' return to life, as an indispensable pillar of genuine Christianity. Behind the amazing drama of the supernatural origin from a virgin, the Gospel preaching and healing ministry of Jesus, his crucifixion, resurrection, ascension and promised return at his future Second Coming to initiate a new political and social order on earth, is the unseen hand of the God of Abraham, Isaac and Jacob, who was also the God of Jesus.

I have no reason to suppose that the resurrected Jesus was imagined by his followers. They had no motive at all for lying about what their senses had taught them to be factual and true. In an unvarnished way they affirm that they "ate and drank with him [Jesus] after he rose from the dead" (Acts 10:41). "God raised him from the dead and he appeared to those who had come up with him from Galilee to Jerusalem, who are now his witnesses to the people" (Acts 13:30-31). I believe that — on the basis of the testimony of those who lived closest to these events and were thus in a position to report them accurately. I have no reason to think that Luke, for example, was inventing fairy tales when he recounted the events of Jesus' supernatural beginning in Mary, preaching ministry, and execution at the hands of cruel, bigoted Romans and Jews. Luke has

12 *Foundations for Belief in God and His Son*

been proven over and over again to be well informed in his knowledge of history and contemporary affairs. He gives no indication that he has abandoned his intention to report historical events, or drifted off into mythology when he tells us that the resurrected Jesus delivered a six-week course of instruction on the Kingdom of God to his chosen students (Acts 1:3).[6]

Paul's sermon in Pisidian Antioch presents the Christian facts in a transparently simple way, commanding our attention and belief. I find Paul here totally convincing. Not only does he believe that Jesus came back to life from death, he sees the biblical drama as centering around God and Jesus, not God and God.

> From this man's [David's] descendants *God*, according to his promise, has brought to Israel a savior, *Jesus*. John heralded his coming by proclaiming a baptism of repentance to all the people of Israel; and as John was completing his course, he would say, "What do you suppose that I am? I am not he. Behold, one is coming after me; I am not worthy to unfasten the sandals of his feet." My brothers, children of the family of Abraham, and those others among you who are God-fearing, to us this word of salvation has been sent. The inhabitants of Jerusalem and their leaders failed to recognize him, and by condemning him they fulfilled the oracles of the prophets that are read sabbath after sabbath. For even though they found no grounds for a death sentence, they asked Pilate to have him

---

[6]Jesus certainly did not set a time limit for the coming of the Kingdom. On one occasion he spoke of his followers seeing the Kingdom before they died, and this prediction was fulfilled in the *vision* (Matt. 16:9) of the Kingdom. Peter explained later that the "transfiguration" event was a vision of the future Kingdom," the Parousia, the Second Coming (2 Pet. 1:16ff). When Jesus spoke of "this generation" not passing before all the events of his prophetic discourse were fulfilled, he referred not to a period of 70 years, much less to a period of 40 years beginning in 1948! "Generation" (Mark 13:31) here has the sense of "present evil society," "brood" (cf. Prov. 30:11-14; Ps. 24:6; Luke 16:8; Acts 2:40; Mark 8:38) which will continue until Jesus introduces the future age of the Kingdom of God on earth. Jesus made it quite clear that fixing a time for the Kingdom is impossible. He stated that clearly in Mark 13:32 and Acts 1:7. The New Testament also speaks of the second coming "after a long time" (Matt. 25:19; Luke 20:9). The Kingdom and Day of the Lord is always "at hand," as the prophets said, 700 years before the first coming of Jesus (Isa. 13:6).

put to death, and when they had accomplished all that was written about him, they took him down from the tree and placed him in a tomb. But God raised him from the dead, and for many days he appeared to those who had come up with him from Galilee to Jerusalem. These are now his witnesses before the people. We ourselves are proclaiming this good news to you that what *God* promised our ancestors he has brought to fulfillment for us, their children, by raising up *Jesus*, as it is written in the second psalm, "You are my son; this day I have begotten you." And as for the fact that he raised him *from the dead* never to return to corruption he declared in this way, "I shall give you the benefits assured to David." That is why he also says in another psalm, "You will not suffer your holy one to see corruption." Now David, after he had served the will of God in his lifetime, fell asleep, was gathered to his ancestors, and did see corruption. But the one whom God raised up did not see corruption. You must know, my brothers, that through him forgiveness of sins is being proclaimed to you, (and) in regard to everything from which you could not be justified under the law of Moses, in him every believer is justified. Be careful, then, that what was said in the prophets not come about: "Look on, you scoffers, be amazed and disappear. For I am doing a work in your days, a work that you will never believe even if someone tells you" (Acts 13:23-41).

I find Luke's and Paul's courtroom testimony style compelling and rational. I have taught the New Testament for many years in a Bible college, working through the text word by word in a classroom setting, perusing the Greek originals, consulting the best biblical scholarship available in English, French and German. The New Testament displays those noble qualities of honesty, purity, courage and zeal which commend themselves and win our approval in other fields of endeavor.

It is of course eminently likely and reasonable that the great Creator would not leave His creatures in ignorance about His plan for humanity. He has in fact revealed His Plan through Holy Scripture, the Hebrew Bible and the Greek New Testament, and supremely and finally in Jesus' Gospel preaching and teaching and that of his Apostles. The resurrection of Jesus simply validates the whole story, putting God's own stamp of approval on the entire drama, still to be completed.

It would be much harder for me to believe that the Bible writers were fraudulent. What motive did they have for creating such a brilliant hoax, if that is what the New Testament story about Jesus and his followers really is? Imagine if their story was deliberately false. What could they possibly gain by reporting with joy their conviction, based on face-to-face contact with Jesus who had come back to life after being killed, that God had performed a marvelous creative miracle by restoring the crucified Messiah to life? If God had created man in the first place, what objection could one have to His bringing a man back to life? Why would those heroic early Christians incur the wrath of hostile religious and secular leaders by trading on what they knew was a grand falsehood — that their beloved leader had been restored to them visibly after he had died?

Is it anything but a form of insanity for people removed from the events by some two thousand years to claim that they know better what happened than those who were able to consult actual witnesses to the Christian story?

Though I believe with a passion the extraordinary and yet eminently sane claims of the New Testament writers, I have the strongest reservation about what the Church, claiming to be followers of Jesus, *later* did with the faith of those original Christians. I believe that history shows an enormous difference between what has through the centuries come to be known as the Christian faith and what we find reported as first-century Christianity. I think that a radical deterioration and distortion took place soon after the death of the Apostles, John, who died around the end of the first century, being the last of them.

Proof of the significant change in the belief system which overcame the post-biblical Christians is nowhere more obvious than in the *shift* which occurred in the matter of defining who God and Jesus are. The heart of Christianity as it was first brought to us by Jesus was permanently and adversely affected. I think that the Church suffered severe damage when the One God, the Father of the Lord Jesus, was turned into two and three, and the human Jesus, the Son of God, was obscured. I think I can demonstrate the radical change for the worse which took place, by simply citing the clear evidence of what Jesus said about God and himself in relation to God, and comparing it with what the *later* institutionalized Church, after centuries of internal struggle and often violent argumentation, proclaimed as its view of God and Jesus.

As is well known, what claimed to be the correct ("orthodox") view about God and Jesus was finally set in stone in the church creeds, notably at the council of Nicea in 325 and Chalcedon in 451. This was only after centuries of bitter and bewildering argumentation. Even after Chalcedon disputes over how to describe who Jesus was continued and, according to the frank admission of a contemporary expert in the history of Christianity, "the demand for a complete reappraisal of the church's belief in Christ right *up to the present day* is an urgent one."[7]

This urgent need for reappraisal is highlighted for me in a dramatically interesting quotation from an informative book by a learned professor of systematic theology at Trinity Evangelical International University. Towards the end of a full historical examination of doctrine he deplores what he sees as a current departure from the classic creeds which have formed the backbone of traditional Christianity. He thinks we are moving, regrettably, beyond the Council of Chalcedon, which formulated in 451 AD the famous "two-nature" doctrine about Jesus:

> In theology, we have to say that we now seem to have entered a post-Chalcedonian era. The transformation this development portends is greater than anything that has yet happened within Christianity. It can be compared only to the transition within biblical monotheism itself, from the unitary monotheism of Israel to the trinitarianism of the Council of Chalcedon. The difference is symbolized by the transition from the prayer *Shema Yisroel,* of Deuteronomy 6:4 ("Hear, O Israel: The Lord our God is one Lord…"), to the confession of the Athanasian Creed, "We worship one God in Trinity, and Trinity in unity."

This is a staggeringly interesting comment. The professor asks:

> Was the transition from the personal monotheism of Israel to the tripersonal theism of Nicea a legitimate development of Old Testament revelation? Christians affirm that it is, holding

---

[7]Aloys Grillmeier, *Christ in Christian Tradition*, Westminster John Knox Press, 1975, 1:557.

that Nicea represents a fuller unfolding, not a distortion, of the self-disclosure of the God of Israel.[8]

What strikes me as astounding in this quotation is firstly the professor's candid admission that the shift from the unitary monotheism of Jesus to the Trinitarian doctrine of Nicea did happen and was indeed momentous. What alerts me to the risk of an uncritical acceptance of "tradition" for tradition's sake, what raises my suspicions, and drives me to the investigation conducted in these chapters is this: that the professor has not apparently noted that *Jesus* was the one fully ascribing to the unitary monotheism of Israel. *Jesus* gave no indication that a "transition" to another form of "monotheism" is conceivable or legitimate. Indeed how could Christians possibly imagine moving beyond the creed which Jesus stated to be the heart and core of the true knowledge of God?

The professor appears to ask the question whether it is permissible to abandon what Jesus taught about God, about Jesus' theology. He seems untroubled that we have in fact moved away from the theology of Jesus. He seems not to be concerned that Jesus spoke of "the Lord *our* God," the God, that is of Israel, who was definitely not a triune God.

That question raised by Professor Brown provides the thesis of my inquiry. My findings may cause something of an uproar, but if they do I think a good purpose may be served. I will argue that any failure to listen to Jesus as our rabbi is perilous. His teachings are laced with warnings that his words are to be heeded. To an alarming degree, I believe churchgoers are approaching faith mindlessly, blithely unaware of where their beliefs come from. In that condition I fear they may be wide open to deception, and deception must be avoided at all costs, and "the love of the truth for salvation" (2 Thess. 2:10) promoted as the first priority in the Christian life. If bumper stickers on cars are to identify their drivers as those who have "got Jesus," should we not be absolutely certain that in fact they have not drifted away from the actual Shema-reciting *Messiah* Jesus of the first century?

---

[8]Harold O.J. Brown, *Heresies*, 431.

Historical Background

The churchgoing public seems little interested in the history of dogma and they are prone to misinformation in that vacuum of information. Even the history of the development of the Trinitarian concept of God has been misrepresented. This raises my suspicions as well as confirming my belief that both Jesus and Paul spoke prophetically when they warned about coming apostasy from the faith. Jesus, understanding human nature as well as the cunning of Satan as he did, wondered if the true faith would manage to exist up to the time of his future return (Luke 18:8). Paul spoke of original truth being replaced by imaginative fictions masquerading as Christianity, of the popular clamor for "heaping up teachers" who preach to people not truth, but what they want to hear (2 Tim. 4:3-4). What if those predictions have been realized?

The fudging of historical fact does not convince me of the objectivity of some authorities in their approach to the truth of our controversial subject. R.P.C. Hanson, a leading expert on the development of doctrine, deplores the travesty which goes under the guise of a true account of how the traditional doctrine of God was developed. Professor Hanson rehearses the well-known battle over God and over orthodoxy:

> The version connected with the Arian controversy, which lasted from 318-381, to be found until very recently in virtually all the textbooks, runs something like this: In the year 318 a presbyter called Arius was rebuked by his bishop Alexander of Alexandria for teaching erroneous doctrine concerning the divinity of Christ, to the effect that Christ was a created and inferior god. When the controversy spread because Arius was supported by wicked and designing bishops such as Eusebius of Nicomedia and his namesake of Caesarea, the Emperor Constantine called a general council at Nicea which drew up a creed which intended to suppress Arianism and finish the controversy. But owing to the crafty political and ecclesiastical engineering of the Arians, this pious design was frustrated. Supporters of the orthodox point of view such as Athanasius of Alexandria, Eustathius of Antioch and later Paul of Constantinople were deposed from their sees on trumped up charges and sent into exile. But Athanasius resolutely and courageously sustained the battle

for [Trinitarian] orthodoxy, almost alone until in the later stages of the controversy he was joined by other standard-bearers of orthodoxy such as Hilary of Poitiers, Pope Damasus and the three Cappadocians, Basil of Caesarea, Gregory of Nazianzus and Gregory of Nyssa. Ultimately by the aid of the Emperor Theodosius right prevailed, the forces of error and wickedness represented by the Arians were defeated and crushed and the formulation of Constantinople in 381 of the revised Nicean Creed (325 AD) crowned the triumph of the true faith.

This conventional account of the controversy, which stems originally from the version given of it by the victorious party, is now recognized by a large number of scholars to be *a complete travesty*...At the beginning of the controversy nobody knew the right answer.[9] There was no "orthodoxy" on the subject of "how divine is Jesus Christ?" It is a priori implausible to suggest that a controversy raged for no less than sixty years in the Church...over a doctrine whose orthodox form was perfectly well known to everyone concerned and had been known for centuries past.[10]

Hanson then adds this interesting fact:

The Creed of Nicea of 325 produced in order to end the controversy signally failed to do so. Indeed it ultimately compounded the confusion, because its use of the words *ousia* [essence] and *hypostasis* [person] was so ambiguous as to suggest that the fathers of Nicea had fallen into Sabellianism [God is one Person in three modes], a view recognized as heresy even at that period.

Hanson concludes his historical survey by stressing that the mistakes and faults "were not confined to the upholders of any one particular doctrine, and cannot all be grasped under the heading of a

---

[9]Professor Karen Armstrong makes the same telling point: "Today Arius's name is a byword for heresy [particularly since his views are connected with those of the Jehovah's Witnesses], but when the conflict broke out there was no officially orthodox position and it was by no means certain why or even whether Arius was wrong" (!) (*A History of God*, Gramercy Books, 2004, 108).

[10]R.P.C. Hanson, "The Doctrine of the Trinity Achieved in 381," *Scottish Journal of Theology* 36 (1983): 41-57.

'wicked Arian conspiracy.' The most serious initial fault was the misbehavior of Athanasius in his see at Alexandria."

That brief account of the struggles which led to the standard concept of God in Christendom should alert the reader to the fact that none of what led to "orthodoxy" bears the marks of the peaceable and truthful spirit of Jesus, whose concept of God provoked none of the chaos to which that later history testifies. What is needed is a fresh look at the whole question about God and the Son of God.

This book hopes to make some small contribution to that much-needed overhaul of the basic structures of "received" Christianity. I want to show you that the alteration which affected the very core of the belief system of Jesus and his earliest followers has had tremendous and far-reaching effects on the history of religion. Whole bodies of believers in God have been set in opposition to each because of disagreement over the most important of all theological questions: Who is God? And who is Jesus? And what is his relationship to the God of the Bible?

The Issue

The issue to be dealt with in these chapters can be boiled down to this: Does Jesus' transparently simple and scriptural declaration that "the Lord our God is one Lord" (Mark 12:29) really warrant the centuries of disputation as to who God is, or have churches simply rejected their Jewish founder and Savior at the most fundamental level? Is Jesus' statement about the identity of God really that hard to understand? Is it really some incomprehensible mystery? Or have we introduced a fearful complication into Jesus' definition of God? Does the creed, as so many modern apologists for "orthodoxy" tell us, really defy description and remain inscrutable and not accessible to the laws of language and logic? Is Jesus' creed negotiable for any reason? Has the Church, rather than the Bible, created a problem about who God is and then spent its energy needlessly trying to unravel its own enigma?

Is there perhaps also a deplorable anti-semitic prejudice against accepting the Jewish Jesus and his creedal definition of God? If so, the Church needs to confess this and reach out in reconciliation to others whom it has rejected as "heretics." The Church needs to reassure itself that its traditions have not ruled out of court Jesus' own basic belief about the identity of God.

What I am *not* saying is that we can understand everything about God! I am proposing that God *has* clearly revealed to us in the Bible how many He is. Agreement on this question could vastly ease the tensions now existing between major religious groups. A start could be made towards seeing who the real God is, "the only true God," "the one who alone is truly God" as Jesus called Him (John 17:3; 5:44), and what He has revealed in His unique Son Jesus.

Are not Christians supposed to be following Jesus Christ, and if so, why are they not unanimously reciting *his* creed? Could it be that a departure from Jesus' creed brought on the Church an inevitable confusion — a penalty for disturbing the proper understanding of who God is? Does the New Testament sanction thousands of differing and disagreeing denominations?[11] Does it ever sanction a departure from the clear teaching of Jesus about who God is?

I propose that the Church, driven in some curious way by a distaste for things Jewish, has jettisoned the very Jewish creed of its Jewish founder and Savior, Jesus. The results of the giant ecclesiastical muddle which has ensued are visible all around us. Church history is replete with embarrassingly obvious disputes, excommunications, even killings, all over the question of who God and Jesus are. These conflicts are not the fruit of the spirit. Jesus never sanctioned the killing of other believers over doctrine. Yet this has happened. Protestants and Roman Catholics have been guilty of amazing cruelty to any who challenged their theological authority, even to the point of killing their opponents. Rather than reach out with love and patience towards those perceived as "heretics," the Church took up the physical sword against them. And information about such senseless murder in Jesus' name has often been kept away from the churchgoing public.

Christianity is fragmented into many thousands of competing groups. Billions of Muslims and Christians have mutually exclusive understandings of who God and Jesus are. And Jews along with Muslims are forbidden by their adherence to their strict monotheism to make common cause with Christians, who claim that the Jewish Messiah who has come (and is coming again) *was God. For Jews and Muslims that would obviously imply belief in two Gods, and belief in*

---

[11]Recent statistics tell us that there are some 34,000 differing Christian denominations.

two who are God is not monotheism. That would be a clear departure into paganism.

My thesis is certainly no new invention. Scholars of the first rank,[12] past and present, have in their various ways made the same complaint as I offer in this book, but their works are read mostly by specialists, or hidden in inaccessible libraries, and their words seem seldom to make any impact outside the world of academia. The average pew-sitter knows little or nothing about what they have said. Nor do most churchgoers seem to care much about how they came by the beliefs they hold. Somehow the fact that so many good people have held those traditional beliefs for thousands of years seems to make them unquestionably true. A soporific approach to matters of what is often disparagingly called "doctrine" seems to have overcome the church community.

Very few who sit in church hear sermons explaining how and why it is that they gather under the auspices of a triune God. They do not know the chaotic history and the interminable wrangles which led to the accepted creed. Nor do they know that the concept of God as three Persons was not taught continuously from the New Testament onwards. The Trinitarian idea of God emerged as fixed dogma only after a prolonged struggle lasting for several centuries. The victorious party was not necessarily in the right. The victorious party suppressed the protests and often the literature of its opponents. The question about who God is ought at least to be open for reasoned discussion on the basis of biblical and historical facts. Those who know that God demands that we love Him with all our "minds and strength" should feel the need to be informed. To do less is to risk being deceived.

At present:

> Most of those who profess and call themselves Christians...are in the habit of saying that Jesus Christ is God. This is the current opinion; it is taught by the Church; it is laid down in the Creeds. But if you come to examine the average Englishman, you will find that he holds this opinion in rather a vague and loose sort of way. He has not thought out exactly what he means by it, nor considered just what it involves. If you asked him whether God is our Heavenly

---

[12]Interested readers would enjoy tracing the anti-Trinitarian passion of Sir Isaac Newton, the poet John Milton and Christian philosopher John Locke, and of course thousands of other "dissenters." The literature is vast.

Father, he would almost certainly answer "Yes." If you then asked, "Well, then, is Jesus Christ our Heavenly Father?" he would certainly say "No." But if you went on, "Are there, then, two Gods?" he would entirely repudiate the suggestion. So that he carries about with him in his mind these four propositions: 1) "Jesus Christ is God"; 2) "God is our Heavenly Father"; 3) "Jesus Christ is not our Heavenly Father"; 4) "There are not two Gods." Yet he has never considered how to reconcile these four separate opinions of his together; it probably has not occurred to him that they are inconsistent with one another...The average Englishman has not troubled himself with the matter.[13]

The inconsistency and contradiction involved in the view of many believers suggests that something has gone awry at the basic level of defining God and Jesus.

Tradition as a Danger

Jesus warned almost daily about the dangers of ecclesiastical traditions. He knew how easily they can pose a threat to divine revelation in Scripture. Jesus observed that God, his Father, was seeking men and women to worship Him within a framework of spirit and truth: "Those who worship Him must worship Him in spirit and in truth" (John 4:24). This would mean that acceptable service of God must be informed by revealed truth and not be marred and rendered ineffective by untrue tradition, however hallowed and cherished.

A wise scholar, the late Professor F.F. Bruce observed this in correspondence with me many years ago: "People who adhere to belief in the Bible only (as they believe) often adhere *in fact* to a traditional school of interpretation of *sola scriptura*. Evangelical Protestants can be as much servants of tradition as Roman Catholics or Greek Orthodox, only they don't realize it is tradition."[14] Being an evangelical "born again" Christian is in itself no guarantee that one has learned the Christian faith from the Bible rather than traditions imposed on the Bible.

Surprisingly, it seldom seems to occur to faithful members of churches that their own fundamental "taken-for-granteds" may be

---

[13]Richard A. Armstrong, *The Trinity and the Incarnation*, 1904, rep. Kessinger, 2005, 7-8.
[14]Letter, June 13, 1981.

entirely at odds with the teaching of the one whom they claim as the pioneer and originator of their faith, the Messiah Jesus. That striking mismatch between Jesus' definition of who God is and the almost universal definition of God on the books of mainline Christianity should be a matter of concern for all who claim that the Bible is the only ultimate standard for believers. I am confident that a glaring difference in the definition of the Deity authorized by Jesus and the definition required by church members today is demonstrable. The facts are not very complicated, though the introduction of alien views of God and His Son has made them appear dauntingly complex. There has been a massive departure from the "simplicity" presented by Jesus himself. His creed — his definition of the true God — is lucidly simple. It asks simply to be believed.

Creeds remind us of the basic framework of our religion.[15] These are a statement of belief in concise form reminding those who gather in church week by week of the substance of their convictions about God, Jesus and salvation. Many of us remember for a lifetime the words of the creeds we recited dutifully in church. Not that we necessarily understood what we were saying, but our weekly utterance seemed to have gained an untouchable sanctity by its sheer antiquity, and by the immense learning and weight of unbroken tradition with which apparently it was backed. How many of us could have explained how it was that Jesus had "descended to hell"? That seemed to be the last place he ought to have gone to, in view of what we understood by "hell." No one bothered to explain the complete shift in meaning which had taken place in the word "hell." In the case of Jesus, it meant in Scripture simply that he had gone at death to the

---

[15]"Many important English words are derived from the Latin language. This is particularly true of theological terms because the ecclesiastical language of Western Christendom was exclusively Latin for more than one thousand years. The term *creed* comes from the Latin *credo*, meaning 'I believe.' The opening line of the Apostles' Creed in Latin reads *Credo in Deum* — 'I believe in God.' Creeds are considered authoritative pronouncements that set forth in summary form the central articles or tenets of the historic Christian faith. Four formal creeds have become known as the ecumenical creeds of Christendom. These creeds, which were formulated at various points in church history, include the Apostles' Creed, the Nicene Creed, the Athanasian Creed, and the Creed of Chalcedon" (Kenneth Richard Samples, "The Ancient Christian Creeds," www.augustinefellowship.org).

place of rest where all the dead are. The Church seemed somehow to tighten its grip on us by allowing the creeds to transmit an atmosphere of mysticism, even incomprehensibility. Perhaps they were really not meant to be intelligible.[16] Could religious belief really be so rational and logical that it could be conveyed in intelligible words?

On the other hand Jesus seemed to reason and dispute in a tight logical fashion as he sought to defend his claims against fierce opposition. Jesus obviously argued, from the Old Testament, the Bible of his time. Would not a Christian do the same thing, adding the New Testament Scriptures to his source of divine information? And if he claimed to believe in scriptural words understood in their normal, logical and grammatical sense, would it not be rather suspect to hear theologians telling us that language is inadequate to explain the mystery of the Trinity? The Bible never hints at the inadequacy of the inspired language used by God to *reveal* who He is (not to mystify us).

Christianity, it is assumed, is based on the recorded teachings of Jesus, who claimed to be the Son of God and Messiah and who congratulated his leading disciples for their brilliant God-given insight in recognizing him as such — "the Christ [the Messiah], the Son of God" (Matt. 16:16-18). On that impregnable rock foundation Jesus promised to build his Church. He thus provided the central basis for sound views of who he was, guarding against the ever-present threat of rival Jesuses, distortions of his true identity or of other claimants to religious devotion.

The New Testament world of thought may well seem strange to us in the 21st century. Do we still view the battle for truth as a constant life and death struggle? Jesus and Paul obviously did. Neither Jesus nor Paul was advocating just good morals or a refined humanism. People are not persecuted and hounded for such programs. Jesus warned his followers that they would have to take up their cross daily, and he meant the cross of crucifixion. They would have to expect opposition from "the establishment" which had proven so intractably hostile to him as the Messiah of Israel. Most startling of all, Jesus foresaw the worst form of persecution arising from a

---

[16]The same anti-intellectual approach to religion seems to prevail when some Roman Catholics request that the Mass not be celebrated in English but as earlier in Latin. They apparently prefer an unintelligible church service because they think its very "mystery" draws them closer to God.

religious quarter: "The time will come when anyone who kills you disciples of mine will think they are doing a holy service for God" (John 16:2). Such a situation can arise only if a huge deception of religious people has occurred.

Jesus the Messiah and Son of God

Our New Testament records report unanimously that Jesus claimed before his followers as well as before Jewish officials at his trial, to be the Messiah promised by his own Hebrew heritage in the Hebrew Bible. Jesus defined "Messiah" from that library of writings we call the Old Testament, whose limits Jesus defined precisely as "the Law, prophets and the writings" (Luke 24:44). These precious documents had promised from the beginning that a unique Savior, King and final prophet would be born to Israel. Jesus obviously treated the Hebrew Bible as a repository of divine, authoritative truth about what his God, the Creator and the God of Israel, was doing in the history of humankind. Jesus' central role in the unfolding divine plans was his unique position as "the Christ, the Son of God." Based on the understanding of that staggering truth his own followers were to be united in one Church, the assembly of the faithful (Matt. 16:16-18). Their confession of Jesus was as the Lord Messiah, the promised son of David. Some discerning members of the public appealed to him as "Lord, son of David" (Matt. 15:22; 20:31). Paul was convinced that recognizing Jesus as originating from the family line of King David was an essential part of the saving Gospel (2 Tim. 2:8). The heart of the apostolic message of Christianity was, and remains, that that Jesus or Yeshua of Nazareth was indeed the long-promised Messiah. To accept that fact was to place oneself on the road to salvation. To reject it was to oppose the will of the God of Israel who had sent His Son as the long-awaited Savior and Messiah.

One cannot go more to the core of the issue than by reminding ourselves of what Jesus considered absolutely primary and fundamental. Our loyalty to Jesus demands that we take him very seriously when he spoke of the rock foundation of the Church he founded. Jesus was intensely interested in who Peter thought he (Jesus) was. Various public opinions were held, but Jesus wanted to assure himself that Peter had the absolute truth about the identity of Jesus.

It is at this point that Jesus could have said so easily, "I am God, and on this rock I will found my Church." That affirmation appears to be required today for membership in the mainline churches. But Jesus said nothing at all like that. Once again we suggest that the churches have betrayed their rabbi and master by departing from Jesus' own clear definition of what is fundamental to faith. "Who do you say that I am?" Jesus inquired of the leading Apostle, Peter. "You are the Christ, the Son of the Living God," was Peter's confident reply. This correct creedal answer delighted Jesus: "Blessed are you, Peter. Flesh and blood did not reveal this to you, but my Father in heaven. On that rock foundation I will build my Church" (Matt. 16:15-18).

Could anything be clearer than the mind of Jesus on this central question? Surely not. Not a hint or word about Jesus being God Himself! Jesus is the Christ. He is the *Son* of God. Both titles appear in the Hebrew Bible, in Psalm 2, a key Messianic passage. The Christ and Son of God in that Psalm is the King whom God is going to place on Mount Zion, to whose authority all the nations are advised in their best interests to bow. Jesus is called Christ, that is "the Messiah," 527 times in the New Testament. Such overwhelming evidence ought to convince every reader of the New Testament. Jesus is to be identified as the Son of God, the Messiah. Jesus declared that this designation of him, and no other, provides the rock foundation of true belief. Peter's confession is the ultimate Christian confession since it gained the enthusiastic approval of Jesus. He is "the Christ, the Son of the living God." "Sons of the living God" was a prophetic title for Israel the nation (Hos. 1:10; Rom. 9:26). It is unthinkable to imagine therefore that Jesus was claiming to be God!

The Shift from Messiah, Son of God, to Jesus as "God"

Lee Strobel in his well-known investigation of the Christian faith spoke with evangelical scholar Ben Witherington. The conversation proceeded as follows. Strobel asked:

> "[Jesus] tended to shy away from forthrightly proclaiming himself to be the Messiah or Son of God. Was that because he didn't think of himself in those terms or because he had other reasons?"
>
> "No, it's not because he didn't think of himself in those terms," Witherington said…"If he had simply announced, 'Hi, folks; I'm God,' that would have been heard as 'I'm

Yahweh,' because the Jews of his day didn't have any concept of the Trinity. They only knew of God the Father—whom they called Yahweh—and not God the Son or God the Holy Spirit."[17]

Two comments are necessary. Yes, Jesus exercised a restraint before the public about his identity as the Messiah. It was a politically charged title.[18] But he left not a shadow of doubt in the minds of his chosen followers about who he was. We have just seen that Jesus viewed the understanding of him as the Christ, the Son of God, as the essential basis of the Christian faith, the rock creed. Peter was warmly congratulated by Jesus for his insight. The New Testament confirms that truth every time it refers to Jesus as the Christ, which of course happens over and over again. He is in fact introduced to us in Luke 2:11 as the "Lord Messiah." Even before that Elizabeth, as an expert in Messianic affairs, greeted Mary as the "the mother of my lord," i.e., the Messiah, "my lord" of Psalm 110:1.

Secondly Witherington concedes that belief that Jesus *is God*, a member of the Trinity, is impossible according to the records of Jesus' teaching. He is absolutely right when he states that if Jesus had said, "I am God," he would have meant "I am Yahweh, the God of Israel." The claim to be the God of Israel would have been nonsensical. No Jew could possibly have understood it, much less accepted it as true. Nor did Jesus believe he was Yahweh. He claimed to be Yahweh's Son.

And Witherington is absolutely right to say that Jews of Jesus' day knew nothing of a triune God. Such a concept would have been a radical and shocking, even a blasphemous innovation. This is essential background information and fact, as we proceed with our investigation.

Who, then, did Jesus think was God? Jesus himself claimed in conversation with a Jew, as we are going to see in detail, that he subscribed to the Jewish unitary monotheistic creed, the Shema — the

---

[17]Lee Strobel, *The Case for Christ*, Zondervan, 1998, 133.

[18]The New Testament nowhere downplays the political role of the Messiah as God's commissioned agent for establishing a new political order on earth at the Second Coming. Jesus in fact stated that the gift of royal position in the coming Kingdom was the heart of the New Covenant (Matt. 19:28; Luke 22:28-30 — where the promise of royal office is *covenanted* to the disciples).

"Hear, O Israel" (Deut. 6:4). The Shema proclaimed that God is one Person. That really settles the whole issue we are discussing. Jesus is on record as reciting and affirming that strictly monotheistic creed of the Jews (Mark 12:28-34). He also said that "salvation is of the Jews" and "we Jews know whom we worship" (John 4:22). And everyone should know that it was not a triune God. Jesus invariably identified his Father with his own God and that of the Jews. "If I glorify myself, my glory is nothing; it is my Father who glorifies me, of whom you say, 'He is your God'" (John 8:54).

Amen, indeed, to Witherington's correct statement, "The Jews of Jesus' day didn't have any concept of the Trinity." But neither did Jesus! He believed exactly the same as his colleague Jews about the central affirmation of Judaism, that *God is a single Person.* The creed of Jesus ought to be the creed of the Church. That it is not should be cause for alarm. Jesus was a unitarian, believing that God the Father alone was truly God (John 17:3).

The issue is very clear. How faithfully has Jesus' understanding of God and of himself as the Messiah been relayed to us over the many centuries since Peter uttered his historic words about the critically important identity of Jesus as Christ and Son of God (Matt. 16:16-18)? I want to propose that essential elements of that rock foundation of truth have been lost to churches. The transmission of the most central of all spiritual information, the identity of God — as Jesus defined Him — and Jesus' own identity, has suffered a subtle and amazing distortion. And this distortion of original truth was well under way as early as the middle of the second century, a little over a hundred years after the death of Jesus. Earlier, the Apostles had battled hard against the various counter-ideas which threatened to obscure who God and Jesus are. Soon after their death, with the stabilizing power of apostolic authority removed, a subtle invasion of new and contrary views of Jesus and his identity, as well as the identity of God affirmed by Jesus, took place. The son of David, God's unique Son, was replaced by a strange Gentile God.

The results of that *later* theological thinking, enshrined in the creeds, continue to hold sway over the minds of countless dedicated churchgoers. They are mostly unaware of the shift in understanding at the heart of the faith which has taken place. They have been persuaded in large numbers to believe that the New Testaments they carry to church, containing the very teachings of Jesus and his agents the Apostles, are the same teachings as they have learned in Church. I think that assumption needs to be challenged in the interests of plain honesty as well as the need for us all to share the mind of Christ.

I propose that the foundational belief of all true religion has been shifted "off-base" by post-biblical church authorities, who actually refused the creed which Jesus had declared the most important spiritual truth of all.

A whole school of professional opinion, remarkably confirmed by leading British and German Bible specialists of current times, backs my central thesis that what we now have as "the faith" is in important respects quite unlike the faith known to Jesus. We are urged to embrace the faith which Jesus' half-brother Jude was so keen to preserve. The faithful are to cling tenaciously to *original* Christianity in the face of opposition which *within the first century* was attempting to undermine "the faith once and for all delivered to the holy people" (Jude 3).

The Challenge of Discipleship

If you are prepared to accept the New Testament records as a faithful account of the teachings of the Jesus of history, Jesus of Nazareth, are you willing to search out Jesus' view of the authentic orthodox creed? Does our acceptance of Jesus as "lord" extend to a willingness on our part to accept and embrace with enthusiasm Jesus' teaching about who God is?

That would not seem to be unreasonable, unless of course we invest in the "Church" the right to supersede the opinions of Jesus. That could not be, you may say. But don't be too sure that such a transference of authority from Jesus to "Church" has not in fact occurred. It may be easier for Protestants to see this obvious transfer in the Roman Catholic Church. But has it happened in their own circles too? It is safer to inquire of the original documents themselves which are now so readily available to us. Calling Jesus "lord" presumably means believing and obeying his teachings, especially in the matter of the central creed which defines God.

Calling Jesus "Messiah," "Lord Messiah," "my Lord," "the Lord Jesus," "the Lord Jesus Christ" or "our Lord Jesus Christ" is obviously the practice of early apostolic Christianity. It is universally attested in our New Testament.

Calling him "the Lord God," "our Lord God" or "your Lord God" is unknown to our New Testament. "Lord God," "the Lord our God," or "the Almighty" are biblical titles reserved exclusively for the Father of Jesus and are never used for Jesus. This fact arises from the fundamental creed of Jesus and Israel, that God is one single Person, designated "the God" (*o theos*) not less than 1317 times in the New Testament. The article in Greek points to *the one* God recognized by the writer and those he writes to. Obviously the Son, who is another person, could not possibly *also* be the Almighty Lord God. A catastrophic departure into polytheism would be unavoidable.

That would amount to two Gods. In the strictly monotheistic atmosphere in which the New Testament documents were produced, that is just a self-evident fact hardly needing to be stated. Today however, with the crushing weight of church tradition bearing down on us, we need to look again at how Jesus described the God whom he loved and served.[19]

---

[19]The last letters of the first and last words of the *Shema* (Deut. 6:4) are in large type in the Hebrew Bible, creating the word "witness." If the "D" at the end of *echad* (one) were altered to "R," making the word "other," rabbis say that "you destroy the world." This could turn out to be profoundly true. Jesus calls the world back to Israel's God.

Chapter 2

Who Was the God of Jesus and His Followers?

"Jesus taught no new doctrine of God...The God of whom Jesus speaks is the one God of Israel (Mark 12:29)."[1]

What then are the facts in the case we are examining? The Bible taken as a whole presents a strict numerically singular view of God. The Greek word for "God," in the singular form of this noun, appears consistently in the New Testament as the designation of the Father of Jesus. This is pure unitarianism. God is the Father, as distinct from Jesus. If one takes the evidence of Scripture as a whole, there is not a single occasion on which the word "God" means the triune God! There are some twelve thousand occurrences of this word "God."[2] The fact that no writer ever meant "the triune God" when he said "God" informs the unbiased reader that biblical writers were not Trinitarians. Writing the word "God," the authors of the Bible never meant the Trinity.[3]

A unitarian understanding of God is reached by looking at the whole range of Scripture. It is a fact that the word "three" occurs in no biblical verse next to the word God, while singular verbs and pronouns designate God, thousands upon thousands of times.

---

[1] Hans Hinrich Wendt, *The Teaching of Jesus*, T & T Clark, 1892, 184.

[2] YHVH, the personal name of God, occurs some 7000 times, always with singular verbs and pronouns; *elohim* (God) some 2300 times; *Adonai*, the Lord God, 449 times; and in the Greek New Testament *ho theos* about 1317 times.

[3] James White in *The Forgotten Trinity*, Bethany House, 1998, cites no examples from Scripture of "God" meaning the triune God.

Christians claim to be following the historical grammatical understanding of the sacred text. Words carry their normal meanings. It would seem reasonable to expect believers in God, when they find Him constantly represented by singular personal pronouns to understand that He is a singular Person. This impression is confirmed, surely, by the presence of thousands of occurrences of the singular nouns for "God." Is anyone prepared to contradict ordinary rules of communication and claim that the God who speaks in the Bible as "I" really means "I three"? When David addressed his God and said "You alone are God" (Ps. 86:10), did he have in mind a triune God of three Persons?

Jews for all their history and as custodians of the sacred text never mistook the meaning of the words "I," "Me," "He," and "Him" as designating the true God.

Unfortunately some evangelicals disregard the massive evidence of the Hebrew Bible and make this sort of claim:

> In the process of history God has revealed Himself as one God, subsisting in three Persons. God as revealed in the Bible is not a simple undifferentiated Subject; but His being is in three objectively distinguished Subjects...That the being of God is complex, in the sense of objectively distinguished Subjects, is a basic presupposition of many OT passages. Psalm 110:1, "Jehovah saith unto my Lord, Sit thou at my right hand until I make thine enemies thy footstool."[4]

As we shall see, this statement, in addition to its disregard for the single Person who speaks as God, contains a remarkable "clanger." The word "lord" (in the form "my lord") at the beginning of the verse quoted from Psalm 110 never means the Lord God, but always a superior who is *not* God! This error of fact has been repeated in article after article even in standard works. To prove the Deity of the second member of the Trinity based on a title which never indicates Deity is astonishing!

To make our case for the Jewish creed of Jesus and the New Testament certain defining statistics need to be kept always in mind. In the New Testament the Greek word for God — *ho theos* ("the God") — is found no less than 1317 times as a description of the

---

[4]"Trinity," Merrill C. Tenney, ed., *The Zondervan Pictorial Bible Dictionary*, 1967, 871.

Father of Jesus, as distinct from Jesus who is His Son. Thus God and Father are repeatedly linked in the mind of the reader. Moreover that same God is called "God and Father," "God, "the Father," "God our Father." When mentioned next to Jesus, His unique Son, God is "the God and Father *of our Lord Jesus Christ.*" While Jesus is never called "the true God" or "the only true God" or "the Almighty" *(pantocrator)*,[5] the Father alone is given those descriptions, in addition to the mass of material just mentioned, which pictures Him as one Divine Person. Every form of language available attaches to the Father of Jesus the idea of complete singleness, supremacy and exclusivity. "There is none beside Him." God the Father is said to be in His own class, unique and unrivaled — a position which He guards with an appropriate divine jealousy. Of Himself the God of Israel states, "I alone stretched forth the heavens and earth. No one was with me" (Isa. 44:24). "The God of Israel" is mentioned as such 300 times in the Bible, and in both Testaments. He is never said to be "begotten," which means brought into existence. By direct contrast, the Son of God is said to be "begotten," meaning of course that he had a beginning of existence and by definition cannot therefore be the supreme God.

Jews as custodians of the oracles of God (Rom. 3:2) for their entire history have never admitted belief in a God who is three Persons. Jesus was a Jew, and on the evidence available to us he certainly was not a Trinitarian.

Jesus and the Identity of God

May I invite you to join me in an exploration of a massively important episode in the teaching life of Jesus. This occurred towards the end of his short, strenuous itinerant ministry as a teacher and preacher of the Gospel of the Kingdom of God. It is an event with the potential to affect dramatically your journey of faith — an event able to change radically the way we think about our Christian faith.

The story I am referring to is found in Mark 12, beginning with verse 28. Mark records here an encounter between Jesus and a Jewish theologian, a scribe. The gospel accounts of Jesus were written of course as "tracts" to commend the Christian faith to readers. We should read these documents as appeals to us to align ourselves with

---

[5]Rev. 1:8 is a reference to the Father and not to Jesus.

the Christian faith. We are obviously intended to pay close attention
to this important interchange recorded by Mark. Jesus is here found in
conversation with a perceptive member of the ecclesiastical guild.
The exchange between Jesus and the Jewish theologian is profoundly
important for our worship of God in spirit and truth (John 4:26). The
story is in fact unique in the New Testament. Jesus, in this
interchange, is seen uncharacteristically as being in perfect agreement
with a Jewish religious expert. Here is how the New Living
Translation captures the fascinating conversation between Jesus and
that professional Bible teacher:

> One of the teachers of religious law was standing there
> listening to the discussion. He realized that Jesus had
> answered well, so he asked, "Of all the commandments,
> which is the most important?" Jesus replied, "The most
> important commandment is this: 'Hear, O Israel! The Lord
> our God is the one and only Lord.[6] And you must love the
> Lord your God with all your heart, all your soul, all your
> mind, and all your strength.' The second is equally important:
> 'Love your neighbor as yourself.' No other commandment is
> greater than these." The teacher of religious law replied,
> "Well said, teacher. You have spoken the truth by saying that
> there is only one God and no other.[7] And I know it is
> important to love Him with all my heart and all my
> understanding and all my strength, and to love my neighbors
> as myself. This is more important than to offer all of the burnt
> offerings and sacrifices required in the law." Realizing this
> man's understanding, Jesus said to him, "You are not far
> from the Kingdom of God." And after that, no one dared to
> ask him any more questions.

It is important to note that a question about the most important
theological issue is nevertheless a highly practical question. A parallel
passage in Matthew 19:16-17 shows that the issue of defining who
God is and loving Him was related to the question of salvation itself.
To find out who the true God is and to love Him is inextricably bound
up with the hope of salvation in the age to come, everlasting life. In
Matthew 19:17 Jesus replied to an inquirer who wanted to know how

---

[6]There is no difference in sense between the various translations: "The Lord
our God is one Lord," "the only Lord," etc.
[7]Or "no one else besides Him."

to be saved: "Why do you ask me about what is good? There is one alone who is good. But if you wish to enter into life, keep the commandments."

Jesus makes the same point to the scribe who asked him about the most important of the commandments. He connects the scribe's good theological understanding with his closeness to salvation in the Kingdom. Jesus and the scribe first agree about there being One God and "no other besides Him." Finding the scribe to be sound in his definition of God, Jesus then reassures him that he is "not far from the Kingdom of God," that is, he is close to being a candidate for salvation in the future Kingdom as a follower of Christ.

An interesting comment from the New Testament background can be found in the words of Josephus, the Jewish historian, speaking of his nation's creed, the "Hear, O Israel" cited by Jesus. The only God in question is of course Yahweh, the God of the Hebrew Bible, our Old Testament. Josephus asks: "What then are the precepts and prohibitions of our Law? They are simple and familiar. The first, which leads all of the commandments, concerns God." Josephus was referring as we all know to his nation's cardinal unitarian creed. So was Jesus in Mark 12:28-34.

Our New Testament passage fits the contemporary background perfectly. It presents the Lord Jesus as firmly rooted in the Jewish belief that God is a single Person. Christianity's founder, in laying down the Christian creed, is thoroughly Jewish. He defines God as "one single Lord." Jesus' God is the God of Abraham, Isaac and Jacob, the God of the Hebrew Bible — the God of the first-century Jewish theologian, "our [Israel's] God." Jesus defines God precisely as one Person and one Lord. But the Christian Church does not.

Comments which Illuminate or Confuse

Massively influential spokesmen like C.S. Lewis divert us from the real definition of Jesus, when they say he must have been "mad, bad or God."[8] What Lewis does not offer us is the real definition: that he was the Messiah, *Son* of God. And Lewis seems to forget that Jesus vigorously subscribed to the non-Trinitarian creed of his heritage in Israel. Logicians call this technique of Lewis "false dilemma." We are pushed into choosing one of the options offered us.

---

[8]See C.S. Lewis, *Mere Christianity*, HarperCollins, 2001, 52.

But what if the right option escapes Lewis and does not appear on his list of choices? Why does Lewis write also that "We must remind ourselves that Christian theology does not believe *God to be a person.* It believes Him to be such that in Him a trinity of persons is consistent with a unity of Deity"?[9] This sounds extraordinarily unlike the theology of Jesus. It flatly contradicts the findings of the writer on the names of God in a leading Bible dictionary who writes, "There is only one supreme and true God, and he is a Person."[10]

H.H. Hamilton, D.D., writing in 1912, felt the force of the episode in Mark 12:28-34 and how beautifully it rooted Jesus in his own environment. He started by referring to the creedal statement quoted by Jesus from Deuteronomy 6:4: "This passage as it stands in the Old Testament expresses the very essence of the Jewish claim to a monopoly of religious privilege. Yahweh is one. There is no God but He. Therefore all other objects of worship must be shunned." Hamilton notes that it is inconceivable that Jesus did not intend the word "Lord" to be taken in the exclusive sense in which it is used in the Old Testament. Jesus could not have altered its sense. "The scribe who raised the question must have understood Jesus to refer to the national God of Israel alone." Thus both to the scribe and to Jesus "it must have sounded like a restatement of the ancient claim of the Jews, that no other worship but that which Israel offered was in reality the worship of the Living God."

The scribe's attitude is fully exposed when he immediately restates what he has heard Jesus say: "You are right, master; you have well said that He is one and there is none other but He, and to love Him...is much more than all burnt offerings and sacrifices." H.F. Hamilton reaches the only possible conclusion: "It seems impossible to doubt that those who witnessed the scene understood Jesus to mean precisely the same thing as the scribe. For it is recorded that 'when Jesus saw that he answered intelligently, he said "You are not far from the Kingdom of God.""'[11]

Jesus offered here a resounding statement of the unitary monotheism required of people at all times for a right relationship with God. Jesus put his stamp of approval upon the Hebrew Bible's

---

[9]Lewis, *Christian Reflections*, 79.
[10]*The Illustrated Bible Dictionary*, Tyndale House, 1980, 1:571.
[11]*The People of God: An Inquiry into Christian Origins*, Oxford University Press, 1912, 239.

definition of God as a single Person. But is this creed of Jesus clear in our churches?

I have often suggested to students studying to be in ministry that they "read themselves into the biblical text." Place yourself in the shoes of that inquiring Bible expert, who had obviously some acquaintance with Jesus and was anxious to put him to the test, not necessarily in a hostile way. This was not a trick question designed to trap Jesus. I suspect the scribe was duly impressed by the rabbi Jesus' teaching ability.[12] He had probably decided to "check him out" further. He wanted to know Jesus' priorities and agenda. How sound was his theology? So he poses this test question: What command from the God of Israel is the most important of all?

Obeying and Following Jesus

The answer Jesus gives to this question is highly significant for Christians at all times. Salvation in the New Testament is by grace, but grace does not allow us to disregard the commands and teachings of Jesus! "Salvation is given to those who obey Jesus" (Heb. 5:9; Acts 5:32). "Not everyone who says 'lord, lord' will enter the Kingdom, but those who do the will of my Father who is in heaven" (Matt. 7:21). He who obeys the Son has life. He who refuses obedience will not see life (see John 3:36). "He who hears my words and does them is like a man building his house on a rock" (Matt. 7:24). Others who disregard Jesus' words are building their spiritual house on sand. "He who rejects me by rejecting my words will be judged by those words" (see John 12:48). "He who is ashamed of me and my words, of him I will be ashamed when I come back" (see Mark 8:38). He who departs from "the health-giving words, namely those of our Lord Jesus Christ, is ignorant and proud" (see 1 Tim. 6:3).

And of course the well-loved and often-quoted saying of Jesus: "If you love me you will keep my commandments" (John 14:15; 15:10). And its counterpart which makes the same plea for adherence to what Jesus taught: "Why do you call me 'lord, lord' and yet refuse to do what I say?" (Luke 6:46). The urgency of paying the closest attention to what Jesus taught comes to us clearly on every page of the gospel accounts — and in the rest of the New Testament:

---

[12]Jesus strongly encouraged his followers to recognize him as both rabbi and lord. "You call me rabbi and lord and you do well" (John 13:3).

Salvation was first announced by the Lord [Jesus] and is granted to those who obey Jesus (Heb. 2:3; 5:9) and "God gives His holy spirit to those who obey Him" (Acts 5:32). In defining the creed, Jesus spoke of the most important of all *commandments*. There is an issue of obedience here.

There is also the compelling voice of the Father from heaven who exhorts us to "listen" to His unique Son: "This is My Son. Listen to him!" (Luke 9:35). In the same vein Peter urges the crowd to pay rapt attention to the final prophet: "Moses said, 'the Lord God will raise up for you a prophet like me from your brethren; to him you shall give heed to everything He says to you. And it will be that every person who does not heed that prophet shall be utterly destroyed from among the people'" (Acts 3:22, referring to Deut. 18:15-19).

What then do we learn, as we hang on every word of the rabbi-Savior (recalling his memorable statement that we do well to call him rabbi and Lord, John 13:13)? What do we hear as we listen to Jesus urging us to "hear, O Israel"?

If we are listening carefully to Jesus in conversation with the Jewish scholar (Mark 12:28-34 above), one crucial fact stands out. Jesus' definition of who God is harmonizes precisely with that of the Jewish scribe. The scribe is in complete agreement with Jesus about the first principle of all sound worship of God. Both the Jewish theologian and Jesus, the ultimate Jew and theologian as well as the Christian Savior, confirm the classic words of sacred Scripture. The first command, or imperative, Jesus recited and repeated was, "*Listen, Israel!*" This is a direct command of the Lord Jesus.

Then he continued with the cardinal proposition of all biblical theology: "The Lord our God is one Lord." Jesus reckons this command, "Listen carefully to the proposition that God is one Lord" as the key to all sound thinking and action. It is the pinnacle of all true religion: to give our full attention to a statement defining who the God is whom we are to worship and love — who the God is who is to be loved with all of our hearts, souls, minds and strength. The second command to love our neighbors goes with the first, of course.

May I startle you by putting a very simple fact before you? The creed announced by Jesus is the creed of Israel, of the Hebrew Bible, the creed of the Jews. Jesus was a Jew and he and the Jewish scribe had no disagreement at all about who the God of the Bible is. Can one possibly argue otherwise? The story is plain and clear, essentially simple and delightfully free of the tangled and abstruse definitions of God in which *later* post-biblical theology became embroiled.

The Jewish Creed of Jesus

Each morning and evening every Jewish man had to recite Deuteronomy 6:4-9; 11:13-21 and Numbers 15:37-41. This was the daily confession of faith. Jesus made no innovations here. He answers the questioner by quoting the texts which they had in common and which both believed to be sacred and ultimately authoritative. In defining the true God, Jesus has nothing to say which is different from what Israel had known from the law throughout her history. All historians and all Jews know that their God is a single Person.

There is no ambiguity about Jesus' response to the inquirer — none at all about how many God is. Jesus knows of no other God than the one revealed in the creed of Israel. This is the God of his own Jewish heritage, the God who had appointed him as Messiah. This same God is the God of Abraham, Isaac and Jacob. He is the God of the Hebrew Bible. He is defined as "one Lord" (Mark 12:29). We are urged by Jesus to listen as he, Jesus, provides us with the only right definition of God. If Jesus is to be our guide, his utterance here about the basis of true worship and the one true God is of paramount importance to us as believers. Jesus is the one of whom God his Father had said, "This is My beloved Son. *Listen to* him" (Mark 9:7).

"Listen, Israel, the Lord our God is *one Lord*" (Deut. 6:4; Mark 12:29). "Is not the God of the Jews the God of the Gentiles also? Yes, of the Gentiles also" (see Rom. 3:29). Is the Church really listening?

There is no need for an army of theologians to help us discern the meaning of Jesus' statement about who God is. The language is simple and precise — a plain proposition, a logical unit of intelligible communication. None of us has the slightest difficulty with statements of this kind. We all know what the number "one" means, and no one could possibly misunderstand the singular noun "Lord." Jews for the whole of their history had no problem with the cardinal tenet of the national faith. God was a single, undivided Divine Person, designated in their holy writings by thousands of singular personal pronouns and designating Himself as the one, single Lord of the universe, the one Divine Person who alone is God. This One God used every device known to language to convey the concept that He and no one else is God, that there is no other God. Singular personal pronouns define a single Person. Christians claim to be rooted in the grammatical method where the standard laws of grammar are decisive.

These statements are beyond any doubt as clear as language can make them: "To you it was shown that you might know that the LORD, He is God; there is none other besides Him...Know therefore today and take it to your heart that the LORD, He is God in heaven above and on the earth below. There is no other" (Deut. 4:35, 39). "So that you may understand that I am He. Before Me there was no God formed and there will be no other after Me. I, even I, am the LORD and there is no Savior besides Me...So you are My witnesses, declares the LORD, and I am God" (Isa. 43:10-12). "I am the LORD and there is no other; besides Me there is no God" (Isa. 45:5). "I the LORD am the Maker of all things, stretching out the heavens by Myself and spreading out the earth all alone" (Isa. 44:24). "Truly you are a God who hides Himself, O God of Israel, Savior" (Isa. 45:15).

Bathe your minds in these Bible words and see if the one speaking is really three Persons. Is the God speaking here a Person, or is He as contemporary Trinitarians claim a "what" — a "substance" existing in *three* Persons?

Imagine the chaos which the introduction of a triune God would bring to these matchless texts. Singular personal pronouns[13] of all forms are provided by Scripture to put beyond any possible doubt the fact that the God of the Bible is a single Person. To speak of the Holy One of Israel as the Holy Three, or tri-personal, does violence to language and theological truth. Worse, it is to defy the words of Jesus. Yet that is effectively what church tradition has done — and to the distraction and horror of the Jewish community to whom the Old Testament was committed, as Paul wrote: "What then is the superiority of the Jew? To them were entrusted the oracles of God" (Rom. 3:2). Those oracles present God as a unitary Person. Unitary monotheism, not Trinitarian monotheism, is the creed of Hebrew Scripture. Jesus never attempted to alter that magnificent fact. He reiterated it and called it the Great Commandment, the greatest commandment. And that God of the Old Testament, the God of Israel, is also the God of the Gentiles. Paul again: "Or is God the God of

---

[13]The Hebrew language uses verbs in the singular to speak of the One God, Yahweh.

Jews only? Is He not the God of Gentiles also? Yes, of Gentiles also" (Rom. 3:29).

Paul's Creed

What God did Paul claim to be serving? There is no doubt about the answer to that question. Paul is on record stating in the presence of a Roman governor, "This I admit to you, that according to the way they call a sect, I am serving the God of our fathers, believing everything which is in accordance with the Law and that is written in the prophets" (Acts 22:14; 24:14).

I would ask the reader whether one can honestly read this text as follows: "I am serving the triune God of our fathers." I suggest that this would be to deface the text and import into it a blatantly foreign concept. Paul, like his Savior Jesus, was unitarian to the core, believing in the God of Israel. "Do we not all have one Father? Has not one God created us?" (Mal. 2:10). Along with the thousands of singular personal pronouns denoting a single Divine Individual, this text cries out against the paganization of Christianity which happened when that matchlessly simple creed of Israel and of Jesus was abandoned, on the pretext that it was being "modified," "expanded," or even "enriched." But these are mere ruses to cover up the mistake. It is time for the Church to retrace its steps to Christ, the Lord Jesus whose avowed confession of God we have disregarded.

May I suggest this challenge? Are you convinced that Paul's God was the non-Jewish Trinitarian God? Could he without misleading his audience claim to be serving the God of the Hebrew Bible, the God of Judaism, the "God of his ancestors," if he believed that the true God was the triune God of later Christianity? Paul followed this claim to be a servant of the unitarian God of Israel by stating his conviction about the future resurrection of the dead (Acts 24:15). In view of this, Paul went on, "I also do my best to maintain always a blameless conscience both before God and men." The triune God? Hardly. Only a very deficient sense of history would permit the impossible notion that Paul believed the God of Israel to have been the Trinitarian God. This is widely admitted.

The Church and the Jewish-Christian Creed

The *New Bible Dictionary* in its article on "Trinity" states:

The Old Testament witness is fundamentally to the oneness of God. In their daily prayer, Jews repeated the Shema of Deuteronomy 6:4, 5: "The Lord our God the Lord is one." In this they confessed the God of Israel to be the transcendent creator without peer or rival. Without the titanic disclosure of the Christ event *no one would have taken the Old Testament to affirm anything but the exclusive, i.e., unipersonal monotheism* that is the hallmark of Judaism and Islam.[14]

Note carefully this candid admission. Reading the Hebrew Bible, on which Jesus was reared and which he affirmed as holy Scripture and which Paul claimed he believed, no one could possibly have imagined God to be more than one divine Person. The Hebrew Bible, says the dictionary, affirmed the unipersonal, non-Trinitarian God. Jesus echoed that affirmation precisely.

But now notice how the dictionary begins to take away with one hand what it just conceded with the other. "The robust monotheism of the Old Testament concedes only a few hints of plurality within the one God." The author then goes on to describe six examples of those supposed hints. Then he admits, "It is unlikely that any of these was understood by the Old Testament authors or their contemporary readers to denote personal distinctions within Israel's one God."[15] In other words neither Moses nor the prophets could possibly have imagined God to be a Trinity. Jews, to whom "the oracles of God were entrusted," never did, and to this day do not. Remember again the dictionary's admission: *"No one would have taken the Old Testament to affirm anything but the exclusive, i.e., unipersonal monotheism."*

The dictionary is suitably tentative about the presence of the Trinity in the New Testament: "The incipient Trinitarianism of the New Testament remained implicit and as yet undefined."[16] The reader is left wondering exactly what that means.

Jesus' own emphasis on the Jewish Shema should settle our question definitively. Jesus quoted the Hebrew Bible's definition of God as the most important command of all (Mark 12:28-34). Jesus did nothing to hint to the Jewish scribe that the One God was now really composed of three Persons. To do this, without the slightest

---

[14]"Trinity," *New Bible Dictionary*, Intervarsity Press, 1996, 1209.
[15] Ibid.
[16]Ibid., 1211.

indication of the radical change, would make the Lord Jesus guilty of dissembling. The Jewish scribe with whom he spoke was convinced by Jesus' plain affirmation of Deuteronomy 6:4 that the true God was the God of Israel, understood in the sense required by Deuteronomy 6:4, on which Jesus and the scribe had perfect agreement. Jesus' public confirmation of the creed of the Hebrew Bible, in conversation with a Jewish scholar, establishes beyond question how Jesus Christ defined God. It defines, therefore, the Christian creed.

Demonstrably then, both Jesus and Paul, who cites the same Shema in 1 Corinthians 8:4-6, were unitarian believers, and of course Jesus constantly claimed to be Messiah and Son of God. Paul equally claimed Messiahship as the proper category for Jesus. Paul was a believer in the unitary monotheism of Israel. He loved that One God of Israel and the fathers. Here is Paul's wonderful doxology in 1 Timothy 1:17: "Now to the king eternal, incorruptible, invisible, *the only God*, be honor and glory forever. Amen." He was addressing the Father.

I ask the reader to ponder this address to God. Is Paul here addressing a triune "essence" of God? Is he thinking of three Persons, all of whom are equally God and yet comprise one God-essence? Is Paul praising the "one what" of Hank Hanegraaff and James White's theology?[17] He defines the one and only God as the eternal king. The king is not "one what" but "one who." What would Jesus and Paul have made of C.S. Lewis' famous quotation that "we must remind ourselves that Christian theology does not believe God to be a person"?[18]

When Trinitarians have finished their voluminous attempts to explain the Trinity as "three who's in one what" they fail entirely to tell us of a single reference to God in the Bible as a "What." This is because no writer believed in God as a triune essence! Of some twelve thousand references to "God" in the Bible, not a single one can be shown to mean "the triune God." None speaks of God as "one essence."

---

[17]The definition offered by "Bible Answer Man" Hank Hanegraaff and by James White in his book *The Forgotten Trinity*. White says, "We dare not mix up the *what's* and *who's* regarding the Trinity" (27).
[18]*Christian Reflections,* 79.

More on the Jewish-Christian Creed

William Mounce in the *Word Biblical Commentary* is quite clear about Paul's thinking in his doxology in 1 Timothy 1:17 (above): "The only God." This is the central affirmation of Judaism as the Shema so eloquently states: "Hear, O Israel: the Lord our God is one Lord" (Deut. 6:4; cf. Mark 12:29, 32; cf. 1 Tim. 2:5; 6:15-16; cf. John 5:44; 17:3; Rom. 3:30; 1 Cor. 8:4-6; Eph. 4:6; Jude 25). The Shema was repeated every day at the synagogue and is still part of the daily prayer life of the pious Jew. It was perhaps this confession more than any other that made the Judeo-Christian outlook unique in the ancient world. Paul began this paragraph by thanking Christ. He closes it by ascribing to God honor and glory.[19]

Paul had never heard of a triune God, or if he had he would have dismissed such an idea as alien. As was Jesus, Paul was committed to the unitary monotheism of Judaism. Paul and Jesus were following the creed of Israel. They never expanded it or revised it. They repeated it. Of course they knew also of the Son of Man, Jesus, as the one now exalted to the right hand of the One God, the Father. But this did not "modify" the creed of Israel defining who the One God is. The coordination of the unique man Jesus with God introduced the stupendous concept that there was now a glorified *human being*, "*the man* Messiah Jesus*" (1 Tim. 2:5), elevated to a unique position next to the One God. It was God Himself who had carried out this wonderful plan. It is the measure of the incomparable destiny of man in the new creation.

None of the New Testament writers suggests a modification, in any way, of the unitary creed of their heritage. They would not have dared to imagine altering it in any way. The later second-century Gentile-controlled church leaders did not have such scruples. They prepared the way for later developments in the definition of God. Their successors eventually, but only after centuries of conflict, *shifted* the One God from One God, the Father to one essence, the Father, Son and Holy Spirit. That is a new and unbiblical creed.

---

[19]*Word Biblical Commentary: Pastoral Epistles,* Thomas Nelson, 2000, 61.

Two Is Not One

At the simplest level, the unwarranted promotion of Jesus to the status of the One God created confusion. Two cannot be made into one. Cardinal J.H. Newman recognized this stark fact of the universe when he said of the Trinity, "The mystery of the doctrine of the Holy Trinity is not merely a verbal contradiction, but an incompatibility in the human ideas conveyed...We can scarcely make a nearer approach to an exact enunciation of it, than that of saying that one thing is two things."[20]

Can the Church afford to be trading on a contradiction? Christians lay claim to the heritage of Israel and profess to be followers of Israel's Messiah. But in the matter of creed, it appears that Christianity has departed from the thinking of its founder. While the Jesus of history believed in and worshipped as God the single Person Yahweh of the Hebrew creed, Christians have expanded that creed to *include two other Persons.* And then, as if to register some embarrassment at this departure from Jesus, they maintain that despite believing in three who are all equally God, they really still believe that God is at the same time one. But that one, by being also three, is not the One God defined by the Bible and by Jesus. It is a redefinition. A tectonic shift occurred when the One God mysteriously became *three* in one. This happened in post-biblical times and was later set in stone by church councils which do not possess the authority of Scripture (a fact to which Christians pay at least lip service). On what basis may the Church legitimately claim the Bible as its authority and at the same time abandon Jesus' definition of the One God?

Erickson and the Creed

Where does the Bible ever hint at a creed so complex that it provoked centuries of often acrimonious debate, ecclesiastical upheaval, hair-splitting arguments over terminology, excommunication and even killing? History records that explaining how one can at the same time be three has exhausted the ingenuity of the most brilliant theologians. Evangelicals' contemporary leading apologist for the view that God is three Persons, Millard Erickson,

---

[20]John Henry Newman, *Select Treatises of St. Athanasius*, James Parker and Co., 1877, 515.

candidly admits after an extensive discussion that it is surprising that
the Trinity gets no direct mention in the Bible:

> It is claimed that the doctrine of the Trinity is a very
> important, crucial, and even basic doctrine. If that is indeed
> the case, should it not be somewhere more clearly, directly,
> and explicitly stated in the Bible? If this is the doctrine that
> especially constitutes Christianity's uniqueness, as over
> against unitarian monotheism on the one hand, and
> polytheism on the other hand, how can it be only implied in
> the biblical revelation?...Here is a seemingly crucial matter
> where the Scriptures do not speak loudly and clearly.[21]

Erickson responds: "Little direct response can be made to this
charge. *It is unlikely that any text of Scripture can be shown to teach
the doctrine of the Trinity in a clear, direct and unmistakable
fashion.*"[22] Erickson goes on to rescue himself from this quandary by
hoping, nevertheless, to "look closely at the Bible and see if the
witness to the Trinity there may not be clearer and more broadly
based than may have been thought."[23]

When he discusses the logical structure of the Trinity, Erickson
quotes author Stephen Davis who feels "he is dealing with a
mystery."[24] Erickson then makes the astonishing admission that Davis
"has perhaps been more candid than many of us, who when pressed
may have to admit that *we really do not know in what way God is one
and in what different way he is three.*"[25] Davis did not risk saying
what is obviously not true of the Bible's God, that He is "one *what* in
three *who's.*"

God Is a Single Divine Person

A straightforward reading of the Bible reveals that God is
presented as a single Person, with all the characteristics of a Person.
He is not a "What" but a "Who."

Admissions that "language is inadequate" to spell out the Trinity
clearly have not prevented the printing of oceans of words attempting
to explain the Trinity, using the non-biblical language of Greek

---

[21]Millard J. Erickson, *God in Three Persons*, Baker Books, 1995, 108-109.
[22]Ibid., 109, emphasis added.
[23]Ibid.
[24]Ibid., 258.
[25]Ibid., emphasis added.

philosophy, that the One God of the Bible is three hypostases in one essence, and that the Son of God was, incredibly, "man" but not "a man." (Did you know that this is what official Christendom believes?) The Bible nowhere, however, calls God "an essence" and never speaks of "three hypostases." And any reader of the New Testament should be able to see that Jesus was a man.

And if language is unable or inadequate to tell us how many God is, or how three is really one, then it is the Bible which has failed to do this. Is God unable to communicate to us through the number "one"? The biblical language is entirely adequate as revelation about what God intends us to understand, at least in terms of His single personality.

It is a matter of astonishment to us that Erickson in his 350-page defense of the Trinity omits entirely any reference to Mark 12:28-34 where Jesus publicly affirms the authoritative creed, that of Israel. Erickson mentions "passages of distinction" like Psalm 110:1, which "speak of one Lord and another Lord, thus drawing some distinction between them (Ps. 110:1; Acts 2:34)."[26] But this is much too vague. The presence of two lords in no way proves that both are God! The second lord, as we shall see, is expressly *not* God, that is, not given the title of Deity. And if "Yahweh is *one* Lord" (Deut. 6:4), it should be obvious that another cannot be Yahweh! Another can of course *represent* Yahweh or act for Yahweh, reflect Yahweh's character, or carry out the will of Yahweh — and Jesus did all of those things — but if Yahweh is one Person, Jesus cannot *be* Yahweh. Two Yahwehs do not make one Yahweh. And the Son is always described in the New Testament (and by prophecy in the Old) as a person distinct from his Father, who is another and different Person. They enjoy, as has been said, an "I-Thou" relationship. And Jesus speaks of himself and his Father as "we" and "us," and as parallel to two individual witnesses (John 8:16-19). He also confessed his subordination to the Father: "The Father is greater than I" (John 14:28).

There seems to be a conspiracy in Christian literature generally to hide this very simple piece of information about Jesus' Jewish creed. Ought not the creed of Jesus Christ to be sufficient for his followers? And need more be said than the creed of Paul in 1 Timothy 2:5 that "there is one God and one mediator between God and men, the man

---

[26]Ibid., 53.

Messiah Jesus"? Understanding that fact about the constitution of the universe Paul has just called "coming to the knowledge of the truth" and "being saved" (1 Tim. 2:4).

I am thankful nevertheless for Professor Erickson's candor. He admits that the introduction of the *logos* (word) concept of John 1:1 as meaning *the preexisting Son of God* "legitimized the incorporation of philosophical speculation, specifically, Neo-Platonic philosophy within the creed of the church."[27] Paul however issued a severe warning against trying to define God in terms of philosophy (Col. 2:8). It happened nevertheless. It needs to be corrected, so that we can worship God in the spirit and truth taught by Jesus, basing ourselves on the very words of Jesus about who God is.

A Simple Creed

How can one possibly miss the New Testament confirmation of the unique status of God as one Person? A well-known investigation into the Trinity reports: "The Jews believed in one God whom they called the Father...For an understanding of the growth of the doctrine of the Trinity the title 'Father' is of special importance, because in the Trinity one of the Persons is God the Father."[28] Arthur Wainwright then presents the following New Testament texts to show "how New Testament writers expressed their belief in the unity of God and described Him as Father."[29]

This last statement would appear to be a practical admission that the New Testament writers were unitarians! What do you as a reader make of these statements?

---

[27]Ibid, 54. John did not of course write "In the beginning was the *Son*," but "In the beginning was the *word*." Cf. Dr. Colin Brown's very telling challenge: "It is a common but patent misreading of [John 1:1] to read it as if it said: 'In the beginning was the *Son*'" ("Trinity and Incarnation: In Search of Contemporary Orthodoxy," *Ex Auditu* 7, 1991, 89). It would be an extraordinary exegetical step to suppose that John in one sentence turned God into two! Not least because Jesus clearly knew only of the God "who alone is truly God," and he was addressing his *Father* in that statement (John 17:3), as a good Jewish unitary monotheist.

[28]*The Trinity in the New Testament*, SPCK, 1980, 41.

[29]Ibid., 41, 42.

Jesus:
"Why do you call me good? None is good except one, namely God" (Mark 10:18).
"The Lord our God is one Lord" (Mark 12:29).
"Call no man your father on earth; for one is your Father, who is in heaven" (Matt. 23:9).
"And the glory which comes from the only God you do not seek" (John 5:44).
"And this is eternal life: that they should know you, the only true God, and him whom you sent, Jesus Christ" (John 17:3).

Paul:
"...if so be that God is one. We know that no idol is anything in the world, and that there is no God but one...Yet to us there is one God, the Father" (1 Cor. 8:4-6).
"For God is one and will justify the circumcised on the basis of faith and the uncircumcised through faith" (Rom. 3:30).
"Now a mediator is not a mediator of one; but God is one" (Gal. 3:20). "God is only one Person."[30]
"One God and Father of all" (Eph. 4:6).
"Now to the King, eternal, incorruptible, invisible, the only God, be honor and glory forever and ever" (1 Tim. 1:17).
"For there is one God and one mediator between God and men, the man Messiah Jesus" (1 Tim. 2:5).

James and Jude:
"You believe that God is one; you do well" (James 2:19).
"One is the lawgiver and judge, who is able to save and destroy" (James 4:12).
"To the only God our Savior, through Jesus Christ our Lord, be glory, majesty, dominion and power, before all time and now and forever" (Jude 25).

"God" is here the Father, as is true some 1317 times in the New Testament. God is explicitly distinguished from Jesus Christ. Wainwright comments on the list of texts above: "The evidence shows that God was regarded as one; *and the one God was believed to*

---

[30]*Amplified Version.*

be the Father of the Lord Jesus Christ. Statements of this nature hardly seem to provide fruitful ground for the growth of a doctrine of the Trinity." He then says that "if they are taken in connection with other statements in which the divinity of Christ is affirmed or implied, they lead immediately to the Trinitarian problem."[31]

Wainwright is right about the Trinitarian "problem." The problem does not arise however until the unitarian texts above are rejected. As to statements about Jesus' "divinity," none of them challenges the statements about the Father being the only God. If they did challenge those unitarian statements they would contradict them. This in turn would lead to the conclusion that the New Testament contradicts itself in its definition of God. This I do not accept. And Jesus, the Jew and founder of our faith, as well as his chosen Apostles, knew who God was.

Once the New Testament unitarian texts are accepted for what they plainly say (in harmony with the whole of the Old Testament and with Jesus in Mark 12:28-34), the verses describing the so-called "divinity" of Jesus can easily be explained as descriptions of Jesus as the man Messiah, in whom the One God was uniquely active through His spirit, and who was exalted to the supreme position assigned to him by God the Father, as predicted in Psalm 110:1. Jesus in the New Testament is seen as the unique agent and reflection of the One God. His "equality" with his Father does not make him God. He is still the man Messiah. The truth then emerges that there is indeed still "one God," but He has next to Him now "one mediator, *the man* Messiah Jesus," as 1 Timothy 2:5 says so lucidly and simply.

Jesus: A Fully Human Person

The crowning and amazing truth which results from this analysis is that Jesus Christ really is a human being, that is to say a unique human being, sinless and virginally begotten, and resurrected to immortality as the first of the new creation. This paradigm allows the One God to remain in His unrivaled position as "the only one who is truly God," as Jesus said in John 17:3, referring to his Father. And Jesus is seen to be the Son of that One God, supernaturally procreated as Luke 1:35 so plainly states. This paradigm above all allows Jesus' definition of who God is to remain undisturbed. The *later* creedal

---

[31]*The Trinity in the New Testament*, 42.

statements by church councils have in fact undermined and contradicted Jesus' own declaration of the unitarian creed of Israel (in Mark 12:29). The biblical position is not that God *was* Christ but that "God was *in* Christ, reconciling the world to Himself" (2 Cor. 5:19).

The Church has sometimes enforced its own non-biblical creed with the strong arm of state law, even executing or burning to death objectors. The spirit thus demonstrated is not the spirit of Jesus.

Has the Church created its own problem creed, and then wearied itself trying to make sense of it, while at the same time both obscuring the simple words of Jesus and antagonizing myriads of Muslims and Jews?

Would a God of love offer us an ambiguous or confusing statement about who He is? Would a God who is three not provide a single Bible verse in which the word three and God appear together? An understanding of who He is enables us to flee every form of idolatry and the menace of promoting others than He as God, as the object of religious worship. God is, Jesus said, "one Lord" — one, not two, not three Lords — certainly not one abstract "essence." He is definitely one Person, since a Lord is a Person — one Person, so designated thousands of times both by nouns and singular personal pronouns. He is the One God of Abraham, Isaac and Jacob, the God of Jesus himself.

It should come as something of a shock then when I suggest that contemporary churches, intent no doubt on serving and obeying Jesus as Messiah, do *not* proclaim the creed obviously adhered to by Jesus. Consult your church statement of faith, its defining creed. In its constitution, the reason for its existence, you will find this: "We believe that God exists in three Persons."

This is certainly not the creed of Jesus. It is fundamentally different. The difference is immediately apparent to every reader. God has become mysteriously "three." But for Jesus, God was strictly one — one Lord. Addressing his Father, Jesus said, "You are the only one who is truly God" (John 17:3). Jesus is here speaking to the Father. He defines Him as "the only one who is truly God." He distinguishes himself in the same sentence from the only God, by calling himself the Messiah, commissioned by God. Yet churches maintain that there are two others who are equally the true God.

Has God been denied the supreme, unequalled, unrivaled position He claims for Himself over and over again in Scripture?

Do We As Christians Learn our Creed from Jesus?

Evangelical apologist Carl Henry wrote: "The triune God is indeed the 'ontological premise' on which the historic Christian faith is founded."[32] But Jesus said nothing of the sort. He knew nothing of any triune God. He was no Greek philosopher concerned with questions of "ontology." His premise for sound faith is belief in the unipersonal God of Israel. Such is the testimony of Scripture to the creed of Jesus.

Is Jesus then not the source of the creed of "the historic Christian faith"? Has the One God suffered a stolen identity when more are added as candidates for the status of Deity? I suggest that this patent difference between the creed of Jesus and the creed of the Church ought to be cause for concern, indeed for alarm. I say this on the basis of Jesus' intense warnings that it is perilous to disregard him as teacher and lord. The announcement that Jesus had been born as "the Lord *Messiah*" (Luke 2:11) places him as God's appointed head of the human race and demands our loyal service of him at every level. But on no account are we at liberty to change his public affirmation of his own creed, the creed of Israel and the Bible, that God is to be understood as one single Lord and God — indeed as "the God and Father of the Lord Jesus" (2 Cor. 11:31).

When commentators discuss the roots of the Christian faith, they subconsciously dismiss Jesus as the real foundation of Christian belief. When *The Interpreter's One-Volume Commentary on the Bible* arrives at Mark 12:29, it hastens to tell us that the commandments to love God and neighbor present "a central doctrine of early Gentile Christianity."[33] That is certainly true, but the commentary changes its tune suddenly when it comes to Jesus' quotation of Deuteronomy 6:4 as the introduction to the command to love. We are told that Jesus' affirmation of Deuteronomy 6:4 "would be satisfactory to all Jews. These are the most treasured verses of Judaism."[34] But are they not the most precious treasure of Christians who desire to love and follow Jesus? Why not? A curious divorcing of Israel's creed from what is thought to be Christianity is evident here. But how can the Christian faith safely disconnect itself from its founder without serious damage and loss?

---

[32]F.F. Bruce et al., *The Origin of the Bible*, Tyndale House, 2003, 25.
[33]Abingdon Press, 1971, 664.
[34]Ibid.

Textbooks on the Bible are keen to provide this information. Probably the earliest Christian creedal statement was the simple yet profound proclamation "Jesus is Lord!" (Rom. 10:9; 1 Cor. 12:3; 2 Cor. 4:5; Phil. 2:11). Saying "Jesus is Lord" was the basic creed of early Christians. The more fundamental question is, How did Jesus define God?

In this typical statement about Jesus as "Lord," the earlier creed of Jesus himself has vanished! Jesus is detached from his Jewish roots in the minds of churchgoers and then reattached to the Church's creed, and not permitted to maintain his own Christian creed, which is the ancient unitarian creed of Israel. Now inspect the creed of mainstream churches. There is no attempt there to reproduce the words of Jesus' creed. Rather we are asked to submit to a very different concept of God. God is one, it is said, but — and here the switch is obvious — "He exists as three Persons." Lip service is paid to the biblical creed, while it is immediately altered to mean something quite different. If we inquire further about this strange proposition we are told that God is three Persons but one substance or essence. Is not the difference quite obvious between God as a single Person and God as one "What"? Jews and Muslims certainly recognize that difference instantly, and they shrink from the notion that God's oneness is an "Essence" composed of three Persons. What Bible verse states that God is "one What"? Anyone who makes such a claim has been taught by post-biblical creeds, certainly not by Scripture. In Scripture God is one Person, never one "What" or essence.

Could Jesus have affirmed that Trinitarian creed? On the contrary. The Jewish creed of Jesus defines the God of the Bible and of Israel as "one Lord." One Lord is a single Lord, one Person — certainly not three Persons. Surely this question should engage our intense interest. It must be of great significance that we are defining God in a way which Jesus, speaking of the most important of all commandments, did not!

I doubt if churchgoers have given this much thought. It appears that not many sermons are given these days on the creed, on the definition of who God is. It is simply assumed that the church councils (Nicea in 325 and Chalcedon in 451) faithfully handed down the right understanding and definition of God for us. Everyone is supposed to know that the Church is based on belief in a triune God.

Those councils are said to have expressed the sum of what the Bible teaches about God. But did they? Is the creed of Jesus the same creed as the creed of the councils and your church? Would it not be plain common sense to recite in church the creed which Jesus himself recited?

The articles of the Church of England wisely warned that "councils may err."[35] The belief system of Jesus himself appears to have suffered a severe blow when councils and churches adopted a strange "three-in-one" view of God, about which Jesus knew nothing.

Jews Were Never Trinitarians

Everyone with even a minimal grasp of the history of Israel knows that Jews never, ever believed in a three-Person God. Jews were passionately and resolutely attached to the belief that God is one Divine Person. They are what theologians helpfully call "unitarians,"[36] or better "unitary monotheists." Jews for all of their history were never believers in a triune God. To this day, they recoil in horror at such a departure from the cardinal tenet of their revealed religion.

Jesus was a Jew. Jesus was an unflinching unitarian. Jesus is also the teacher and Lord of all professing Christians (John 13:13).

An Oxford professor of theology, lecturing on the Trinity, makes our point:

> Christianity, as I said last week, began as a trinitarian religion with a unitarian theology. It arose within Judaism and the monotheism of Judaism was then, as it is still, unitarian. How was the Christian church to state a theology adequate to express the new knowledge of God which had come to it through Jesus Christ? In what terms could the Christians think of God as He was revealed to them in the practice of their religion? Were they to repudiate monotheism and assert a tritheistic theology? Or could the monotheism be revised so as to include the new revelation without ceasing to be monotheistic? That was the problem with which the Church was wrestling in those early centuries in which the creeds

---

[35]Church of England article of faith XXI.
[36]I am writing unitarian with a lower-case "u" to distinguish it from the modern Unitarian Universalists, whose theology would be rather different from that presented here.

were formulated. Last week we were considering one aspect of that piece of Christian history, and we saw that Christian thought developed through the intercourse of its religious beliefs inherited from Judaism with the Greek tradition of philosophical thinking. I shall now try to show that the upshot of this development was a revision both of the theological idea of monotheism and of the philosophical idea of unity.[37]

This statement demands careful analysis. The faith of Judaism was always unitarian, belief in God as a single Person. But the Church, so argues the professor, revised its original unitarian view of God and turned God into three Persons, calling that view monotheism.

Listen to the impassioned objection of Jews to the Trinitarian creed adopted by those claiming to follow the Jew Jesus:

Room for the Master of Nazareth within the structure of Jewish thought is only possible on the condition of a clear distinction between the Christ of the Christian dogma and Jesus the *Jew*...The Christian perception of Jesus in terms of the Holy Trinity rests upon a tragic misunderstanding...the rehabilitation of the "historic Jesus" at the expense of the orthodox Son of God...It is only a vague and diluted Christian theology which imagines it possible to come to terms with Judaism. In reality there is no understanding between the two faiths: They possess no common denominator which could form the basis for a "bridge theology"...Montefiore is well aware of the difficulty as can be seen from an earlier remark: "The center of the teaching of the historic Jesus is God: the center of the teaching of the Church is he (i.e. Jesus himself). It is this peculiar attitude to Jesus which divides forever the Church from the Synagogue."[38]

The same writer underlines the Jewish view of the unity of God:

The essence of Judaism is the doctrine of the absolute and unmodified unity of God. Prof. Moore's masterly definition of the Jewish conception of that unity can hardly be surpassed. He calls it "the numerically exclusive and uncompromisingly personal monotheism." With it Judaism

---

[37]Leonard Hodgson, *Christian Faith and Practice*, Blackwell, 1952, 74.
[38]Jacob Jocz, *The Jewish People and Jesus Christ*, SPCK, 1962, 262.

stands or falls. Indeed the absolute unity of the God of Israel together with the Torah, i.e., the revelation of this one and only God, form the heart and essence of Judaism. The rest of Jewish thought and practice is of secondary importance when compared with these two fundamental truths...This most vital tenet, as conceived by orthodox and liberal Judaism alike, stands thus in direct opposition to the Trinitarian doctrine of the Christian Church.[39]

But who decides what creed Christians are to accept? What happened to the creed of Jesus himself, which is recorded by our gospels as the unitarian creed of Israel? Late in his ministry Jesus affirmed as the most critically important spiritual issue of all, the fact that God is one and that this One God is to be loved with all our being. Jesus, we submit, did not in any way revise the creed of his own Jewish heritage. Jesus nowhere authorized a new definition of God! The professor (Hodgson, above) may speak of the "wrestling" of the Church as they struggled to express faith in Jesus. But who said that the creed could be altered, or needed to be altered, and become unrecognizable as the creed of Jesus? Who said that the creed of the Bible is something to wrestle over?

Neither Paul nor any New Testament writer attempted to "improve on" the creed of Jesus or their Jewish heritage. It was the *later*, post-biblical Church which through a torturous process gradually slipped away from its biblical heritage, grounded in the very words of Jesus. In 325 AD after bitter struggles, the monotheism of Jesus was officially revised to include three Persons. Revised? Can one safely alter the creed, and brush aside the words of Jesus?

Concessions of Scholars

There are lots of very competent scholars who have shown that the language of the creeds which churches accept is very different from the language of the Bible. Most obviously, there is a glaring difference between Jesus' creed in Mark 12 and that of churches announcing belief in God who is three.

The *Encyclopedia Britannica* in its 15th edition observes correctly that:

---

[39]Ibid., 262-265.

Neither the word Trinity, nor the explicit doctrine as such, appears in the New Testament, nor did Jesus and his followers intend to contradict the Shema in the Old Testament, "Hear, O Israel, The Lord our God is one Lord" (Deut. 6:4). It was not until the fourth century that the distinctness of the one and three and their unity were brought together in a single orthodox doctrine of one essence and three persons.

Dr. Marvin Wilson, an expert on the Hebrew roots of Christianity, comments well on Jesus' unmistakable confirmation of the creed of Israel:

> Of the 5,845 verses in the Pentateuch, "Hear, O Israel..." sounds the historic keynote of all Judaism. This fundamental truth and leitmotif of God's uniqueness prompts one to respond by fulfilling the fundamental obligation to love God (Deut. 6:5). Accordingly, when Jesus was asked about the "most important commandment," his reply did not contradict this central theme of Judaism (Mark 12:28-34; cf. Matt. 22:34-40). With 613 individual statutes of the Torah from which to choose, Jesus cited the Shema, including the command to love God; but he also extended the definition of the "first" and "great" commandment to include love for one's neighbor (Lev. 19:18)...Yahweh is the Supreme Being, wholly unlike all other things in the universe, which have been created by Him.[40]

Wilson then mentions that some scholars have seen God as a "complex unity." He wisely makes no attempt to justify this attempt to read later theology back into the simple words of the Hebrew Bible. But he strangely seems unalarmed that the Church he belongs to does not subscribe to the creed affirmed by Jesus himself.

Dr. Wilson provides excellent historical comment on the creed recited by Jesus. He states that the Shema "is one of the most crucial Old Testament texts for the foundational teachings of *both Jesus and Judaism.*"[41] But that foundational creed of Jesus is nowhere to be found on the books of mainline churches. For all of his good history and presentation of the facts, Professor Wilson seems unable to

---

[40]*Our Father Abraham*, Eerdmans, 1989, 124-125.
[41]Ibid., 122.

protest the Church's — his own church's — failure to uphold the creed of Jesus.

Unless, then, it can be shown that belief in three Persons who are God can be reconciled with the Shema affirmed by Jesus, Christians have a defective creed. They have been mistaken for centuries. They have abandoned Jesus at a fundamental level (as well as keeping many Jews and Muslims away from considering the claims of Jesus).

Let us do some further comparing. We have seen what creed Jesus established as the foundation of true religion: "the Lord our God is one Lord." Now let us hear what Christians were supposed to recite as creed some 500 years after the time of Jesus.

From the Jew Jesus to a New Gentile Creed

Below is the so-called Athanasian creed. I will not quote it in full, but give you enough to show how it unpacks the summary statement that "God exists in three Persons."

> Whoever wants to be saved, before all things it is necessary that he hold the catholic [universal] faith; which faith unless everyone keeps it whole and undefiled, without doubt he will perish everlastingly. And the catholic faith is this: that we worship one God in Trinity, and Trinity in Unity; neither confounding the persons nor dividing the substance...The Father eternal, the Son eternal and the Holy Spirit eternal, and they are not three eternals but one eternal...So likewise the Father is almighty, the Son almighty, and the Holy Spirit almighty. And yet they are not three almighties, but one almighty. So the Father is God, the Son is God and the Holy Spirit is God. And yet they are not three Gods, but one God. So likewise the Father is Lord, the Son Lord and the Holy Spirit Lord; and yet they are not three Lords but one Lord. For just as we are compelled by the Christian verity to acknowledge every Person by himself to be God and Lord, so we are forbidden by the catholic religion to say there are three Gods or three Lords...And in this Trinity none is before or after another; none is greater or less than another. But the whole three persons are coeternal and coequal. So that in all things, as aforesaid, the Unity in Trinity and the Trinity in Unity is to be worshipped. He who wants to be saved must thus think of the Trinity.

Note the heavy threats leveled at any who might question this amazing dogma. But could Jesus have possibly subscribed to that creed? Or would Jesus himself have fallen under the cruel anathemas of this "Christian" creed? The appalling possibility is that Jesus would have fled from association with this bizarre document, which presents the ordinary reader with rather obvious non-sense.

Jesus patently knew nothing about the creeds of Nicea or the so-called Athanasian creed. Jesus perfectly taught and carried out the will of his Father. Jesus' own affirmation of the creed of Israel is testimony to the greatest fact of the universe — that there is a God, and that He is one divine Person. Could even the God of Jesus possibly believe in the Trinity?

I believe that the professor of church history was precisely right when he observed:

> The Old Testament is strictly monotheistic. God is a single personal being. The idea that a Trinity is to be found there is utterly without foundation... There is no break between the Old Testament and the New. The monotheistic tradition is continued. Jesus was a Jew, trained by Jewish parents in the Old Testament scriptures. His teaching was Jewish to the core; a new gospel indeed but not a new theology...And he accepted as his own belief the great text of Jewish monotheism: Hear, O Israel, the Lord our God is one God.[42]

Standard works on the Bible are quite clear about the facts. Here is an excerpt from the *Exegetical Dictionary of the New Testament* in its entry on the word "one": "Early Christianity consciously adopts from Judaism (Deut. 6:4) the monotheistic formula 'God is one.' According to Mark 12:29, 32, Jesus explicitly approves the Jewish monotheistic formula."[43] Paul was equally "Jewish" in his core belief about God: "There is one God and one mediator between God and men, the man Messiah Jesus" (1 Tim. 2:5). That creedal statement of Paul, reflecting Jesus' view of God, should have been enough. But the Church went beyond and outside the Bible. Church history witnesses to the chaos which has ensued.

Hugh Anderson in his commentary on Mark speaks amazingly of the "Church that did not any longer recite the Shema," while "Jesus

---

[42]L.L. Paine, *A Critical History of the Evolution of Trinitarianism*, Houghton Mifflin and Co., 1900, 4.
[43]*Exegetical Dictionary of the New Testament,* Eerdmans, 1990, 399.

stands foursquare within the orbit of Jewish piety."[44] What then
happened to the Church? Did it forget its founder? There was surely
nothing inadequate about the Savior's theology and his confession
that his God was the God of his Jewish heritage. Why do we as
Christians not remain within Jesus' Jewish orbit of piety?

Jesus' unitarian confession is a fixed belief from the Shema of
Deuteronomy 6:4 handed down through the prophets of Israel to Jesus
himself in Mark 12. Leading Jews of the time of Jesus echoed the
same creed. Josephus was typical: "To acknowledge God as one is
common to all the Hebrews."[45] And Philo: "Let us, then, engrave deep
in our hearts this as the first and most sacred of commandments, to
acknowledge and honor one God who is above all, and let the idea
that gods are many never even reach the ears of the man whose rule
of life is to seek for truth in purity and goodness."[46] Jesus' creed "is in
conformity with the Jewish confession."[47]

Does our Lord Jesus not have the right to tell us who God is?
Would it not be perilous and arrogant for us to ignore the Lord Jesus'
understanding of monotheism?

I return to the striking comments of a leading contemporary
systematic theologian. In his classic evangelical work on the
development of doctrine Professor Harold O.J. Brown considered in
1984 that we have now "entered a post-Chalcedonian era." He regrets
this trend:

> The transformation this development portends is greater than
> anything that has yet happened within Christianity. It can be
> compared only to the transition within biblical monotheism
> itself, from the unitary monotheism of Israel to the
> trinitarianism of the Council of Chalcedon. The difference is
> symbolized by the transition from the prayer *Shema Yisroel,*
> of Deuteronomy 6:4 ("Hear, O Israel: The Lord our God is
> one Lord..."), to the confession of the Athanasian Creed,
> "We worship one God in Trinity, and Trinity in unity." Was
> the transition from the personal monotheism of Israel to the
> tripersonal theism of Nicea a legitimate development of Old

---

[44]*Gospel of Mark (New Century Bible Commentary),* Eerdmans, 1981, 280.
[45]*Antiquities* 5. 112.
[46]*Decalogue* 65.
[47]Eduard Schweizer, *The Good News According to Mark*, John Knox Press,
1970, 251.

Testament revelation? Christians affirm that it is, holding that Nicea represents a fuller unfolding, not a distortion, of the self-disclosure of the God of Israel. Indeed, the trinitarianism of Nicea and the Christological definitions of Chalcedon are seen as the valid and necessary interpretation of the claims of Jesus Christ in the context of the Old Testament witness to the God who is One.[48]

What the professor seems not to notice is that the transition he approves was in fact a transition which moved the Church away from Jesus himself! His remark is symptomatic of the giant ecclesiastical muddle which allows theologians to forget that Christianity is supposed to be based on Christ himself. Abandoning the creed of Jesus must amount to abandoning him.

Brown's concession that the Church has altered the creed of Jesus clashes with the plain statement of the *Dictionary of Christ and the Gospels*: "To Jesus, as to His people through many centuries, God was one. *He did not modify this ancient belief.*"[49]

Very much to the point is the perceptive remark of Professor Hiers who notes that "interpreters of Christian persuasion have ordinarily not been especially interested in what Jesus intended and did in his own lifetime,"[50] and Professor Loofs who warned about the Hellenizing of the faith and a "camouflaged introduction of polytheism into Christianity"[51] and Professor Martin Werner who deplored the paganization of the faith.[52]

Unless it can be demonstrated from Scripture that Jesus authorized a new creed, the Church must confess to having adopted a definition of God which is not Christ's and thus not strictly Christian. A revolution is needed if we are to take Jesus seriously in the matter of defining who God and he is. The Reformation of the sixteenth century must be reevaluated as very partial and in many ways inadequate. At issue is the question as to whether the Reformers really meant what they said when claiming that the Church is always

---

[48]Harold O.J. Brown, *Heresies*, 431.
[49]"God," *A Dictionary of Christ and the Gospels*, 1:650.
[50]Richard Hiers, *Jesus and the Future*, 1.
[51]Paul Schrodt, *The Problem of the Beginning of Dogma in Recent Theology*, Peter Lang, 1978, 121.
[52]*The Formation of Christian Dogma*, Harper, 1957, 298.

reforming[53] in order to recover its original status. Might not this question about who God is be a key to the solution of the vast problems which afflict Christendom, as well as the wider world of relations with Judaism and Islam?

---

[53]*Semper Reformanda.*

Chapter 3

Biblical Fact and History Against Dogma

"Granted that the New Testament does not say, in so many words, that Jesus of Nazareth was actually God, it is natural to ask how the Christian Church came to assert that he was."[1]

"Has any historian had the audacity to contend that Israel's doctrine of God in Jesus' day or afterwards was anything but the strictest monotheism?"[2]

Christians are urged by Paul to flee from any teaching which is not in harmony with the health-giving words — namely those of our Lord Jesus Christ:

> If anyone teaches a different doctrine and does not agree with the sound words of our Lord Jesus Christ and the teaching that accords with godliness, he has an over-high opinion of himself; being without knowledge, having only an unhealthy love of questionings and wars of words, from which come envy, fighting, cruel words, evil thoughts (1 Tim. 6:3).

This warning of the Apostle would seem to apply well to the hairsplitting wars of words which raged around the development of the post-biblical creeds. Ought it not to have been sufficient to rest in the creed of Jesus that none is the supreme God but his Father? "The Lord our God is one Lord" is a proposition easily understandable by

---

[1]Peter Hinchliff, "Christology and Tradition," in *God Incarnate: Story and Belief*, A.E. Harvey, ed., SPCK, 1981, 81.
[2]Pastor William Wachtel, "Christian Monotheism: Reality or Illusion," *The Restitution Herald*, April, 1985, 7.

any with a childlike attitude to truth, an approach which Jesus commended so highly.

Jesus is said in Scripture to be the Apostle of the Christian faith, "the apostle of our confession" (Heb. 3:1). The same verse names him our High Priest. Mention is often made of the Apostles' Creed, which is not in the Bible but reflects an early confession of Almighty God and Jesus. What could be wrong with appealing to the creed of *Jesus*, our *Apostle*: I believe that "the Lord our God is one Lord" (Mark 12:29)? Its parallel in John 17:3 records Jesus' own strict monotheism. He declared that "You, Father, are the only one who is truly God." These are easy propositions which should have been left in all their pristine purity. Years of conflict and confusion could have been avoided.

Ancient Voices of Protest

The celebrated poet John Milton was one of three distinguished minds of the seventeenth century, along with Sir Isaac Newton and John Locke (and many other learned dissenters), who protested against the Trinitarian creed of the churches. Milton's timely advice to us was to rely on Scripture alone:

> Let us then discard reason in sacred matters, and follow the doctrine of Holy Scripture exclusively...It is most evident...from numberless passages of Scripture that there is in reality but one true independent and supreme God; and as He is called one (inasmuch as human reason and the common language of mankind, and the Jews, the people of God, have always considered him as one person only, that is, one in a numerical sense) let us have recourse to the sacred writings in order to know who this one true and supreme God is. This knowledge ought to be derived in the first instance from the Gospel, since the clearest doctrine respecting the one God must necessarily be that copious and explanatory revelation concerning Him which was delivered *by Christ himself* to his apostles, and by the apostles to their followers. Nor is it to be supposed that the Gospel would be ambiguous or obscure on this subject; for it was not given for the purpose of promulgating new and incredible doctrines respecting the nature of God, hitherto utterly unheard of by his own people, but to announce salvation to the Gentiles through Messiah the

Son of God, according to the promise of the God of Abraham. "No man has seen God at any time; the only begotten Son, who is in the bosom of the Father, he has explained Him" (John 1:18). Let us therefore consult the Son in the first place respecting God.

According to the testimony of the Son, delivered in the clearest terms, the Father is that one true God, by whom are all things. Being asked by one of the scribes (Mark 12:28, 29, 32) which was the first commandment of all, he answered from Deuteronomy 6:4, "The first of all the commandments is, 'Hear, O Israel, the Lord our God is one Lord'"; or as it is in the Hebrew, "Jehovah our God is one Jehovah." The scribe assented; "there is one God, and there is none other but He"; and in the following verse Christ approves this answer. Nothing can be more clear than that it was the opinion of the scribe, as well as of the other Jews, that by the unity of God is intended His oneness of person. That this God was no other than God the Father is proved from John 8:41, 54, "We have one Father, even God...It is my Father who honors me; of whom you say that He is your God." John 4:21: "Neither in this mountain, nor yet at Jerusalem, shall you worship the Father." Christ therefore agrees with the whole people of God, that the Father is that one and only God. For who can believe it possible for the very first of the commandments to have been so obscure, and so ill-understood by the Church through such a succession of ages, that *two other persons*, equally entitled to worship, should have remained wholly unknown to the people of God, and debarred of divine honors even to that very day?...Christ himself therefore, the Son of God, teaches us nothing in the Gospel respecting the one God but what the Law had before taught, and everywhere clearly asserts him to be his Father. John 17:3: "This is eternal life, that they might know You, the only true God, and Jesus Christ whom You have sent." 20:17: "I ascend to my Father and your Father; to my God and your God." If therefore the Father be the God of Christ, and the same be our God, and if there be no other God but one, there can be no God beside the Father.[3]

After examining the plainly unitarian statements of Paul, Milton reflects on the prodigious efforts that the Church has made to confuse such simple truth, that God is one Person:

> Though all this [the numerical singularity of God] be so self-evident as to require no explanation — namely, that the Father alone is a self-existent God, and that a being which is not self-existent cannot be God — it is wonderful with what futile subtleties, or rather with what juggling artifices, certain individuals have endeavored to elude or obscure the plain meaning of these passages; leaving no stone unturned, recurring to every shift, attempting every means, as if their object were not to preach the pure and unadulterated truth of the Gospel to the poor and simple, but rather by dint of vehemence and obstinacy to sustain some absurd paradox from falling, by the treacherous aid of sophisms and verbal distinctions, borrowed from the barbarous ignorance of the schools.[4]

Isaac Newton

One of the most distinguished scientists of all time, Sir Isaac Newton (1642-1727) was a passionate opponent of the Church's understanding of the One God as triune. Because of his prominent public position his theological writings, which were immense, were guarded in their criticism of "orthodoxy." Nevertheless, Newton was familiar with the anti-Trinitarian writings of his time and he argued as did Arians and Socinians (anti-Trinitarians) of the seventeenth century that the word "God" in the Bible should be understood of the Father of Jesus and that the very occasional use of "God" for Jesus does not make him part of a co-eternal Godhead. Even Moses, Sir Isaac pointed out, was called God in an honorary sense.

Karen Armstrong explains Sir Isaac's dislike for the imaginative concept of God in Trinitarianism:

---

[3]John Milton, "On the Son of God and the Holy Spirit," rep. *A Journal from the Radical Reformation*, 5:2, 1996, 56-58.
[4]Ibid., 60.

His total immersion [was] in the world of *logos*...In his view, mythology and mystery were primitive and barbaric ways of thought. "'Tis the temper of the hot and superstitious part of mankind in matters of religion ever to be fond of mysteries and for that reason to like best what they understand least." Newton became almost obsessed with the desire to purge Christianity of its mythical doctrines. He became convinced that the a-rational dogmas of the Trinity and the incarnation were the result of conspiracy, forgery and chicanery...The spurious doctrines of the incarnation and the Trinity had been added to the creed by unscrupulous theologians in the fourth century. Indeed, the Book of Revelation had prophesied the rise of Trinitarianism — "this strange religion of the West," "the cult of three equal Gods."[5]

In his *Two Notable Corruptions* of 1690 Newton anticipated the work of many later scholars who have shown that the Greek manuscripts of our New Testament have been tampered with in certain verses with the intention of promoting the "Deity" of Jesus.[6] Newton was an advocate of simplicity: "In disputable places of Scripture" he loved "to take up what I can best understand."[7] Newton contended for simplicity against a backdrop of corrupting and complicating influences from philosophy and metaphysics. Newton believed that Scripture is reasonable and composed in the tongue of the vulgar. Thus there is an expectation that the Bible is written in plain and lucid language. Newton's professed desire to avoid introducing hypotheses into natural philosophy aligns with his suspicion about infusing metaphysics into Scripture." He argued also that one should "prefer those interpretations which are most according to the literal meaning of the Scriptures."[8]

Karen Armstrong affirms that Newton was correct in his analysis of the Trinity as irrational. She points out that the makers of Trinitarian dogma did not intend the doctrine to be subject to reasoned analysis:

---

[5]Karen Armstrong, *The Battle for God*, Ballantine Books, 2001, 69.
[6]See for example Bart Ehrman, *The Orthodox Corruption of Scripture*, Oxford University Press, 1993.
[7]Stephen Snobelen, "'God of gods and Lord of lords': The Theology of Isaac Newton's *General Scholium* to the *Principia*," *Osiris* 16, 2001, 198.
[8]Ibid., 199.

Ultimately…the Trinity only made sense as a mystical or spiritual experience: it had to be lived, not thought, because God went far beyond human concepts. It was not a logical or intellectual formulation but an imaginative paradigm that confounded reason. Gregory of Nazianzus made this clear when he explained that contemplation of the Three in One induced a profound and overwhelming emotion that confounded thought and intellectual clarity. "No sooner do I conceive of the One than I am illumined by the splendor of the Three; no sooner do I distinguish Three than I am carried back into the One. When I think of any of the Three, I think of him as the whole, and my eyes are filled, and the greater part of what I am thinking escapes me."[9]

One of the chief architects of the finished Trinitarian dogma considered that three men ought really to be thought of as one since they share a common humanity!

The atmosphere of such language and thought is far removed from that of Scripture. One's suspicions are further confirmed when we learn that Athanasius, chief architect of the Trinity, attempted to create an artificial connection between his teaching about God and the famous desert ascetic St. Antony. "Athanasius tried to show how his new doctrine affected Christian spirituality."[10] The real Antony:

comes across as a human and vulnerable man, troubled by boredom, agonizing over human problems and giving simple, direct advice…However, Athanasius presents him in an entirely different light. He is, for example, transformed into an ardent [pro-Trinitarian] opponent of Arianism; he had already begun to enjoy a foretaste of his future apotheosis [deification], since he shares the divine *apatheia* [inability to suffer pain] to a remarkable degree. When, for example, he emerged from the tombs where he had spent twenty years wrestling with demons, Athanasius says that Antony's body showed no signs of aging. He was a perfect Christian.[11]

Athanasius had no reservations about outright trickery in support of the justice of his case for the triune God.

---

[9]Karen Armstrong, *A History of God*, 117.
[10]Ibid, 113.
[11]Ibid., 113.

"Orthodox" clergy have been burdened with the problem of expressing their view of God at the peril of misstating it. This points to the awful complexity of Trinitarian theory as compared with the non-complex unitarian creed of Jesus. The Anglican Bishop Beveridge of the seventeenth century wrote:

> We are to consider the order of those persons in the Trinity described in the words before us in Matthew 28:19: First the Father, then the Son, and then the Holy Ghost, every one of which is really and truly God. A mystery which we are bound to believe, and must have great care how we speak of it, it being both easy and dangerous to mistake in expressing so great a truth as this is. If we think of it, how hard it is to imagine one numerically divine *nature* in more than one and the same divine *person*. Or, three divine persons in no more than one and the same divine nature. If we speak of it, how hard it is to find out words to express it. If I say, the Father, Son and Holy Ghost be three, and everyone distinctly God, it is true. But if I say they are three, and everyone a distinct God, it is false. I may say God the Father is one God and the Son is one God and the Holy Ghost is one God, but I cannot say that the Father is one God, and the Son is another God, and the Holy Ghost is a third God. I may say that the Father begat another who is God, but I cannot say that He begat another God. And from the Father and the Son proceeds another who is God, yet I cannot say, from the Father and the Son proceeds another God. For all this while, though their nature be the same, their persons are distinct. And though their persons are distinct, yet still their nature is the same. So that though the Father be the first person in the Godhead, the Son the second and the Holy Ghost the third, yet the Father is not the first God, the Son the second and the Holy Ghost a third God. So hard a thing it is to word so great a mystery aright; or to fit so high a truth with expressions suitable and proper to it, without going one way or another from it.[12]

The bishop went on to lament the fact that the chief complaint of the Koran is that Christians believe in a Trinity of persons in the

---

[12]William Beveridge, cited in Charles Morgridge, *The True Believer's Defence*, 1837, rep. Christian Educational Services, 1994, 13-14.

divine nature. Since each was designated God, the doctrine was rather obviously tritheistic in the eyes of a Muslim.

A contemporary of Bishop Beveridge offered us this by way of a description of the Trinity:

> There is one divine nature or essence, common to three Persons incomprehensibly united and ineffably distinguished; united in essential attributes, distinguished by peculiar idioms and relations; all equally infinite in every divine perfection, each different from the other in order and manner of subsistence. And there is a mutual inexistence of one in all, and all in one; a communication without deprivation or diminution in the communicant, an eternal generation and an eternal procession, without precedence or succession, without proper causality or dependence; a Father imparting his own, and the Son receiving his Father's life, and a Spirit issuing from both without any division or multiplication of essence.[13]

The admission of Professor Moses Stuart (1780-1852), one of the most learned Trinitarians of his day, shows how far "orthodox" definitions have departed from the biblical blueprint. Speaking of the definition of "persons" or "distinctions" in the Godhead, he wrote:

> I do not and cannot understand them. And to a definition I cannot consent, still less *defend* it, until I do understand what it signifies. I have no hesitation in saying that my mind is absolutely unable to elicit any distinct and certain ideas from any definition of *person* in the Godhead, which I have ever examined.[14]

Archbishop John Tillotson of the Church of England commented on the "jargon and canting language" of the schoolmen:

> I envy no man the understanding of these phrases, but to me they seem to signify nothing, but to have been words invented by idle and conceited men, which a great many ever since, lest they should seem to be ignorant, would seem to understand. But I wonder most what men, when they have amused and puzzled themselves and others with hard words, should call this *explaining* things.[15]

Another scholar wrote wisely:

[13]Barrow's *Works*, cited in *The True Believer's Defence*, 15.
[14]Cited in *The True Believer's Defence*, 15.
[15]Tillotson's *Works*, cited in *The True Believer's Defence*, 16.

The language of Scripture is the language of common sense;
the plain, artless language of nature. Why should writers
adopt such language as renders their meaning obscure; and
not only obscure, but unintelligible, and not only
unintelligible, but utterly lost in the strangeness of their
phraseology?[16]

Among repeated candid admissions of the extreme difficulties
bequeathed to the Church by the very non-Jewish creed of the church
fathers, there is this example of perplexity from Dr. John Hey:

When it is proposed to me to affirm, that "in the unity of the
Godhead there be three persons, of one substance, power, and
eternity, — the Father, the Son and the Holy Ghost," — I
have difficulty enough! My understanding is involved in
perplexity, my conceptions bewildered in the thickest
darkness. I pause, I hesitate; I ask what necessity there is for
making such a declaration...But does not this confound all
our conceptions, and make us use words without meaning? I
think it does. I profess and proclaim my confusion in the most
unequivocal manner: I make it an essential part of my
declaration. Did I pretend to understand what I say, I might
be a Tritheist or an Infidel; but I could not both worship the
one true God, and acknowledge Jesus Christ to be Lord of
all.[17]

Relief for the doctor's agonizing is provided simply by the
creedal words of Jesus: "You, Father, are the only one who is truly
God" (John 17:3). Jesus is His commissioned human Messiah. Jesus
referred to his Father as "my commissioning Father" (John 5:37;
6:44).

In our time the public is exposed to *The World's Easiest Guide to
Understanding God*. A conversation proceeds between two believers:

"All you need to remember is that there is one God," Dan
continued.

"Oh, so you don't consider Jesus to be a god," Jay
offered.

"Oh, yes I do," Dan emphasized. "Jesus is absolutely
God. And the Holy Spirit, He is God too."

---

[16]Dr. Dwight, cited in *The True Believer's Defence*, 16.
[17]Cited in John Wilson, *Unitarian Principles Confirmed by Trinitarian
Testimonies*, rep. University of Michigan, 2005, 322.

"All right," Jay said with a sigh, "so we've got the Father, who is God, Jesus who is God, and the Holy Spirit who is God. That adds up to — "
"One God," Dan finished. Jay slapped his forehead..."Okay, maybe it's as confusing as it sounds," Dan acknowledged.[18]

The author does little to ease the confusion:

> If the Trinity is not the most confusing and least understood aspect of the Christian faith, it is easily in the top five. It is not that the subject is unfamiliar. Most Christians can tell you that the Trinity is made up of the Father, Son and Holy Spirit. Beyond that, though, things get a little fuzzy.[19]

They do indeed. The proposition X is God, Y is God and Z is God and that makes one God is just nonsense. It can only be resolved into some sort of sense by the proposition that X, Y, and Z amount to one God in a sense different from that predicated of the three. 3X cannot equal 1X, but 3X can equal 1Y. The problem which remains unsolved is how to square any of this with the words of Jesus who declared the true God to be one Lord and a single Father.

Would it not be a resolution of all the confusion to admit with J.H. Newman (1801-1890): "The mystery of the doctrine of the Holy Trinity is not merely a verbal contradiction, but an incompatibility in the human ideas conveyed...We can scarcely make a nearer approach to an exact enunciation of it, than that of saying that one thing is two things"?[20] The same bewilderment was expressed by an Anglican Bishop Hurd (1720-1808): At the Trinity "reason stands aghast, and faith herself is half confounded."[21]

Statistics

In no verse in the Bible (and there are some 31,102 verses) is the word *three* ever associated with the word God. God is never said to be numerically three. None of the 810,677 words of the Bible provides a sample of the word "God" meaning a triune God. Yes, of

---

[18]Randy Southern, *The World's Easiest Guide to Understanding God*, Northfield, 2003, 84, 85.
[19]Ibid., 84, 85.
[20]*Select Treatises of St. Athanasius*, 515.
[21]Cited in Andrews Norton, *A Statement of Reasons for Not Believing the Doctrines of Trinitarians*, 1833, rep. University of Michigan, 2005, 82.

course, the Father, the Son and the Spirit are mentioned together often in the New Testament, but never once does any Bible writer arrive at the proposition that God is to be defined as three Persons. It is one thing to speak of the Father, Son and Holy Spirit together. It is quite another to say that each of these three is coequally God and that together they amount to one God! The so-called Trinitarian passage in Matthew 28:19 may sound like the much later doctrine of the Trinity. But it does not say that the three linked together as a triad amount to one God! Nor of course does the doxology in 2 Corinthians 13:13: "May the grace of our Lord Jesus Christ, the love of God, and the fellowship of the Holy Spirit be with you all." This statement says nothing at all about the triad being equal to one God.

Bible writers never mean a triune God when they say "God." Since the words "God," "Lord God," and LORD appear over twelve thousand times, they had about twelve thousand opportunities to make that equation "God = God in three Persons," but they never did.

They constantly say that God is a single Person and in the New Testament they equate that divine Individual with the *Father* of Jesus, who is everywhere said to be the Father's *Son*. Exhaustive studies by both Protestant and Catholic scholars affirm that the word God, used absolutely, in our New Testament documents refers to the Father of Jesus on page after page.[22] In no case, throughout the whole of Scripture, does the word "God" mean "God in three Persons." The tri-personal God is therefore never mentioned as such in the Scriptures. This fact surely calls for a public investigation.

The absence of the triune God as such would seem to rule out any suggestion that the Father and the Son are both *equally* to be thought of as God. While "God" in the New Testament describes the Father over 1300 times, the same word "God" is used of Jesus on two occasions for certain in the New Testament. There are a few verses where Jesus *may* be referred to as "God," but because of grammatical ambiguity this cannot be maintained with certainty.[23] The "one Lord"

---

[22]There is a very rare exception. On two occasions for certain the term "God" is applied to Jesus. But it should be remembered that the judges of Israel could be called God (Ps. 82:6) and that Moses was said to be God to Pharaoh (Exod. 7:1). The Roman emperor at the time of Jesus could also be addressed as "Lord and God."

[23]1 John 5:20; Rom. 9:5. 1 John 5:7 in the KJV is known by all modern commentators to be a forgery which is no part of the original text.

of the creed which we hear Jesus affirming as the basis of true religion (Mark 12:28-34, citing Deut. 6:4) is unambiguously a reference to the God and Father of Jesus. Jesus never hinted that he was overturning his whole Hebrew heritage in the matter of defining who God is, by including himself in the Godhead.

To say that he was God while acknowledging his Father as God would quite evidently confront his audiences with the proposition that there were two Gods. This Jesus never imagined. Nor did he accept for one moment any accusation that he was interfering with the creed of Israel. He was not accused of deconstructing the monotheism of his Hebrew heritage. On the contrary as we have seen in Mark 12:29, Jesus affirmed that strict, unitary monotheism of Judaism, making it the basis of the greatest of all commandments. In John's account of Jesus' teaching, Jesus identified his God as the God of the Jews, holding the Jewish creed in common with Jews: "We know whom we worship, for salvation is from the Jews" (John 4:22).

At what point, a church member today might reasonably inquire, was that greatest commandment of God and of Jesus rescinded? Are churches meeting in the name of Jesus free to disregard the heart of his theology of God and redefine the creed? Are they at liberty to reshape the meaning of ultimate reality?

An enormous fuss is made in America about the sanctity of the Ten Commandments, but how many are agitated by the fact that the Church has forgotten the greatest commandment — Jesus' own definition of who God is? It seems to be sailing under false colors.

Historian Karen Armstrong

There is no doubt at all about the historical facts:

> Christianity began as another of the first-century movements that tried to find another way of being Jewish. It centered on the life and death of a Galilean faith healer who was crucified by the Romans in about 30 CE. His followers claimed that he had risen from the dead. They believed that Jesus of Nazareth was the long-awaited Jewish Messiah, who would shortly return in glory to inaugurate the Kingdom of God on earth. He was "the son of God," a term they used in the Jewish

sense of someone who had been assigned a special task by God and enjoyed a privileged intimacy with him.[24]

Karen Armstrong's brief summary is equally helpful when she goes on to point out that:

The ancient royal theology had seen the king of Israel as the son and servant of Yahweh; the suffering servant in second Isaiah, who was associated with Jesus, had also suffered humiliation from his fellow humans and had been raised by God to an exceptionally high status. Jesus had no intention of founding a new religion and was deeply Jewish.[25]

We should modify this last statement slightly. Jesus did not just repeat the Judaism bequeathed to Jews by Moses. Claiming an astonishing authority as the unique spokesman for the One God, his Father, he went beyond the letter of the Torah of his own heritage in some areas.[26] What he certainly did *not* do was to undermine or alter in any way the central tenet of his and Israel's faith that God his Father was the sole God of the universe, who at the beginning had "made them male and female" (Mark 10:6). In this conviction he was strictly in line with the great prophet Isaiah who had reported that the God of Israel created all things by Himself, unaccompanied (Isa. 44:24).[27] On no occasion did Jesus ever claim to be the Genesis creator.

When a young man addressed Jesus as "good teacher," he immediately challenged this greeting by pointing out that "one only is good, the one God" (Mark 10:17-18).

In none of his recorded sayings did Jesus state, "I am God." If he had said this, he would have been heard to say, "I am the Father,"

---

[24]Karen Armstrong, *The Great Transformation*, Alfred A. Knopf, 2006, 382, 383.

[25]Ibid., 383.

[26]Mark 7:19 provides what is probably an editorial comment as to how Jesus was seen to have modified the Torah in the matter of food laws (cf. Rom. 14:14, 20 where Paul speaks as a convinced Jewish Christian). Paul did not affirm the law of circumcision required of all wanting to be part of the Old Covenant (see Gen. 17:10-14; cf. I Cor. 7:18, 19; Gal. 5:2).

[27]There are at least 50 verses in Scripture which state that God, not Jesus, created the heavens and the earth. He was alone in this process (Isa. 44:24), His hands made everything and He (God) rested on the seventh day after completing the creation (Heb. 4:4).

since he constantly referred to God as his Father. At his trial the worst his accusers could say of him was that he claimed to be *"the Son* of God" or "Messiah, a king" (John 19:7; Luke 23:2). When Jesus was accused by hostile Pharisees of claiming to be "equal with God," he immediately denied that he was capable of doing anything on his own (John 5:18-19). He was totally dependent on the One God, his Father. It is preposterous to suppose that Jesus meant that as God he was dependent on God or that as God he always did what God his Father told him to do.[28] Over and over again Jesus declared himself to be God's *Son* and as such to be subordinate to his Father as every son ought to be. Any such talk of more than one person being God is totally ruled out by the unitary monotheism which governs our New Testament documents.

More Evidence from the Standard Authorities

Standard Bible dictionaries give us the fullest support for the monotheism of Jesus. Hastings' *Dictionary of the Bible* states:

> In Mark out of 20 quotations, of which all but one are sayings of our Lord, 16 are either exact, or very slightly altered, quotations of LXX [the Greek version of the Old Testament]…Mark 12:29-30 (Deut. 6:4-5) is the great Shema, which from its frequent use in devotion was probably known to Greek Jews in its Hebrew form.[29]

Jesus was simply repeating the great creedal statement of his heritage and hoped to pass it on to us his followers.

The *Dictionary of Christ and the Gospels* in its article on "Trinity" says:

> We must never forget that *Christianity was built upon the foundation of Jewish monotheism.* A long providential discipline had secured to the Jewish people their splendid heritage of faith in the One and Only God. "Hear, O Israel, Jehovah our God is one Jehovah…" This was the corner-stone of the religion of Israel. These were perhaps the most

---

[28]Referring to John 8:28, C.K. Barrett writes, "It is simply intolerable that Jesus would be made to say, 'I am God, the supreme God of the Old Testament, and being God I do as I am told,'" and in John 13:19, "I am God, and I am here because someone sent me" (*Essays on John*, SPCK, 1982, 12).
[29]James Hastings, ed., *A Dictionary of the Bible*, Charles Scribner's Sons, 1902, 4:186.

familiar of all sacred words to the ears of the pious Jew. They were recited continually. Our Lord Himself had them frequently in His mind (Matt. 22:37; Mark 12:29, 30; Luke 10:27). That He thought of God always as the Supreme One is unquestionable.[30]

But why did the Church not follow him in this matter of creed and definition of who God is? The claim that Christianity is in fact built on the foundation of Jewish monotheism may turn out to be a hollow boast.

A German professor of the Bible, Hans Hinrich Wendt,[31] wrote in *The Teaching of Jesus*:

> Jesus taught no new doctrine of God...The God of whom Jesus speaks is the one God of Israel (Mark 12:29), the God of Abraham, Isaac and Jacob. Jesus has based his view on the Old Testament revelation of God and the knowledge of the nature of God, as derived from this revelation, he accepted as valid. Nowhere do we find him stating and teaching anything as the nature of God which was impossible on the basis of the Old Testament religion...When he affirmed that none were good but God only (Mark 10:18)...he sought to unfold no new view of God, which would have required a special explanation and basis for the Jewish mind. But he appealed to those features of the Divine character whose recognition he could take for granted...He employs the name of Father to designate God.[32]

Designating God as the Father, and calling Him unique God, is of course to declare oneself a unitarian. It is impossible to imagine Jesus promoting in any way a strange triune God. Loyalty to Jesus would seem to require that we agree with him about who God is and how many He is.

The celebrated *Peake's Commentary on the Bible* tells us: "The Shema was repeated daily by the Jews. It was the foundation-text of their monotheism."[33] Why was there any need to go beyond Jesus?

More recently, world-famous theologian N.T. Wright states:

---

[30]"Trinity," *A Dictionary of the Christ and the Gospels*, 2:761.
[31]Professor of theology at Heidelberg and later at Jena.
[32]Wendt, *Teaching of Jesus*, 184, 185.
[33]Thomas Nelson and Sons, 1919, 695.

The answer Jesus gave [to the question about which is the greatest commandment of all] was thoroughly non-controversial, quoting the most famous Jewish prayer ("Hear O Israel. YHVH our God, YHVH is one"). The Shema, the prayer which begins with these lines, was central to Judaism then as it is now, and the coupling of it with the command to love one's neighbor was not unknown, either...The scribe receives from Jesus an accolade.[34]

But would Jesus celebrate the Church's departure from his creed? Why was the creed of Jesus not left intact as a standing testimony to the most refreshing and unifying truth of the universe?

Why is this Great Commandment not taken with utmost seriousness by followers of Jesus today? No one would quarrel with Jesus' teaching about loving one's neighbor and loving God. But Christians do not seem willing to accept Jesus' definition of who that God is who is to be loved with all our hearts. This is confusing and inconsistent.

State of the art in evangelical scholarship, the *Word Biblical Commentary*: "Jesus' affirmation of the Shema...is neither remarkable *nor specifically Christian.*" This remark is revealing indeed — Jesus' teaching is not "specifically Christian." "Exalting the Jewish Law is hardly what one would expect an early Christian to do...If the exchange [between Jesus and the Jew] is thoroughly Jewish in perspective and advanced nothing of the early church's distinctive claims, why was the tradition preserved?"[35]

Why was it preserved?! Because Jesus said it was the most important spiritual truth in the universe! "The scribe's assertion would be reassuring and of some apologetic value." An affirmation, indeed, of the very creed of Jesus. "Having come to the point of agreeing with Jesus' answer, the scribe is now drawing closer to the kingdom,"[36] i.e. to being saved. What is so difficult about this? Why might it not simply be the truth and the most important summary of all truth? Was not Mark an evangelist for the true faith, addressing us all and presenting his beloved hero as a resolute believer in the One God of Israel?

---

[34]*Jesus and the Victory of God*, Augsburg Fortress, 1997, 305.
[35]Craig A. Evans, *Word Biblical Commentary: Mark 8:27-16:20*, Thomas Nelson, 2001, 261.
[36]Ibid., 262, 263.

The affirmation that "the Lord our God is one Lord" is implicitly an injunction to recognize and obey the only God. The only God is identified as YHWH. The commandment proper that follows presupposes this identity. A comment in Josephus reflects similar thinking "…The first that leads (all of the commandments) concerns God"…Jesus' affirmation of Deuteronomy 6:4b-5 is thoroughly Jewish and is, as already stated, unremarkable…Jesus' double-commandment summary of the Law places him *squarely in the center of Jewish piety.*[37]

On what authority are we at liberty to remove Jesus from "the center of Jewish piety"? What does this say about Christians, who seem quite uninterested in the Great Command of Jesus? Is the creed of Jesus really "unremarkable" in view of the fact that his words were later replaced with a creed he would not have known about? What is truly remarkable is the patent fact that Jesus was a non-Trinitarian believer. He is also the head of the new creation, to which Christians claim to belong as members of his Church.

"Jesus is not presenting Israel with some new, strange doctrine."[38] But the Church does exactly that. It claims Jesus' approval, contrary to Jesus' express words, for a strange new doctrine of God, and then expresses its persecuting fury against any follower of Jesus who questions it. History demonstrates repeatedly that the "heretic" has been the brunt of every imaginable form of unloving treatment. Jesus, however, killed no one, but rather allowed himself to be killed.

The Loss of Original Truth

In his *Introduction to Christian Doctrine*, John Lawson writes:

The primitive Church went before the world preaching two imperative religious interests — from its Jewish background in the Scriptures, that there is one sovereign God; and from its *experience* of salvation that Christ is divine. As and when the Church developed the talent and leisure for intellectual speculation it was realized that there is a tension between these two interests. How could they both be safeguarded? Thus the fathers of the Church had to construct a doctrine of God which would enable them to say that their Lord was a

[37]Ibid., 263-265, emphasis added.
[38]Ibid., 267.

divine Savior, in the full and proper sense of the word, and at the same time make it plain that there is *only one God*. The fruit of this admittedly exacting intellectual quest is the doctrine of the Trinity.[39]

The result of this painful effort was to abandon the words of Jesus in the name of "experience." But who authorized the idea that "experience" is the ultimate criterion of truth? It is not. The words and teachings of Jesus are. Who authorized the church fathers "to construct a doctrine of God," when Jesus and the Bible had provided a clear creed? The tragic fact is that the most important teaching of all, loving the One God of the Hebrew Bible, was compromised. The human Messiah was promoted from Son of God to Deity. Deity was thus assaulted, and the fundamental unity of God promoted from one end of the Bible to the other was sabotaged.

Could it be that Mary and later dead "saints" were promoted to the rank from which Jesus had been improperly removed? In a sort of theological "musical chairs," Jesus was moved into the place reserved in the Bible for the One God. Mary was then needed to fill Jesus' role of human intercessor.

On the principle that if we refuse one part of Scripture, in this case its primary doctrine, we are abandoned to our own devices with dire consequences, it is worth pondering what has happened to the Jewish Jesus. In a miniature way this principle was illustrated when Zacharias refused to believe the words of God through the angel. He was rendered dumb. Failure to believe has its consequences: "Because the love of the truth they did not embrace in order to be saved, God gave them over to a spirit of delusion to believe what is false" (see 2 Thess. 2:10-11).

John Lawson admits: "Christian theology speaks of God as He and not It."[40] But is the triune God truly a Person? C.S. Lewis says the opposite: "We must remind ourselves that Christian theology *does not believe God to be a person*. It believes Him to be such that in Him a trinity of persons is consistent with a unity of Deity."[41] While Jesus speaks of God as a Person, his Father, developed Trinitarianism has shifted the meaning of God to a substance or essence. Architect of the

---

[39]John Lawson, *Introduction to Christian Doctrine*, Francis Asbury, 1980, 11.
[40]Ibid., 11.
[41]*Christian Reflections*, 79.

Trinity, the church father Basil of Caesarea wrote, "We confess one God not in number but in *nature*."[42] But Jesus confessed one God in number, "one Lord." The Hebrew word for the number one, *echad*, appears some 970 times in the Hebrew Bible, meaning "only one, unique, alone, the numeral one, one single."[43]

It is unquestionable that Jesus never imagined the One God as Father, Son and Holy Spirit. He would have been offended at such a deviation and distortion of the biblical teaching about God, shared with his fellow Jews.

The *Dictionary of Christ and the Gospels* in its article on "Monotheism" reports that the suffering of Israel and the teaching of the prophets "had fixed immovably in the conscience and conviction of the entire nation the faith that Jehovah was the one God of the whole earth." The New Testament speaks of the:

> unique obligation of worship and service to the one only God (Matt. 4:10; Luke 4:8); in the emphatic affirmation of a common Fatherhood and Godhead (John 20:17; cf. 8:41) [but he refers to the omniscience of the Son]...There are also passages in which the epithet "one" or "only" is directly applied to the Divine Ruler, thus claiming for Him with more or less emphasis the sole dominion and the exclusive right to homage. "The Lord our God is one Lord" (Mark 12:29 from Deut. 6:4, cf. v. 32). The God who forgives sins is *eis* [one] (Mark 2:7), or *monos* [alone] (Luke 5:21); He is unique in goodness (Matt. 19:17; Mark 10:18; Lk. 18:19); *the sole Father* (Matt. 23:9); and the only God (John 5:44)...
>
> Moreover, in one passage (Jn. 17:3) there is found a perfectly distinct and unequivocal assertion of monotheistic doctrine; eternal life is to gain a knowledge of the only true God. Other phrases, in themselves less definite or comprehensive, must clearly be received and interpreted in the light of this, if an adequate conception of Christ's teaching concerning the Father is to be reached...The whole is

---

[42]Epistle 8. 2.

[43]Ernst Jenni and Claus Westermann, *Theological Lexicon of the Old Testament*, Hendrickson, 1997, 1:78-80. Brown, Driver and Briggs, *Hebrew and English Lexicon of the Old Testament*, Oxford University Press, 1968, 25. Koehler-Baumgartner, *Hebrew and Aramaic Lexicon of the Old Testament*, Brill, 2001, under *echad*.

to be construed and expounded by means of the loftiest and most comprehensive statements of doctrine, not to be attenuated to those which may be more particular or obscure. The conclusion, therefore, is that a monotheistic belief is everywhere assumed in the Gospels; and if it is rarely formulated, the reason is to be sought in the universal assent with which it was received. Christ did not need to teach with definiteness and reiteration, as though it were a new truth, that there is one only Lord of heaven and of earth; for this belief was common to Himself and to His hearers, and formed the solid and accepted foundation of their religious faith.[44]

Today that unitary monotheism is regarded as heretical, and Jesus as alien because of his failure to accept God as three in one.

All examinations of the issue of who God is in the Bible should start with the God texts, and especially those that bear directly on the question of creed. Jesus' own creed should be taken as the only legitimate starting point. That creed demonstrates that the Messiah was firmly grounded in the Hebrew Bible and the God revealed in those Scriptures. Only when the definition of God has been derived from these primary texts can we then fit the position of Jesus into the proper unitary monotheistic framework which he himself provides.

In their *The Mission and Message of Jesus* Major, Manson and Wright say of Jesus' encounter with the scribe: "The scribe is deeply appreciative of the teaching of Jesus and Jesus warmly commends the insight of the scribe."[45] Jesus' faith was rooted in the One God of Israel. Jesus was a unitary monotheist, as was the scribe who questioned him.

Ian Wilson in *Jesus: The Evidence* writes:

From all that we know of Jesus, is it possible that he regarded himself as God? The gospels' answer is clear. In the Mark gospel, the most consistent in conveying Jesus' humanity, a man is represented as running up to Jesus and addressing him with the words "Good Master." Jesus' response is a firm rebuke: "Why do you call me good? No one is good but God alone" (Mark 10:18)... If Jesus had wanted to institute a

[44]"Monotheism," *A Dictionary of Christ and the Gospels,* 2:201, 202.
[45]H.D.A. Major, T.W. Manson and C.J. Wright, *The Mission and Message of Jesus*, E.P Dutton and Co., 1953, 152.

formula for the religion he taught there is one moment in Mark's gospel when he had the perfect opportunity to do so. A scribe is reported as having asked him, "Which is the first of all the commandments?" It was an occasion to which Jesus could have imparted one of his characteristic twists, bringing in something new, something involving himself if he wished us to believe that he was a member of a Trinity, on an equal footing with God, the Father.

Instead he unhesitatingly looked to his traditional Jewish roots. "This is the first: 'Listen Israel, the Lord our God is one Lord, and you must love the Lord your God with all your heart, with all your soul, with all your mind and with all your strength'" (Mark 12:29, 30)...Jesus was confirming in the most emphatic way possible that the Jewish faith was the absolute bedrock of his belief. The quotation is not just a passage from Deuteronomy 6:4-5. It is the great Shema Israel ("Listen Israel"), the confession of faith which every practicing Jew recites morning and evening every day of his life, a confession instituted by Moses in these terms...It is difficult therefore to believe that Jesus could have intended the elaborate and un-Jewish formulations of "faith" that Nicea and later councils devised in his name and which still represent the way he is *supposed* to be understood by the present-day Christian.

[For a leading Jewish scholar, Dr. Geza Vermes] the one overwhelming stumbling block for Jews is the verdict of Nicea. In his view Jesus certainly never imagined he was God. To a pious Palestinian Jew of his time, the very idea would have seemed inconceivable, pure blasphemy.[46]

The evidence from Mark 12 teaches us that since the establishment of the creeds in the fourth and fifth centuries, Christians have betrayed their Master and Lord at the fundamental level of defining who God is. They have been lured into a Gentile creed promoting a triune God, a God never mentioned as such in the Bible and a God of whom Jesus knew nothing. This would seem to call for an urgent investigation for all those who love the Messiah and hope to win his approval on the conditions which he taught, that is,

---

[46]Ian Wilson, *Jesus: The Evidence*, Harper & Row, 1984, 176, 178.

intelligently hearing and doing God's will by following Jesus' teachings and believing in his Kingdom of God Gospel (Mark 1:14, 15) and in his death and resurrection. Can churches afford to remain a moment longer in defiance of Jesus' statement about the constitution of the universe, the true God, and about the only sound basis for worshipping that God? "The Lord our God," says the Lord Jesus Messiah, "is one Lord." That is the most important of all propositions to be heeded and promoted by all who love Jesus.

Bishop N.T. Wright in *The Meaning of Jesus* observes:
> Jesus belonged within a world where (what we call) theology and politics went hand in hand...The theology was Jewish monotheism...The Jews believed *their* god, YHWH, was the only god, and that all others were idols, either concrete creations of human hands or abstract creations of human minds. Jesus shared the belief that Israel's god was the only true god.[47]

Yes, and he defined that belief in the One God of Israel first by affirming the creed of Israel which declared that fact and secondly by addressing the Father as "the only one who is truly God" (John 17:3). In the same breath Jesus placed himself in a position distinct from that One God, defining himself as the commissioned Messiah. Wright later says, "The first stroke in my historical sketch of Jesus as a first-century Palestinian Jew is therefore: Jesus was a first-century Jewish prophet."[48]

Wright again: "Classic Jewish monotheism, then, believed, first, that there was one God, who created heaven and earth and who remained in close and dynamic relation with his creation; and, second, that this God had called Israel to be his special people."[49]

How then is Wright to square this solid historical evidence with what the post-biblical Church did by way of revising Jesus' creed? He thinks Paul achieved this revision of the definition of God:
> In 1 Corinthians 8:6, within a specifically Jewish-style monotheistic argument, [Paul] adapts the Shema [Jesus did not!] itself, placing Jesus within it: "For us there is one God — the Father, from whom all are all things and we to him;

---

[47]Marcus Borg and N.T. Wright, *The Meaning of Jesus: Two Visions*, HarperCollins, 2000, 31.
[48]Ibid., 33.
[49]Ibid., 159.

and one Lord, Jesus Christ, through whom are all things and we through him."[50]

Why does not Wright simply compare Paul with Jesus and permit Paul to be following Jesus? Jesus spoke about who God is. He recited the unitary monotheistic creed of Israel (Mark 12:28-34), and he then went on to speak of himself as "Lord." But in what sense Lord? Jesus defined his own lordship *with reference to Psalm 110:1* (Mark 12:35-37) exactly as Peter later did in Acts 2:34-36. Peter said that Jesus is Lord *in the sense determined by the oracle in Psalm 110:1*. Jesus likewise spoke of his lordship by reciting the same Psalm. What perfect concord and what a marvelous example of one mind on the question of the lordship of Jesus.

Paul in his own words said he was serving the God of his ancestral heritage, "the God of this people Israel" (Acts 13:17), who was not a Trinitarian God. Paul confessed publicly that he was "worshipping the God of our fathers, believing everything according to the Law and as written in the Prophets" (Acts 24:14). He was also in the service of the Lord Messiah, defined as the "my lord" of Psalm 110:1. It is simply incredible that Paul could describe the God of his fathers as the triune God, or that such a God was found in the Law and the prophets. To imagine this is to depart from any sound approach to history and biblical truth. Moreover the ancient cry of first-century Christians, *maranatha*, "our Lord come," demonstrably defines Jesus as "our Lord," a title which is from every angle impossible for the word Yahweh, who is not ever "our Yahweh."

Why should not Paul have followed Jesus and Peter in his definition of Jesus as Lord? He obviously did. Having defined the Father as the One God, besides whom there is no one else, in a truly Jewish manner (Deut. 6:4; Mark 12:28-34), Paul then goes on to say that Jesus is the one Lord *Messiah*. This is exactly what Jesus and Peter had done. They had used the massively important prophetic oracle of Psalm 110:1 to define what it means for the Messiah to be lord. It was a position conferred on Jesus not because he was the One God but because that One God had promoted Jesus to the righthand position as *adoni*, "my lord" of Psalm 110:1, the Lord Messiah. *Adoni* in Psalm 110:1 is a title which in all of its 195 occurrences never means God, but someone who is a non-Deity superior.

[50]Ibid., 161.

It is at this point that standard works seem unaware of the critical distinction between the two lords of Psalm 110:1. *The Wycliffe Bible Commentary* on Mark 12:36 imagines that Psalm 110:1, against all the evidence of the Old Testament, slips in a second member of the Trinity: "[Christ's] purpose in using David's words was to press home from the Scripture itself the truth of *the deity of the Messiah.*"[51] But he did no such thing. He defined his own status at the right hand of God according to the prophetic oracle of David. He is the *adoni* ("my lord") of David, positively not *Adonai,* the Lord God!

In their *1001 Bible Questions Answered,* Pettingel and Torrey fall into the same trap of thinking that Psalm 110:1 speaks of two who are God: "What then must a teacher confess about Jesus of Nazareth? The answer is that he must confess that Jesus of Nazareth is the Christ of the Scriptures. The Scriptures demand and declare that Christ is Himself *God.*"[52] Amongst verses cited in proof of Jesus' Deity we are offered Psalm 2:7, 2 Samuel 7:14 and Psalm 110:1. But Psalm 110:1 speaks of the One God Yahweh and the human lord Messiah, *adoni,* which, we repeat, in none of its 195 occurrences ever refers to God.

Of course Luke had already explained what it means for Jesus to be the Son of God, as the one procreated by miracle (Luke 1:35). Luke had then called Jesus "the Lord Messiah" (2:11) and reported Elizabeth's reference to Jesus as "my lord" (1:43), reminding us again of the great Psalm 110:1 ("my lord") which acts as an umbrella text over the whole New Testament. Psalm 110:1 is the text from the Old Testament quoted in the New Testament more often than any other verse.

A great deal of confusion has arisen when authorities, as distinguished as the *Encyclopedia Americana,* boldly misrepresent the Hebrew word for the second lord in Psalm 110:1:

> In Psalm 110:1 "Yahweh said to *Adonai:* Sit at my right hand." This passage is cited by the Christ to prove that he is Adonai seated at the right hand of Yahweh (Matt. 22:44). But *Adonai,* my Master, as a proper name is used exclusively of the Deity, either alone, or in such a phrase as Yahweh Adonai; instead of the ineffable name Yahweh the pious Jew

---

[51]Charles Pfeiffer and Everett Harrison, eds., Moody Bible Institute, 1990, 1015.
[52]William Pettingill and R.A. Torrey, *1001 Bible Questions Answered,* Inspirational Press, 1997, 325.

read Adonai. It is clear, then, that in this lyric, Yahweh addresses the Christ as a different Person yet identical in Godhead.[53]

Amazingly, the whole argument is flawed, built on a failure to read the Hebrew text. The Hebrew word in this centrally important Psalm is *not Adonai at all*. If it were, God would be speaking to God. The word is *adoni*, not *Adonai*. *Adoni* in none of its 195 occurrences ever refers to Deity. It is the form of *adon* (lord)[54] which deliberately identifies anyone so designated as a non-Deity!

A leading writer on evangelism, Dr. Michael Green, emphasizes Psalm 110:1 as "the most favored" of all Old Testament passages, and then explains that the title "lord" for Jesus "takes us back to Psalm 110:1." He builds his case for the Deity of Jesus by claiming that "the crucified peasant has the right to the name *Adonai*, Lord."[55] However, the title granted to the risen Jesus as the "Lord" of New Testament believers is not the divine title *Adonai*, but rather the title of non-Deity, *adoni* (Ps. 110:1) The Lord God and the Lord Messiah have become confused in the mind of evangelicals, and a frequent misreporting of the Hebrew word in Psalm 110:1 is symptomatic of the problem.

The Loss of the Simplicity of the Creed

The Bible's simple unitary monotheism and messianism was turned into chaos by later theology which spent its energy arguing over definitions for God and Jesus in terms completely alien to the Bible. They crowned this dismal endeavor by finally forcing a view on believers that the One God was one "essence," and at the same time mysteriously three eternal Persons. The unitary personal God of the Bible was deposed from His unique position (at least in the minds of the theologians). The precious definition of God given by Jesus himself had to give way to a different God who was mysteriously one abstract "essence" in three "subsistencies." Church members are at a

---

[53]*Encyclopedia Americana*, 1949, 6:624.
[54]The form *adon* (lord) is used of both God and man. The same word with the suffix added, *adoni*, "my lord," is never used of the Deity. It tells us that the one so designated is man (occasionally an angel) but not God, who is 449 times *Adonai*, the Lord. More on this important distinction is given in chapter 7.
[55]*Evangelism Now and Then*, Intervarsity Press, 1979, 65, 75, 60.

loss to know how to articulate clearly what those three subsistencies or hypostases are. They are left with the confusing proposition that each member of the Trinity is fully God and that this is still one God. There is no analogy for this in our common experience of language. "This is a book, this is a book, and this is a book. That makes one book!" These are nonsense propositions. The problem is akin to placing three billiard balls on one spot. It is an impossible task.

The whole patristic struggle over the creed, leading to the councils of the Church in 325, 381 and 451 AD, is light years removed in language and tone from the superlatively lucid definitions of God and Jesus provided by Scripture.

Bishop N.T. Wright says that Paul in 1 Corinthians 8:6 "adapts the *Shema* itself, placing Jesus within it."[56] If so, he thus changed the meaning of the Shema, to the horror of Jews and one would hope of Christians. But Paul has done nothing of the sort. He is strictly a Jewish monotheist. "To us there is one God, the Father and no other God besides Him." That is precisely what the Jewish scribe had echoed back to Jesus, agreeing with Jesus on the unitary creed of Israel. Paul repeats the same view of God as a single Person: "There is one God and one mediator between God and men, the man Messiah Jesus" (1 Tim. 2:5). "God is one person" (Gal. 3:20). God is in the Greek *eis,* one, masculine, i.e. one person, just as Jesus is the one seed, the one (*eis*) person who is the seed (Gal. 3:16), and the one (*eis*) teacher of the faithful (Matt. 23:8).

In the hope of justifying the later departure from the creed of Jesus, it is popular today to argue that Paul describes Jesus as the "one Lord." Thus, we are asked to believe, Paul has now distributed the creed which defines the one "Lord our God" between the Father as God and Jesus as Lord. If "no one is God except the Father" excludes Jesus from Godhead, then so the argument goes, would not Jesus being the "one Lord" exclude the Father from Lordship?

The fallacy is obvious. It is assumed that God and Jesus are both Lord *in the same sense.* This is quite false. Paul is careful to say that there is "one Lord Jesus *Christ.*" There is firstly one God, the Father who is the Lord God of the Shema. Then there is the one Lord *Christ* who is Jesus, now exalted to the right hand of the One God. There are

---

[56]"The Divinity of Jesus," in Marcus Borg and N.T. Wright, *The Meaning of Jesus: Two Visions,* 161.

two Lords but only one God. The second Lord cannot also be God. He is the Lord *Messiah* and he is so designated by the angel at the time of his birth: "Today...is born to you a Savior, who is the Lord Christ" (Luke 2:11) — not the Lord God. That "Lord Christ" is further described as "the Lord's Christ" (Luke 2:26). The Lord Christ belongs to the one Lord God. Jesus is the Lord Messiah, or the Lord's anointed.

None of this is in any way problematic provided the famous Messianic Psalm 110:1 is kept in mind, along with the whole unitary monotheistic heritage of the Old Testament. Psalm 110:1, which Jesus had discussed immediately after laying down the Shema of Israel as the foundation of all true worship (Mark 12:28-34), had spoken of the two distinct lords. The first was Yahweh, the God of Israel. The second "my lord," *adoni* was as both rabbis and Jesus agreed the Messiah. That Messiah was not a second "God" member of a Trinity, but the royal human "my lord" elevated to the highest position in the universe next to God. In that position he receives the authority of Yahweh himself, without of course actually being that One God.

If Paul had expanded the creed of Israel, and allowed another person into it, he would be proposing two eternal beings, and that is not monotheism at all. Paul did not contradict the Shema, nor did he expand it in any way. This would have been to alter the teaching of Jesus as to God's revealed definition of who He is. Neither Paul nor Jesus would have dared to turn the one-Person God of Scripture into a two- or three-fold God as *one Essence*, which is quite a different idea. Jews to this day are properly aghast at this development, and we should remember that Jesus is "the same yesterday, today and forever" (Heb. 13:8). He has not forgotten or rescinded his classic statement to Israel about who God is recorded in Mark 12:28-34 and massively elsewhere in his teaching — and throughout the New Testament including John's gospel.

It appears to us a matter of verbal quibble that Professor Richard Bauckham has to speak of Paul not "adding" Jesus to the Shema but "including" him in it.[57] In either case, Paul would have been meddling with the creed of his Jewish heritage. The inclusion of Jesus as the One God would in fact be an addition to the Godhead, an unthinkable

---

[57]*God Crucified: Monotheism and Christology in the New Testament*, Eerdmans, 1999, 40.

idea. The God of Israel's position is in no way compromised by His choice to elevate His own sinless human Son to the position of authority next to the divine throne. Psalm 110:1 provides the inspired oracle in regard to this paradigm.

Cambridge New Testament scholar J.A.T. Robinson observed in his *Twelve More New Testament Studies*, correctly, that:

> John is as undeviating a witness as any in the New Testament to the fundamental tenet of Judaism, of unitary monotheism (cf. Rom. 3:30; James 2:19). There is the one, true and only God (John 5:44; 17:3): everything else is idols (1 John 5:21). In fact nowhere is the Jewishness of John, which has emerged in all recent study, more clear.[58]

As A.J. Maclean observes, even ancient documents recall the clear distinction made by Jesus and the Apostles between God and His human Son, the point made also by Arians, that the Son of God could not be in the highest sense "God":

> The *Clementine Homilies* (which used to be thought to be of the 2nd or 3rd cent., but are now usually, in their present form, ascribed to the 4th,[59] make the same distinction [between God and Son of God]. St. Peter is made to say: "Our Lord...did not proclaim Himself to be God, but He with reason pronounced blessed him who called Him the Son of that God who has arranged the universe." Simon (Magus) replies that he who comes from God is God; but St. Peter says that this is not possible; they did not hear it from Him [Jesus]. "What is begotten cannot be compared with that which is unbegotten or self-begotten." Sanday refers to this passage as an isolated phenomenon; but now that the book has been with much probability assigned to the later date, we may say that the teaching just quoted was not heard of, as far as the evidence goes, till the 4th century.[60]

How then did God as one Person become God as three Persons? Theologians admit that ecclesiastic "remaking" of God as three Persons led to endless discussion about how the three members of the Godhead discoursed with each other in eternity. It was an exercise of

---

[58]SCM Press, 1984, 175.
[59]*JTS* 10, 1908-09, 457.
[60]*Dictionary of the Apostolic Church*, Charles Scribner's Sons, 1916, 1:462.

"pious" imagination without biblical foundation. "In speaking of the eternal relations within the Godhead itself we are again in the sphere of the inscrutable where the only truth for us is in the form of analogy or myth," wrote Oliver Quick, the Regius Professor of Theology at Oxford in 1938. He concludes his discussion about God and Christ with this astonishing remark: "It cannot be the best expression of the unity of God to declare that God is a single person."[61] He claims John's gospel for support and seems unaware of his direct contradiction of Jesus and John. He has scrapped the creed of Israel and of Jesus. When John speaks of the Son as in the bosom of the Father (John 1:18), the professor simply reads his preexisting Son into the text, and does not imagine that the *historical* Jesus was in the closest communion with the One God.

If what the professor states is right, then Jesus was certainly terribly mistaken. But for believers, Jesus affirmed the best possible understanding of God when he declared that "the Lord our God is *one Lord*" and in John's account that the Father is "the only one who is truly God," as distinct from the Messiah whom he commissioned (John 17:3). For Jesus and the whole Bible, God is a single divine Person. And if we claim Jesus as the foundation of the Christian faith, Christianity needs to be reestablished on its original strictly monotheistic foundation. It should rest upon a monotheism based on the very creedal words of Jesus himself. "The Lord our God is one Lord" is hardly a difficult proposition. There is no hint of mystery about the meaning of the word "one." *Eis* in Greek (like *echad* in Hebrew) means "one, a, an, single, only one." Does anyone have the slightest difficulty understanding that "God is a single Lord"?

Once the single Lord God is accepted as the God of Scripture and of Jesus himself, there will be no need to "expand" or "modify" the Bible's unifying monotheistic truth. It has been repeatedly stated in thousands of works on Christology that the characteristic way of describing Jesus in the New Testament was to call him "lord." That does not make him God! The title "lord" goes back to the earliest

---

[61]*Doctrines of the Creed*, Nisbet, 1938, 139. How strikingly contradictory is this "orthodox" view to the plain reading of L.L. Paine, professor of Ecclesiastical History, who remarks that in the OT "God is a single personal Being" and that Jesus did not come to destroy the law or the prophets and "accepted as his own belief the great text of Jewish monotheism" in Deut. 6:4 (*A Critical History of the Evolution of Trinitarianism*, 4).

Jewish Christology as is shown by the prayer to Jesus: "*Maranatha!* Come, our Lord." Jesus is the Lord *Messiah* and definitely not the Lord God.

As "our Lord," Jesus is given the royal title suitable for God's vice-regent and perfect agent. The Hebrew Bible never refers to Yahweh as "our Yahweh." This is an impossibility. However the king and other human superiors are addressed as "my lord" and "our lord." And this is the fixed basis and origin of the application of the title "lord" to Jesus. He is our lord the king, our Lord Messiah. He is introduced from the very start as Elizabeth's "my lord" (Luke 1:43) and as "Messiah Lord" (Luke 2:11). It is as the "my lord" of Psalm 110:1 that Jesus attains his supreme position at the right hand of the Father. Peter makes this abundantly clear in his definitive statement about the exaltation of Jesus. "God has *made* him [Jesus] both Lord and Messiah" — and as proof and in the same breath he has just quoted Psalm 110:1 in support (Acts 2:34-36). It is in the sense provided by that key proof-text that Jesus is the "lord" and hence "the Lord Jesus Christ." But the meaning there is not "the Lord Yahweh," but the Messianic and human lord Messiah. When this basic truth is reinstated the Shema will regain its proper significance and Jesus will be hailed as the unique human Messiah, and certainly not God Himself, making two Gods.

Chapter 4

The Titanic Struggle of Scholars to Find the Triune God in the Bible

"The phrase Son of God indicates Jesus' importance but by picturing him as a truly obedient Israelite, not as the second Person of the Trinity."[1]

"A complex structure has been erected upon the systematic misunderstanding of biblical language of sonship...Indeed, to be a 'Son of God' one has to be a being who is *not* God!"[2]

"After the third century anyone who at that time still kept to the original sense of ['only-begotten Son'] and refused to acknowledge the new interpretation was branded a heretic."[3]

Theological literature and particularly evangelical apologetic writing in support of the Trinity makes its case against an increasing volume of opposition from solid exegetical and lexical fact and the historical examination of the Bible. The best that such apologetics can do is assemble a few isolated verses, mostly from John's gospel and a handful from Paul. It can find no text in Scripture with the word "God" meaning a triune God. And little attention is paid to the plain unitarian statements of Jesus recorded by John. Paul's constant affirmation of the God of his Israelite heritage does not deter the determined Trinitarian. The obviously unitarian concept of God

---

[1] E.P. Sanders and Margaret Davies, *Studying the Synoptic Gospels*, SCM Press, 1991, 272.
[2] Colin Brown, "Trinity and Incarnation," *Ex Auditu* 7, 1991, 92, 88.
[3] Adolf von Harnack, cited in Karl-Josef Kuschel, *Born Before All Time? The Dispute over Christ's Origin*, Crossroad, 1992, 49.

presented by the Old Testament is bypassed. Some employ fanciful methods, including the redefinition of simple words, to make the Hebrew Bible a Trinitarian book. Language is thus insulted and those who support the Jewish custodians of Old Testament Scripture and the Jewish monotheistic heritage are appalled and offended.[4]

The overwhelming mass of unitary monotheistic statements about God as the Father of Jesus are given scant attention, while a few ambiguous texts are advanced in favor of Jesus being "God." Their weight, however, is slight compared with the obvious description of God across the range of Scripture as a single divine Person. A very occasional use of the word "God" for Jesus is parallel to the occasional use of "God" for important human agents such as Moses. Altering the unitary monotheistic creed of the Hebrew Bible on the basis of two (for certain) references to Jesus as "God" involves an unfair treatment of the biblical data.

If the Church is serious about being rooted in Jesus, it would be wise for believers to return to the creed of Jesus and the *theology* of Jesus. A failure to attach ourselves to Jesus by believing him and his teaching would seem to open the doors to widespread deception. Perhaps this is why Jesus warned that the majority of "Christians" would one day be disappointed to find out that they were sailing under false colors (Matt. 7:22-23).

A clear picture of the real Jesus as a devoted worshiper of the One God of Israel is now coming to the public's attention from various quarters. A distinguished German Roman Catholic systematic theologian supports our thesis:

> There is no indication that Jesus would have understood the "Father"...differently than the monotheistic God of Judaism...Jesus himself stood in the tradition of Jewish monotheism...His thinking and acting were geared towards this One God by whom he felt himself to have been sent and to whom he felt close, so that — again following early Jewish

---

[4]The plural ending on *Elohim* provides no support of any sort for the idea that God is more than one. The Messiah is not plural, but he is called Elohim. Moses was Elohim to Pharaoh (Exod. 4:16; 7:1) but Moses was not plural. Four "us" texts, which say nothing about a triune Godhead, are advanced against the evidence of 20,000 singular verbs and singular personal pronouns designating the One God as not triune, but a single Person. No verse hints at God being "one Thing" or "one What."

practice — he called him Father...If it is certain — and there seems to be no getting around this assumption — that Jesus himself knew only of the God of Israel, whom he called Father...by what right can a doctrine of the Trinity then be *normative?*[5]

This question could not be more pointed.

Professor Ohlig's candor is refreshing. As a historian he knows that the Trinity did not "fall from heaven" in New Testament times. It was a painful and lengthy development, and it left the Church with a legacy which separated it from its Jewish founder. Ohlig concludes his masterly account of the problems the Church faces promoting a view of God and the Son which has no roots in the New Testament:

> The doctrine of the Trinity thus appears to be an *attempt to combine monotheism, monism and polytheism, hence all of the important world-religious and advanced cultural conceptions of God*...Perhaps the fascination of the doctrine of the Trinity can be explained by the fact that it seeks to combine the merits — in a suspenseful way - of all of the conceptions of God which have been mentioned: the warmth and the potential for hope that the monotheism awakens; the rational plausibility of a final immanent principle as well as the communicative and social liveliness of polytheism..."the middle between the two opinions" [Gregory of Nyssa], between polytheism and Jewish monotheism[6]...What the religious scholar is able simply to state, however, signifies at the same time a question for theology about the legitimacy of such a construct. If it is certain — and there seems to be no getting around this assumption — that Jesus himself knew only of the God of Israel, whom he called Father, and not of his own later "deification," by what right can a doctrine of the Trinity then be *normative?*...How...can one legitimize doctrinal development that actually first began in the second

---

[5]Karl-Heinz Ohlig, *One or Three? From the Father of Jesus to the Trinity*, Peter Lang, 2003, 31, 121, 129, emphasis his.

[6]So also Harnack observes that the Christian conception of God as developed by church fathers was "the midway point between the polytheism of the heathen and the monotheism of the Jews" (*Lehrbuch der Dogmengeschichte*, Wissenschaftliche Buchgesellschaft, 1983, 1:702). But was this the monotheism of Jesus, or a rather obvious compromise with paganism?

century?...No matter how one interprets the individual steps, it is certain that the doctrine of the Trinity, as it in the end became "dogma" both in the East and — even more so — in the West, possesses no Biblical foundation whatsoever and also has no "continuous succession."[7]

Ohlig was preceded by other historians of dogma who call our attention to the very great difficulty in justifying the rather obvious pagan tendencies of the Church since the second century:

The world of the second century was marked in its philosophy and religion by a strong syncretism [mixing of alien systems of thought]. The highest expression of this tendency was, of course, Gnosticism. Within its dualism between spirit and matter, cosmological speculations and progressive emanations (Aions) from the highest God linking via these aions to matter, there was found also a place for a revised Gospel of salvation through Christ...

With the Church this hellenization has remained and is to be found first amongst the apologists of the second century...The Church's monotheism always retained a certain heathen, philosophical pluralistic coloring. This strange coloring of the doctrine of God began with the taking over of the heathen-philosophical notion of Logos, which in the heathen background had a different meaning. In John's gospel the Logos is tied to the notion of "teacher" and "teaching." In the philosophy of that time it was, on the contrary, only one Aion of the Most High God. It was in this last meaning that the apologists [Justin Martyr and others] read Philo's doctrine of the Logos into Scripture.[8]

But Jesus was far removed from those later developments and compromises with paganism. William Barclay, known for his sober scholarship and painstaking analysis of the biblical texts, comments on Jesus' exchange with the Jewish scribe:

This scribe came to Jesus with a question which was often a matter of debate in the rabbinic schools. In Judaism there was a kind of double tendency. There was the tendency to expand the law limitlessly into hundreds and thousands of rules and

---

[7]Ohlig, *One or Three?* 129-130, emphasis his.
[8]Paul Schrodt, *The Problem of the Beginning of Dogma in Recent Theology*, 64. Schrodt is discussing the views of Friedrich Loofs.

regulations. But there was also the tendency to try to gather up the law into one sentence, one general statement which would be a compendium of its whole message.[9] Hillel was once asked by a proselyte to instruct him in the whole law while he stood on one leg. Hillel's answer was, "What thou hatest for thyself, do not to thy neighbour. This is the whole law, the rest is commentary. Go and learn."…

> For answer Jesus took two great commandments and put them together. (i) "Hear, O Israel, the Lord our God is one Lord." That single sentence is the real creed of Judaism…It was the sentence with which the service of the synagogue always began and still begins…(ii) "You shall love your neighbor as yourself."…The new thing that Jesus did was to put these two commandments together.[10]

Barclay reminds us that the Shema "is the declaration that God is the only God, the foundation of Jewish monotheism." He then notes that "When Jesus quoted this sentence as the first commandment, every devout Jew would *agree* with him."[11]

What has happened, then, to render the Church's affirmation of God as three in one an obstacle and offense to every devout Jew? Jesus' description of God has been discarded and replaced with an "improved" creed which rightly offends Jews and ought to alarm Christians who claim devotion to Christ.

The startling fact emerges from this evidence that Jesus' creed did not and, since he remains the same yesterday, today and forever (Heb. 13:8), *does* not match the Trinitarian creed so beloved by his modern disciples. This would seem to call for a deliberate inquiry by churches of all denominations. Something could be systematically wrong with the traditional Christian doctrine of God as Trinity.

Dr. McGrath

Attempts to sustain a Trinitarian view of God from Scripture are unimpressive and often confusing. A leading modern exponent of the Trinity, Alister McGrath, rightly tells us that Jesus Christ reveals

---

[9]Cf. Mark 1:14, 15 as a compendium of the whole point of the Christian faith: Repentance with a view to belief in God's Gospel about the coming Kingdom of God (see also Luke 4:43).
[10]*The Gospel of Mark*, Westminster John Knox, 1975, 293-295.
[11]Ibid., 295.

God. He makes no mention of Jesus' express revelation of God as the One God of Israel. He notes that one can find three examples in the whole New Testament of the term "God" being applied to Jesus. McGrath attributes the sparseness of references to Jesus as "God" to the fact that the writers were mostly Jews. But, one might ask, weren't they also authentic Christians, and did they not know which God to worship? Were they not apostolic exponents of the Christian faith? McGrath says:

> The New Testament was written against a background of the strict monotheism of Israel...Given the strong reluctance of New Testament writers to speak of Jesus as "God," because of their background in the strict monotheism of Israel, these three affirmations are of considerable significance [John 1:1; 20:28; Heb. 1:8].[12]

Dr. McGrath's remarks provide eloquent evidence that Jesus and his followers did not alter the Jewish creed. If they were strongly reluctant to speak of Jesus as God, could this not simply be because their creed, affirmed by Jesus, forbade them to call anyone but the Father the supreme God? They show no sign of being Trinitarians. Nor, of course, did Jesus.

The three examples of the word "God" for Jesus, as compared with over 1300 references to the Father as "God" in the New Testament, are easily explained.[13] They provide no justification at all for departing from the creed of Jesus, who believed that "The Lord our God is one Lord" (Mark 12:29).

When it comes to the Trinity itself McGrath remarks:

> The casual reader of Scripture will discern a mere two verses in the entire Bible which seem, at first glance, to be capable of a trinitarian interpretation: Matthew 28:19 and 2 Corinthians 13:14. Both these verses have become deeply

---

[12]Alister McGrath, *Christian Theology: An Introduction*, Blackwell, 2006, 280, 281.

[13]John 20:28 is in the context of Jesus saying he is going to ascend to "my God and your God" (v. 17). Thomas had failed to recognize that in seeing Jesus one was seeing God at work (14:7, 9). Thomas' exclamation "My Lord and my God!" beautifully summarizes his realization that in meeting his Lord Jesus, he is also meeting the One God who is at work in him. The address is to both "my Lord" (the Messiah) and "my God," the God of Jesus and of Thomas. See further Appendix 1.

rooted in the Christian consciousness...Yet these two verses, taken together or in isolation, can hardly be thought of as constituting a doctrine of the Trinity.[14]
This is a significant admission. McGrath then goes on to give us twenty pages of post-biblical historical development of the Trinity. He has only a page and a half to offer us for its biblical foundation. Then comes this amazing statement. How securely does he really find the Trinity in the New Testament?

The doctrine of the Trinity can be regarded as the outcome of a process of sustained and critical reflection on the pattern of divine activity revealed in Scripture, and continued in Christian experience. *This is not to say that Scripture contains a doctrine of the Trinity*; rather, Scripture bears witness to a God who demands to be understood in a trinitarian manner. We shall explore the evolution of the doctrine and its distinctive vocabulary in what follows.[15]

I suggest that Dr. McGrath's faith is rooted firmly in post-biblical tradition, against his own Protestant principle of *sola scriptura.* He seems internally conflicted. There is no doctrine of the Trinity in the Bible, he admits, and yet in its pages, God demands belief in the Trinity.

I invite some prolonged reflection on the statement italicized above: "This is not to say that Scripture contains a doctrine of the Trinity." Yet God "demands to be understood in a Trinitarian manner." There is curious illogicality and irrationality at work here. Can anyone explain how the absence of a Trinitarian doctrine in the Bible is good evidence that God demands to be worshipped as a Trinity? If Scripture is taken as the foundation of faith, as Protestants claim, its pages yield no information about "God in three Persons." The God of Jesus and of the New Testament is a single divine Person, the Father of Jesus and of Christians.

Frank admissions about the creed of the earliest Christians are found frequently in standard works on the New Testament: "The first Christians were orthodox Jews who had been brought up to believe that God was one. They never abandoned their belief that God was one, but they gradually came to understand the oneness of God in a

---

[14]McGrath, *Christian Theology,* 248.
[15]Ibid., 249, emphasis added.

new way."[16] But was that novelty justified? Were later disciples of Jesus authorized to abandon his unitarian creed?

Jewish sources have no doubts at all about the origin of the monotheism which Jesus obviously shared. *The Encyclopedia of Jewish Knowledge* under its entry "Monotheism" says:

> Belief in one God...Abraham was its discoverer. Moses proclaimed it in the Shema, which, through the ages, acquired a sanctity equalled by nothing else in Judaism...The Monotheistic idea was clarified by Amos and Isaiah...The Jews...became the "Swiss Guard of the Almighty"...Nothing remained but a sublime faith in the indivisible, omnipresent Creator, without beginning and without end, until the Jews became a "God-intoxicated people"..."I am that I am" [*o ohn*, Ex. 3:14, LXX]...It is not improved...by philosophic or theological speculation. The profession of the Unity is the supreme act of faith. It is the climax of the Atonement service, the last utterance of the conscious dying Jew. It was the death avowal at the stake, and it is Judaism's greatest contribution to the spiritual growth of the human race.[17]

Speaking of the Jewish creed, the same source emphasizes that belief in the One God was the single most important article of faith for Jews. "Refusal to worship idols" was the only real creed of Judaism.[18] Maimonides proclaimed, "He alone is our God, who was, is, and will be."[19]

Jesus was versed in the law and the prophets and never departed from the core belief of his Jewish heritage. H.H. Rowley wrote:

> When in the New Testament we find the essence of the Old Testament law summarized in two of its provisions, it is made clear that they are set before the followers of Christ as valid for them no less than for the children of the Old Covenant. These two laws are "You are to love the Lord your God" and "you are to love your neighbor as yourself." The love of God, if it is to be the love of the God who is revealed in the Bible,

---

[16]Colin Chapman, *The Case for Christianity*, Eerdmans, 1981.
[17]Jacob de Haas, ed., *The Encyclopedia of Jewish Knowledge*, Behrman's Jewish Book House, 1938, 364.
[18]Ibid., 111.
[19]From his 12th-century statement of faith. Cf. Rev. 1:8 for the same creedal statement from John and Jesus.

The Titanic Struggle of Scholars to Find the Triune God in the Bible 101

must result in the love of man. The covenant, whose establishment is recorded in the Law, called first and foremost for obedience. The principles of humanity so dear to the prophets are expressed with power in Deuteronomy, and there we read the great word which has been cherished by Jews in all ages, *and which was declared by our Lord to be the first law of life for all men.* "You are to love the Lord your God."[20]

This is beautifully said. But might it not be added that obedience to those laws includes, or rather, is introduced by the command to listen carefully *to who that God is* who is to be loved? Neither Jesus nor the Law which he quoted permits God to be defined as "Father, Son and Holy Ghost." The text does not say "The Lord your God is three Lords in one." Surely the words of Scripture have been assaulted when our traditional terms describing God are no longer the words of Jesus himself. And, as Rowley says, these words of the Law are put before readers of the New Testament as "valid for them." Jesus, indeed, insists on strict monotheism as the continuing basis of genuine Christian faith.

Tom Harpur expresses his discomfort that the central dogma of Christianity today is not found in the Bible:

What is most embarrassing for the Church is the difficulty of proving any of these statements of dogma from the New Testament documents. You simply cannot find the doctrine of the Trinity set out anywhere in the Bible. St. Paul has the highest view of Jesus' role and person, but nowhere does he call him God. Nor does Jesus himself anywhere explicitly claim to be the Second Person of the Trinity, wholly equal to his heavenly Father. As a pious Jew, he would have been shocked and offended by such an idea...

This research has led me to believe that the great majority of regular churchgoers are, for all practical purposes, tritheists. That is, they profess to believe in one God, but in reality they worship three. Small wonder Christianity has always had difficulty trying to convert Jews and Muslims. Members of both these faiths have such an abhorrence of anything that runs counter to their monotheism, or faith in the

---

[20]*The Unity of the Bible*, Living Age, 1957, 81, 44.

unity of God, that a seemingly polytheistic gospel has little appeal for them.[21]

Standard authorities make this important point: "Early Christianity consciously adopts from Judaism (Deut. 6:4) the monotheistic formula, 'God is one'...According to Mark 12:29, 32, Jesus explicitly approves the Jewish monotheistic formula."[22]

Jewish historians and theologians have no doubt about what first-century Jews believed about God. Otto Kirn, PhD, ThD, professor of dogmatics at the University of Leipzig, commented:

> Early dogmaticians were of the opinion that so essential a doctrine as that of the Trinity could not have been unknown to the men of the Old Testament. However, no modern theologian who clearly distinguishes between the degrees of revelation in the Old and New Testaments can longer maintain such a view. Only an inaccurate exegesis which overlooks the more immediate grounds of interpretation can see references to the Trinity in the plural form of the divine name *Elohim,* the use of the plural in Genesis 1:26, or such liturgical phrases of three members as the Aaronic blessing of Numbers 6:24-26 and the Trisagion of Isaiah 6:3.[23]

Dr. William Smith warned against the imaginative attempts to find the Trinity in the Hebrew Bible: "The plural form of Elohim has given rise to much discussion. The fanciful idea that it referred to the *trinity of persons* in the Godhead hardly finds now a supporter among scholars."[24]

Doctor of Theology Wolfhart Pannenberg stated:

> Jesus is what he is only in the context of Israel's expectation. Without the background of this tradition, Jesus would never have become the object of a Christology. Certainly this connection is also clear in other titles and generally throughout the New Testament, especially in Jesus' own message. His message can only be understood within the horizon of apocalyptic expectations, and the God whom Jesus

---

[21]Tom Harpur, *For Christ's Sake*, Beacon Press, 1987, 11.

[22]*"Eis"* ("One"), *Exegetical Dictionary of the New Testament,* Eerdmans, 1990, 399.

[23]*The New Schaff-Herzog Encylopedia of Religious Knowledge*, Baker, 1960, 12:18.

[24]*A Dictionary of the Bible*, Thomas Nelson, rep. 1986, 220.

called "Father" was none other than the God of the Old Testament. This context is concentrated in a most particular way in the title *Christos*...This justifies the formulation of the content of the confession of Jesus...he is the Christ of God.[25] How very confusing then to say he *is* God.

To the men of the NT, God was the God of the OT, the living God, a Person, loving, energizing, seeking the accomplishment of an everlasting purpose of mercy, the satisfaction of His own loving nature...Perhaps it would be more correct to say that the monotheism of the OT was never abstract, because the God of the OT was never a conception, or a substance [essence], but always a *Person*. Personality, indeed, has never the bare unity of a monad.[26]

Murray Harris in *Jesus as God* attempts to justify the traditional view of Jesus as fully God. His findings however leave him admitting that the Trinity is not easy to detect! Harris discovers no instance of a triune God in the pages of Scripture:

It was not the Triune God of Christian theology who spoke to the forefathers by the prophets...It would be inappropriate for *Elohim* [God, 2,570 times] or *Yahweh* [6,800 times] ever to refer to the Trinity in the OT when in the NT *theos* regularly refers to the Father alone and *apparently never to the Trinity.*[27]

Harris concludes:

No attempt has been made in the preceding summary to be exhaustive. But we have seen that throughout the NT *(o) theos* [God] is so often associated with and yet differentiated from *kurios Yesous Christos* [Lord Jesus Christ] that the reader is forced to assume that there must be both a hypostatic distinction and an interpersonal relationship between the two. The writers of the NT themselves *supply the key* by speaking not only of *o theos* and *Yesous* but also of Father and Son, of the Son of God and of the God and Father of our Lord Jesus Christ. God is the Father (in the trinitarian

---

[25]Wolfhart Pannenberg, *Jesus – God and Man*, Westminster Press, 1968, 32.
[26]Thomas B. Kilpatrick, Prof. of Systematic Theology, Knox College, Toronto, "Incarnation," *A Dictionary of Christ and the Gospels*, 1:807.
[27]*Jesus as God: The New Testament Use of Theos in Reference to Jesus*, Baker, 1992, 47n, emphasis added.

sense), Jesus is the Lord (1 Cor. 8:6). When *o theos* is used, we are to assume that the NT writers have the Father in mind unless the context [twice for certain] makes this sense of *o theos* impossible.[28]

In a footnote he adds:

A related question demands brief treatment. To whom did the NT writers attribute the divine action described in the OT? To answer "the Lord God" is to beg the question, for the authors of the NT wrote of OT events in the light of *their trinitarian understanding* of God.[29]

Yet above he just said God never refers to the Trinity.

A clear *distinction* must be drawn between what the OT text meant to its authors and readers and how it was understood by the early Christians who lived after the advent of the Messiah and the coming of the Spirit.[30]

Harris goes on:

Certainly the person who projects the trinitarian teaching of the NT back into the OT and reads the OT through the spectacles of the dynamic or trinitarian monotheism of the NT is thinking anachronistically. On the other hand, it does not seem illegitimate to pose a question such as this: To whom was the author of Hebrews referring when he said (1:1), "At many times and in various ways *God* spoke in the past to our forefathers through the prophets"? That it was not the Holy Spirit in any ultimate sense is evident from the fact that in neither the OT nor the NT is the Spirit called "God" *expressis verbis* [in so many words]. And, in spite of the fact that the LXX equivalent of YHVH, viz. *kurios*, is regularly applied to Jesus in the NT so that it becomes less a title than a proper name, it is not possible that *o theos* [God] in Heb. 1:1 denotes Jesus Christ, for the same sentence (in Greek) contains, "(the God who spoke...) in these last days has spoken to us in a Son (*en 'uio*)." Since the author is emphasizing the continuity of the two phases of divine speech

[28] Ibid., 47.
[29] Ibid., 47n.
[30] Ibid., 47n.

("God having spoken, later spoke"), this reference to a Son shows that *o theos* was understood to be "God the Father."[31] And of course no New Testament writer ever wrote "God the Son." Harris adds:

> Similarly, the differentiation made between *o theos* as the one who speaks in both eras [throughout the entire Bible] and *uios* (Son) as his final means of speaking shows that in the author's mind *it was not the Triune God of Christian theology who spoke to the forefathers by the prophets.* That is to say, for the author of Hebrews (as for all NT writers, one may suggest) "the God of our fathers," Yahweh, *was no other than "the God and Father of our Lord Jesus Christ"* (compare Acts 2:30 and 2:33; 3:13 and 3:18; 3:25 and 3:26; note also 5:30). Such a conclusion is entirely consistent with the regular NT usage of *o theos*. It would be inappropriate for Elohim [2,570 times] or Yahweh [6,800 times] ever to refer to the Trinity in the OT *when in the NT theos regularly refers to the Father alone and apparently never to the Trinity.*[32]

He later says:

> In classical Greek *to theion* [the Godhead] often signifies divine power or activity or the divine nature considered generically, without reference to one particular god. There appears to be no NT instance where *theos* signifies merely *to theion*, deity in general, although both Philo and Josephus use *to theion* of the one true God of Israel's monotheism. In Acts 17:29 *to theion* is used of "the Deity" that is often represented "by the art and imagination of man."[33]

With this massive evidence for "God" as the consistent description of the Father of Jesus, Harris finds references to Jesus as God "certainly in John 1:1; 20:28; very probably in Rom. 9:5; Titus 2:13; Heb. 1:8; 2 Pet. 1:1; probably in John 1:18; possibly in Acts 20:28; Heb. 1:9; 1 John 5:20."[34]

Harris concludes with admirable candor that "nowhere is it appropriate to render *o theos* by 'the divine Essence' or 'the

---

[31]Ibid., 47n.
[32]Ibid., 47n.
[33]Ibid., 48, n. 113.
[34]Ibid., 49.

Godhead.'"[35] This is astonishing. No New Testament writer ever once put in writing the concept of God as three!

It would be a giant understatement to say that finding the Trinity in the Bible is hard work! Harris throws in occasional use of the word "Trinitarian" despite his own findings. The relevant literature is full of expressions like "the problem of the Trinity" and how "the Church was struggling" to find ways of expressing what it was experiencing, in terms that the Greek world would find "meaningful."

All the while, however, I believe, the simplicity of Jesus, which Paul warned about losing (2 Cor. 11:3), was in fact being lost! Is it really too much to ask the reader to consider the fact that God would be pleased to have us confess and celebrate the creed of His own unique Son? Is that complicated? Hardly. Our New Testament presents Jesus the Savior as imploring us to believe in him by understanding and believing and practicing *his words*. How could we disparage and spurn that teaching? How can we turn down his constant appeal and warning that we must listen to "these words of mine" (Matt. 7:24), words which "will not pass away" (Matt. 24:35) because they are more permanent than our present heaven and earth?

Of countless talented writers on Jesus some catch the spirit and style of his ministry vividly:

> As the Gospel narratives run on we meet successively the Roman centurion, women of Samaria, of Syro-Phoenicia, of Bethany, and many more, children, scribes, beggars, Nathanael and Nicodemus, the leper, the demon-ridden outcast, and to each and all Jesus turns as though the human contact matters more than all else in the world. He seems oblivious of politics, of philosophy, even of theology. Nothing matters save man in the purposes of God. Nothing matters save God in the life of any and every man.[36]

And by "God" our writer means the God of Israel.

> [The disciples] were Hebrews, with all the teaching of the Old Testament to shape their thought of God...He was...the God of Israel, just and yet loving, "slow to anger and of great kindness"...What they saw in Jesus did not contradict all this.

---

[35]Ibid., 271.
[36]L.W. Grensted, *The Person of Christ*, Nisbet & Co., 1933, 45.

The monotheism of Judaism has remained a foundation-stone of Christian thought.[37]
But has it? Jews and Jewish theologians do not believe so. Is Trinitarian monotheism really the monotheism of Jews and of Jesus? It is the most obvious and straightforward fact of the entire Bible that the God of the Old Testament, the God of the Hebrews was "a living personality who became deeply engaged in the life and struggles of the Hebrew people."[38] Israel indeed knew that there were many gods, but they were urged by prophet and priest to adhere to their one God, the God of Abraham, Isaac and Jacob, and the God of Shadrach, Meshach and Abednego, who was so far superior to the useless gods of the nations that He could bring them safe and alive from a burning cauldron. All the fury of a tyrannical, fiendish pagan ruler like Nebuchadnezzar was no match for the incomparable God of Israel.

Their knowledge of this one true and only God convinced Israel that He had spoken to them through Moses. As the "Almighty" — a title never given to Jesus once in the Bible — God had addressed Abraham and Isaac and Jacob. Melchizedek the mysterious priest had spoken to Abraham of the unique Most High (*El Elyon*). That same Most High was the one who announced later that His Messiah was to be David's and God's son and receive from Him "the throne of his father David" (Luke 1:32, 35). That same all-powerful God of Israel had revealed Himself to Moses as YHVH, the LORD (Exod. 3:14). This "identifies the Jewish God as the one who is always present and active."[39]

The same author, William La Due, says, echoing thousands of good articles on the God of the Hebrews, that the Jewish God of the Bible is:

> an active, abiding presence who never grows weary and is ever vigilant (Isa. 40:28), a holy God who swears by the divine holiness. From the outset Yahweh would not tolerate the worship of other gods (Exod. 20:3). During the exile (ca. 587-538 BC) Yahweh wanted the Hebrews to see him as a shepherd who nourishes his flock and carries his sheep in his

---

[37]Ibid., 46.
[38]William J. La Due, *The Trinity Guide to the Trinity,* Trinity Press International, 2003, 1.
[39]Ibid.

arms, leading them with great care (Isa. 40:11). Nonetheless, Yahweh frequently proclaimed Godself as a jealous God...Yet Yahweh treated them with the gentleness of a father (Hos. 11:1-3)...and regarded them with the affection of a lover (Hos. 2:9-16)...Yahweh called himself the Father of Israel (Exod. 4:22-23)...

In the forging of the covenant, the Hebrew Deity was given an explicitly personal character...by no means an impersonal power...Eager to portray God as warm and personal, the prophets frequently referred to his love and his sorrow, his fear and his jealousy...The Shema (Deut. 6:4-9) set out once and for all the classic statement of Jewish monotheism...The ancients saw in the wind and in human breath...a symbol of the activity and the nearness of the divine...They associated this spirit of life with the Lord's word, and these two agents — spirit and word — were responsible for establishing Yahweh's sovereignty over the whole of creation (Ps. 33:6)...The spirit is best understood as a vitalizing force, and the word as the living expression of Yahweh's thought and will.[40]

Our author concludes his section on the God of the Hebrew Bible with this:

Yahweh and his intermediaries [word, spirit, wisdom] constitute the intimations of Trinity in the Old Testament, but *they do not emerge as distinct and equal personalities, for the rigid and uncompromising monotheism of the Jewish faith would not countenance such a development.*[41]

Neither, we propose, did Jesus for a single moment countenance such a "development." Jesus was relentlessly and vigorously attached to the Jewish monotheism of his heritage. This is proven beyond any doubt by his wholehearted agreement with Deuteronomy 6:4 and with a Jewish scribe. That confession of Jesus himself ought to be the gold standard by which all confessions are judged. At present churches seem to have forgotten that Jesus was a Jew, and worse, that he recognized no God as God but the God of the Hebrew Bible, his own Father.

---

[40]Ibid., 2-6.
[41]Ibid., 14, emphasis added.

Jesus' affirmation of the unitary creed of Israel ought to have closed the door forever on any variation in the definition of God. Commentators very frequently admit the enormous change which overcame later discussions about who God is: "The theological treatises on God as revealed in the Judeo-Christian tradition took a far different shape compared with the data in the Old Testament."[42]

Revealing also are the findings of a number of leading theologians: "For [Karl] Rahner, the Yahweh of the Israelites *is a particular person* with a proper name, *who* created everything that is and *who* intervenes in the life of his people."[43] James White's definition of God as one "what" and three "who's" cannot be matched with Rahner's definition. White's attempts to find the Trinity in the Bible are quite unconvincing.

Karl Rahner

When this leading Roman Catholic theologian produced an exhaustive examination of the word "God" in the New Testament he concluded with these extraordinary admissions:

> We may outline our results as follows. Nowhere in the New Testament is there to be found a text with *o theos* which has unquestionably to be referred to the Trinitarian God as a whole existing in three Persons [God as Trinity].[44] In by far the greater number of texts *o theos* refers to the Father as a Person of the Trinity…In addition, *o theos* is never used in the New Testament to speak of the holy spirit.[45]

In a footnote he adds:

> Thus, for example, the whole Old Testament saving history is ascribed to the God who sends Jesus, thus to the Father (Acts 3:12-26; cf. Heb. 1:1). In Acts 4:24, Eph. 3:9 and Heb. 1:2,

---

[42]Ibid., 17.

[43]Ibid., 18.

[44]According to a standard authority, Calvin says the opposite: "When the word God is used without particular reference to any of the 'Persons,' it designates indistinguishably the three." The same source speaks of "Calvin's strong insistence that the one who wishes to talk about the one, true God must at all times talk about the triune God, since all else is vanity and idolatry" (Richardson and Bowden, eds., *Westminster Dictionary of Christian Theology*, SCM Press, 1983, 588).

[45]Karl Rahner, *Theological Investigations*, Helicon, 1963, 1:143.

the God who created all things is clearly characterized as the Father in virtue of his distinction from the "Son" ("Servant," "Christ"). Now if creation and saving history are ascribed to God the Father, there can hardly be a single statement about *o theos* which is not included therein...

Where Christ's Person and Nature are to be declared with the greatest theological strictness and precision, he is called the Son of God...For [the NT writers] the expression *o theos* was just as exact and precise as "Father"...When in consequence of all this we say that *o theos* in the language of the New Testament signifies the Father...all that is meant is that when the New Testament thinks of God, it is the concrete, individual, uninterchangeable Person who comes into its mind, who is in fact the Father and is called *o theos*; so that inversely, *when o theos is being spoken of, it is not the single divine nature that is seen, subsisting in three hypostases, but the concrete Person who possesses the divine nature unoriginately*, and communicates it by eternal generation to a Son too, and by spiration to the Spirit.[46]

Rahner and Harris, as leading experts representing respectively the Roman Catholic Church and evangelical Protestantism, virtually concede our point that "God" in Scripture almost invariably means the Father of Jesus. Most significant of all as a challenge to Trinitarianism is Scripture's united testimony that "God" cannot possibly describe a triune God. The God of the Bible and of Jesus was and is not the Trinity of traditional theology.

Rahner's conclusion to his detailed study is very similar to that of Murray Harris. The greatest number of references in the New Testament to "God" clearly refer to the Father. The six texts which might refer to the Son are "hesitant and restrictive" — hardly a firm foundation for altering the monotheism of Israel. "God," adds Rahner, "is never used in the New Testament to speak of the holy spirit."[47] And when "God" is spoken of in the New Testament it is the person of the Father who is referenced, the individual "Person who possesses the divine nature unoriginately."[48] This is of course pure unitarianism and has been pointed out by objectors to the Trinity for centuries.

---

[46]Ibid., 143-146.
[47]Ibid., 143.
[48]Ibid., 146.

Rahner concedes also that in post-biblical times Justin Martyr, Irenaeus and Tertullian speak of the Father as God *par excellence!* This too is a unitarian perspective. The Church of the second century, although it had mistakenly extended the Son's life into prehistory, was far from establishing his Deity.[49]

Roman Catholic scholar Raymond Brown's biblical studies are well-known and highly acclaimed. Brown says that "Jesus is never called God in the Synoptic Gospels, and a passage like Mark 10:18[50] would seem to preclude the possibility that Jesus used the title of himself." He says also that "even the fourth Gospel never portrays Jesus as saying specifically that he is God." Brown notes that there are five New Testament passages in which Jesus may be identified as God, but "often these five examples are rejected by scholars...on the grounds that the use of 'God' for Jesus is rare in the New Testament and therefore always to be considered improbable." He concludes that there are only three "texts where Jesus is clearly called God" (Heb. 1:8-9; John 1:1 and John 20:28).[51]

But in what sense is he called God on those three rare occasions? In the Hebrews passage, the author immediately speaks of the "God" Messiah as himself *having a God* who anoints him. And we know that human beings can be called "God" in a secondary sense. John speaks of the *logos* (word) as God, but does not equate the Son with the preexisting *logos*, but speaks of the Son existing only when he appears as flesh (John 1:14). John is the writer who very clearly defines God from the words of Jesus as "the only one who is truly God" (John 17:3) and who describes Jesus as refusing the accusation that he is "making himself God" (see John 10:33-38). Raymond Brown is right that even the fourth gospel never reports Jesus as saying specifically that he is God. Brown observes that the New Testament as a whole shows that "while Jesus was associated with God and was called the Lord or the mediator, there was a strong tendency to reserve the title 'God' to the Father who is the one true God." This could most easily be explained on the basis of the simple fact that Jesus and the New Testament authors were unitarian and

---

[49]Tertullian is supposed to be the father of western orthodoxy, yet he himself says that the Son did not exist from eternity. "There was a time when neither sin existed with [God], *nor the Son*" (*Against Hermogenes*, ch. 3).
[50]"Why do you call me good? No one is good except one, and that is God."
[51]*Jesus: God and Man*, MacMillan, 1967, 23, 30.

monotheists of the strict Jewish type. Most revealing is the fact that the greatest of the Nicene fathers, Athanasius, admitted that the Trinitarian formula of Nicea "was going beyond anything said explicitly in the New Testament."[52]

Brown has hardly produced overwhelming evidence that Jesus' conviction that "You, Father, are the only one who is truly God" and the Hebrew monotheism which underlies that proposition have been overthrown and replaced by belief in a triune God, incompatible with the Hebrew Bible. John 17:3 identifies one Person (not "a What"), the Father, as the only one who is truly God.

Equally decisive are the conclusions of another theologian, the French scholar Yves Congar. Examining Paul's writings he finds that there are "forty or more quasi-trinitarian formulas in Paul, but there are no clear statements revealing a trinity of persons in the one divine nature." That has been the claim of unitarians for centuries. Congar judges that "it is almost impossible to draw any real conclusions even from the Gospel of John regarding the dogma of the Trinity." Then he adds that it was John's "trinitarian view" that inspired Ignatius (d. ca. 110), Justin (d. ca. 165) and Irenaeus (ca. 140-200). He observes a most significant fact as a corrective to the widely held but erroneous notion that the Trinity can be traced in an unbroken line back to the New Testament: Athanasius (ca. 295-373) and Basil the Great (ca. 330-379) "stopped short of calling the Spirit 'God' because they did not want to move beyond the data found in the Scriptures."[53]

William La Due observes:

> [In the New Testament] the Deity is identified again as the God of Abraham, Isaac and Jacob (Mark 12:26-27), as well as the Father of Jesus (Eph. 1:3)...*Theos* regularly refers to the first person of the Trinity [the Father], and occasionally to the Son, but the term is apparently never used of the Holy Spirit...Jesus is not called God in the Synoptic Gospels, nor does he specifically refer to himself as God in the Gospel of John. There is some dispute as to whether Paul unambiguously identifies Jesus as God...Not even the Pauline writings could support the trinitarian doctrine we profess today.[54]

---

[52]Ibid., 9, xii.
[53]La Due, *Trinity Guide to the Trinity*, 25, 26.
[54]Ibid., 27.

It seems to us a cruel injustice for churches today to threaten with loss of salvation anyone who questions the Trinitarian Deity of Jesus. The evidence as admitted by staunch Trinitarians themselves is ambiguous at the very least. Very often Trinitarian scholars concede their whole case to the unitarian cause. If the Bible is to be our guide, as is the cry of Protestantism, why could we not settle the ambiguity once and for all by simply saying that Jesus resolved the issue for us? It is only for us to believe his words. God has not teased us with ambiguities, uncertainties, and hairsplitting arguments about how many He is. It is very unfair to hand a person a Bible, recording the teaching of Jesus, and then to maintain that the triune God of the Church is easily identified with the God of Jesus and the Apostles.

Jesus simply and clearly affirmed the unitarian creed of Israel. Paul did likewise: "For us [Christians] there is one God, the Father, and no other besides Him" (see 1 Cor. 8:4-6). Paul confessed Jesus not as God, but with the rest of the New Testament as the Lord Messiah (1 Cor. 8:6). Paul said also, "God is one Person" (Gal. 3:20). The Trinity adds two more who are God. This creed is not the creed of Jesus, and Jesus is to be Lord, master and rabbi of his followers.

Chapter 5

The Son of God: Protestant Loss of Jesus' Teaching and His Promotion to Deity

"The Shema comes from the Torah...Deuteronomy 6:4-9 is the Shema. By the first century, we find evidence that it was standard practice for Jews to recite the Shema as a form of their prayer life and confessional life, the way many Christians recite the Apostles' Creed [150 AD] or the Lord's Prayer."[1]

"Why is it necessary to improve on the foundational Christian confession, 'You are the Christ, the Son of the living God,' and thus alter its clear meaning? In order to understand God and Jesus and their relationship, we must begin with this confession...This biblical confession of faith represents the central biblical message."[2]

It is an easy matter to demonstrate that our New Testament writers, some of whom had known Jesus personally and heard him teach day after day in the temple, were committed to the belief that Jesus was "the Son of God." This is the precise claim Jesus made for himself in John 10:36: "I said that I am the Son of God." It was the accusation of Jesus' enemies at his trial that he had claimed to be "the Son of God" (John 19:7). This was the worst they could say of him.

---

[1]Scott McKnight, "What Jesus Believed," Interview by Paul O'Donnell, www.beliefnet.com/story/154/story_15466_1.html
[2]William Clark, *Catechism of the Catholic Church*, German ed., Oldenbourg, 1993.

In John 10:36 Jesus is intent on putting the record straight when angry members of the religious establishment charge him with inadmissible claims and what they consider a blasphemous challenge to the authority of God. Jesus had claimed to be a unique agent of the One God and to be performing God's will perfectly. He rejected entirely their suggestion that he was somehow replacing God, and protested that he was able to do nothing of himself, but only what God permitted or ordained: "The Son can do nothing of himself unless it is something he sees the Father doing" (John 5:19).

This reply of Jesus to his accusers is very often omitted from evangelical literature, since it would expose as wrong the notion that Jesus was claiming actually to *be* God. Jesus vigorously rejected the idea that he was God Himself. What he did claim was to be blamelessly performing the will of God. There is an equality of function in Jesus' activity. And he spoke the words of God (John 3:34). But far from working out of his own "Deity" he can do only what he "sees the Father doing. Whatever the Father does the Son does it in the same way" (John 5:19). By no stretch of the imagination does this constitute Jesus a second uncreated Person of the Godhead. It proves him rather to be the perfectly submitted, sinless human being. As C.K. Barrett remarked with humor on John 8:28, "It is simply intolerable that Jesus should be made to say, 'I am God, the supreme God of the Old Testament, and being God I do as I am told.'"[3]

The later Catholic Church, losing touch with the Jewish Jesus of the Scriptures, invented a new identity for Jesus which he would not and could not have accepted. The Son who in Scripture came into being (was *begotten*) was replaced by an eternal being who was transmuted into a human fetus. And so it remains to this day: The creed of the Church and the creed of Jesus are at odds.

In John 10:34-36 Jesus answers his accusers by arguing that even the judges of Israel, who were entrusted with God's revelation, were called in Psalm 82:6 "gods" (*elohim*). Why then would it be wrong for him as the specially appointed promised Messiah of Israel, the ultimate prophet promised by the Hebrew Bible (Deut. 18:15-19), to claim to be the *Son* of God? (John 10:36). How easy it would have been for him to declare unambiguously, "I am God, an uncreated

---

[3]*Essays on John*, 12.

second member of a triune Godhead." He says no such thing. Far
from claiming to *be* God, he claims to be God's *Son*.

Son of God

It is a very easy task to demonstrate that within the pages of the
Bible "Son of God" never means God. The very word "son" implies
— both in and outside the Bible — origin, derivation and
subordination. Adam is called "son of God" (Luke 3:38). Adam was
not God. Israel, as God's chosen nation, was called God's "son"
(Exod. 4:22; Hos. 11:1). This did not elevate them to the status of
Deity. They were still members of the human race. Angels as "sons of
God" were definitely created beings (Job 1:6; 38:7). Created persons
could on rare occasions even be called "God." The king of Israel had
been called "God" (Ps. 45:6),[4] and this same title was applied in
Hebrews 1:8 to Jesus as Messiah. It is well known that in the Bible
the human kings of Israel are meant to reflect the One God who
appointed them. No one imagined they were actually the Creator God.
No Israelite, reading his Scriptures and eagerly anticipating the
promised Son to be born as a descendant of David, could have
remotely supposed that God Himself was going to arrive from
heaven, as a member of the Godhead become man.

In the Old Testament the One God appointed Moses to be "God
[*elohim*] to Pharaoh" (Exod. 4:16; 7:1). What we learn here reveals
the marvelous status that God is able, if He wishes, to assign to
selected human agents. Adam, indeed, as the beginning of the human
creation, was appointed as the son and "image of God" (Gen. 1:27)
which in Middle Eastern cultures meant that he was a direct
representative of the Deity on earth. The distinguished professor of
systematic theology at Fuller Theological Seminary states
categorically a fact which can be confirmed in a good modern Bible
dictionary:

> To be a 'Son of God' one has to be a being who is *not* God! It
> is a designation for a creature indicating a special relationship

---

[4]The Roman Catholic translation of the Bible (NAB) very helpfully has
"Your throne, O god, stands forever; your royal scepter is a scepter for
justice." The notes observe that "god" is a courtly royal title describing a
human being who represents God. The *Theological Dictionary of the New
Testament* confirms that "In Ps. 45:6 the *Elohim* undoubtedly refers to a
man, i.e., the king, and not to Yahweh" (Eerdmans, 1965, rep. 2006, 3:96).

with God. In particular, it denotes God's representative, God's vice-regent. It is a designation of kingship, identifying the king as God's son.[5]

Had attention been paid to this rather elementary fact about the term "Son of God," centuries of pointless dispute leading to the Trinity could have been avoided. "Son of God" is the Messianic title marking Jesus as the one whom God promised as son of Abraham, David and of God Himself.

The confusion created by churches which lift the biblical term "Son of God" out of its biblical context and redefine it to mean something quite different, continues to blight reasonable discussion of the controversial issue about who God and Jesus are.

Church members who have not examined these issues of identity carefully are liable to react with alarm to the proposition that "Son of God" does not mean God. Cherished tradition causes an automatic reflex making them equate "Son of God" with the later phrase "God the Son." But in terms of Scripture, to which Protestants say they are committed as sole authority, not only does the title "God the Son" not appear,[6] but "Son of God" describes a creature related in some way to God, but certainly not God Himself. The very idea of two who are God should cause churchgoers to shrink in horror from such potential polytheism. But centuries of indoctrination seem to have desensitized them to the awful prospect that the monotheism of Jesus has been violated by their traditions. They have not pondered the troubling problem involved in believing that one who is God (the Son) left his home in heaven while another who is God (the Father) did not. Does this situation not point to an on obvious ditheism, belief in two Gods? One who is fully God on earth and another who is fully God in heaven makes two Gods.

[5]Colin Brown, "Trinity and Incarnation: In Search of Contemporary Orthodoxy," *Ex Auditu* 7, 1991, 88.
[6]There is a single text in John 1:18, the authenticity of which is disputed by critics. This speaks of "an [not 'the'] only begotten god." John has just said that "no one has seen God at any time." He then describes the Son as "an only begotten god." If this text is genuine it still does not make the Son the supreme God, but as F.J.A. Hort said, a uniquely begotten Son is the "highest form of derivative being" (*Two Dissertations 1876,* rep. Kessinger, 2004, 13).

Believing that Jesus is the *Son* of God and thus by biblical
definition not God Himself (a proposition which would immediately
lead to belief in two Gods, since the Father of Jesus was obviously
God) was the core of right belief according to Jesus. The New
Testament makes a proper understanding of who he is and was a
crucial issue. Jesus asked this test question of his chosen executives,
the leaders of the Church which he founded. In view of various public
misunderstandings about who Jesus was — some thought he was
Jeremiah or another prophet who had returned to life — Jesus posed
the question of questions: "Who do *you* say that I am?" The
resounding and correct reply came from Peter: "You are the Christ,
the Son of the living God" (Matt. 16:15-16).

Jesus greeted this recognition of him as the Messiah and Son of
God with warm enthusiasm. With the assurance that Peter had been
given this correct identity of Jesus by divine revelation, Jesus then
promised to found the Christian Church on Peter's insight: Jesus is
the Messiah, Son of God (Matt. 16:17-18). That is what New
Testament Christianity is all about. Note that this fact immediately
links Christianity to its Jewish roots in the Hebrew Bible. The
designation of Jesus as *the Christ* is repeated hundreds of times, in
every book of the New Testament except 3 John. "Christ" is simply
our English translation of the Greek word *Christos* and the Hebrew
Mashiach. The Christ is God's unique son and King (Ps. 2:2, 6, 7).
The heart of the faith is shaken when definitions are produced which
(no doubt in the name of "progress") go beyond the core biblical
belief that Jesus is the Son and Messiah.

As reported in the corroborating accounts of Mark and Luke,
Peter said, "You are the Christ" (Mark 8:29), "the Christ of God"
(Luke 9:20). John records Jesus as being rightly identified as "the
holy one of God" (John 6:69). Matthew's addition of the explanatory
phrase "Son of the living God" (Matt. 16:16) does not mean that
"Messiah" and "Son of God" were radically different in meaning. The
predicted king of Israel had been called "Messiah" in the Hebrew
Bible. He had also been called "Son of God." Psalm 2 treats as virtual
synonyms the titles "Messiah" (anointed), "Son" and "My [God's]
King." And in John's opening presentation of the key figure of
Christian belief, various associates of Jesus recognize him as "Son of
God," "King of Israel," and "Lamb of God," "the one of whom Moses
in the Law and the prophets were writing" (John 1:29, 36, 45, 49).

These are all titles for the same person. They have nothing at all to do with designations of Jesus by *later*, post-biblical theology, i.e., "God the Son," or God. For John "King of Israel" and "Son of God" are synonyms. Nathanael, the man "without guile," declared of Jesus, "You are the Son of God; you are the King of Israel" (John 1:49). Of Israel in its ideal future converted state as God's people the prophet Hosea had written, "It will be said to them, 'You are sons of the living God'" (Hos. 1:10; Rom. 9:26). They were not thus to be Deity but transformed human beings. Jesus is the forerunner of just that ideal. He was recognized by those gifted to know he is "the Christ, the son of the living God" (Matt. 16:16).

The definitive descriptions of Jesus as Son of God and Messiah are found with equal emphasis in the latest of the four gospels, John. Since it is to the gospel of John that some appeal for the *later* definition of Jesus as the second member of the Trinity, those introductory designations of Jesus (cited above), using titles which could not possibly mean he is "God," are particularly significant. Equally impressive, and to be noted with special care, is John's explicit and concluding statement about why he had written his whole gospel. "These things are written," he states, "that you [the reader] may believe that Jesus *is the Christ, the Son of God,* and that by believing this you may have life in his name" (20:31). Since this is exactly the definition of Jesus provided much earlier by Peter and acclaimed by Jesus as the essential rock foundation of Christian faith, we see that the Apostles were in complete harmony about the identity of their rabbi, lord and savior. Not unreasonably Christianity is centered in the belief that Jesus was and is the *Christ. "Everyone who believes that Jesus is the Christ has been born from God"* (1 John 5:1). This confession is synonymous with believing that "Jesus is the Son of God" (1 John 5:5). Indeed, "he who has the Son has life and he who does not have the Son of God does not have life" (1 John 5:12).

This is the impassioned conviction which pervades apostolic Christianity, forming its backbone and substructure. To require of church members a belief that "Jesus is God" is to demand allegiance to a Jesus not known to the pages of the New Testament. It is alien to John's writings to maintain that believing in the Christ or the Son means that one holds the view that Jesus is fully God and fully man. To say "I believe that Jesus is Christ" and "I believe he is God" is to give with one hand and take back with the other — a disturbing self-contradiction.

We see, then, that there has been no evolution or change within the canon of the New Testament in the basic identity of Christianity's founder. Peter, in conversation with Jesus in the 30s AD, provides the creedal statement about Jesus as Messiah, Son of God. And John writing probably in the 90s makes the same identity of Jesus the whole point of his gospel-writing. This should put an end to any theories of "progress" within the New Testament period. It is not seldom claimed that it is only when we come to John that we find Jesus elevated as a member of the Godhead. This is patently not so, since everything John included in his gospel was to demonstrate the Messiahship and Sonship of Jesus (John 20:31). Neither of these titles, provided we stay within their New Testament meaning, provides evidence that he is God!

If on the other hand we approach the New Testament doctrines armed with the concept that "Jesus is Almighty God," we may be able to justify the traditional view from a very few texts, but only at the cost of ignoring the thousands of singular verbs and nouns, notably the personal name of God, Yahweh, and singular personal pronouns, which in the biblical languages, as in English, denote a single person.[7] The triune God contradicts the plain unitarian, creedal statement of Jesus and the Apostles (Mark 12:29; John 17:3; 1 Cor. 8:4-6; 1 Tim. 2:5). The Messianic title "Son of God" is distorted when it is turned into "God the Son." The concept of an eternal "God the Son" demolishes the birth narratives of Matthew and Luke, which do not describe the arrival of a divine being from another realm, but the begetting of a baby in Mary. This is conception and begetting, not transmutation or transformation or Incarnation, which is a concept completely at variance with Matthew's and Luke's meticulously detailed account of the genealogical pedigree of Jesus as the son of David and Abraham (Matt. 1:1), indeed of Adam himself (Luke 3:38).

---

[7]The Hebrew Bible speaks of a person as a *nephesh* or living soul. This is equivalent to an "individual." Even God Himself is said to be a person or soul and speaks of Himself, of His own Person, as "My soul" (Isa. 42:1; Lev. 26:11). He is a single individual or soul, the Father and the One God (Mal. 2:10). For *nephesh* as "self," "person of man" "individual," see Brown, Driver, and Briggs, 659, 660.

If Scripture is a revelation at all it speaks to us in intelligible language using established rules of grammar and syntax. It is sometimes said that descriptions of God, because He is God and not man, must go beyond reason and logic. Foggy assertions are frequently advanced to the effect that language is inadequate to describe God. This allows for a waffly retreat into "mystery."

An argument which tries to skirt the ordinary meaning of personal pronouns is invalid, once we accept Scripture as verbal revelation. The human language by which God has chosen to disclose what He desires to be known of Him (and of course there is much He has not revealed) is entirely adequate to the job. God describes Himself as a single, undivided divine personality. He describes His unique Son Jesus as a distinct person. "Person" is to be understood according to normal rules of grammar and language. Jews as custodians of Scripture have known this for the totality of their history. Hence their horror at any tampering with their creed, which is so repeatedly and explicitly "unitarian," that is, describing God as a single Person.

For Christians there remains the inescapable fact that Jesus is reported as endorsing the Jewish unitary monotheistic creed of his own biblical heritage. Unless Jesus is to be disallowed as the arbiter of what the true creed is, Christians should feel themselves dutybound as Jesus' disciples to follow their Master. At present we are faced with a bizarre situation: Churchgoers gather under the umbrella of a creedal statement unknown to Jesus. The words of the Father that Jesus is "My Son," and that we are to "hear him" (Luke 9:35) appear to allow no other view of the creed than the one announced by Jesus himself as the most important of all theological considerations.

Mark's inclusion of Jesus' interchange with a Jewish scribe over the truly orthodox creed roots the Christian creed in the creed of Israel, as far as defining God is concerned. There can be no mistaking the fact that Jesus' creed, and therefore the creed of Christianity, must be the ancient and hallowed creed of Scripture and of Israel. The creed recited by Jesus is not the property of Israel alone. On the contrary it becomes via Jesus the property of all who profess belief in and allegiance to the one whom we believe to be the promised Messiah. It seems to me that the reader of Mark 12 is invited to bring his intelligent understanding to bear on the Savior's words and to question how closely Jesus has been followed by traditional Christianity in this respect. If Jesus' God and his service of that one

God are embedded in Judaism, ought not Christians to be following suit?[8]

The amazing capacity of the Jew to survive seems not to be true of their monotheistic creed, when it was passed from the hands of Jesus' chosen Jewish Apostles into the hands of second-century Gentiles, who apparently thought that the creed of their claimed Savior needed "upgrading." This fatal development has caused Jews of all generations to discount the claims of the professed followers of Jesus. They rejected them out of hand for the very reason that the Trinitarian creed was something their own Scriptures had forbidden them to embrace. This could turn out to be one of history's great ironies. The spiritual and intellectual heritage of the Jews, undergirded by their pure monotheism, should have passed into the Christian Church unchanged. Jesus could have been claimed as the greatest proponent of such a transfer of creed to the whole world. Israel's and Jesus' God could have been proclaimed worldwide. But this has not happened. The Church betrayed her master at a most fundamental level. This was made possible by Protestant neglect of Jesus as their teacher and rabbi. A double tragedy occurred: The Christians disregarded the unitarian creed of Jesus, and Jews were strengthened in their refusal of the Messiah because Christians misrepresented Jesus in the matter of creed.

Nowhere was Jesus more clearly the Jewish teacher of salvation than in Matthew, Mark and Luke. It was these books which enshrined Jesus' own declaration about the true God. These records of the Jewish Jesus, however, lost their primary and central place in Protestant theology. How this happened is not difficult to investigate.

Luther and Anti-Semitism

A contemporary British scholar reminds us that:

> One of the "lies" of which [Luther] accused the Jews is that they claimed that Christians believe in more than one God. Thus the Jewish perception that the doctrine of the Trinity is not monotheistic was put forward as a reason for condemning

---

[8]This is not to say that the New Testament requires those under the New Covenant to adopt a Jewish calendar or food laws. Acts 15, the first church council and later Paul (Rom. 14:14, 20; Galatians) deal expressly with this issue. But there is no suggestion ever in the New Testament that the definition of God has been altered.

the Jewish people. Luther's recommendations included burning down the synagogues or schools of "the Jews," destroying their houses, confiscating all copies of their prayer books...and forbidding their rabbis to teach on pain of death.[9] Maurice Casey alerts us to the fact that "with these recommendations, the architect of the Reformation erected a signpost to the holocaust. He is often thought to have provided the key to understanding St Paul: but in Paul the cross is to be borne, not inflicted."[10] The violent approach to those who did not accept "orthodoxy" should provide a warning signal that all was not well with "orthodoxy." Instead of a loving appeal to Jews and to Christian "dissenters," the mainstream of traditional Christianity threatened them with death for their non-conformity to dogma. The faith as modeled by Jesus was thus turned on its head. Jesus had warned that misguided religious opponents were the ones most likely to be dangerous to the Christian's life (John 16:2).

The root of Luther's problem as with much evangelicalism today was that he was selective in his use of the New Testament. His selectivity gave preference to the letters of Paul over the synoptic records of Jesus' own teaching. But the Jewish Jesus is most clearly presented in precisely those books which Luther tended to disregard. Not widely recognized by Protestants is Luther's prescription for elevating certain portions of the New Testament over others, ensuring thus that we do not look too closely at the teaching of Jesus. That teaching was of course for Paul fundamental (1 Tim. 6:3). The Protestant tendency, however, with its heavy emphasis on Romans as the heart of the Gospel, has been to twist Paul and reject Jesus. The New Testament presents Jesus, not Paul, as the author of the Gospel of salvation (Mark 1:14, 15; Heb. 2:3; 1 Tim. 6:3; 2 John 7-9). And Jesus throughout his ministry appealed to all who heard him teach, never to forget that his *words* provided the only basis for the knowledge of God and His plan of salvation.

Luther Versus the Canon of the Bible

Luther's principle of selection in the use of Scripture has called forth some strong criticism:

---

[9]Maurice Casey, *From Jewish Prophet to Gentile God,* Westminster/John Knox Press, 1991, 175.
[10]Ibid.

Martin Luther, in accord with his posture of supreme self-importance *as restorer of Christianity*, even presumed, inconsistently, to judge various books of the Bible, God's holy Word. Luther feels himself entirely able and duty-bound — as a lone individual — to judge the canonicity and even overall value of Old Testament and New Testament books which had been securely in the canon for over 1100 years. Most of these sentiments (especially concerning the New Testament) can be found in Luther's prefaces to various books of the Bible. Scanning some of those in one primary source produced by the United Lutheran Church in America, I see that Luther rejects the apostolicity of Hebrews, James, Jude, and Revelation, although he does say they are "fine" books. Yet of James, Luther states that it is "flatly against St. Paul and all the rest of Scripture." Logical consistency was not one of Luther's better qualities, needless to say.

If a book in the Bible contradicts another, then it is clearly not God-breathed (as God can't contradict Himself or be in error about anything), hence not inspired, and therefore not part of Scripture at all. And that is basically Luther's conclusion, although the overwhelming weight of tradition pertaining to the biblical canon required him to retain these books in his Bible, albeit separately, as a sort of New Testament "Apocrypha." Luther clearly had little patience with the book of Revelation: In his Preface to Revelation, from 1522 — from the time period in which he was translating the Bible — he states with amazing boldness: "I miss more than one thing in this book [the book of Revelation], and this makes me hold it to be neither apostolic nor prophetic...I think of it almost as I do of the Fourth Book of Esdras, and can in no way detect that the Holy Spirit produced it. It is just the same as if we did not have it, and there are many far better books for us to keep. Finally, let everyone think of it [Revelation] as his own spirit gives him to. My spirit cannot fit itself into this book. There is one sufficient reason for me not to think highly of it — *Christ is not taught or known in it*; but to teach Christ is the thing which an apostle is bound, above all else, to do, as He says in

Acts 1, 'Ye shall be my witnesses.' Therefore I stick to the books which give me Christ, clearly and purely."[11]

Of special interest and relevance is Luther's Preface to the New Testament (1522; revised 1545), where he says some astonishing things (including the famous "epistle of straw" remark). After expounding generally for a few pages, the alleged restorer of the gospel concludes with this evaluation of John's gospel as compared with Matthew, Mark and Luke: "From all this you can now judge all the books and decide among them which are the best. John's gospel is the one, tender, true chief gospel, far, far to be preferred to the other three and placed high above them. So, too, the Epistles of St. Paul and St. Peter far surpass the other three gospels — Matthew, Mark, and Luke. In a word, St. John's gospel and his first Epistle, St. Paul's Epistles, especially Romans, Galatians and Ephesians, and St. Peter's first Epistle are the books that show you Christ and teach you all that is necessary and good for you to know, *even though you were never to see or hear any other book or doctrine.* Therefore St. James' Epistle is really an epistle of straw, compared to them; for it has nothing of the nature of the Gospel about it."

We see the legacy of this tendency to emphasize certain New Testament books to the neglect of others in Protestantism to this day. It was clear that St. Paul's writings (especially Romans) and John's gospel were the favorites, and the books Luther liked less are too often neglected (especially Hebrews and James). Revelation is popular in some circles (particularly the Dispensationalists).[12]

---

[11] *The Works of Martin Luther,* trans. C.M. Jacobs, Muhlenberg Press, 1932, 488, 499, emphasis added.

[12] Dave Armstrong, "Luther vs. the Canon of the Bible," ic.net/~erasmus/RAZ325.HTM (since deleted). We should add that Revelation has become the victim of a "pre-tribulation rapture" system which contradicts the plain words of Jesus that he will gather the elect "post-tribulation": "Immediately *after* the tribulation of those days...he will gather his elect" (see Matt. 24:29-31). Paul likewise would have no patience with modern innovative theories of a pre-tribulation rapture/resurrection. He obviously expected Christians to have to endure tribulation until the coming of Jesus in visible power and glory to raise the faithful dead (1 Cor. 15:23)

Luther biographer Hartmann Grisar, S.J. (author of a massive six-volume biography) writes:

[Luther's] criticism of the Bible proceeds along entirely subjective and arbitrary lines. The value of the sacred writings is measured by the rule of his own doctrine. He treats the venerable canon of Scripture with a liberty which annihilates all certitude. For, while this list has the highest guarantee of sacred tradition and the backing of the Church, Luther makes religious sentiment the criterion by which to decide which books belong to the Bible, which are doubtful, and which are to be excluded. At the same time he practically abandons the concept of inspiration, for he says nothing of a special illuminative activity of God in connection with the writers' composition of the Sacred Book, notwithstanding that he holds the Bible to be the Word of God because its authors were sent by God...Thus his attitude towards the Bible is really burdened with "flagrant contradictions," to use an expression of Harnack, especially since he "had broken through the external authority of the written word," by his critical method. And of this, Luther is guilty, the very man who elsewhere represents the Bible as the sole principle of faith! If, in addition to this, his arbitrary method of interpretation is taken into consideration, the work of destruction wrought by him appears even greater. The only weapon he possessed he wrested from his own hand, as it were, both theoretically and in practice. His procedure regarding the sacred writings is apt to make thoughtful minds realize how great is the necessity of an infallible Church as divinely appointed guardian and authentic interpreter of the Bible.[13]

---

and "to give relief to you who are afflicted and to us as well when the Lord Jesus will be revealed from heaven with his mighty angels in flaming fire, dealing out retribution to those who do not know God and to those who do not obey the gospel of our Lord Jesus" (2 Thess. 1:9).
[13]*Martin Luther: His Life and Work*, Newman Press, 1930, 263-265. An infallible Church, however, is an impossible solution. What we do have is inspired Scripture as the basis of the faith as originally taught (Jude 3).

From a Protestant point of view also Luther does not escape criticism in regard to his "canon within the canon." The *Hastings Dictionary of the Bible* observed:

With Luther the Reformation was based on justification by faith. This truth Luther held to be confirmed (a) by its necessity, nothing else availing, and (b) by its effects, since in practice it brought peace, assurance and the new life. Then those Scriptures which manifestly supported the fundamental principle were held to be *ipso facto* inspired, and the measure of their support of it determined the degree of their authority. Thus the doctrine of justification by faith is not accepted because it is found in the Bible; but the Bible is accepted because it contains this doctrine. Moreover, the Bible is sorted and arranged in grades according as it does so more or less clearly, and to Luther there is "a NT within the NT," a kernel of all Scripture, consisting of those books which he sees most clearly set forth the gospel. Thus he wrote: "John's Gospel, the Epistles of Paul, especially Romans, Galatians, Ephesians, and 1 Peter — these are the books which show thee Christ, and teach all that it is needful and blessed for thee to know even if you never see or hear any other book, or any other doctrine. Therefore is the Epistle of James a mere epistle of straw (*eine recht stroherne Epistel*) since it has no character of the gospel in it" (Preface to NT, 1522; the passage was omitted from later editions). Luther places Hebrews, James, Jude, and the Apocalypse at the end of his translation, after the other NT books, which he designates "the true and certain capital books of the NT, for these have been regarded in former times in a different light."[14]

Luther at first (Preface in Translation of NT, 1522) expressed a strong aversion to the book [of Revelation], declaring that to him it had every mark of being neither apostolic nor prophetic...He cannot see that it was the work of the Holy Spirit. Moreover, he does not like the commands and threats which the writer makes about his book (22:18, 19), and the promise of blessedness to those who keep what is written in it (1:3, 22:7), *when no one knows what that is*, to

---

[14]*Hastings Dictionary of the Bible* (one vol.), rep. Hendrickson, 1989, 116.

say nothing of keeping it, and there are many nobler books to be kept. Moreover, many Fathers rejected the book..."Finally, every one thinks of it whatever his spirit imparts. My spirit cannot adapt itself to the book, and a sufficient reason why I do not esteem it highly is that *Christ is neither taught nor recognized in it*, which is what an apostle ought before all things to do." Later (1534), Luther finds a possibility of Christian usefulness in it...He still thought it a hidden, dumb prophecy, unless interpreted, and upon the interpretation no certainty had been reached after many efforts...He remained doubtful about its apostolicity, and [in 1545] printed it, with Hebrews, James, Jude, as an appendix to his New Testament, not numbered in the index...Zwingli [a leading Reformer] regarded Rev. as "not a Biblical book"; and even Calvin, with his high view of inspiration, does not comment on 2 and 3 John and Revelation.[15]

Calvin showed a curious unease with the historical records of Matthew, Mark and Luke. He even ventured to suggest a different order for Matthew, Mark, Luke and John, making John the gospel of first choice, and an introduction to the other three:

The doctrine, which points out to us the power and benefit of the coming of Christ, is far more clearly exhibited by [John] than by the rest...The three...exhibit [Christ's] body...but John exhibits his soul. On this account, I am accustomed to say that this Gospel [John] is a key to open the door for understanding the rest...In reading [the four gospels], a different order would be more advantageous, which is, that when we wish to read in Matthew and the others, that Christ was given to us by the Father, we should first learn from John the purpose for which he was manifested.[16]

One might well ask why Luke's answer to the question of Jesus' purpose was not adequate. "I came to preach the Kingdom of God. That is the reason for which I was sent" (Luke 4:43). But Calvin was horrified at the question asked by the disciples after they had been thoroughly schooled in the Gospel of the Kingdom for three years and

---

[15]Hastings, *A Dictionary of the Bible* (1902), 4:241, emphasis added.
[16]*Commentary on the Gospel According to John,* Baker, 1847. 1:21-22.

another six weeks (Acts 1:3): "Is it now time for you to restore sovereignty to Israel?" (Acts 1:6). From Calvin's non-Messianic point of view, this was entirely the wrong question! "There are as many errors in this question as words," he wrote.[17] Jesus did not think so at all. He merely told the disciples that the time for the arrival of that Messianic Kingdom on earth was not to be revealed (Acts 1:7).

Readers should reflect on the remarkable fact that churches have continued to place considerable faith in the spiritual leadership of Calvin and Luther, despite the former's hesitancy about the Apocalypse — Calvin wrote no commentary on Revelation — and the latter's apparent failure to heed the warnings of Jesus given in the Revelation:

> I testify to everyone who hears the words of the prophecy of this book, if anyone adds to these things, God will add to him the plagues written in the book; and if any one takes away from the words of the prophecy, God will take away his part out of the book of life, and out of the holy city, and from the things which are written in this book (Rev. 22:18, 19). Blessed is he who keeps the sayings of the prophecy of this book. Blessed is he who reads and they who hear the words of this prophecy and keep the things which are written in it: for the time is at hand (Rev. 1:3).

This hardly sounds as if the book could be safely relegated to an appendix! The book of Revelation appears in Scripture as a message *directly from Christ* to the churches. It is every bit as authoritative as the teaching of Jesus prior to his death. Jesus has certainly not altered his belief in the One God of Israel affirmed during his ministry on earth. "Who will not fear and glorify your name, O Lord? For you alone are holy" (Rev. 15:4). This is the purest Jewish-Christian monotheism, unaffected by the exaltation of Jesus to the right hand of God. Yet Luther was blind enough not to heed the powerful warnings from Jesus that his words in the Revelation are of supreme value.

In Revelation, as is well recognized, Jesus draws together the strands of Old Testament prophecy (it contains hundreds of allusions to and quotations from the Hebrew Bible) and describes the establishment of the Kingdom of God on earth at the Second Coming. It is the fitting climax to the expectations of both Old and New

---

[17]*Commentary upon the Acts of the Apostles,* Baker, 1:43.

Testament, depicting the triumph of the Kingdom of God, to be
established by the returning Messiah on a renewed earth, over a
hostile world.

This unfortunate tendency of Protestants not always to take
seriously the *teaching* of Jesus as the basis of faith is almost universal
in evangelical circles. Christians often imagine, contrary to the
repeated warnings of Jesus, that the faith somehow began with Paul
and that Jesus may be safely relegated to some sort of pre-Christian
status: This unfortunate, widespread tendency is reflected in the
following quotation from D. James Kennedy:

> Many people today think that the essence of Christianity is
> Jesus' teachings, but that is not so. If you read the Apostle
> Paul's letters, which make up most of the New Testament,
> you will see that there is almost nothing said about the
> teachings of Jesus. Throughout the rest of the New
> Testament, there's little reference to the teachings of Jesus,
> and in the Apostles' Creed, the most universally-held
> Christian creed, there's no reference to Jesus' teachings.
> There is also no reference to the example of Jesus. Only two
> days in the life of Jesus are mentioned — the day of His birth
> and the day of His death. Christianity centers not in the
> teachings of Jesus, but in the Person of Jesus as Incarnate
> God who came into the world to take upon Himself our guilt
> and die in our place.[18]

Paul in fact was a follower of Jesus and thus of his teaching. Paul
followed the great commission and preached the Kingdom of God as
the heart of the Gospel (Acts 19:8; 20:24-25; 28:23, 31). Dr. Kennedy
reflects the tendency which causes churchgoers to lose their roots in
Jesus the rabbi and savior, whose passion for the one God of Jewish
monotheism is never in doubt, and who constantly insisted on the
absolute necessity of hearing and following his words and teachings.

Jesus as the Source of the New Testament Writings

Jesus promised to communicate everything necessary through his
agents (John 14:26; 16:13). Paul recognized this important fact: "We
have used the very words given us by the Holy Spirit" (1 Cor. 2:13).

---

[18]"How I Know Jesus Is God," *Truths that Transform*, Nov. 17, 1989.

In the New Testament prophets are subject to Apostles (1 Cor. 14:29-30; Eph. 4:11).
When in the Protestant Reformation all things were being reexamined, some of the reformers sought means of reassuring themselves and their followers about the canon of Scripture. This was in some ways an unfortunate aspect of reformation thinking, because once God in his providence had determined for his people the fixed content of Scripture, that became a fact of history and was not a repeatable process. Nevertheless, Luther established a theological test for the books of the Bible (and questioned some of them)– "Do they teach Christ?" [Luther said Revelation did not.] Equally subjective, it would seem, was Calvin's insistence that the Spirit of God bears witness to each individual Christian in any age of church history as to what is his Word is and what is not...The tests of canonicity proposed by both Luther and Calvin are improper.[19]

The selective process of the reformers tended to put the *teaching* of Jesus into the background. One of many results of this tendency was the loss of Jesus' own Jewish definition of God as a single Individual.

There is evidence that all the gospels and Paul's letters were being used within 30 years of the death of John. Clement of Rome (95 AD) shows knowledge of many New Testament books. Jesus puts his stamp of authority on the canonization of the New Testament by promising that the spirit will remind them of everything. There is therefore no justification at all for selecting some books and playing others down. The fact that the books were not officially canonized before the fourth century does not mean that they were not recognized as apostolic from the start.[20]

Paul speaks of his words as commandments of the Lord (1 Thess. 4:2). Paul is taken as Scripture by Peter (2 Pet. 3:16). 1 Timothy 5:18 quotes Deuteronomy 25:4, not "muzzling the ox" as Scripture and combines it with Luke 10:17. Thus there is an equivalence of authority in both Old and New Testaments. The New Testament was written within a period of 50 years. Peter speaks of the prophets as

[19]F.F. Bruce et al., *The Origin of the Bible*, 75-77.
[20]Just as Sunday was observed as a memorial of the resurrection early and yet legislated formally later by Constantine.

holy (2 Pet. 3:2) and of Jesus giving commands through his Apostles.
The Apostles are also "holy apostles" (Eph. 3:5).

Moving Jesus Back into the Old Testament and Losing Him
A whole new approach to the Bible is evident early in the second
century. It was a departure from the view point of the New
Testament. The Son of God has mysteriously become an active figure
in Old Testament history, appearing as the angel who wrestled with
Jacob. The bedrock teaching of Jesus about the One God and himself
as the son of David underwent a radical change. F.F. Bruce writes:

> With the coming of Christ and the new understanding of the
> New Testament Scriptures as bearing witness to him, a new
> dimension of biblical understanding was opened up. But the
> Christian interpretation of the Old Testament in the New
> Testament is restrained and disciplined by contrast with what
> we find *in the post-apostolic period*. There is no reference to
> wrestling Jacob in the New Testament nor yet in the apostolic
> fathers. But Justin Martyr [150 AD] in his dialogue with
> Trypho asserts confidently that the mysterious wrestler,
> whom the narrator describes as "a man," and of whom Jacob
> speaks of as God, must be the one whom Christians
> acknowledge as God and man. Trypho [a Jew] is increasingly
> bewildered as he listens to the flow of Justin's argument.
> *Such application of sacred Scripture is entirely foreign to him*
> and he cannot understand how anyone can understand it in
> such a sense as Justin expounds. But to Justin this
> understanding of the incident is all of a piece with his
> understanding of other Old Testament incidents in which
> God, or His angel, appears or speaks to human beings in the
> form of a man. The Christological exposition of such
> incidents is hardly attested, if at all, in the New Testament
> documents; but it is a well established tradition by Justin's
> time, for Justin can scarcely be supposed to have initiated it.
> Once established the tradition was actively maintained.[21]

---

[21]F.F. Bruce, *Canon of Scripture*, Intervarsity Press, 1988, 328, 329,
emphasis added.

Charles Wesley likewise moved far beyond the terms of Scripture when he wrote: "And when my all of strength shall fail, I shall with the God-man prevail."
What we witness in the mid-second century is a clear departure from the New Testament. This falling away from apostolic faith led to a new doctrine of God and His Son. George Purves sensed the startling difference between Christianity during and very soon after New Testament times:

> In post-apostolic literature the New Testament doctrines are often reproduced in a fragmentary way. They are mixed with other ideas foreign to apostolic Christianity. The latter is unintentionally distorted and misrepresented. The points of view from which the New Testament authors presented their religion had been, it would appear, frequently lost by their successors, so that apostolic phrases were not seldom repeated with changed meanings.[22]

The Bible's Messianic Story

The concept that the Son of God was *already active* in Old Testament times disturbed the promised program of salvation laid out in the Bible. Stephen did not imagine that the angel of the Lord was Jesus himself (Acts 7:35, 38). As history proceeded, the God of Israel continued to confirm in Abraham and David and the prophets His ancient promise that the "seed" of Eve would arrive as Savior of mankind (Gen. 3:15). The story unfolds as the eager expectation that a son will be *born* in Israel (Isa. 9:6) and a prophet like Moses (Deut. 18:15-19) will originate from among the people of Israel. The program is severely disrupted by the completely different idea that a second member of a triune God (about whom Israel knew nothing) would descend from heaven and be transmuted into a human fetus.

But we find this counter-story well developed as early as the writings of Justin Martyr in 150 AD. Even earlier some of the letters of Ignatius refer to Jesus as "our God." With this the blurring of the clear unitary monotheism of the New Testament is under way. The Son of God's genealogy is to be traced to Judah and to Abraham. The "orthodox" system traces the origin of the Son beyond those

---

[22]"The Influence of Paganism on Post-Apostolic Christianity," rep. in *A Journal from the Radical Reformation* 8:2, 1999, 25.

designated ancestors. The Messiah is thus traced off the biblical map
and made into an essentially non-human person no longer traced to
the line of David. To qualify as Messiah, the Son of God must be
rooted in the genealogy of David and the history of Israel.

The whole point of the biblical story is that the Son of God has to
be a biological descendant of Eve, Abraham and David. He must be
truly a Jew by lineage. He must stem from the line of David. He must
be an Israelite, as the "prophet like Moses." If suddenly a brand new,
non-human personage from heaven is inserted into the story-line, the
whole of the divine plan is derailed, confused and vastly complicated.
The promise of the Savior's continuous lineage from Abraham and
David becomes impossible. The Savior is no longer essentially
human. Instead of talking about "him," the promised Messiah, the
Church altered the scheme to speak about "his humanity," in very
abstract terms. The Messiah of Israel and the world has been replaced
by a strange being arriving from another world. From this
unmessianic Messiah the Church needs to retreat and rediscover its
Jewish, Messianic roots. The Church should once again confess its
true roots in the creed of Jesus and Israel. It should abandon the
bizarre opinion of Augustine that Jesus at his arrival from a supposed
preexistence took "to Him what He was not."[23]

Paul warned about the danger of zeal without knowledge (Rom.
10:2). He was keen to affirm that his colleague Jews were zealous for
God, but it was an uninformed enthusiasm. His aim was to save them
from their misguided religion. What they needed was "knowledge." A
good grasp of Jesus and his Kingdom of God Gospel was the solution,
because John reported that "the Son of God came to give us an
understanding that we might know God" (1 John 5:20). This was an
echo of the ancient prophecy of Isaiah 53:11 — this text gets almost
no mention in evangelical preaching — that the Messiah would
"make many righteous by his knowledge."

It has been very unfairly quipped that Jesus could have benefited
from a course in friendship evangelism. In fact Jesus was the
deliberate friend of tax gatherers and the non-religious. There is today
a large number of "unchurched" seekers after God for whom a return
to the creed of Jesus would be a welcome relief from what is
perceived by many as a mystification of God, that He is three in One.

---

[23]*Tractates on the Gospel of John*, 17. 16; 8. 3.

The Bible is vastly more readable and cogent when read through the spectacles of its Hebrew authors and atmosphere and its strongly unitarian view of God.

The one and only exclusive God of the Jews and of Jesus still remains as the untried rallying point for a simpler Christianity with a worldwide appeal. The Jews worshipped an invisible God and because Yahweh never dies He did not need to be resurrected. Even some Jews however fell under the spell of Greek philosophy despite warning from the rabbis who repeated the appeals of the prophets of Israel. The question is a reasonable one: Did the Church commit suicide by surrendering its monotheism to the culture? There is validity in the challenge of Dr. Norman Snaith who warns that "neither Catholic nor Protestant theology is based on biblical theology. In each case we have a domination of Christian thought by Greek thought. *Pagan ideas* have largely dominated Christian thought."[24] Canon Goudge was right to warn us that "the Greek mind and the Roman mind in turn, instead of the Hebrew mind, came to dominate [the Church's] outlook: from that disaster the Church has never recovered, either in doctrine or in practice."[25]

One indication of that loss of original truth can be traced to unfair translation, promoting Jesus to the Trinitarian status of God. Our standard translations of the Scriptures are geared to perpetuating the myth that what we teach as doctrine is readily found within the pages of the Bible. This illusion is fostered by a number of subtle distortions in translation. One blatant example is the use of the word "worship" to create the impression in readers' minds that Jesus must be God because "worship" is offered to him. Jesus never demanded worship as God.

Worship

Jason BeDuhn in his *Truth in Translation* reminds us of an elementary biblical fact: "In the Jewish tradition, the Messiah is merely a chosen human being: there is no suggestion that he is a divine being."[26] He is of course not "just a man," but the unique

---

[24]*Distinctive Ideas of the Old Testament*, Epworth Press, 1944, 188, 189, *emphasis added.*
[25]"The Calling of the Jews," in *Judaism and Christianity*, 1939, 50.
[26]BeDuhn, *Truth in Translation*, University Press of America, 2003, 43. The word "divine" is used in different ways in our time. Jesus was certainly

virginally begotten, sinless Son of God, the only member of the
human race to achieved his destiny as an immortal man now sitting
next to God in heaven.

Another contemporary scholar is among many who fully know
that the later disputes over the identity of Jesus are far removed from
the concerns of Jesus and the Apostles.

Titles provide one way of speaking about Jesus' identity.
Another way is to speak of his being: Was Jesus God? Was
he human? Was he both? The church followed this way as it
struggled with doctrinal controversies, especially in the fourth
and fifth centuries, culminating in the Nicene Creed and the
definition of Chalcedon. *That concern belonged neither to
Jesus nor to the authors of the New Testament, not even to
John.*[27]

A powerful propaganda in favor of "orthodoxy" has invaded our
standard translations of Scripture. The public has been miseducated
into believing that if someone is "worshipped" in the Bible they must
be Deity. This is not so, as many examples from the Hebrew Bible
and the New Testament demonstrate. Jesus predicts that the day is
coming when his followers, who are certainly not God, will be
"worshipped" (Rev. 3:9).

We all recognize that Nebuchadnezzar did not think that Daniel
was God Himself. Nebuchadnezzar was in fact "doing homage" to the
prophet (Dan. 2:46). The KJV says that the king "worshipped"
Daniel. We all know that David the King was not God. Nevertheless
David was "worshipped" alongside God. The KJV tells us in 1
Chronicles 29:20 that "all the congregation…worshipped the Lord,
and the king." A specially appointed representative of the One God is
worthy of "worship" or obeisance. But that does not mean he *is* God.

The New Testament recognizes Jesus as "a teacher come from
God," (John 3:2), "a man approved by God by miracles and wonders
and signs which God performed through him" (Acts 2:22). Jesus is
the "man" whom God has appointed to administer the world in
righteousness" (Acts 17:31). John's gospel contains a single instance

---

"divine" in the sense that he was sinless, virginally conceived and reflected
the mind and character of his Father uniquely, but he was not Deity, coequal
with two other members of a triune Godhead.

[27] R. David Kaylor, *Jesus the Prophet: His Vision of the Kingdom on Earth*,
Westminster John Knox Press, 1994, 206, emphasis added.

reporting the "worship" of Jesus. The blind man worshipped him (John 9:35). As far back as 1837 a member of the clergy, Charles Morgridge, was making the point that "there is nothing but the mere sound of the English word 'worship' that favors the idea that Jesus was worshipped *as* God. Had the translators [of the KJV] rendered Matthew 8:2 as 'did him obeisance,' there would be nothing to favor the belief that supreme adoration was intended."[28]

Morgridge makes the excellent point that the association of Jesus with God as the object of praise should not lead to the conclusion that Jesus *is* God. In Exodus 14:31 "the people feared the Lord and believed the LORD and his servant Moses." Similarly in 1 Samuel 12:18, "all the people greatly feared the Lord and Samuel." 2 Chronicles 31:8: "And when Hezekiah and the princes came and saw the heaps, they blessed the Lord and his people Israel." In the New Testament the close association of God and His agents does not mean that the agent is God Himself: "It seemed good to the holy spirit [God in His operational presence and power] and to us" (Acts 15:28). "You are witnesses and God also" (1 Thess. 2:10). This reflects the Old Testament passage in which David says to Abigail who worshipped David as king (1 Sam. 23:25): "Blessed be the Lord God of Israel who sent you this day to meet me, and blessed be your advice, and blessed be you" (1 Sam. 25:32-33).

In the book of Acts Cornelius was so impressed with the status of the Apostle Peter that "fell down at his feet and worshipped him" (Acts 10:25). Cornelius did not confuse Peter with God. Cornelius certainly did not intend a gesture of "divine service" to Peter. Peter pointed out merely that as a human being he expected no such reverential behavior. Jesus recognized that there are situations in which honor paid by one person to another is not inappropriate. In one of his parables the wise guest is told to sit down in the lowest seat and when the one who invited you comes, he will say "Friend, go up higher." "Then you will have 'worship' in the presence of those eating with you" (Luke 14:10). This does not mean that the one "going up higher" would be honored as God. Jesus in another parable

---

[28]*The True Believer's Defence Against Charges Preferred for not Believing in the Deity of Christ.* Morgridge observes that even in his day Archbishop Newcombe had correctly rendered "worship" in Matt. 8:2 as "did him obeisance."

recognized that a servant might "fall down and worship" a human master (Matt. 18:26).

I have taken these quotations from the King James Version to illustrate the fact that "worship" in 1611 was the appropriate word both for reverence for God and *in another sense* homage due to superior human beings. Modern translations, recognizing that we no longer use the word "worship" for human superiors, have often replaced the word "worship" (*proskuneo*) with phrases like "to do obeisance to" "to do homage to."

But what policy are they to adopt when "worship" is directed to Jesus? Clearly they have a choice. If they want you to believe that Jesus is God, then the appropriate word to put before you, as a modern English speaker, is "worship." Knowing that "worship," as we use the word today, is due only to God, you will draw the conclusion desired by the "orthodox" translators that Jesus must *be* God because the Bible says he is worshipped, and we know that only God is to be worshipped.

However, the translators have forced this impression on you and misled you. They have not allowed you to know that *proskuneo* is a "flexible" word with a range of meaning describing acts of deference offered to persons of different rank, including of course God who is the highest personage of all. Translators of the modern Bibles read by the public bring their theological bias to the task of translation. They create a false impression about who Jesus is by having him "worshipped." As Messiah and King he was and is certainly to be honored in the highest sense, short of making him completely equal with the one God.

When the wise men bowed before the newly born Messiah most modern versions tell you that they "worshipped" the baby (Matt. 2:11). This would encourage belief in the Deity of Jesus as second member of the eternal Trinity. The Roman Catholic translation (the New American Bible, NAB), and the New Revised Standard Version (NRSV) are distinguished for their fair treatment of the text in the passage involving the magi. They report that the wise men prostrated themselves before Jesus and "did him homage," or "paid him homage" (Matt. 2:11). They do not try to tell us that Persian astronomers from the East believed they had come to visit the "baby God." Their joy was to have discovered the Messiah of Israel.

The two versions which sense the correct modern sense of "worship" as "do homage to" acknowledge that the word "worship" applied to Jesus does not in itself demonstrate his Deity. A contemporary scholar who examined this issue carefully in various translations warns Bible readers. He points out that:

> translators' biases lead them to restrict what they will allow the reader to be able to consider...The Reformation fought for the access of all believers to the Bible and the right of the individual to directly encounter and interpret the text. Modern translators undermine that cause when they publish interpretations rather than translations, still trying to direct readers to the understanding acceptable to the beliefs and biases of the translators themselves.[29]

Arthur Wainwright's highly-respected study of *The Trinity in the New Testament* concludes after a thorough investigation that the use of the word "worship" of Christ does not lead us to conclude that he was worshipped *as God*:

> The examples of *proskunein* [to worship] which have been discussed do not greatly strengthen the evidence for the worship [in the sense of worshipping Deity] of Christ. The ambiguity of the word *proskunein*, which can be used of oriental obeisance, as well as actual worship [of Deity] makes it impossible to draw certain conclusions from the evidence.[30]

This has not prevented scores of writers from overlooking these language facts. Wainwright also finds not one example of worship offered to the Holy Spirit. This is because in the New Testament the Spirit is never regarded as a third Divine Person. The Spirit is the operational power and presence of God. No one in the Bible ever prayed to the holy spirit, or praised the holy spirit. The strange appeal "Come, holy spirit," heard in charismatic quarters today, as though the spirit is a third member of the Godhead, is utterly alien to Scripture.

Typical of a disregard for the meaning of the biblical words for "worship" is the statement of Peter Toon in *Our Triune God*:

---

[29]BeDuhn, *Truth in Translation: Accuracy and Bias in English Translations of the New Testament*, 49.
[30]*The Trinity in the New Testament*, 104.

The first Christians, apostles and disciples, were thoroughly committed to the living God, to his unity and his uniqueness. Yet very quickly and without losing their passionate commitment to the unity of YHWH, they began to speak of and *worship* the resurrected, ascended and glorified Lord Jesus Christ in such a way as to confess that he is divine as is the Father.[31]

He makes this statement while paradoxically admitting that the confession of the Hebrew Bible in Deuteronomy 6:4 "is accepted and confirmed by Jesus" (Mark 12:29; Matt. 22:37; Luke 10:26) and by his Apostles (Rom. 3:30; 1 Cor. 8:4, 6; Gal. 3:20). Toon notes also:

The climax of the response of Jesus to his testing is to cite Deuteronomy 6:13, "You shall worship the Lord your God and him only shall you serve" (Matt. 4:10) [*latreuein*, to do service to Deity]. Equally striking is the answer of Jesus to the rich young man, "No one is good but God alone" (Mark 10:18).[32]

Toon speaks of "the simple task of noticing the clear commitment to monotheism within the New Testament." He admits that:

everywhere in the New Testament the truth of the monotheistic formula is taken for granted — "God is one — *eis o theos.*" In fact, God is "the only true God" (John 17:3); he is "the only God, our Savior" (Jude 25) and "the only wise God" (Rom. 16:27). So "to the King of ages, immortal, invisible, the only God, be honor and glory for ever and ever. Amen" (1 Tim. 1:17).[33]

Toon leaves us with the impression of complete contradiction. On the one hand Jesus affirms the unitary monotheism of the Hebrew Bible. On the other the Apostles do not bat an eyelid at introducing a "mutation in monotheism," a "redefinition of Jewish monotheistic devotion by a group that has to be seen as a movement within Jewish tradition of the early first century C.E."[34] This expansion or alteration of the creed of Jesus was unknown to Mark writing late in the New Testament period, when with the other synoptic gospels Jesus is

[31]Peter Toon, *Our Triune God*, Victor Books, 1996, 113.
[32]Ibid., 114.
[33]Ibid.
[34]Ibid., 115, citing Larry Hurtado, *One God, One Lord: Early Christian Devotion and Ancient Jewish Monotheism.*

presented as adhering strongly to the unitary monotheism of his heritage, which he calls the most important proposition of all. We must therefore register a protest against Toon's assertion that "Jesus was given the devotional attention which was reserved only for God himself in the Jewish tradition,"[35] if by that is meant that Jesus was thought to be God, coequal in every sense with the Father.

Toon's attempt to justify from the New Testament a "major mutation" of the Jewish-Christian definition of God promoted by Jesus himself, must be judged a failure. It is gallant but flawed. No redefinition of the express confession of Jesus is permissible for Christians. There is no new binitarian understanding of God in the Bible. Toon's argument progresses by almost unnoticeable stages. He *has* to arrive at what he thinks of as "orthodoxy." But it is not the orthodoxy of Jesus. He thinks he has found in the New Testament "a new form of Christian monotheism." He believes that there is a "general trinitarian consciousnesss" in the pages of the New Testament "out of which there arises an implicit trinitarianism."[36]

Toon hopes to convince us with Michael Ramsey, Archbishop of Canterbury, that "the first Christians began with the monotheism of Israel, and without abandoning that monotheism, were led by the impact of Jesus upon them to worship Jesus as divine."[37] But Jesus authorized no such "development." One cannot worship God as one and also as three and then claim that one has not tampered with the bedrock instruction of Jesus and the Bible. Amazingly, Toon has to admit that the New Testament Christians did not speak of "*theos* as a Trinity because for them God, *theos*, was (with a few exceptions) always the Father."[38] This, of course, concedes the whole case for unitary monotheism.

But Toon appears entirely conflicted. He goes on to cite B.B. Warfield who confidently refers to "the simplicity and assurance with which the New Testament writers speak of God as a Trinity...The whole book is Trinitarian to the core...[The Trinity] is not so much inculcated as presupposed."[39]

---

[35]Ibid., 115.
[36]Ibid., 121, 125.
[37]Ibid., 126.
[38]Ibid., 127.
[39]Ibid., 128.

Toon seems uneasy with Warfield here. He adds that "Warfield does not mean that the ecclesiastical dogma of the Holy Trinity is found in the New Testament." Toon "would prefer to speak of a vision, or conviction, or a consciousness of the Trinity."[40]

But notice that Toon has now moved by almost imperceptible steps from "a general trinitarian consciousness," "an implicit trinitarianism" to "a consciousness of the Trinity" — remarkable is the advance from lower case "t" to the capitalized Trinity.[41]

The whole exercise, I suggest, is invalid. Jesus is not worshipped as God in the New Testament, and calling him "lord" is not the same as calling him "God." Jesus founded his Church on the proposition that he is the Messiah, not God. Astonishingly Toon provides no discussion of the vital distinction between the two "lords" in Psalm 110:1,[42] the text which more than any other biblical verse provides the right framework for discussing the relationship between the One Lord God and the Lord Jesus Messiah.

Warfield's comment that the Trinity is "presupposed" in the New Testament is true in fact of the presupposition which these scholars bring to the pages of the Bible. It is they who are equipped with the presupposition that the Trinity is a New Testament doctrine and must somehow be extorted from the monotheism of Jesus.

Toon is careful to point out that "Jesus did not exist before he was conceived." But "the Son of God existed before Mary existed." When Toon explains that "the preexisting Son of God took human nature in Mary's womb," he is describing post-biblical dogma, not what Luke and Gabriel report. He urges us to believe that in Luke 1:35 "we have the Incarnation of 'the Son of the Most High,' who is 'the Son of God'; this becoming man is because of the unique presence and action of 'the Holy Spirit.'"[43]

Gabriel presented no such doctrine. The Son of God is the direct result of the divine begetting of *the Son* in Mary: "For this reason precisely he will be called the Son of God" (Luke 1:35). There is no preexisting Son of God as distinct from Jesus who did not preexist. Toon admits that Jesus did not preexist but believes that the Son of

---

[40]Ibid., 128, 129.
[41]Ibid., 125, 129.
[42]Toon's Scripture index contains no reference to Ps. 110:1, though a single reference to Ps. 110 appears in parenthesis without comment on page 118.
[43]Ibid., 197, 198, 199.

God did. To posit a preexisting Son of God who is not yet Jesus is to present us with two persons, one eternal and the other beginning (begotten) as a human being. On this scheme the promised son of David and of God has been ousted by a preexisting Son who is not traceable to the line of David and is not therefore the Messiah.

Honoring the Messiah as God's Agent

In the Old Testament we find suitable reverence offered to the Messiah who is seen in vision as the Son of Man. *Palach* is used in biblical Aramaic generally for divine service, but it is applied to saints in Daniel 7:27 and to the Messiah in 7:14. The Septuagint chooses *latreuo* (worship) in 7:14, but Theodotian, another Greek version of the Old Testament, uses the verb *douleuo,* a neutral word meaning to serve. The word *latreuo,* used in the Greek New Testament only of divine service, is not applied to Jesus. Jesus was not worshipped as God. Only the Father is said to be worshipped as receiving the activity described by the Greek word *latreuo.*[44]

We noted that in one version of the Septuagint *latreuo* is used of the Messiah, in Daniel 7:14. However the Son of Man in that vision incorporates the saints to whom the Kingdom of God will be given. It is impossible to conclude from the single use of *latrueo* here that "Jesus is God." Referring to service of the Son of Man in 7:27 Theodotian's *douleuo* and the Septuagint's *peitho* allow for no dogmatic statements about the status of the Messiah in Daniel. So the Aramaic does not distinguish divine from human service with *palach.* Or one could say that saints *and* Jesus receive divine worship, in which case the words are ambiguous as to the object. The word worship, by itself, does not tell you anything for certain about the status of the one receiving it.

The worship of Jesus in the book of Revelation certainly points, as does the whole New Testament, to the supreme elevation of the man Messiah to the right hand of the Father. Doxologies are sung to Jesus. He sits with God on God's throne. Songs are sung in praise of the Messiah, but the word "worship of deity" (*latreuo*) is reserved for the Father. Revelation 22:3 is apparently no exception, since as the *Translators' Translation* observes in its notes "John is writing a little

---

[44]Arthur Wainwright notes that "there is no instance of *latreuein* [to do religious service to] which has Christ as its object" (*The Trinity in the New Testament*, 103).

loosely. If a translation is to be more explicit, the main reference in the paragraph is to God, see verse 4."[45] The only other use of *latreuo* in Revelation is found in 7:15 where God is the object. It should be carefully noted again that the broader term for "worship" (*proskuneo*) is offered to glorified saints (3:9) and this does not lead us to believe that they are God!

The identity of Jesus is emphasized at the end of the book of Revelation. "I am the root and offspring of David, the bright morning star" (Rev. 22:16). The word root means descendant. A plant grows upwards and downwards. The shoot is derived from the ancestor, in this case David.[46] Jesus in the last verses of the New Testament is presented, as throughout the New Testament, and from its opening words (Matt. 1:1), as the promised Messiah, of the tribe of Judah and son of David. His genealogy is "traced to Judah" (Heb. 7:14). That, in all its Messianic simplicity, is the single identity of the Jesus of history, now risen and ascended and coming again. Paul's Gospel contained the same central information that Jesus is "the seed of David" (2 Tim. 2:8). There are no New Testament grounds for disturbing the unitary monotheism of Jesus and the Bible.

The argument that because Jesus is thanked, appealed to[47] or sung to, or that he walks on water, he must be part of the eternal Godhead is false. The task of the investigator of the question about God and Jesus is not to start with a presupposition about what is possible for a human being. Walking on water does not prove that Jesus is God. Peter was invited to do what Jesus did. What if God ordains homage and reverence for his unique human Son? What if angels are commanded to "worship" the human Jesus (Rev. 5:9)? We cannot rush to the conclusion that no man is worthy of such honor. God is the one who decides who is fit to die for the sins of mankind, to be our High Priest and to receive the praise of the church and of angels.

---

[45]Prepared by New Testament scholars and missionary linguists, British and Foreign Bible Society, 1973, 550.

[46]The same word "root" meaning shoot is found in Isa. 11:10 which speaks of the offspring of Jesse, as well as in Isa. 14:29, describing the offspring of a viper.

[47]In John 14:14 Jesus says, "If you ask me anything in my name, I will do it." The pronoun "I" here strongly suggests that a request can be made of Jesus.

Such is the elevation of Jesus by God Himself that the Son is honored alongside his Father. The sponsor is honored in his special agent. This does not however make the Son coequal with the uncreated God. God the Father remains the one of whom it is said in both Testaments, "You alone are holy" (Rev. 15:4), "You alone are God" (Ps. 86:10). Jewish, biblical monotheism is still very much intact.

Hymns are sung in honor of Jesus (Rev. 5:9, 12). Jesus is equipped like God to "search the hearts and minds" (Rev. 2:23; cf. Ps. 7:9). Yet he was the mortal human being, "the lamb" who *died*, and such a person cannot by definition be the one immortal God of all creation. Jesus enjoys divine titles conferred on him. He like the Father is the ultimate, "the alpha and omega," of God's great plan, "the author and finisher of our faith" (Heb. 12:2). But this does not turn God into two or three Persons. Jesus, not God, is the "alpha and omega" who *died* (Rev. 1:17). God cannot die (1 Tim. 6:16).

The comment of the writer on "Christ, Christology" in the *Dictionary of the Apostolic Church*, C. Anderson Scott, is instructive:

> The writer [of Revelation]...carries the equating of Christ with God to the furthest point short of making Them eternally equal. Christ is still "the beginning of the creation of God" (3:14), by which is probably to be understood (cf. Col. 1:18, "the beginning, the first born from the dead"; also Col. 1:15) that *He Himself was part of the creation*.[48]

With that fine statement the learned writer recovers the Messiah Jesus for the human race. He is the first to have achieved immortality and is thus the inspiring model for us all. If he were God, his achievement would be reduced to some sort of charade. It is the same professor whose eyes were open to the supreme problems involved in finding the Trinity in the New Testament. "St. Paul had no doctrine of the Trinity," he declared with confidence.[49]

We are much encouraged in our quest for the truth about the identity of Jesus by Frances Young who wrote:

> If we avoid reading the New Testament with spectacles colored by later dogma, we find emerging a christological picture — or rather pictures — *quite different from later*

---

[48]*Dictionary of the Apostolic Church*, 1:185.
[49]Ibid., 1:189.

orthodoxy. If we look at the contemporary environment, we discern not only the cultural factors which led the fathers to the dogmatic position from which the New Testament has traditionally been interpreted, but also the inherent difficulties of their theological construction.[50]

A return to a biblical identity of Jesus will be strongly encouraged when the word "worship" is properly examined. There is, as we have seen, an ambiguity in the word "worship." Playing on this, modern translations invite readers to think that Jesus is God because he is "worshipped." A warning appeared in Hastings' celebrated *Dictionary of the Bible*, in the article "Worship in the New Testament": "Some indefiniteness attaches to this subject, partly owing to the two senses in which the Greek word *proskuneo* is used, and partly owing to the ambiguous usage of the word *kurios* [lord]." The writer then referred to a Bampton Lecture in which the speaker had claimed proof of the Deity of Jesus from various occasions when Jesus was "worshipped." He went on:

> But it cannot be proved that in any of these cases…more than an act of homage and humble obeisance is intended. Josephus uses the word *proskuneo* of the high priests…The physical act of prostration in profound humility, and as rendering great honour, is all that can be meant…The homage offered to Christ would vary in its significance from the simple prostration of the leper before the Great Healer to the adoration of Mary Magdalene and Thomas in presence of the risen Christ, its significance depending wholly on the idea of His nature that had been attained, and therefore not to be determined by the mere statements of the outward acts which we find in the Gospels.[51]

This is profoundly true, and should put an end to all assertions that Jesus is God himself, because he is "worshipped." That the Messiah is worthy of the praise of angels is clear. That the Father is, in Jesus' words, "the only one who is truly God" or "the only God" or the one who "is alone holy" (Rev. 15:4) remains as a barrier against any disturbance of the creed professed by Jesus himself.

---

[50]John Hick, ed., *The Myth of God Incarnate*, SCM Press, 1977, 14, emphasis added.
[51]Hastings, *A Dictionary of the Bible*, 4:943.

The Amazing Achievement of the Human Son of God

The status of Jesus is unique. His elevation to the right hand of God marks a brand new departure in the history of the world. God has promoted his firstborn Son to immortality, an immortality which would be a laughable sham, if he had had it in eternity. What then would he have gained? And what would have happened to the Trinity (if such a thing existed) if three coequal Persons eventually added to themselves a "human nature." The "shape" of God would have been permanently altered.

The simplicity of the Messianic story presented in Scripture has been turned into a nightmare of complexity by orthodox dogma. That shift of the identity of God to so-called "Trinitarian monotheism" has been encouraged by the unconsidered meaning of "worship" in Scripture. It is more important to examine God's own story as He prepared to bring his unique Son on to the scene of history, "when He brought the firstborn into the world" (Heb. 1:6). "In the fullness of time God sent forth his Son, *coming into existence* from a woman" (Gal. 4:4).[52]

The whole point of the biblical story is that the Son of God must be a biological descendant of Eve, Abraham and David. He must be truly a Jew by lineage. He must be an Israelite. If suddenly a brand new, non-human personage from heaven is inserted into the story-line, the whole of the divine plan is derailed and confused. The promise of the Savior's continuous lineage from Abraham and David becomes impossible. The Savior is no longer essentially human. The Messiah has been replaced by a strange being arriving from another world. From this unmessianic Messiah, the Church needs to retreat.

Jesus' true identity is that he is "the Lord's Messiah" (Luke 2:26), "the holy one of God" (John 6:69). "Holy one" is the equivalent to the New Testament word "saint," the title given to Christians — "saints, holy ones." The Messianic title "holy one of God" is applied to Samson in the Septuagint of Judges 13:7. A person so described is one set apart, consecrated by God. To be God's "anointed" indicates a special relationship, between Jesus and God. Christians, as well as the patriarchs are God's anointed. "Do not touch my messiahs; do my

---

[52]Note the deliberate and unusual use of *ginomai* here and in Rom. 1:3 to express the beginning of existence, not just birth. Compare the *genesis* of Jesus in Matt. 1:18. Note that the normal word to express birth is *gennao* (see Job 14:1; 25:4).

prophets no harm" (Ps. 105:15). "Now He who establishes us with you in Christ and anointed us is God" (2 Cor. 1:21).

"Son of God" in the Messianic sense is the biblically "orthodox" definition of who Jesus is, rooted in the Hebrew Bible's royal title (Ps. 2:7). Even the centurion calls the crucified one "Son of God" (Mark 15:39). Jesus affirmed his own identity when asked by the Sanhedrin; he said he was the Messiah, Son of God (Mark 14:61-64). The same combination of Son of God and Messiah occurs in Paul's reference to the Gospel (just as in Mark's opening definition in Mark 1:1) at the beginning of Romans in verses 1:1-4. Jesus was born God's Son (Rom. 1:3) and equally the descendant of David (Rom. 1:3) and his status as Son of God was declared with power by his resurrection (Rom. 1:4). At the most fundamental level, and as the bedrock of New Testament revelation, he is the son of David, properly addressed as "lord," Messiah (Matt. 15:22; 20:31).

Chapter 6

Jesus as "My Lord" Messiah: The Golden Key of Psalm 110:1

"Probably the earliest Christian creedal statement was the simple yet profound proclamation 'Jesus is Lord!' (Rom. 10:9; 1 Cor. 12:3; 2 Cor. 4:5; Phil. 2:11). Saying Jesus is Lord (Greek: *Kyrios Iesous*) was the New Testament Greek equivalent of saying 'Jesus is Yahweh.'"[1]

"We are *not* to suppose that the Apostles identified Christ with Jehovah. There were passages which made this impossible, for instance Psalm 110:1."[2]

In Paul "there are no clear statements revealing a trinity of persons in the one divine nature."[3]

The quotations at the head of this chapter point to the confusion which has overtaken the Church. There is no Trinity in Paul, says one commentator. It was impossible to identify Jesus with Yahweh, says another. But another contradicts him by claiming that Jesus is identified with Yahweh. Who is right?

To confess Jesus as Lord in the first century set Christians apart both from Judaism and the Romans' worship of Caesar as Lord.

---

[1]F.F. Bruce, *Jesus: Lord and Savior*, Intervarsity Press, 1986, 203, but see also his view in footnote 493.
[2]Charles Bigg, D.D., *1 Peter, International Critical Commentary*, T&T Clark, 1910, 99, emphasis added.
[3]La Due, *Trinity Guide to the Trinity*, 25, referring to the work of Yves Congar.

Confessing Jesus as Lord, however, certainly did not mean that Christians had abandoned the unitary monotheistic creed fully endorsed by their founding hero, Jesus. The New Testament is violated if one suggests that its writers proposed that two Persons were both Yahweh!

Paul over and over again makes the clearest distinction between God, by which he meant the Father, and Jesus the Lord Messiah. God, for Paul, was the "God and Father of our Lord Jesus Messiah" (Rom. 15:6; 2 Cor. 1:3; Eph. 1:3). He uses that precise phrase to convey his understanding of the difference between God and Jesus. He never wrote "God the Son." Not once did he speak of "God and God." Nor did he use the phrase "God from God," as later creeds did. Paul knows of "one God and Father over all" (Eph. 4:6). This is a thoroughly Jewish definition of God. Luke in Acts reports Paul as expressing belief in the God of his Jewish heritage (Acts 24:14), and that God was never triune. Ananias, who was dispatched by the risen Jesus to inform Paul of his commission, spoke for "the God of our fathers" (Acts 22:14). Peter likewise spoke of "the God and Father of our Lord Jesus Christ" (1 Pet. 1:3).

Coequal "Gods" cannot be said to be related as "God *of* God" or "Father of God." Jesus speaks of "my God," recognizing the Father as both his God and the God of Christians (John 20:17). The Trinitarian idea throws the New Testament documents into confusion, importing into it the much later thinking of the Church.

Paul defines Jesus, as does the New Testament, as the Christ or Messiah. He refers to Jesus as "Jesus Christ our Lord,"[4] "Christ Jesus our Lord,"[5] "the Lord Jesus Christ,"[6] "the Lord Christ."[7] Jesus is the unique Son of God and God is beautifully described as "the God of our Lord Jesus Christ, the Father of glory" (Eph. 1:17). Paul, Peter, John and Jude each refer to the One God as "God the Father," "God, even the Father" (Eph. 5:20). Over and over again the Lord Jesus Christ is distinguished from the Lord God who is said to be his Father. Some 1317 references to God (*o theos*[8]) in the New Testament

---

[4]Rom. 1:4; 5:21; 1 Cor. 1:9.
[5]Rom. 6:23; 8:39; 1 Cor. 15:31; Eph. 3:11; 1 Tim. 1:2; 1:12; 2 Tim 1:2.
[6]19 times in Paul. Also James 1:1.
[7]Col. 3:24; cf. Luke 2:11.
[8]Our transliterations of Greek words reflect a modern Greek pronunciation of Greek rather than the traditional Erasmian pronunciation.

refer to the Father of Jesus and not one of them can be shown to mean "the triune God." The Bible is silent about any triune God, since the word "God" throughout Scripture never describes a God in three Persons. The triune God is rather obviously foreign to the Bible. The words "three" and "God" occur together in no Bible verse. And Yahweh who speaks as "I Myself" provides an entirely adequate description of his single personality (Jer. 29:23, etc.).

Paul was a highly trained Pharisee before his sudden and spectacular conversion to belief in Jesus as the promised Messiah of Israel. He knew God as the God of his Jewish heritage and never wavered in that conviction. He spoke of the God of the Jews as the same God as the God of the Gentiles (Rom. 3:29). Paul contradicted the Trinitarian idea of God with his claim that the God of both Testaments was the same One God, and by declaring in Galatians 3:20 that "God is [only] one Person."[9]

Today churches assemble under the umbrella of belief that the true God is composed of three Persons. The biblical creed has undergone an obvious revision. Instead of God being a single Person, the Father of Jesus, He has become a composite Being consisting of three Persons. Jews and Muslims sense that the unitarian creed of Scripture, and of Jesus himself, has had to give way to a post-biblical redefinition of God. The foundations of theology have undergone a radical change. Jesus has been divorced from his own stated creed, yet he is claimed as the founder of churches assembling in the name of a creed not known to him.

There are over 1300 references to "God" in the New Testament. The word for the One God is *o theos* in the original Greek manuscripts, and the one so designated is the Father, as is quite clear to all readers. The "Father" never means "Father, Son and Holy Spirit." This is obvious from the immediate context of the references to God as the Father. "God the Father" simply confirms that God in the New Testament means the Father. And He is both the God and the Father of His Son Jesus. These defining titles for God and Jesus are perfectly obvious to any reader and may be confirmed, for example, by looking at the introductory words of Paul's letters to the churches. Greetings are sent from God who is the Father of the Lord Jesus Christ. Greetings are sent from the Messiah Jesus. Greetings are never

---

[9]Amplified Version.

sent from the holy spirit, because, as we shall see later, Paul did not think of the holy spirit as a third member of a triune God. For Paul and the other New Testament writers the spirit of God was not a different Person from God Himself, any more than "the spirit of Elijah" (2 Kings 2:15; Luke 1:17) meant a person other than Elijah. The spirit of God was the operational presence and power of God or, after the ascension, of Jesus operating in the world in various ways.

God and Jesus thus share a common spirit, but it would be to rush to a false conclusion to say that this means that Jesus is God! It would without any proof rule out the possibility that God can impart His spirit to specially selected human beings, Jesus being the supreme and unique example of a human being endowed with the spirit of his Father.

Most readers of the New Testament approach the biblical text with the foregone conclusion that the later creeds of Nicea and Chalcedon were right in their assessment of the biblical data. They read the Bible with Nicene eyes, and the translators of our English Bibles have helped them along in this process by some editorial capital letters (which do not appear in the original Greek), forcing them to see the holy spirit as the "Holy Spirit," a third person. Translations prejudice the reader against the original understanding of the holy spirit as the personal spirit of God, His influence and power in action, by using masculine pronouns for the spirit. The Greek does not require this at all. The spirit may be legitimately thought of as "it" rather than "he." (An example of this is found in the KJV in Rom. 8:16, 26: "the Spirit itself.") If translators render the pronouns as "he," the later belief that God is three Persons and not one is imposed on the text. Translation is of course the subtlest form of commentary. The translator or translators have the power to direct the reader's thinking beyond what the original Greek had meant, "helping" him to read the New Testament as though its writers agreed with the *later* Christian creeds.

To impose later creeds on the New Testament is an inadmissible way to deal with the documents preserving apostolic faith. It is an anachronism to talk of the Bible as though it reveals a tri-personal God. It is akin to asking what sort of software Paul had on his computer. Paul knew as little about a triune God as he did about computers. If Paul was aware of competing "Gods" he warned against them and insisted on the creed of the Scriptures on which Jesus himself had built his own faith.

If one starts with belief in the triune God, a doctrine forged over a period of more than three hundred years marked by the creedal decisions of Nicea, Constantinople and Chalcedon in the fourth and fifth centuries, one will find what one is looking for in *some* verses in the New Testament. But this is to examine the issue with a preconceived bias that the New Testament is properly represented by the later creeds. What if this is not the case?

Do we need a Trinitarian "solution" to make sense of the biblical data? Or can we rest in the creed of Jesus himself which was not Trinitarian? The latter solution would appear to be the only one consonant with the conviction that Jesus is the one who is authorized to tell us who God is. Only when Jesus is rejected as our rabbi and theological guide is it possible to ascribe to him a creed he did not believe in.

I propose that the Trinitarian theory is completely unnecessary for explaining the New Testament data about God and Jesus. Worse than that, since the Trinity is an alien doctrine imposed on the text and read back into it, it actually confuses the very Jewish theology of Jesus and the Apostles. It diminishes the amazing achievement of the human Jesus. The Trinity complicates the Godhead by adding two Persons to it, and at the same time it blunts the fact that Jesus was a human being — but not just an average human being, of course! He was certainly not "just" a man, if that means an ordinary man, not a "mere man" (whatever that is supposed to mean), but the uniquely begotten and sinless Son of God, resurrected from the dead, appointed as High Priest to the human race, authorized in the future to raise and judge the dead (John 5:22, 27) and to rule the world in the coming Kingdom (Acts 17:31).

High priests, according to the book of Hebrews, are "chosen from among men" (Heb. 5:1). They have to be fully human. The Jesus who is believed to be God Himself does not fit that category. He is presented in the New Testament as the uniquely begotten or generated Son of the One God of Israel. The essential question to be answered is this: How are we to define that special and unique relationship of the Son of God to his Father? I propose that the Trinity, calling Jesus coequal with God and part of the eternal Godhead, has pushed him far beyond any of the designations given him by the New Testament.

And to make its case, Trinitarianism has to destroy the meaning of some key biblical words.

Putting two (or three) billiard balls on one spot is an impossible task. Trying to put the second one on the same spot as the first displaces the first. They will not both fit. Claiming that Jesus is God, while holding of course that the Father is God, introduces a second God, if language has any meaning. The term "God" in the Bible appears as a title. It becomes in fact virtually the proper name of God. "God is our Father," the Jews protest (see John 8:41), and they mean that the Person, God, is our Father. They learned this fact about the true God from one end of the Hebrew Bible to the other. They learned to cling to that One God after bitter historical disasters caused them to return to the unitarian view of God they were supposed to present to the pagan world. "Do we not all have one Father? Has not one God created us?" (Mal. 2:10). To say that "Jesus is God" means that there are now two Persons who are God. This is not the strict monotheism of the Bible proclaimed by the prophets of Israel and adhered to by Jesus.

Any duality or Trinity in the Godhead complicates the cardinal proposition that God is "one Lord" (Yahweh) or the one "Lord God," so designated as a single personal Being by thousands of singular personal pronouns. Calling Jesus God immediately raises the question as to how he can be a real human being without being two different persons. The proposition "The Father is God, and Jesus is God" suggests to the mind that there are two Gods. When theologians protest that the faith can accommodate two who are God, by insisting that they are joined in one unity *of essence*, they are quite unconvincing. They have departed from the categories of thought provided by Scripture. Let them show us that the Bible ever proposes that God is one substance or essence, a united Godhead of two or more Persons. Such a theory eliminates the very personal One God of Scripture who never presents Himself as an "essence" or a "What."

The addition of Jesus to the Godhead raised the awful problem of a damaged monotheism. A distinguished professor of New Testament writing from the University of Jena, H.H. Wendt, pointed out that the inclusion of Jesus as a member of the eternal Godhead undermined monotheism, though Christians claimed that it did not:

> The ancient Church Christology is burdened by very serious difficulties. These are difficulties which are connected to its

very core and center, that is to say with the fundamental concept that the Deity to be recognized in Jesus was a preexisting personal Being, the Logos, the eternal Son of God...Monotheism is damaged by this view of Christ, and monotheism is no side-line for the Christian view of God, but something fundamental and essential.

No harm would be done to monotheism when the being incarnated in Jesus is viewed as personal but not essentially Deity, nor if it is seen as essentially Deity but impersonal. But monotheism is inevitably damaged when these two factors are combined: personality and essential Deity. If the Logos which belongs to the essential Being of God is a *Person*, and as such clearly distinguished from the Person of God the Father, there arises a *plurality* in God and pure monotheism is dissolved...Further, the ancient Christology of the Church makes the spiritual being of the historical Jesus unclear and incomprehensible...The combining of a personal Logos belonging to God with a complete human being, with a human spiritual existence, means that the historical Jesus contains within himself a duality which contradicts the idea of a spiritually united personality...The incomprehensibility which pertains to God has nothing to do with the irrationality of the Trinity.[10]

None of these abstruse, brain-teasing problems arises if the pure Jewish-Christian monotheism of Jesus and his Apostles is upheld as the core of Christian faith in God. But one has only to enter a contemporary Christian bookstore to find out that the unitary monotheism of the Shema in Deuteronomy 6:4, and of Jesus, has been ruled out of court for Christians. The NIV Study Bible notes tell us that the Shema "became a Jewish confession of faith recited daily by the pious."[11] The Scofield Reference Bible states that "the Shema is meant to emphasize the monotheistic belief of Judaism."[12]

Apparently, then, Jesus, who considered the Shema to be the crowning proposition of true faith in God, is disallowed as a Christian teacher. Christianity as we know it seems to have moved away from

---

[10]Hans Hinrich Wendt, *System der Christlichen Lehre*, Vandenhoeck and Ruprecht, 1906, part 2, 368-370, translation mine.
[11]Note on Deut. 6:4.
[12]Note on Deut. 6:4.

and beyond Jesus whom it claims as its founding hero. This should be an issue of public concern, lest we fall under the criticism of Jesus himself who complained in his day that religions fall for manmade doctrine in place of scriptural truth (Matt. 22:29). It is dangerous to our spiritual health to render Scripture invalid by imposing human tradition on it. The critical standard to which Jesus and the New Testament call us is the standard set by Jesus' own Gospel and words. "If anyone is ashamed of me and my words in this faithless and sinful generation, I will be ashamed of him when I come in the glory of the Father" (Mark 8:38).

Psalm 110: A Master Key: Two Lords but Only One God

Luther referred to Psalm 110 as "the true, high, main Psalm of our beloved Lord Jesus Christ." Jesus used the key verse in Psalm 110:1 as the theme of a penetrating interchange with his opponents. He was able to silence all objectors (Matt. 22:46). No confusion would have arisen had we paid attention to the episode recorded by the gospel writers, immediately following Jesus' encounter with the scribe in Mark 12:28-34. Having replied to the Jewish inquirer by setting his seal on the unitary monotheism of his Jewish heritage, Jesus reversed the role he had played with the scribe and chose to address a question to his listeners. The gist of the question was, "How is it that David under inspiration called the Messiah 'lord'? How can the Messiah be both the son of David and also his lord?" (see Mark 12:37).

It is at this point that Trinitarianism displays an unusual carelessness with the facts. Recognizing the immense significance throughout the New Testament of Psalm 110:1, it fails entirely to give us the proper definition of the two Lords mentioned in that verse. It either neglects to inform us about the meaning of the second lord, or completely misstates the facts about the Hebrew word there. Misrepresenting the Hebrew word for "my lord" in Psalm 110:1 is remarkable, since there is no doubt at all about the word *adoni*, my lord, which appears in that verse and which provides the key to the relationship of God to the Messiah.

When Norman Geisler wrote the *Baker Encyclopedia of Christian Apologetics*, he thought he had found clear evidence for at least two elements of a Trinitarian God in Psalm 110:1: "The Lord said to my lord, 'Sit at My right hand until I make your enemies your footstool'":

The Bible also recognizes a plurality of persons in God. Although the doctrine of the Trinity is not as explicit in the Old Testament as the New Testament, nonetheless, there are passages where members of the Godhead are distinguished. At times *they even speak to one another* (see Ps. 110:1).[13]

But the second "lord" in Psalm 110:1 is not Deity at all. He is expressly *not* God. In a section "Jesus' Claim to Be God," Geisler firstly states that humans can be called *Adonai*. He refers to Genesis 18:12, where the Hebrew word is in fact not *Adonai*, but *adoni*. He then misquotes Psalm 110:1: "The Lord (*Yahweh*) speaks to my Lord (*Adonai*)."[14] The second lord of the Hebrew text is not *Adonai*, the title of Deity, but the human title *adoni*.

Even such a prestigious authority as the *Encyclopedia Americana* is confident that it has established good reason for believing in at least two members of the Trinity in Psalm 110:1. Walter Drum, S.J., professor of Scripture at Woodstock College, Maryland wrote:

> In Psalm 110:1 "Jahweh said to *Adonai*, Sit thou at my right hand." This passage is cited by the Christ to prove that he is *Adonai*, seated at the right hand of Yahweh (Matt. 22:44). But *Adonai*, "my Master," as a proper name is used exclusively of the Deity, either alone or in such phrases as Yahweh *Adonai*; indeed, instead of the ineffable name Yahweh the pious Jew read *Adonai*. It is clear, then, that in this lyric, Yahweh addresses the Christ as a different Person and yet identical in Godhead.[15]

The learned professor's statement would be fine were it not for his misreporting of the key Hebrew word. It is not *Adonai* at all, but *adoni*, a title never applicable to Deity. He is right that *Adonai* is used exclusively of Deity. But it is not the word used of the Messiah in this Psalm.

The Scofield Reference Bible on Psalm 110:1 first notes the supreme importance of this Psalm measured by its very frequent quotation in the New Testament: "The importance of the 110th Psalm is attested by the remarkable prominence given to it in the New Testament." Scofield then asserts: "Psalm 110:1 affirms the Deity of

---

[13]Norman L. Geisler, *Baker Encyclopedia of Christian Apologetics*, Baker, 1999, 730, emphasis added.
[14]Ibid., 129, 130.
[15]*Encyclopedia Americana*, 1949, 6:624.

Jesus, thus answering those who deny the full divine meaning of his New Testament title 'Lord.'"

Scofield's claim is extraordinary, since the text in fact presents the very opposite information. The second "lord" here is *adoni*, a word which in none of its 195 occurrences ever refers to Deity. *Adoni* is the form of the word "lord" (*adon*) in the Hebrew Bible which expressly tells us that the one so designated is *not* God, but a human superior.[16] *Adoni* is the "profane" title, that is, not the title of Deity. How then can its appearance in this Psalm affirm "the Deity of Jesus"? It affirms, in fact, that however exalted his position, the Messiah is not Deity. He is "my lord" (*adoni*), the king. He is the supremely exalted man.

The following information will I think convince the reader that Bible commentary has committed itself, in this matter of the lordship of Jesus, to some extraordinary misinformation, presumably copied from one "authority" to another without bothering to consult the Hebrew Bible. This issue has become something of a "saga," provoking intense disagreement over what is in fact a rather simple issue. More is at stake here than meets the eye, but a little investigation points to the vulnerable nature of "orthodoxy," when it blithely tells us that both the Father and Jesus are to be recognized as equally and fully Deity, but that this does not make two Gods.

At the popular level many authorities simply do not read the Hebrew and they misstate the facts about the Hebrew word for the second lord in Psalm 110:1. Charles Spurgeon mistranslates: "Jehovah said unto my *Adonai*." Spurgeon is convinced that "though David was a firm believer in the Unity of the Godhead, he yet spiritually discerns the two persons."[17] Matthew Henry's commentary defines "my Lord" as the Trinitarian eternal Son. Catholic Answers maintains that "God the Son" is called Lord by David. Nave's Topical Bible uses Psalm 110 as proof of the "divinity of Jesus." *The Evangelical Dictionary of Biblical Theology* refers to our verse as ascribing "full deity" to Jesus. The dictionary concedes, however, that Jesus' "essential oneness with God the Father and full divinity as

---

[16]Occasionally an angelic superior.
[17]*The Treasury of David*, Baker Book House, 1983.

second Person of the Trinity have been widely rejected as Hellenistic embellishment of the earliest Christian belief."[18]

It is a matter of surprise that commentators of the caliber of Campbell Morgan report that Psalm 110:1 is to be read, "Jehovah said to *Adonai*," adding that "both these titles are used often of God."[19] Even more startling is *The Bible Knowledge Commentary* written by Dallas Seminary faculty. They present Jesus as asking the question in Matthew 22:42-45:

> If the Messiah were simply an earthly son of David, why did he ascribe deity to him? Jesus quoted from a messianic Psalm 110:1 in which David referred to the Messiah as my Lord. "Lord" translates the Hebrew *Adonai*, used only of God (e.g. Gen. 18:27; Job 28:28). If David called his son "Lord" he certainly must be more than a human son.[20]

This comment reflects an extraordinary desire to find in the text what is not there. The word *Adonai* in all of its 449 occurrences is indeed the divine Lord God. But the second lord in the Hebrew of Psalm 110:1 is not *Adonai*, but *adoni*, which is specifically the designation of non-Deity. So much for a failed Trinitarian proof text, repeated scores of times. So keen are commentators to think of the Messiah as God that they copy uncritically from each other a very obvious misstatement about the indisputable second "lord" of Psalm 110:1, who in the biblical text is not *Adonai*, but *adoni*.

The Jehovah's Witnesses are upbraided by Ron Rhodes for their non-Trinitarian understanding of Jesus. He writes: "David's reference to 'my Lord' [Ps. 110:1] also points to the undiminished Deity of the Messiah, since 'Lord' (Hebrew *Adonai*) was a title for deity."[21] *Adonai* was indeed the title of Deity. But David, as recorded for us in Scripture, wrote *adoni*. Rhodes' suggested apologetic question to the Witnesses falls flat: "Ask: Did you know that the same word used for 'Lord' (*Adonai*) in Psalm 110:1 of Jesus Christ is also used of the

---

[18]"Jesus Christ, Names and Titles," *Evangelical Dictionary of Biblical Theology*, Baker, 1996, 409.

[19]*Notes on Psalms*, Fleming Revell, 1947.

[20]John Walvoord and Roy Zuck, eds., *The Bible Knowledge Commentary*, Victor, 1983, 73.

[21]*Reasoning from the Scriptures with the Jehovah's Witnesses*, Harvest House, 1993, 162.

Father numerous times in Scripture (Exod. 23:17; Deut. 10:17; Josh. 3:11)?"[22]

The texts he references do not contain the form *adoni,* the word found in Psalm 110:1, and the Father is never once addressed as *adoni,* my lord.[23] But Jesus is so addressed in this centrally important Psalm. One mistake compounds another here.

When Rev. V.A. Spence Little prepared a substantial booklet on the Deity of Christ, he devoted a chapter to "The Deity of Christ Implied in the Old Testament." He then refers to "the striking passage in the opening verse of Psalm 110, 'The Lord (Jehovah) saith unto my Lord (*Adonai*).'" He tells us that the use of "this Lord *Adonai* is acknowledged both in the Psalm and in many New Testament interpretations of it as a Divine Personage and on equality with Eternal Deity."[24]

He has not read the Hebrew. The second "lord" is not *Adonai* at all but *adoni,* the title for someone who is expressly *not* Deity.

The MacArthur Study Bible seems not to know the difference between divine and human titles. Dr. MacArthur asserts that when Jesus cited Psalm 110:1, referring it to himself as Messiah, "the inescapable implication is that Jesus was declaring his deity."[25] A professor of Biblical Studies at The Master's College is likewise certain that Psalm 110:1 "records a conversation between two members of the Godhead...A literal translation of the first phrase is 'Yahweh said to my *Adonai*...'" This is then said to be proof of plurality in the Godhead.[26]

John MacArthur seems unimpressed by Jesus' insistence on the non-Trinitarian creed of Israel. He notes that Jesus "confirmed the practice of every pious Jew who recited the entire Shema (Num. 15:37-41; Deut. 6:4-9; 11:13-21) every morning and evening."[27] He goes on to imply a contradiction of the Shema by Jesus! Referring to

[22]Ibid., 162.
[23]The form *adon,* lord, is found as a title for both God and man. But the suffixes found respectively on *adoni* and *Adonai* always distinguish non-Deity persons from Deity.
[24]*The Deity of Christ,* Covenant Publishing, 1956.
[25]The MacArthur Study Bible, Thomas Nelson, 1997, 1426.
[26]William Varner, *The Messiah,* cited in Patrick Navas, *Divine Truth or Human Tradition,* Authorhouse, 2007, 138.
[27]The MacArthur Study Bible, 1479.

Jesus' citation of Psalm 110:1, MacArthur tells us that "the second word for 'Lord' is a different word [i.e., not *Yahweh*] that the Jews used *as a title for God.*"[28] But the second lord is not *Adonai*, but *adoni*, a title which never refers to God. Jesus believed with the whole of Scripture that God is a single divine Person.

The misstatement about the Hebrew word for the second lord in Psalm 110:1 is widespread and shocking as coming from scholars who normally read the Hebrew text accurately. J. Barton Payne in his massive *Encyclopedia of Biblical Prophecy* quotes "Yahweh said to my Lord" and comments that "my Lord" "implies the latter's deity."[29]

But the second "lord" in Psalm 110:1 is not *Adonai*. The Hebrew reads not *Adonai*, the title of Deity, but *adoni*, a title never used of Deity! A giant terminological muddle has afflicted the system and all because of a failure to distinguish God from man. Jesus allowed for no possible doubt about that distinction when he grounded the Christian faith in the unitary monotheistic creed of Israel (Mark 12:28-34).[30]

Getting the Facts Right

Some earlier authorities and many modern sources are much more careful with the data. Although Dean Farrar in *The Cambridge Bible for Schools and Colleges* did not verify the Hebrew of Psalm 110:1, "In the Hebrew it is 'Jehovah said to my Lord *(Adonai)*,'"[31] he very helpfully includes the Septuagint reference to the begetting of the Son: "From the womb, before the morning star, did I beget you"[32] — pointing to the real origin of the Messiah as "from the womb," prior to the arrival of the Kingdom at the dawn of the coming New

---

[28]Ibid., 1479-80, emphasis added.
[29]Baker Book House, 1973, 274.
[30]David Cooper, ThM, PhD, was confident that the God of Israel was triune and ventured this mistranslation of the *Shema*: "The Lord our Gods is the Lord a unity" (*The Messiah: His Redemptive Career*, Biblical Research Society, 1938, 68). On page 67 he alleges wrongly that Jehovah is addressed as *adoni*. It is in fact the angel who is not Deity, but Deity's representative, who is addressed as *adoni* and not *Adonai* in Judges 6:13. The angel is distinguished from God in verses 12, 22.
[31]F.W. Farrar, *The Gospel According to St. Luke*, Cambridge University Press, 1902, 311.
[32]Ps. 110:3; in the Septuagint this is Ps. 109:3.

Age. Isaiah spoke also, prophetically, of the servant as having been "formed from the womb" (Isa. 49:5). The servant's origin is similar to Jeremiah's in his mother's womb: "Before I formed you in the womb I knew you" (Jer. 1:5). Job likewise speaks of the origin of all human persons as coming into existence by formation in the womb. "Did not He who made me in the womb make him, and the same one fashion us in the womb?" (Job 31:15). Indeed it was the "spirit of God which fashioned me" (Job 33:4). Christians, knowing that the suffering servant had been likewise "formed in the womb" (Isa. 49:5), could not possibly expect the Messiah to have any different place of origin. He would be a human person though begotten as a direct result of God's intervention.

A.F. Kirkpatrick, also writing in *The Cambridge Bible for Schools and Colleges*, and as Regius Professor of Hebrew, correctly removes the capital from the second lord in Psalm 110:1 and replaces it with "my lord," noting that the Revised Version of 1881 "rightly dropped the capital letter."[33] He points out that "my lord" (*adoni*) "is the title of respect and reverence used in the O.T. in addressing or speaking of a person of rank and dignity, especially a king (Gen. 23:6; 1 Sam. 22:12; 1 Kings 1; 18:7; and frequently)." The professor observes that the capital on "Lord" in most translations is "of the nature of an interpretation."[34] This is a kind and understated way of telling us that it in fact manipulates the text. The clarity and precision of the Hebrew text was marred by the "curse of the capital."

It is the policy of many translations to write "Lord" throughout the Old Testament when the Hebrew word behind it is *Adonai*, the title of Deity, all 449 times.[35] Translators profess to write "lord" in the case of *adoni*, thus showing that the person so designated is *not* Deity. However consistency was abandoned in Psalm 110:1 under the pressure of "orthodoxy."[36] This gave rise to a mass of commentary

---

[33]*The Book of Psalms (XC-CL)*, Cambridge University Press, 1901, 665.
[34]Ibid., 666.
[35]The professor also points out that in Ps. 110:5 the Lord (*Adonai*) is God, who in this different image is at the right hand of the Messiah as his support. This picture of God helping a human person is found also in Ps. 16:8; 73:23; 109:31; 121:5.
[36]The same inconsistency made the KJV put a capital on the lord of Dan. 12:8 and Judges 6:13 in the mistaken belief that this was the Son preexisting as God. The RV corrected the error, writing "my lord."

alleging, against the actual fact, that the second "Lord" here was *Adonai*, the Lord God. This in turn allowed commentators and readers to find evidence for two Persons within the Godhead. The attempts to read later "orthodoxy" into the Hebrew Bible, and indeed the whole Bible, have been relentless.

A Surprising Analysis of Psalm 110:1

In a 1992 issue of *Bibliotheca Sacra* of Dallas Theological Seminary, professor Herbert Bateman turned his attention to Psalm 110:1 and noted that traditionally the Psalm has been recognized as David's prophetic address to "his Messianic Lord, his divine Lord"[37] (by "divine" he means the "Deity" of the Messiah). However Bateman as a Trinitarian feels the need to remove the reference to Jesus and assign David's oracle to "an earthly lord, that is an earthly king of his lifetime." Though he concedes an application to Jesus he is concerned about a primary reference to Jesus because:

> the form *l'adoni* (to my lord) is never used elsewhere in the Old Testament as a divine reference...The Masoretic pointing distinguishes divine references (*Adonai*) from human references (*adoni*). Furthermore when "my lord" (*adoni*) and LORD (YHVH) are used in the same sentence, as in Psalm 110:1, "my lord" always refers to an earthly lord.[38] Thus the phrase "to my lord" (*l'adoni*) apparently indicates that David was directing this oracle from Yahweh to a human lord, not to the divine Messianic Lord, nor to himself.

Bateman mentions that some think David was speaking to himself, but Bateman prefers a reference to Solomon on the basis that the Hebrew title is *adoni* and cannot therefore be a divine Lord.

Bateman could have revised his Trinitarian Christology under the pressure of his correct observation about the word for "lord," and by recognizing that the New Testament has no reserve about the direct and only application of the Psalm to the Messiah, Son of God, a view

---

[37]Herbert Bateman, "Psalm 110:1 and the New Testament," *Bibliotheca Sacra* 149, Oct-Dec., 1992.
[38]These examples may be examined: Men or women to men (Gen. 24:12, 27, 42, 48; Num. 32:27; 36:2; 1 Sam. 1:26; 25:26, 28-29) men or women to a king (2 Sam. 15:21; 24:3; 1 Kings 1:17, 36-37; 2 Kings 5:18), and man to an angelic being (Jud. 6:13).

held by both Jews and early Christians.[39] Peter confirms Jesus' arrival
at the position of supreme exaltation at the right hand of the Father
(Acts 2:34-36). He then tells us that Jesus is Lord, *in the sense
prophetically prescribed by Psalm 110:1.* Had this oracle, which
governs New Testament Christology and acts as umbrella over the
doctrine of the Son in relation to the Father, been heeded, all of the
squabbles and centuries-long debate over God could have been
avoided. Bateman has rendered us a service by pointing to the facts
about the meaning of the second "lord." At least he did not resort to
the desperate evasion produced by other evangelicals, namely that the
Psalm tells us only about the human nature of Jesus, without telling us
about his other "100%." But neither David nor Peter ever imagined a
200% person, much less that God was more than one Person — nor
that the Messiah was to be God Himself. The Hebrew Bible is
however very much concerned, in its careful choice of words, with
distinguishing God from man. Jews took with utmost seriousness
their charge to be custodians of the "oracles of God" (Rom. 3:2).

So confused has this issue of the Hebrew words in Psalm 110:1
become, and under the pressure of reassuring themselves that the
Trinity must surely be in the Hebrew Bible, popular theological
sources continue to misstate the facts and mislead their audiences
about the identity of the Messiah in relation to the One God. Thus the
Lockman Foundation, in its New American Standard Bible comments
in the margin of Acts 2:36, misinforms us that Peter's use of Psalm
110:1 involves the Hebrew word *Adonai* as the second lord.[40] A
leading organization providing biblical information to the public
replied to our question as follows:

> Your question about Psalm 110:1 can be answered quite
> easily. In fact this is an excellent text for supporting the
> plurality of members within the Godhead as well as the
> distinctiveness of the person of the Messiah or Christ. Both
> the psalmist David and our Lord Jesus Christ declare that the

---

[39]Some Jewish writers saw the second lord of Ps. 110:1 as Abraham,
Hezekiah, or Melchizedek, thus demonstrating that no one imagined *adoni*
to be God. Jews have never had the slightest difficulty with this distinction
between divine and human titles.
[40]The editors of the NASB agreed to remove the error in a new printing, but
they did not supply the actual Hebrew word, *adoni.*

second lord (*Adonai*, in Hebrew) refers to a divine being who
would become the Messiah.[41]
C.S. Lewis is brought in to support the idea that Psalm 110:1
"contains a second or hidden meaning...concerned with the
Incarnation." The Christian Research Institute continued with this:
  Also, in your letter, you forgot to accurately quote Psalm
  110:1 (NIV) when you failed to capitalize both "Lords": "The
  LORD (Yahweh or Jehovah) says to my Lord
  (*Adonai*)"...David is writing the Psalm under inspiration of
  the Holy Spirit and in a poetic form about the future reign of
  his Lord Christ, as distinct from another member of the
  Godhead.[42]
The facts are entirely wrong. It is they who wrongly capitalized
the second lord, supposing this to be *Adonai*, which it is not. The
comment appears to be symptomatic of a very widespread inability of
Bible readers to deal with the unitarian creed of the Hebrew Bible and
of Jesus, and a mesmerizing tendency to read into the text, at the
expense of fact, a Trinitarian view of God.
  It is a fundamental error to suppose that these two Lords in Psalm
110:1 were both coequally God. A mass of good scholars of the
Hebrew Bible know the difference between Hebrew words for God
and man. The Hebrew Bible, with its thousands of singular personal
pronouns for God and its seven thousand or so references to YHVH
as a single Person, excluded any possibility of plurality in the
Godhead. The Shema had declared God to be only one Lord and Jesus
confirmed this central fact in Mark 12:28-34. It would be sheer
contradiction to say that there are two Yahwehs when Jesus and the
Shema say that there is only one! If there is one Yahweh and *another*
Yahweh, and *they* speak to each other, it is impossible to avoid the
conclusion that monotheism has been abandoned.
  Psalm 110:1 does not overthrow that massive testimony to God as
a single divine Person. YHVH speaks to David's *lord* in Psalm 110:1.
You will notice the lower case on "lord" here. I am following the RV,
RSV and NRSV in writing "lord" and not "Lord." The reason is that
behind this "my lord" lies the Hebrew word *adoni* (pronounced in
Hebrew "adonee"). It is a form of the word for lord (*adon*), and in this

---

[41] Letter from Christian Research Institute, Aug. 13, 1998.
[42]Ibid.

form (*adoni,* my lord) designates a human (occasionally an angelic) superior, but it never once means God![43] This is highly significant. YHVH in Psalm 110:1 speaks to non-Deity. It would be without precedent in the Hebrew Bible for the One God to speak to another who is equally the One God. That would be impossible. It would contradict the thousands of statements declaring God to be one Person. It would contradict the New Testament monotheistic statements from Jesus and Paul that the Father is "the only one who is truly God" (John 17:3) and that "God is one Person" (Gal. 3:20) and that "to us there is one God, the Father" and "there is no God but one" (1 Cor. 8:4-6). The latter is Paul's strong confirmation of his Jewish monotheism.

The capitalization of the second lord of Psalm 110:1 in many translations is thoroughly misleading. Translators tell us that their practice is to render the divine title *Adonai* as "Lord." The innocent reader will suppose then that *Adonai,* the Lord God, is a legitimate designation of the Messiah. However, since the word for the second lord in Psalm 110:1 is not *Adonai* at all, but *adoni,* a capital letter breaks the translators' own rule. Our Bibles correctly do not capitalize lord when they translate *adoni* ("my [human] lord"). In Psalm 110:1, a key verse for defining who Jesus is, the editorial convention for capital letters has been disregarded. The false impression, then, is given that God speaks to God![44] The creed of Israel and of Jesus is violated.

This confusion over a critically important reference to Messiah is now well recognized by scholars. It is amazing that any confusion over the Hebrew *adoni* vs. *Adonai* could have been allowed to go into print. As Larry Hurtado says, "It would have been quite clear that *kyrios* [lord] here was not used for God but referred to a figure distinguishable from God."[45] This has always been quite clear in the

---

[43]*Strong's Concordance* does not show the important difference between *adoni* (my lord) and *Adonai* (the Lord God).

[44]The King James Bible broke its own rule of capitalization also in Dan. 12:8. Readers were meant to suppose that the "Lord" there (capitalized) was the preexisting Jesus. In fact it was an angel (addressed as *adoni*). Many modern translations have "my lord," not "my Lord" in Dan. 12:8.

[45]*Lord Jesus Christ,* Eerdmans, 2003, 183.

Hebrew text, where *adoni* is never confused with *Adonai*.[46] Modern theologians are supposed to know about the original titles for Deity and for the Messiah. How is it then in the twenty-first century they repeatedly tell us that calling Jesus "lord" proves that the New Testament writers thought that the Messiah was Yahweh, God?

The One Lord Christ
    The Greek of the New Testament speaks of God and Jesus as "one thing." *En*, the neuter form of *eis* meaning one, is the word found in John 10:30 about the oneness of God and His Son. When the masculine form of "one" (*eis*) is used, the meaning is "one person." This elementary point was noted in a discussion of the Trinity in a nineteenth-century work by Rev. Richard Treffry. He wrote, "'I and my Father are one'; *en* in the neuter, one substance;[47] not *eis* in the masculine, one person." [48] Paul spoke in Romans 5:19 of the parallel between Adam and Jesus: "For just as through the disobedience *of one person* the many were made sinners, so through the obedience *of one* [Jesus] the many will be made righteous." Paul uses the same word "one" (*eis*) to refer to Jesus. The meaning is of course "one person," "a single person." The New Testament speaks of God as "one person." A good example is found in Galatians 3:20: "Now a mediator is not for one *party* only; whereas God is *only* one." The sense in both halves of the sentence is "one person." Thus the Amplified Version catches the meaning: "God is only one person." That same phrase "God is one [person]" appears several times in the New Testament. "'Well said, teacher,' the man replied. 'You are right in saying that God is one and there is no other but him'" (Mark 12:32). "There is only one God [God is one, *eis*] and there is only one way of being accepted by him. He makes people right with himself

---

[46]Professor Howard Marshall leaves the significance of *adoni* in Ps. 110:1 somewhat less than clear. He says that the word is *adon* "which can be used of human lords and masters" (*Acts, Tyndale Commentaries*, Eerdmans, 1980, 79). In fact the form of the word is *adoni* which only refers to non-Deity superiors and *never* to God.
[47]Exactly the same oneness describes the relationship of Christians to God. Jesus prayed that believers should be "one" (*en*), just as he and the Father are one (John 11:17, 22).
[48]Richard Treffry, *An Inquiry into the Doctrine of the Eternal Sonship of Our Lord Jesus Christ*, John Mason, 1837, 134.

only by faith, whether they are Jews or Gentiles" (Rom. 3:30). "For there is one God, and there is one mediator between God and men, the man Christ Jesus" (1 Tim. 2:5). In each case God is one person. God is contrasted with Jesus who is also one person. This pervasive fact of the New Testament is incompatible with the later doctrine that God is three Persons.

In Psalm 110:1 YHVH, the God of Israel, addresses the Messiah as *adoni*, my lord. *Adoni* signals the fact that it is not Deity who is being so addressed. The custodians of the text were scrupulously careful to distinguish God from man. *Adoni* is the royal title. It refers to kings.[49] It is thus the eminently appropriate title for the King Messiah Jesus. It may be applied to a husband, or a master. But it never designates the supreme God. When God is addressed or referred to there is another form of the same word "lord," and this is *Adonai*. The Masoretes who faithfully pointed the Hebrew text with meticulous care distinguished between a non-Deity lord and the Deity who was the Lord God. Jews sometimes speculated that the "my lord" of Psalm 110:1 could have been Hezekiah or Abraham. It is clear then that at least they knew that the word there in the sacred text was not *Adonai*, the One Lord God.

This Psalm 110, and in particular its first verse, is a marvelous testimony to the Messiah in David's collection. It is everywhere acclaimed as being of key significance for all the writers of the New Testament. It stands as a shield over the New Testament, beautifully defining the principal players in the divine drama, the God and Father of the Lord Jesus Christ and His Son, the Lord Christ. The latter is bidden to sit in the place of supreme eminence at the right hand of God, pending the time when he will be dispatched to the earth to establish his Kingdom by subduing God's enemies. Psalm 2, of equal Christological significance, deals with the same great events of the divine plan for our earth. There can be no doubt that we have in Psalm 110:1 a major key to the understanding of God and the human Messiah Jesus. So many scholars have observed this rather obvious and telling fact, that this verse from the Psalms controls all of the New Testament thinking about Jesus' status in relation to the One God.

---

[49]"My lord [*adoni*] the king" occurs some 57 times.

To investigate the biblical view of God and the position of Jesus in relation to God, it is now necessary to do more detailed work on that very special Old Testament verse, which New Testament writers quote constantly. They chose this verse because it uniquely spoke of God and the Messiah and the relationship between them. It also revealed in a concise and compressed statement God's whole plan for the world centered in Christ: "The Lord said to my lord, 'Sit at My right hand until I make your enemies your footstool'" (Ps. 110:1).

Here are the two principal players in the divine drama unfolded in the pages of Scripture. First there is Yahweh, the God of Israel. The LORD (Yahweh in the Hebrew, some seven thousand times in the Hebrew Bible) utters a predictive oracle about David's lord. Both Jews and Jesus were quite clear that this Psalm referred to God and the Messiah. Jesus cleverly asked the Pharisees to explain how the Messiah could be both the descendant of David and also his lord. The answer of course is that the Messiah came into existence as a lineal and biological descendant of King David as well as the Son of God. He was later, following his triumphant ministry, elevated by God to the position of David's lord at the right hand of the One God of Israel. The lordship of the Messiah was acquired by Jesus at the end of his ministry on earth. It was a lordship which had nothing to do with an imagined lordship from eternity past, but one conferred on Jesus by God, the Father. Peter in Acts showed how this very text had foretold God's plan to exalt the resurrected Jesus to the right hand of God.

Here is how Peter unfolded God's ongoing plan based on the truth of Psalm 110:1. Following the dramatic outpouring of the spirit at Pentecost, Peter "took his stand with the eleven and raised his voice" (Acts 2:14), declaring the essence of the Christian drama to the Jewish crowd. As we listen to his sermon, we must pay careful attention to Peter's understanding of what had occurred. Did he believe that *God* had been raised to the right hand of God?

> Men of Israel, listen to these words. Jesus the Nazarene, *a man* attested to you by God with miracles and wonders and signs which God performed through him in your midst as you yourselves know — this man delivered over by the predetermined plan and foreknowledge of God, you nailed to a cross by the hands of godless men and put him to death. But God raised him up again, putting an end to the agony of death

since it was impossible for him to be held in its power (Acts 2:22-24).

Peter then goes on to quote Psalm 16:8-11 to confirm the resurrection of Jesus, how God rescued him from the place of the dead (Hades). Peter repeated his point about the resurrection: "This Jesus God raised up again, to which we are all witnesses" (Acts 2:32).

He then described the present status of Jesus at God's right hand — the status which the Son of God, now resurrected and alive for ever, achieved for the first time at his ascension. These are his vitally important words with reference to God and Jesus based on the inspired divine utterance recorded in Psalm 110:1.

Therefore having been exalted to the right hand of God, and having received from the Father the promise of the Holy Spirit, he has poured forth this which you both see and hear. For it was not David who ascended to heaven, but David himself says, "The Lord said to my lord, 'Sit at My right hand until I make your enemies a footstool for your feet.'" Therefore let all the house of Israel know for certain that God *made him both lord* and Christ — this Jesus whom you crucified (Acts 2:33-36).

The story is not complex. There is God and there is the man Jesus. God allowed the man Jesus to be killed (no Jew imagined that the immortal God could be killed!) and God reversed that tragedy by resurrecting the man Jesus and subsequently exalting him to His right hand, thus *making* him "Lord and Christ" *in the sense predicted by the oracle of Psalm 110:1.*

Now imagine that Peter believed that both the Father and Jesus were equally God. Then God had allowed God to be crucified and God had raised God to His right hand? Does this make the slightest sense? God sitting at the right hand of God would present the audience with a blatantly polytheistic system. God is not two. He is only one. The heritage of Israel would have been overthrown if the Messiah were now to be included as an eternal member of a plural Godhead. No Jew could possibly have been prepared for the notion that the Messiah was part of the Godhead. The Hebrew Bible had announced no such thing. It would have been a staggering innovation, requiring pages of explanation, to say that the Messiah, *adoni*, my lord, was really the One God of Israel, who was now mysteriously "two."

Psalm 110:1 provides us with an absolute testimony against any possibility of two who are both God. The LORD (Yahweh, the Father of Jesus) utters an oracle about David's lord the Messiah.

For our investigation it is critically important to underline the status of this one who has been crucified, resurrected and raised to God's right hand. Who is this? Is he God the Son, second member of an eternal Trinity?

What is the rank of that second lord of Psalm 110:1? Is he God in the same sense as the Father is God, as Trinitarian doctrine claims? Peter states that the man Jesus has been exalted to a position of supremacy next to God, and that this is a fulfillment of Psalm 110:1. It is as "lord" in the sense required by Psalm 110:1 that Jesus is now seated next to God. But what status is meant by the "my lord" of our Psalm? Very occasionally *adoni* is an address to an angel. But in the vast majority of its 195 appearances in the Old Testament Hebrew Bible, *adoni* designates a human superior — husband, king, master, etc. *Adoni* never, ever means God. It is the royal title admirably appropriate for Jesus the Messiah and King of Israel (John 1:49).

Peter, on whose brilliant Messianic "rock" confession the Church is to be founded (Matt. 16:16-18), informs us that as from the ascension of Jesus there is a human lord in the supreme position next to the One God, a man who had been brought back from death. That lord *(adoni)* cannot be God Himself. To every reader this would suggest a second God, an absolute impossibility within the Jewish monotheism of the New Testament. Jesus according to Peter and Psalm 110:1, his proof text, repeated some 23 times in the New Testament, is the human being at God's right hand. This is exactly in harmony with Paul's much later statement that "that there is one God and one mediator between God and men, *the man* Messiah Jesus" (1 Tim. 2:5). It is exactly the same picture presented by Stephen in his dying moments: "I see heaven open and the Son of Man [the Human Being] standing at the right hand of God" (Acts 7:56). Jesus evidently shared the same theological paradigm when he warned his persecutors that they would see "the Son of Man [the Human Being] at the right hand of Majesty" (Matt. 26:64).

It has been well said that:

> Luke's understanding does not allow for any deification [of Jesus]...Luke moves wholly within the sphere of Old Testament thought. It is this which fashions Luke's

understanding at this point and, more especially, the ideas suggested by Psalm 110:1...This does not mean that Jesus becomes God, or that he is given a divine status by Luke. The Psalmist calls both God and the king "lord," but he does not give equality to the two. Luke sees Jesus as wholly subordinate to the Father, given a share in the Father's authority, but one which is derived from the Father. He is still the instrument of his Father and is still called His servant (Acts 3:26; 4:30).[50]

The Jewish monotheism of Jesus' own creed is beautifully preserved in all these passages. It would be a major alteration of the text to say that a "God-man" or "God" is now at God's right hand. Psalm 110:1 blocks that possibility, rules it out of court. The one at God's right hand is precisely defined as the human lord Jesus, the first man ever to be brought back permanently to life by resurrection. We might even say that "there is an immortal Jew at the right hand of the One God."

Vowels and Consonants

It is sometimes objected that the word *adoni* ("my [human] lord") differs only from the word *Adonai* (the Lord God) in the matter of vowel points, which were not originally written in the Hebrew manuscripts. The vowel points, it is true, were added much later than New Testament times. They were based on the ancient tradition reflecting synagogue reading of the sacred text. But there is no hint anywhere that the vowel points were added wrongly in Psalm 110:1. The Jews were almost fanatically careful in what they regarded as the sacred task of copying the scriptural text. They knew generation after generation how the text was read in the synagogues and finally that ancient reading was permanently fixed by the addition of the vowel points from around the seventh century AD.

There is no evidence anywhere of any problem with the vowel points in the Hebrew text of Psalm 110:1. And there is another powerful line of evidence which confirms that the Old Testament never imagined that second lord of Psalm 110:1, seated at God's right hand, to be God Himself, making two Gods. This line of reasoning is slightly more technical, involving reference to the Hebrew and to the

---

[50]Eric Franklin, *Christ the Lord*, Westminster Press, 1975, 54.

translation of the Hebrew into Greek (the translation known as the Septuagint, quoted by both non-Christian Jews and New Testament writers).

The evidence will show that Psalm 110:1 as originally written and preserved accurately in the Hebrew manuscripts did indeed distinguish the Messiah as the non-Deity lord. Yahweh in that verse as all know means the Father, the One God. *Adoni*, the second lord in our verse, means "my lord."

Our point is confirmed when we look at the Greek version of the Old Testament current in the time of Jesus and cited by New Testament writers. When we examine the Greek equivalent of the Hebrew Bible we discover that when Jews in BC times translated their Hebrew Bible into Greek, they understood the Hebrew word for "my lord," even before vowel points were added to the written text, to be *adoni*, which title is never used for God. The New Testament, which I take to be inspired Scripture, reflects the same fact: The Greek is *kurios mou* ("my lord") which is the proper translation of the Hebrew *adoni*. No argument can be mounted therefore to doubt that the Hebrew text always read *l'adoni*, meaning "to my lord."[51]

Standard Authorities on the Hebrew Bible

Psalm 110:1 in the Greek of the Septuagint and New Testament simply confirms the very elementary fact that our Hebrew text is correct in defining the Messiah as *adoni*. All of this proves that later creeds which proclaimed that Jesus *was* God, second member a Trinity, go beyond anything taught by Scripture.

There should be no need to have to argue that the Hebrew Masoretic text is correct in Psalm 110:1. There is not a shred of evidence of corruption of the text here. Moreover the Greek translation of the Hebrew made in BC times merely corroborates, as we shall see, the fact that the Hebrew word *adoni* in Psalm 110:1 is perfectly genuine. Confirmation of the very important definition of

---

[51]The article in Smith's *Bible Dictionary* on "Son of God" claims that Ps. 110:1 provides "a convincing proof of Christ's Godhead." A later editor is rightly amazed at this conclusion. In a footnote he writes, "In ascribing to St. Peter the remarkable proposition that God has made Jesus Jehovah, the writer of this article appears to have overlooked the fact that 'lord' refers to 'my lord' (Ps. 110:1), where the Hebrew correspondent is not Jehovah but *adon*, the common word for 'lord' or 'master'" (Baker, rep. 1971, 3090).

"my lord" (wrongly given a capital L in many translations to give the impression that lord means God here) is supplied by the following standard authorities on the Hebrew Bible. The vital distinction between God and man is fully documented as follows:

"*Adonai* and *adoni* are variations of Masoretic pointing to distinguish divine reference from human. *Adonai* is referred to God but *adoni* to human superiors. *Adoni* — ref. to men: my lord, my master [see Ps. 110:1]. *Adonai* — ref. to God...Lord."[52]

"The form *adoni* ('my lord'), a royal title (1 Sam. 29:8), is to be *carefully distinguished* from the divine title *Adonai* ('my Lord')[53] used...of Yahweh...*Adonai*...the special plural form [the divine title] distinguishing it from *adoni* [with short vowel], 'my lords.'"[54]

Lord in the Old Testament is used to translate *Adonai* when applied to the Divine Being. The [Hebrew] word...has a suffix [with special pointing] presumably for the sake of distinction. Sometimes it is uncertain whether it is a divine or human appellative...The Masoretic Text sometimes decides this by a note distinguishing between the word when "holy" or only "excellent," sometimes by a variation in the [vowel] pointing — *adoni, adonai* [short vowel, plural form] and *adonai* [long vowel].[55]

Hebrew *adonai* exclusively denotes the God of Israel. It is attested about 450 times in the Old Testament...*adoni* [is] addressed to human beings (Gen. 44:7; Num. 32:25; 2 Kings 2:19 [etc.]). We have to assume that the word *adonai* received its special form to distinguish it from the secular use of *adon* [i.e., *adoni*]. The reason why [God is addressed] as *adonai* [with long vowel], instead of the normal *adon, adoni*

[52]"*Adon*" (lord), Brown, Driver, Briggs, *Hebrew and English Lexicon of the Old Testament*.
[53]The latest research suggests that *Adonai* means not my Lord but the supreme Lord.
[54]"Lord," *The International Standard Bible Encyclopedia*, Eerdmans, 1986, 3:157. *Adonai* with a short vowel is the rare *plural* of *adoni* and appears as a title for the angels in Gen. 19:2. Uncertainty as to the pointing as a divine or human title is very rare, i.e. Gen. 19:18.
[55]Hastings, *A Dictionary of the Bible*, 3:137.

or *adonai* [with *short* vowel] may have been to distinguish Yahweh from other gods and from human lords.[56]
"The extension of the ā [on adon<u>ai</u>, the Lord God] may be traced to the concern of the Massoretes to mark the word as sacred by a small outward sign."[57]
"The form 'to my lord,' *l'adoni*, is never used in the Old Testament as a divine reference...The generally accepted fact [is] that the Masoretic pointing distinguishes divine references (*adon<u>ai</u>*) from human references (*adon<u>i</u>*)."[58]
"I agree with what you say about Psalm 110:1 (*adoni*). And the LXX is translating correctly...The use of the Psalm in the New Testament does not identify Jesus as *Adonai* [the Lord God]."[59]

Psalm 110:1 in the Septuagint and the New Testament Scripture
If we now examine how the Greek Septuagint deals with the Hebrew *l'adoni*, "to my lord," we simply confirm the accuracy of the standard Hebrew vowel pointing of Psalm 110:1 found in all Hebrew manuscripts. The Greek Septuagint enables us to see how the Hebrew text was being read several centuries before Christ as well as during his time. There should be no need to confirm the Hebrew from the Greek version of the Old Testament. No one has found any trace of a corrupted text in the Hebrew of Psalm 110:1. The following merely shows how completely unproblematic is the designation of the Messiah, not as God Himself, but as "my [human] lord."
When Jews translated the Hebrew text into Greek from the third century BC it is perfectly clear that they were reading *adoni* as the second lord of Psalm 110:1. They rendered "*my* lord" as *kurios mou*, literally "the lord *of me*." Other examples of *l'adoni*, to my lord, in the Hebrew Bible are listed below. The Greek consistently reads the Hebrew *adoni* as "my lord."
1. Gen. 24:36: "Sarah my master's wife bore a son *to my master*" (Hebrew *l'adoni* / Greek *to kurio mou*).

[56]*Dictionary of Deities and Demons in the Bible*, Eerdmans, 1999, 531.
[57]*Theological Dictionary of the New Testament*, 3:1060-61.
[58]George Wigram, *The Englishman's Hebrew and Chaldee Concordance of the Old Testament*, cited in Herbert Bateman, "Psalm 110:1 and the New Testament," *Bibliotheca Sacra*, Oct.-Dec., 1992, 438.
[59]Professor Howard Marshall, letter, Aug., 1998.

2. Gen. 24:54: "Send me away *to my master*" (*l'adoni / pros ton kurion mou*).

3. Gen. 24:56: "Send me away that I may go *to my master*" (*l'adoni / pros ton kurion mou*).

4. Gen. 32:4 (Heb. v. 5): "Thus you shall say *to my lord* Esau" (*l'adoni / to kurio mou*).

5. Gen. 32:5: (Heb. v. 6) "I have sent to tell *[to] my lord* [*l'adoni / to kurio mou*] that I might find favor in your sight."

6. Gen. 32:18: (Heb. v. 19) "It is a present sent *to my lord* Esau" (*l'adoni / to kurio mou*).

7. Gen. 44:9: "We will be servants *to my lord*" (*l'adoni / to kurio emon*).

8, 9. Gen. 44:16: "What can we say *to my lord*?" (*l'adoni / to kurio*).[60] "We are slaves *to my lord*" (*l'adoni / to kurio emon*).

10. Gen. 44:33: "Let your servant remain instead of the lad a slave *to my lord*" (*l'adoni / tou kuriou*).

11. 1 Sam. 24:6: (Heb. v. 7) "Far be it from me because of the LORD that I should do this thing *to my lord* [*l'adoni / to kurio mou*], the LORD's anointed" (David calling Saul the Lord's Messiah, cf. Luke 2:26). This text establishes the equivalence of *adoni* and Messiah.

12. 1 Sam. 25:27: "Let this gift which your maidservant has brought *to my lord* [*l'adoni / to kurio mou*] be given to the young men who accompany *my lord*."

13. 1 Sam. 25:28: "The LORD will certainly make *for my lord* [*l'adoni / to kurio mou*] an enduring house because *my lord* [*adoni*] is fighting the battles of the Lord."

14. 1 Sam. 25:30: "When the Lord does *for my lord* all the good…" (*l'adoni / to kurio mou*).

15, 16. 1 Sam. 25:31: "This will not cause grief or a troubled heart *to my lord* [*l'adoni / to kurio mou*]…When the LORD deals well *with my lord* [*l'adoni / to kurio mou*], then remember your maidservant."

17. 2 Sam. 4:8: "Thus the LORD has given vengeance *to my lord* the king" (*l'adoni / to kurio basilei*).

---

[60]An exception occurs here in the Greek in the case of a direct address to "my lord" (Gen. 44:16). So also 44:33.

18. 2 Sam. 19:28: "For all my father's household was nothing but dead men *before my lord* the king" (*l'adoni hamelech / to kurio emon to basilei*). This establishes *adoni* as the royal title.

19, 20. 1 Kings 1:2: "Let them seek a young virgin *for my lord* the king...that she may provide warmth for my lord the king" (*l'adoni hamelech / o kurios emon o basileus*).

21. 1 Kings 18:13: "Has it not been told *to my master?*" (*l'adoni / to kurio mou*).

22. 1 Kings 20:9: "Tell [*to*] *my lord* the king" (*l'adoni / to kurio emon*).

23. 1 Chron. 21:3: "Are they not all servants *to my lord?*" (*l'adoni/ to kurio mou*).

24. Ps. 110:1: "The LORD says *to my lord*" (*l'adoni / to kurio mou*).

There is not a shadow of doubt that the Hebrew of Psalm 110:1 designates the Messiah not as Deity (*Adonai*) but as a human superior (*adoni*). The evidence for the Hebrew word *adoni* is established long before the pointing added later by the Masoretes. There is no mistake in the Hebrew text as pointed by the Masoretes.

Here are the occurrences of "*and* my lord." Once again the Hebrew *v'adoni* is properly rendered into Greek.

1. Gen. 18:12: "Also *my lord* being old" (*v'adoni / o kurios mou*).

2. Num. 36:2: "And *my lord* [*v'adoni / to kurio emon*] was commanded by the LORD."

3. 2 Sam. 11:11: "And *my lord* Joab..." (*v'adoni / o kurios mou*).

4. 2 Sam. 14:20: "And *my lord* is wise" (*v'adoni / o kurios mou*).

5. 2 Sam. 19:27: (Heb. v. 28) "And *my lord* [*v'adoni / o kurios mou*] the king is like the angel of God."

6. 2 Sam. 24:3: "And *my lord* [*v'adoni / o kurios mou*] the king, why does he still delight in this thing?"

Further samples are provided by "against my lord" (*b'adoni*) and "from my lord" (*me'adoni*).

1. 1 Sam. 24:10: (Heb. v. 11) "I will not stretch out my hand *against my lord*" (*b'adoni / epi kurion mou*).

2. 2 Sam. 18:28: "The men who lifted their hands *against my lord* [*b'adoni hamelech / en to kurio mou*] the king."

1. Gen. 47:18: "We will not hide *from my lord* [*me'adoni / apo tou kuriou emon*] that our money is all spent."

Additional evidence of the very ancient distinction between *adoni* and *Adonai* is provided by the fact that when the Hebrew reads *l'adonai*, "to the Lord [God]," the equivalent Greek is **not** *kurios mou*, but simply *kurios*, "to the Lord." This again confirms how precise the Masoretes were with the divine-human distinction signified by *Adonai* and *adoni*. Here are the examples of "to the Lord [God]":

1. Gen. 18:30, 32: "Let not the Lord be angry" (*l'adonai / kurie*).
2. Ps. 22:30: (Heb. v. 31) "It will be told of the Lord" (*l'adonai / to kurio*).
3. Ps. 130:6: "My soul waits for the Lord" (*l'adonai / epi ton kurion*).
4. Isa. 22:5: "To the Lord of hosts" (*l'adonai Yahweh / para kuriou*).
5. Isa. 28:2: "The Lord has a mighty and strong one" (*l'adonai / kuriou*).
6. Jer. 46:10: "The day of the Lord God of hosts" (*l'adonai Yahweh / kurio to theo*).
7. Jer. 46:10: "For the Lord Yahweh of hosts" (*l'adonai Yahweh / to kurio*).
8. Jer. 50:25: "The work of the Lord God of hosts" (*l'adonai Yahweh / to kurio*).
9. Dan. 9:9: "To the Lord our God belong compassion and forgiveness" (*l'adonai / to kurio*).
10. Mal. 1:14: "Sacrifices to the Lord what is blemished" (*l'adonai / to kurio*).

Based on Psalm 110:1, the key to his identity, Jesus defined his position in relation to the One God (Matt. 22:44). Jesus confirmed the title which most beautifully describes who he is: Lord Messiah and son of David. Paul habitually thought of Jesus as "lord," or "the Lord Jesus Christ," or "the Lord Christ." Paul recognized Jesus not only as the unique, promised Messiah of God but as a skilled theologian.

Professor David Flusser in his *Jesus* notes:

> When Jesus' sayings are examined against the background of contemporaneous Jewish learning, however, it is easy to observe that Jesus was far from uneducated. He was perfectly at home both in holy scripture and in oral tradition, and he knew how to apply this scholarly heritage. Moreover, Jesus'

Jewish education was incomparably superior to that of St. Paul...External corroboration of Jesus' Jewish scholarship is provided by the fact that, although he was not an approved scribe, some were accustomed to address him as "Rabbi," "my teacher/master"...Those numbered among the inner circle of his followers and those who came to him in need addressed him as "Lord." Apparently this is the title that he preferred. This we know, again thanks to the report of Luke: "How can one say that the Messiah is the Son of David? For David himself says in the Book of Psalms, 'The Lord (God) said to my lord (*l'adoni*), Sit at My right hand until I make your enemies your footstool.' David calls him Lord. How then can he be David's son?" (Luke 20:41-44 and par.). The title should not be confused as a sign of his deity (i.e. *Adonai*), but an indication of his high self-awareness.[61]

Jesus did not approve of the pleasure so many Pharisees took in being addressed as rabbi: "Do not be called rabbi, for one is your teacher and you are all brothers. Call no man on earth father [or Abba] for there is but one [person] who is your Father in heaven. Do not be called leaders for you have but one leader, the Christ" (Matt. 23:8-10). God is one Person; Christ is another person. God is one Lord, not two or three. Calling the Father and Jesus equally God makes more than one God.

A Tragic Development

W.R. Matthews in *The Problem of Christ in the Twentieth Century* reminds us of the conflict engendered by the loss of pure monotheism:

Christianity inherited from the Jews the strict monotheism which it was the glory of the Prophets to have established [Paul believed the prophets and so did Jesus], and the Church never intentionally compromised that primary affirmation. How then are we to think of the divine Son as rightly to be worshipped and yet to preserve the unity of the Godhead? As we know, the solution, if that is the right word, was found in the end, in the mystery of the Trinity...The issues involved were vital to Christianity and the decisions of the great

---

[61]David Flusser, *Jesus*, Magnes Press, 1997, 29-30, 32.

Councils have been a norm for the thought and devotion of
the whole Church. Nevertheless, they had tragic
consequences. *They marked the beginning of persecution by
Christians of their fellow believers.*[62]
How very true this is. The climax of such brutality is seen in the
murder, in 1553, of Michael Servetus by John Calvin.[63]

Now was heard for the first time the word anathema
pronounced by fathers in God on members of the flock of
Christ. Political motives and even personal rivalries crept into
the discussion and the deepest mysteries of the faith, and at
the end the Church was left with a series of definitions which
were intended as a means of exclusion from the family of
God. The original creed of the Church was the simple
formula "Jesus is Lord." With this watchword the Church
achieved the first and decisive expansion of Christianity into
the pagan world. In my opinion that earliest creed should
have remained the sole doctrinal test for membership and the
greatest misfortune which followed from the Christological
disputes was the substitution of the criterion of acceptance of
a set of theological propositions by which to judge a genuine
Christian for that which Jesus laid down "by their fruits you
shall know them." The development of theology involved the
entrance of philosophy into the discussion.[64]

Such a dramatic down-turn in the faith prompted this from Albert
Nolan in his *Jesus Before Christianity*:

Many millions throughout the ages have venerated the name
of Jesus, but few have understood him and fewer still have
tried to put into practice what he wanted to see done. His
words have been twisted and turned to mean everything,
anything and nothing. His name has been used and abused to
justify crimes, to frighten children and to inspire men and
women to heroic foolishness. Jesus has been more frequently

---

[62]*The Problem of Christ in the Twentieth Century*, Oxford University Press,
1950, 23, 24, emphasis added.
[63]For an instructive and moving account of this dramatically important
episode we thoroughly recommend Lawrence and Nancy Goldstone, *Out of
the Flames: The Remarkable Story of a Fearless Scholar, a Fatal Heresy
and One of the Rarest Books in the World,* Broadway Books, 2003.
[64]Matthews, *The Problem of Christ in the Twentieth Century*, 24, 25.

honored and worshipped for what he did not mean than for what he did mean. The supreme irony is that some of the things he opposed most strongly in the world of his time were resurrected, preached and spread more widely throughout the world — in his name.[65]

The shameful violence which overtook Christianity when it imagined that doctrine could be enforced by physical punishment is a sign of a troubling development. The root of the difficulty is traceable to the loss of Jesus' creed. Brian Holt makes our point in *Jesus: God or the Son of God?* He refers to Mark 12:32-34: "Does this sound like [the scribe] thought Jesus was the God we were to worship?...He spoke of Jehovah as someone other than Jesus...This man had a viewpoint...that was certainly not Trinitarian. Jesus...strengthened and confirmed it."[66]

The Struggle Against the Messianic Christology of Psalm 110:1

Richard Bauckham recognizes, as every commentator must, that Psalm 110:1 is a major key to the identity of Jesus. Having noted that Judaism's monotheism in the time of Jesus never blurred or bridged "the line of absolute distinction...between God and all other reality," Bauckham observes that "early Christian theology...proceeded primarily by exegesis of the Hebrew scriptures...Psalm 110:1 is the Old Testament text to which the New Testament most often alludes (twenty-one quotations or allusions, scattered across most of the New Testament writings)."[67] He makes no comment about the meaning of *adoni* in the Hebrew text. One would expect an analysis of this critically important title "lord" for Jesus. He does not observe that *adoni* is a title which does *not* speak of Deity, but of human superiority, in this case the supreme exaltation of Jesus. Bauckham tells us that early Christians read the Psalm "as placing Jesus on the divine throne itself, exercising God's own rule over all things."[68] However, this fact does not make Jesus God Himself. It describes him as the uniquely elevated *human* superior, God's Son, placed at the right hand of the One God. The *Deity* of Jesus is hardly proved by the exclusively *human* title given to him in Psalm 110:1!

---

[65]Albert Nolan, *Jesus Before Christianity*, Orbis Books, 1992, 5.
[66]Brian Holt, *Jesus: God or the Son of God?* TellWay, 2002, 167.
[67]Bauckham, *God Crucified*, 25, 29.
[68]Ibid., 30.

Yet this category error is committed over and over again in standard works. A treasury of good information is found in the *Dictionary of the Later New Testament and Its Developments*. But the desire to find there the Deity of Jesus pushes its authors to make fundamental mistakes about who Jesus is. The crucial importance for the entire New Testament of Psalm 110:1 is fully recognized:

> God seats Jesus at God's right hand. Hebrews' extensive use of this image of session shows the importance of Psalm 110:1 for this author, as for New Testament reflection on Christ's status generally. He is exalted above the angels to the extent that a "Son" is greater than "servants" (Heb. 1:4-7, 9).[69]

If only the writers of learned articles about Jesus had paid attention to the meaning of "my lord" in Psalm 110:1! This would have prevented the repetition of the blunder which seems to occur over and over again: "'Lord' represents the attribution of the divine title *kyrios* to the exalted Jesus...The resurrection undeniably revealed Jesus' true identity as the divine Lord, the *kyrios* (Acts 2:36)."[70] But Acts 2:36, quoting Psalm 110:1, defines the lordship attained by Jesus as not that of Deity. He is the *adoni* of Psalm 110:1, a Hebrew form which *expressly distinguishes a human from Deity*. Far from adding Jesus to the Godhead, Acts deliberately quotes Psalm 110:1 to show that Jesus is not God, but God's Messiah.

The same stretching of the evidence occurs when it is stated: "Acts explicitly substitutes 'Jesus' for 'Yahweh' in several Old Testament quotations (Ps. 110:1 at Acts 2:34)...The divine title *Lord*...functions to identify Jesus as participating in Yahweh's divinity."[71] But Jesus is identified not with Yahweh in Psalm 110:1 but with the one addressed by David as "my lord," *adoni*, which every reader of the Hebrew Bible knows is not the divine but the human lord. It is that status as *adoni* which Jesus has achieved. Peter makes that tremendous announcement as the climax to his sermon to the house of Israel (Acts 2:34-36).

The truth is that God exalted Jesus to His right hand and conferred on him, as the supremely exalted human being, the exercise of God's own Lordship. Jesus is given divine prerogatives, acting for

[69]Ralph Martin and Peter Davids, eds., *Dictionary of the Later New Testament and Its Developments*, Intervarsity Press, 1997, 360.
[70]Ibid., 360, 416.
[71]Ibid., 416.

Yahweh, doing what Yahweh does because God has granted that authority to him. But this does not mean that he *is* God. What drives the New Testament drama is the amazing privilege bestowed by God on the human Messiah who has now become Lord of the human race, according to God's foreordained plan.

Commentators seem bent on making Acts fit the mold of much later views of Jesus. "In using *kyrios* of both Yahweh and Jesus in his writings Luke continues the sense of the title already being used in the early Christian community, which *in some sense* regarded Jesus as on a level with Yahweh."[72] Yes, but in what sense? God has given Jesus divine functions, but the person at the right hand of Majesty is still *adoni* and not *Adonai*, man and not God.

So keen are theologians to redefine the creed of Israel and of Jesus that they try to persuade us that Paul has not *added* Jesus to the Shema but *included* him in it. What does that mean? If the Son is included in the Shema by Paul, the implication is that the Shema has been expanded. If Jesus is included in it, he is surely added to it. This is contrary to the express words of Jesus who never claimed to be Yahweh.

Professor Bauckham says:

> Paul exhibits the typically strong Jewish monotheistic self-consciousness; he distinguishes the one God to whom alone allegiance is due from all pagan gods who are no gods; he draws on classic Jewish ways of formulating monotheistic faith; and he reformulates them to express a christological monotheism which by no means abandons but maintains precisely the ways Judaism distinguished God from all reality and uses these to *include* Jesus in the unique divine identity. He maintains monotheism, *not by adding* Jesus to but *by including* Jesus in his Jewish understanding of the divine uniqueness.[73]

If the Shema originally speaks of one single Person as God, and if Paul later includes Jesus in the Shema, Paul has indeed added to the Shema and altered it, which is an impossibility. Jesus is the exalted human being.

---

[72]Joseph Fitzmyer, *The Gospel According to Luke I-IX* (*Anchor Bible*), Doubleday, 1981, 203, emphasis added.
[73]Bauckham, *God Crucified*, 40, emphasis added.

The title "my lord" for the Messiah Jesus is a constant indicator of who Jesus is in relation to God. From the very start "our Lord" and "my Lord" reflect the Messianic titles which tell us who Jesus really is. Elizabeth reflects the "my lord" of Psalm 110:1 when she rejoices that "the mother of my lord" has visited her (Luke 1:43: not "the mother of God," as later taught by Roman Catholicism). "My lord" is the title of Israel's king. Jews had referred to David as "our lord David" or "my lord David." Luke reports that it was the Lord Messiah who was born in Bethlehem (Luke 2:11). And Mary Magdalene bewails the loss of her lord: "They have taken away *my lord* and I do not know where they have laid him" (John 20:13). The blind men who received their sight were blessed for their recognition of who Jesus was. They addressed him as "Lord, son of David" (Matt. 15:22; 20:30). When Paul says that there is "one Lord Jesus Christ" (1 Cor. 8:6; cf. Eph. 4:5) he is not altering the creed of Israel to include two who are God; he is echoing the central Christian conviction of Peter and all the apostles that God "has made this Jesus Lord and Christ" (Acts 2:36).

The ancient cry *maranatha*, "our Lord come" (1 Cor. 16:22), preserves the earliest Aramaic prayer of the Church. Just like "Abba Father," Jesus' customary address to the One God, his Father, so "our Lord come" points to the essential and original meaning of "Lord" as the appropriate title for Jesus. But it is not "Lord=Yahweh." The divine title does not and cannot appear with a personal possessive pronoun. No one in the Old Testament says "our Yahweh" or "my Yahweh." Therefore the address to Jesus, *maranatha*, simply drives home the basic New Testament teaching and conviction that Jesus is our lord the Messiah, certainly not the Lord God Himself. David the king of Israel had been addressed as "our lord King David" (1 Kings 1:43, 47) but no one confused him with God.

There is an ancient tradition of referring to a superior, particularly the king, as "our lord" and "my lord": "my lord, your father David" (2 Chron. 2:14); "our lord David" (1 Kings 1:11). The Messiah is "your lord" in the prophecy of Psalm 45:11. The king of Israel is "our lord King David" (1 Kings 1:43), "your lord the king" (1 Sam. 26:15) "your lord, the man on whom the Lord [Yahweh] has put the holy oil" (1 Sam. 26:16). Another anointed king is styled "your lord Saul" (2 Sam. 2:5).

Jesus is the ultimate in the series of royal anointed persons. "He is your lord; and do homage to him" (Ps. 45:11). "Therefore be on the alert, for you do not know which day your Lord is coming" (Matt. 24:42). He is born the Messiah lord, or "Lord Messiah" (Luke 2:11). In this capacity he belongs to Yahweh who is his Lord God. Thus Luke calls Jesus "the Lord's [Yahweh's] anointed [Messiah]" (Luke 2:26).

There is also "my lord," King Agrippa (Acts 25:26). Paul in Philippians has not for a moment abandoned faith in "Messiah Jesus my Lord" (Phil. 3:8). He clings to the *adoni* ("my lord") of Psalm 110:1. He is in the service of "our/the Lord Christ" (Rom. 16:18; Col. 3:24). Other superiors like angels can also be given the title of lord: "My lord, you are the one who knows" (Rev. 7:14). Then there is "their lord, the king of Egypt" (Gen. 40:1), "Hanun their lord" (2 Sam. 10:3), "their lord, Rehoboam king of Judah" (1 Kings 12:27).

Jesus as Lord Messiah and Distinct from the One God

The importance of Jesus' identity as the Lord Messiah, not the Lord God, is shown by the interesting way in which both Paul and Jesus discuss the unitary creed of Israel and then describe the relationship of Jesus to that One God. Mark 12:28-34 presents Jesus the unitarian, in complete agreement with the Jewish scribe, and in verses 35-37 Jesus immediately goes on to define himself on the basis of Psalm 110:1 as the human lord (*adoni*) exalted to the position next to God. Paul rehearses the same Christian creed by stating first his unitarian conviction that for Christians "there is one God, the Father" (1 Cor. 8:6, alluding to Deut. 6:4; 4:35) and adding that "there is also one Lord Messiah Jesus" (cf. John 17:3). That Lord Jesus is the Messiah, not the Lord God. He is worthy of worship as the exalted Messiah. David had known this much earlier. He described the Messiah as "your Lord" (Ps. 45:11), just as Jesus described himself as "your Lord" (Matt. 24:42). David expected the Messiah to be worshipped, thanked and blessed, even, like Moses, to bear a divine title "God" (Ps. 45:6). But no one imagined that calling Moses (Exod. 4:16; 7:1) or the judges of Israel (Ps. 82:6) or the Messiah "God" (Ps. 45:6) meant that the Godhead had been enlarged.

The notion that the Messiah *was* God is unthinkable. The divine title, *Adonai*, was readily available, but it is not used of the Messiah. After all the Jews understood that there was only One Person who was the supreme God. No one therefore could have imagined that the Messiah would be God Himself. Though the Messiah could certainly as God's agent and emissary perform divine functions, he remained the human Messiah. The "name" of God was indeed invested in the Messiah. As the angel of the Lord of the Hebrew Bible had acted as God's agent — "My name is in him" (Exod. 23:21) — so to an even higher degree, Jesus was given absolute authority to act for the One God, his Father. His position at the right hand of God made him worthy of homage and reverence as Messiah. Requests could be addressed to him (Acts 7:59; John 14:14) and songs sung to him. The honor paid to the risen Messiah simply shows us what is due to the first and so far only immortalized human being. The situation is brand new. A human being has been exalted and placed next to God. This does not mean he *is* God! He is Immanuel (Matt. 1:23) because God is at work in him and because God is thus with us in Christ.[74] Psalm 110:1 speaks of the amazing position granted by God to His unique Son. God has chosen to execute His plan through His appointed human mediator, the Christian High Priest whose ministry has superseded that of Melchizedek and the Levites.

Bible commentators approach the issue of the Son's identity with a presupposition which they read into the text. They set up their own definition of what must be involved in "true humanity." They then declare that Jesus is outside these limits and must therefore *be* God. This method is flawed firstly because it goes beyond the limits imposed by the unitary monotheism of the whole Bible and secondly because it does not allow the position of supreme privilege and power which God has given to the first immortalized human being. He has been made far superior to any angel. He has inherited a position much greater than any other created being. The entire process is wrecked if we suppose that the Son was supreme by virtue of being God from eternity!

Paul in Philippians 2 and Colossians 1

Attempts to undermine the unitary monotheism of Jesus appear often in commentary on a few passages from Paul's letters. Paul is alleged to have believed in a preexisting Son who left heaven and

---

[74]The individuals named Ithiel (Prov. 30:1; Neh. 11:7) were not understood to *be* God! Their name "God [is] with me," like Immanuel, "God [is] with us" signified the confidence that God was active in them.

came to live a human life, while not ceasing at any point to be fully God.[75] According to the Trinitarian idea the baby Jesus, or even before that the fetus Jesus, was, as *God*, upholding the universe. Philippians 2:5-11 is appealed to in support of this Incarnation.[76]

However, Philippians 2 cannot possibly overthrow the accounts of the origin of the Son of God established by Matthew and Luke and elsewhere by Paul himself (Rom. 1:3; Gal. 4:4). Paul in this celebrated passage is urging Christians to follow the model of Jesus. It would be amazing if Paul advocates, in this single passage, belief in a *second* Divine Being from eternity who decides to be born as a human being. This is contrary to the whole Old Testament prediction of the Messiah as son of David. And it is hardly a realistic model for believers. Are they really being asked to imitate the behavior of an eternal Person in heaven who decided to come to earth? Or is Paul urging us to follow the example of the historical human being Jesus, who lived and preached and suffered in Israel and who was the Christian model of servanthood?

Paul's letters were the first of the New Testament documents to be written. Matthew, Mark, Luke and John came later. If Paul subscribed to a view of Jesus as second member of the Trinity, why is this understanding so patently absent from the theology of the gospels, written as testimonies to the Christian faith later than Paul's letters?

Paul's subject in Philippians 2 is *Messiah* Jesus (v. 5). And by Messiah Jesus Paul elsewhere means "*the man* Messiah Jesus" (1 Tim. 2:5). Jesus was indeed in the image of God or the "form of God" (Phil. 2:6). "Form" should not, as modern scholars recognize, be read as a Greek philosophical term. Rather it is similar to the word "image" and thus describes the visible man Jesus. Adam was created as the image of God and Jesus is the second Adam, the image of God as man was intended to be. In 1 Corinthians Paul sees man as "the image and glory of God" (11:7) and in 2 Corinthians he speaks of "the light of the gospel of the glory of Christ, who is the *image* of

---

[75] A theory espoused by some Trinitarians is that the Son emptied himself, so to speak, of Deity while on earth and resumed it at his ascension. This is known as the theory of *kenosis* or self-emptying based on Phil. 2. Other Trinitarians reject this theory and say that God remains unchanged, so that the man Jesus was fully God.

[76] The same concept is presented in 2 Cor. 8:9.

God" (4:4) as well as of "the knowledge of the glory of God in the face of Jesus Christ" (4:6). Paul knows only the historical Jesus, later ascended to the right hand of the Father. He was indeed in the very image of God ("If you have seen me you have seen the Father," John 14:9). Endowed with the very authority of God, being like God his Father, Jesus did not exploit his royal position but acted as a servant (Phil. 2:6-7). He adopted the role of a servant, did not abuse his Messianic privilege, and was prepared to obey God to the point of surrendering his life in an ignominious, torturous death on the cross (v. 8). Therefore God "superelevated him" to a position second only to the One God and for the glory of God, the Father (vv. 9-11). Paul ends his statement with a resounding unitarian phrase, "God, the Father" (v. 11).

The whole teaching of Paul here would be pointless, if in fact Jesus merely returned to the status of Deity which he had enjoyed by nature from eternity. Even at the culmination of his career, Jesus holds his exalted position "to the glory of God, the Father" (v. 11). God is still the equivalent of the Father and this is one of scores of testimonies to biblical unitarianism.

The lesson Paul conveys here is about our imitation of the historical Messiah and sharing his mind and attitude. Enjoying the status of God as God's unique agent, Jesus did not consider such likeness to God as something to be used for his own advantage. Instead he took the role of servant and conducted his whole ministry in the service of human beings, even giving up his life for them. Jesus did not exploit his position for his own purposes. He behaved as a submitted servant of mankind and of the God who commissioned him to be the model of right relationship to God and man. The picture is very much a reflection of the temptation story in the gospels, when Jesus refused to use his status as Son of God to bypass the destiny of suffering which God had prepared for him.

Colossians 1

Colossians 1:15-19 is often read with Trinitarian spectacles and it is imagined, in contradiction to the rest of Scripture, that Jesus was the active agent in the Genesis creation.[77] Rather Paul again describes

---

[77]There are some 50 statements in Scripture defining God, the Father as the Creator of everything, and Isa. 44:24 shows that He was alone as Creator.

Jesus as "the image of the invisible God" (v. 15). Image implies
visibility. We see God at work in Jesus. Paul's subject is the visible,
historical Jesus. He was, as Psalm 89:27 predicted of the Messiah,
God's "firstborn, the highest of the kings of the earth." Firstborn (v.
15) is thus a Messianic title and implies that Jesus is head of the new
creation which begins in him. Colossians 1 is all about reconciliation
in Christ. Jesus is what "wisdom," God's wise plan from the
beginning, eventually became when Jesus was born. Paul's subject is
not here the creation of the material world, but Christian transference
into the Kingdom of God's Son (v. 13), the "heading up of all things"
(Eph. 1:10) in the Messiah who is head of the new creation. Paul is
thinking of the plan of the ages (Eph. 3:11) in which Christ is to be
ruler of all authorities.

"Firstborn" is certainly not a title of Deity. Paul calls Jesus "son
of His [God's] love" (Col. 1:13) and immediately follows with the
title "firstborn." Israel was also God's firstborn (Exod. 4:22) and so
was Ephraim (Jer. 31:9). The Messiah is especially God's firstborn
(Ps. 89:27). In Jewish literature contemporary with the New
Testament Israel is like a firstborn, an only son (Pss. Sol. 18:4). In the
book of Esdras 6:58 Israel calls herself "your people, whom you call
your firstborn, your only son." "Beloved," "uniquely begotten,"
"firstborn" are all titles for the Messiah and describe him not as God,
but a chosen human being. Colossians provides us with a description
of the position of Jesus as Messiah and his destiny by appointment to
head up God's marvelous program of reconciliation. Jesus is certainly
the purpose of God's creation and at the right hand of the Father he
supervises the new creation.

Paul in Colossians 1:13, the *all-important context* to Colossians
1:15-19, sets the stage for his discussion of Jesus' position at the right
hand of God. He says that Christians have been transferred into the
Kingdom of the Son. This has nothing to do with the Genesis creation
but focuses on the *new* creation in Christ. Jesus is certainly the first to
be immortalized in that Kingdom. As God's Messiah and firstborn of
the new creation, "all things are created *in* him" (v. 16).[78] The text
does not read "all things were created *by* him." Paul defines what he
means by "all things" in this context: authorities and principalities

[78]Moulton and Milligan suggest a causal meaning, "because of" for the
preposition *en*, "in" (*A Grammar of New Testament Greek*, T & T Clark,
1963, 3:253).

and powers, a hierarchy of rulers. Paul is not thinking here of the material universe as a whole, but of personal authorities. Jesus is supreme over them all as God's firstborn son, His "uniquely begotten" Son, as John calls him (John 1:14, 18; 3:16, 18).

Jesus, says Paul, is now supreme, "before all things" (v. 17), the word "before" indicating, as it often does, supremacy of rank rather than priority in time. But it remains true that Jesus is chronologically prior to all others in the *new* creation. He is chronologically prior to the world in God's plan to grant him the inheritance of all things. He is the first to gain immortality by resurrection. This is exactly what Paul says in verse 18 where he describes Jesus as "the firstborn from the dead." It was his resurrection from the dead which established him as supreme under God over the whole new creation and all authorities in it. Verse 18 is significant since Jesus' exaltation was "*in order that* he might be in first position.*" This is meaningless if Paul believed that Jesus was during the whole process and from eternity God Himself! Jesus acquired his unique status.

If Paul refers at all to the cosmology of Genesis he thinks of Jesus as the wisdom or wise Plan of God. It was with the Messiah, Son of God in mind that the creation was made. It was made "in him" (v. 16) and Christians were also "in him" before the foundation of the world (Eph. 1:4). It is as head of the new creation that Jesus attained his supreme position next to God, "all authority" (Matt. 28:18) having been delegated to him for his work in that new creation.

Translations mislead when they give the impression that Jesus was instrumental in the Genesis creation as active agent. This would contradict that plain statement of Isaiah 44:24 that the One God created all things unaccompanied ("Who was with Me?"). Jesus himself knew that the Lord God had formed man from the dust of the ground and referred to this event, attributing it to his Father: "God made them male and female" (Mark 10:6). Hebrews 1:1-2 deliberately states that God did *not* operate or speak through a Son in the Old Testament period, and it was God, not Jesus, who rested on the seventh day after creation (Heb. 4:4). One has only to open the *Expositor's Greek Commentary* on Colossians 1:16 to read "this does not mean 'all things were made by him.'" The sense is "in him," not "by him."[79]

The New Testament urges belief in Jesus as the Messiah, certainly not as God. Jesus is the Messianic Lord. This central truth is established as the foundation of the Church, the rock belief. Peter declares Jesus to be "Lord and Christ" in Acts 2:36 and Paul makes the same confession when he states the belief of Christians in "one Lord Jesus Messiah" (1 Cor. 8:6). The Messiah is the son of David and of God by supernatural generation in Mary. He is declared to be Son in power by a mighty act of God resurrecting him from death (Rom. 1:4). No one imagines in the Bible that God dies! The "lamb who was slain" (Rev. 5:6, 12; 13:8), however exalted his present position in association with the One God, was still a mortal being, and therefore not God. God alone has immortality inherently (1 Tim. 6:16). God therefore cannot die. Charles Wesley can pen words of the hymn: "'Tis mystery all: the immortal dies."[80] But this is still contradictory and nonsense. The immortal cannot die. God cannot die. The Son of God did.

"Lord" is used of an ordinary human "boss." "They told their lord all that was done" (Matt. 18:31). As we have seen, throughout Paul's epistles Jesus is "our Lord Jesus Christ, their Lord and ours" (1 Cor. 1:2). In Revelation 11:8 Jesus is still "their Lord [who] was crucified." God, the immortal One God of Israel, was never crucified. The theology of the Bible knows nothing of a mortal supreme God. Jesus is "the first and the last, who was dead and is alive" (Rev. 2:8), "the beginning of the creation of God" (Rev. 3:14), which as we remember from the Bible dictionary means that "He Himself was part of the creation."[81] He is the supreme head of the new creation of immortal human beings, the second Adam. Strict monotheism is jealously guarded provided we stay within the bounds of the New Testament canon. Not until the Greek influence, through the early church fathers, began to call for a theology based on Greek cosmological models involving "a second God," did unitary monotheism suffer a deadly blow.

---

[79] W. Robertson Nicoll, *Expositor's Greek Commentary*, Eerdmans, 1967, 504.
[80] "And Can It Be That I Should Gain."
[81] *Dictionary of the Apostolic Church*, 1:185.

Chapter 7

If Only We Had Listened to Gabriel

"The holy spirit will come upon you, and the power of the Most High will overshadow you; for that reason the holy child will be called the Son of God" (Gabriel, Luke 1:35).

"'For that reason he will be called the Son of God.' Calling brings to expression what one is, so that it means no less than 'he will be.' Interchangeability of the two phrases is seen by comparing Matthew 5:9, 'they will be *called* sons of God' and Luke 6:35, 'you will *be* sons of the Most High.'"[1]

"The miraculous genesis of Christ in the virgin and a real preexistence of Christ are of course mutually exclusive."[2]

"Some key phrases like 'Son of God' continued in use throughout while their meaning was gradually shifting and this helped to disguise the development which was taking place."[3]

In John 10:36 Jesus spoke of his own history: "The Father made him holy and sent him into the world." With this simple account our other gospels agree perfectly. The supernatural coming into existence of the Son of God constituted him a uniquely holy human being and

---

[1]Raymond Brown, *The Birth of the Messiah*, Geoffrey Chapman, 1977, 289.
[2]Adolf Harnack, *History of Dogma,* Dover Publications, 1961, 1:105.
[3]Don Cupitt, *The Debate About Christ*, SCM Press, 1979, 119. Within the New Testament the title Son of God is stable and means the Messiah. After Bible times, from the second century, a gradual shift in meaning led to the loss of Jesus' identity as Messiah, Son of God.

thus Son of God in a matchless way. As Son of God, God's final agent, he was sent by his Father on the mission of preaching the saving Gospel of the Kingdom (Luke 4:43).

Hebrew prophecy had announced the birth of Messiah in Bethlehem (Mic. 5:2). God had "raised up" Jesus, that is, put him on the scene of history,[4] and then sent him as His commissioned agent to deliver the Gospel to Israel (Acts 3:26). This verse should put to rest any suggestion that if God "sent" Jesus it must mean that Jesus was alive and conscious before his conception. Peter says that God first produced the Messiah and then sent him as His authorized representative and prophet. The detail of just how Jesus, God's Son, came to be is the subject also of the united and definitive testimony of Matthew and Luke, who provide by far the longest and most detailed accounts of the origin of the Son of God. Both writers intend to anchor the origin of the Son of God firmly in history. And these writers provide the basic ABCs of Christian theology and are rightly placed at the beginning of our canon.

Neither Matthew nor Luke presents us with a theological problem of vast proportions needing armies of theologians to provide an explanation. The biblical accounts describe the Son of God as the object of age-old Jewish promises — that a biological descendant of the royal house of David would appear as God's instrument for the salvation of Israel and the world. Commentators are so accustomed to thinking of the Son as eternal God Himself that they instinctively imagine that Luke and Matthew agree with them. A writer of a tract on "Who Is Jesus?" tells us that "Luke teaches that the origins of Jesus' *human life* were supernatural." He does not observe that Luke describes the origin of the *person*, the Son of God himself whose life began at conception. There is not the slightest hint that Jesus is other than human originating from his mother. Our writer claims Christ was "to be confessed as Lord and God," but he gives no text from Luke or Acts in support of that amazing statement. He thinks that "Mary's son was called the Son of the Highest by the angel because that is who he was from eternity." But Luke and Gabriel say nothing of the sort. Quite to the contrary, Gabriel links the miracle in Mary expressly to Jesus being and originating as the Son of God. The Son of God is

---

[4]Not inserted into history from outside of history as an already existing being.

entitled to that designation because God was his father by biological miracle (Luke 1:35). No other reason is supplied, and it is quite unnecessary to imagine any other origin for the Son of God. Luke 1:35 is a complete statement about the basis for Jesus being God's Son. But later theology introduced a fatally complicating element into these innocent accounts.

It is a relief to turn from the many tortuous attempts to make Luke and Gabriel into Trinitarians, to the far more scientific and factual accounts of Jesus found in the *Theological Dictionary of the New Testament*. The author approaches his subject from the Old Testament background: "There can be no disputing the link with the OT and Jewish picture of the Messiah. Of the OT Messiah Isaiah says that the spirit of counsel and strength rests upon Him (Isa. 11:2). He calls Him a mighty hero (9:6)."[5] The dictionary happily corrects the mistranslation of some who attempt to read Trinitarian theology into Isaiah and describe the Messiah as "the Almighty God," thus presenting us with the amazing concept of a second Almighty God! Isaiah was speaking of a descendant of David who was to be *el gibbor*, mighty or divine hero.

The dictionary points also to Micah's prediction of the human Messiah: "Micah compares Him with a shepherd and says that He will tend His flock in the strength of the Lord (5:4)."[6] Such a portrait prevents any idea that the Messiah will be God. He works in the power of one who is "*his* God" (Mic. 5:4). The same Messianic agent of God is described in the royal Psalm 110:2: "The Lord [Yahweh] will send the rod of your [Messiah's] royal strength out of Zion." Corroboration of this regal picture of the supernaturally endowed Messiah is found in writings half a century before the birth of Jesus. Psalms of Solomon 17:24, 42, 47 read:

> And may God gird him to defeat unrighteous rulers, to purify Jerusalem of the heathen who trample it to destruction...God has made him strong in the holy spirit and wise in counsel with power and righteousness. And the good pleasure of the Lord is with him in strength and he will not be weak...Strong is he in his works and mighty in the fear of God.

---

[5]*Theological Dictionary of the New Testament*, 2:299. Brown, Driver and Briggs translate this title as "divine hero reflecting the divine majesty" (*Hebrew and English Lexicon of the Old Testament*, 42).
[6]*Theological Dictionary of the New Testament*, 2:299.

The dictionary observes that:
> in all these passages the picture of the Messiah is that of the King. The power granted to Him is victorious power to defeat His enemies. It is the power confessed by the king of Israel: "For who is strong save the Lord?...the mighty One who maketh me strong with strength...and maketh me mighty with strength to battle" (2 Sam. 22:32, 33, 40; cf. Ps. 18:32, 39). The king attributes his success in battle to the power which Yahweh has given him. Messiah is thought of as a king like this, endowed with the strength of Yahweh.[7]

Luke is excited by the picture of the Messiah and he reports the prophetic power of Jesus demonstrated in his ministry. The two disciples who walked with the risen Jesus on the way to Emmaus knew Jesus to be "a man, a prophet powerful in deed and in word" (Luke 24:19).[8] The picture is that of a wonderful "new Moses." Moses was likewise "a man of power in words and deeds" (Acts 7:22). What more does Luke tell us?

> [Christ] is unique in His existence. His existence is peculiarly determined by the power of God. This is the most important feature in the Lucan infancy story...Luke is here describing the conception of Jesus as the miracle of the Virgin Birth...the divine miracle which causes pregnancy...In the background stands the biblical conception of the God who begets His Son by a verbal act which cannot be rationalised...For this reason the Son has a special name not borne by other men, namely, "Son of God"...At the beginning of His existence a special and unique act of divine power...gives Him the title "Son of God"...the linking of the Messianic title "Son of God" with the miracle of conception and birth.[9]

God has not left Himself without powerful witness both in the text of Scripture and in expert commentary. It must be obvious to any unprejudiced reader how far these sublime accounts are removed from the later paganized view of Jesus as an eternal Son of God, begotten in eternity, and entering the womb of his mother from a fully conscious existence as God, second member of the Trinity.

---

[7]Ibid.
[8]As the Greek reads literally.
[9]*Theological Dictionary of the New Testament*, 2: 300.

The Justification of Later Developments
Theological writings frequently tell us that the right definition of Jesus and his relationship to God was discovered only after centuries of painful intellectual struggle. The Bible however seems much more straightforward. It says nothing about a "mystery of the Trinity." This came much later. *Post-biblical* writings invite us into a very different world of thought. J.S. Whale, in his *Christian Doctrine*, asks:

> How did [the doctrine of the Trinity] come to be formulated, and why? What did it mean? As soon as the Church addressed itself to systematic doctrine it found itself wrestling with its fundamental axioms. I use the word "wrestling" deliberately, because those axioms were, on the face of them, mutually incompatible...The first was monotheism, the deep religious conviction that there is but one God, holy and transcendent, and that to worship anyone or anything else is idolatry. To Israel, and to the New Israel of the Christian Church, idolatry in all its forms was sin at its worst. "Hear, O Israel: The Lord our God is one Lord" (Deut. 6:4). "I am the Lord, and there is none else, there is no God beside me" (Isa. 45:5). Monotheism was the living heart of the religion of the Old Testament; it was and is the very marrow of Christian divinity...The systematic thought of the Church inevitably involved *a further definition of monotheism*, an elaboration of the unitary conception of the Godhead, not in terms of Tritheism, but of tri-unity...Christian thought, working with the data of the New Testament and *using Greek philosophy as its instrument,* constructed the doctrine of Trinity in Unity...The popular view of the Trinity has often been a veiled Tritheism.[10]

This account is typical of the voluminous material published to inform us how the Trinity came into being. Unable to face the awful possibility that the Church distorted the New Testament rather than explaining it accurately, our writer speaks in low-key words of "a further definition of monotheism, an elaboration of the unitary conception of the Godhead." At least he recognizes that the creed of Jesus was non-Trinitarian, but rather affirmed unitary monotheism.

---

[10]J.S. Whale, *Christian Doctrine*, Cambridge University Press, 1952, 112, 115, 116, 118, emphasis added.

But does he deal fairly with the disaster which occurred when Jesus' own creed was tampered with? Why is it admissible to redefine the simple creed of the Bible? God is one. He is not three. One will not become three without a major restructuring of God and thus of the universe. The New Testament contains not a word about any "wrestling" with how many Persons in the universe can be called the supreme God. There are indeed struggles over issues of the Mosaic law and its application in the New Covenant. But no one amongst our apostolic writers ever broached the subject of a brand new definition of God, of monotheism. The God of the Old Testament is the God of the New. He is the Creator and the Father of Jesus. No more needs to be said.

But the Gentile pagan mind did not want to submit itself to the Jewish creed of the Jewish founder of the Christian faith. The simplicity found in Jesus needed elaboration in terms of the philosophies of the Greek culture. Hence arose all the conflict over the identity of Jesus in relation to God.

Hence also the Church "wrestled," wrestled itself in fact most unwisely out of the perceived straitjacket of biblical monotheism, the very doctrine which would have spared it so much subsequent agony and division. Not to mention the appalling offense it presented to Jews and Muslims, an offense particularly galling to Jews whose Scriptures the Christians took over and then man-handled to avoid Israel's monotheism, while claiming not to!

Other authorities who comment on our topic are forthright about the facts, particularly if they are historians with less of a theological axe to grind. The 15th edition of the *Encyclopedia Britannica* says: "Neither the word Trinity, nor the explicit doctrine as such, appears in the New Testament, *nor did Jesus and his followers intend to contradict the Shema of the Old Testament*: 'The Lord our God is one Lord' (Deut. 6:4)."[11]

This fact is fundamentally important in view of the later Church departure from the creed, which Jesus, citing it verbatim in agreement with a Jewish scribe, certainly did not contradict! He affirmed it with all the emphasis he could muster. When the Church in post-biblical times no longer held on to the Shema as its creed, this caused Jews to have "the gravest doubts that with our doctrine of the Trinity we were

---

[11]"Trinity," *Encyclopedia Britannica, Micropaedia Ready Reference*, 126.

still speaking of the one God."[12] Since the Church did not find Jesus' Shema adequate as a definition of God, it is clear that a different creed was felt necessary. Three however is not one. And no New Testament writer ever hinted that Greek philosophical language was a necessary aid to explaining the biblical creed. Paul alerted the Church to the danger of the pernicious effects of philosophy (Col. 2:8). And Jesus warned repeatedly that his words are the only safe guide to a proper relationship with God and himself.

It was the Gentile desire to develop a religion based not on a Jewish Savior, but, as was supposed, on a more imaginative and captivating universal figure, which led to the disaster by which the Jewish God and His unique human Savior where replaced. The casualty in the wars of words by which the Church tried to define God and Jesus in terms of Greek philosophy was Jesus himself. The "improved version" of the faith no doubt made its appeal to the pagan mind, prepared by concepts of divine cosmogony, but the Messianic figure of the Son of God and of David found in Scripture was obscured. The final result of the "demessianizing" of Jesus in favor of a paganized universal religious figure was the loss of the descendant of David himself, herald of the coming Kingdom of God on earth. As Martin Werner declared decisively it was a descent into darkness "behind which the historical Jesus completely disappeared."[13]

No departure from the creed of Jesus should have been imagined as valid in any way. Jesus had rooted the Christian faith in the heart of Judaism. The Shema was Israel's single and central dogma, to be clung to at all costs. Jesus as founder of the Christian religion should be heard and followed on this central theological issue.

Luke Calls Us Back to Messiah Jesus

New Testament Scripture provides its own built-in safeguards against any alteration in the understanding of who God and Jesus are. Laying his firm foundation in the originating facts of the faith, Luke supplies us with exactly what we need as the key to the identity of Jesus in relation to God. He reports Gabriel as announcing to Mary the birth of her unique son, who was also, by a biological miracle effected by the creative spirit of God, to be the *Son of God*.

---

[12]Paul van Buren, *A Theology of the Jewish-Christian Reality*, Harper & Row, 1983, 2:12.
[13]Werner, *Formation of Christian Dogma*, 298.

This simple record of Luke should have put an absolute stop to the idea that *more* than one Person was God. Gabriel's inspired explanation of the term "Son of God" blocks any suggestion that the Son was Son for some *other* reason than the historical miracle of begetting caused by the Father in Mary. Few verses are so explicit, so totally unambiguous. Few verses come packaged with their own built-in interpretation. Few verses are more crammed with clear theological definition. And few verses have suffered more at the hands of hostile commentary, either by being twisted or, more effectively, by simply being ignored.

I am referring to Luke 1:35, a text which has received nothing like the attention which should have been accorded to it. Perhaps there is good reason for this. The words of Gabriel are indeed an embarrassment to the Church's later doctrine of Christ, which nullified the information provided by the angel.

In Luke 1:32 Gabriel makes clear that the son of Mary is to be at the same time the Son of the Most High, that is, the Son of God. The Most High is the Lord God who "will give him [Jesus] the throne of his father David, and he will rule over the house of Jacob forever. His Kingdom will have no end" (Luke 1:32-33). The promised son is both Son of God and descendant of David, his "father." Mary already knows that her promised will be "Son of the Most High." But how, since she herself is not yet living with her husband, can she bear a son? And how can he be God's Son?

The answer to her question, when fully taken into account by Bible readers, will change the shape of theology forever. Mary's inquiry is entirely fair and it receives its crystal clear answer: "The spirit of God will come upon you and the power of the Most High will overshadow you. *For that reason precisely* [*dio kai*], the Son to be begotten will be called holy, the Son of God" (Luke 1:35). This is Luke's first reference to Jesus as "Son of God" (those precise words). This is a title which of course pervades the New Testament records, reflected particularly in John with Jesus constantly calling God his Father, more precisely his *own* Father. The point not to be missed is that Luke provides us with an explanation of how, why and when the Son of God will come into existence. The Son is to be begotten, that is, caused to come into existence. The Son of God who is thus miraculously begotten is also the son of Mary and of David. He is caused to exist by virtue of the miracle worked by God in Mary.

According to Gabriel, the constitution of Jesus as God's Son is grounded and rooted in the biological miracle. "For that reason precisely" Jesus is the Son of God (Luke 1:35). Sonship is secured by historical divine intervention.

The angel's announcement harmonizes perfectly with the Hebrew Bible's promise of a son of David whom God would beget and call His own Son (2 Sam. 7:12-14). God promised to make this Messianic Son "My firstborn, the highest of the kings of the earth" (Ps. 89:27). These grand covenant promises find their fulfillment in Jesus. Absent from the biblical story is any hint of a Son who is *alive before his conception*! That imaginative idea introduces an alien element and a fearful complication into the readily understandable promise to David that his descendant would be the Messiah as well as God's Son.

Luke, we remember, is setting out the facts of the faith into which Theophilus had been catechized (Luke 1:1-4). It is unthinkable to imagine that Luke believed in the Incarnation of a *preexisting* Son, and then made it impossible for his readers to understand such an event. Expressly, Luke, through Gabriel, makes it clear that the Son's one and only origin is based on the miracle performed in Mary. The Son is precisely and deliberately the result of that biological wonder — a physical miracle worked here on earth in historical time. There is not a hint of a Son entering the womb from a previous existence, and thus not a hint of any ingredients for a doctrine of the Incarnation and Trinity. For Luke there is no eternal Son. There is a clear reason for Jesus' right to be the Son of God. It is his origin as Son in Mary. Another "eternal Sonship" would make Gabriel's words untrue. And if there is no eternal Son there can be no Trinity, and Jewish-Christian unitary monotheism remains intact.

James Dunn's comment on the Lukan view of the Son deserves much publicity:

> In his birth narrative Luke is more explicit than Matthew in his assertion of Jesus' divine sonship from birth (1:32, 35, note also 2:49 where Jesus recognizes God as his Father). Here it is sufficiently clear that a virginal conception by divine power without the participation of any man is in view (1:34). But here too it is sufficiently clear that it is a begetting, a becoming, which is in view, the *coming into existence of one* who will be called, and will in fact *be* the Son of God, not the transition of a preexisting being to

become the soul of a human baby or the metamorphosis of a divine being into a human fetus.[14]

Dunn's words should be carefully weighed as a perfectly accurate reflection of what Luke wrote. Note how significantly Luke here contradicts the later notion that the Son of God was actually a preexisting Person who never came into existence but was eternally existing. Luke would have failed the Nicene test miserably. That council, reacting against Arius, pronounced a damning anathema against any who would dare to say that "there was a time when the Son did not exist." Luke (and Matthew) declared in the plainest terms that the coming into existence (begetting) of the Son of God was by a miracle, some two thousand years ago, in the womb of the virgin Mary.

There is in this Christology of Luke no preexisting Son and no possibility of such a doctrine, which is expressly excluded on the basis that the Sonship of Jesus is grounded in a single reason. The foundation of Jesus' Sonship is the miraculous creation by God's spirit acting in the human biological chain, and thus securing also the essential blood relationship of Jesus to David as promised in the Hebrew Bible's Davidic covenant as the throbbing heart of hope for salvation.

"Luke's intention is clearly to describe the creative process of begetting."[15] The Son of God is thus presented to us in Scripture in this fully clarifying text, as the Son by biological miracle, brought about in comparatively recent history. The Incarnation of a Son who did *not* begin in his mother's womb and thus the later Trinity are expressly excluded from Luke's view.

German theologian Wolfhart Pannenberg agrees:

> While in Luke the divine Sonship is established by the almighty activity of the divine Spirit upon Mary (Luke 1:35), in Matthew it is apparently thought of even more emphatically in the sense of a supernatural procreation (Matt. 1:18)...Jesus' uniqueness [is] expressed in the mode of his birth...[The virgin birth] explains the divine Sonship literally in such a way that Jesus was creatively begotten by the Spirit of God (Luke 1:35)...

---

[14]*Christology in the Making*, Eerdmans, 1996, 50-51.
[15] Ibid., 51.

Jesus' virgin birth stands in an irreconcilable contradiction to the Christology of the Incarnation of the preexistent Son of God [and thus to the Trinity]...Jesus first *became* God's Son through Mary's conception...[Preexistence] is irreconcilable with this: that the divine Sonship as such was first established in time. Sonship *cannot at the same time consist in preexistence and still have its origin only in the divine procreation of Jesus in Mary.*[16]

Unfortunately, having explained the biblical texts with complete accuracy, Pannenberg dismisses the whole event of the virgin birth as a legend. Its acceptance however relieves theology at once of the tortuous problems of Incarnation, by which the Son of God somehow transited through Mary, having existed consciously before his own begetting! Luke and Matthew know absolutely nothing about this, for them, novel idea. They had no knowledge of an eternal Son and therefore struggled with no "problem" of the Trinity. The acceptance of Scripture in this matter of the origin of Jesus — the exact word "origin," *genesis* is used in Matthew 1:18 — would free our thinking and enable us to resonate with these matchless accounts.

The celebrated Roman Catholic commentator, Raymond Brown, author of the most extensive examination of the birth narratives, observes:

> In the commentary I shall stress that Matthew and Luke show no knowledge of preexistence; seemingly for them the conception was the becoming (begetting) of God's Son...We are dealing with the begetting of God's Son in the womb of Mary through God's creative spirit.[17]

Noting that Luke describes a direct causality between the miraculous begetting and the Sonship of Jesus, Brown observes: "In preexistence Christology a conception by the Holy Spirit in Mary's womb does *not* bring about the existence of God's Son. Luke is seemingly unaware of such a Christology; conception is causally related to divine Sonship for him."[18] This evident discrepancy between Luke and the later "orthodox" view of Jesus as preexistent eternal Son "has embarrassed many orthodox theologians,"[19] and

---

[16]Pannenberg, *Jesus – God and Man*, 120, 142, 143.
[17]Raymond Brown, *The Birth of the Messiah*, 31n, 312.
[18]Ibid., 291.
[19]Ibid., 291.

rightly so. According to the Trinitarian view of Jesus as God the Son, the virginal begetting does *not* bring the Son into existence. The doctrine of the Trinity therefore flatly contradicts the Christology of Luke whose doctrine of the Son cannot possibly match that of later orthodoxy. Luke was evidently a "heretic" if judged by the later councils.

The embarrassment admitted by Raymond Brown ought indeed to trouble the hearts of churchgoers and Bible readers. The "received" dogma about a Son of God who was Son before being begotten is a contradiction of Luke (and Matthew). According to Gabriel the intervention of God to beget, bring into existence, His Son in history provides us with the Savior Jesus. According to "orthodoxy" this is not the case. Mary simply took into herself, supplying an "impersonal human nature," a Son who was already God and second member of a Trinity.

So far the embarrassment has not led the Church to abandon its own "received" view of Jesus in favor of the biblical one. When this eventually happens the Bible will have been rescued from the layers of contradictory traditions which have been so heavy-handedly imposed upon it.

Some of the most brilliant and instructive passages of the New Testament are found in Matthew's and Luke's descriptions of the origin and birth of Jesus. The proposition that "Jesus is God" cannot possibly fit these accounts. Mary did not conceive God in her womb or bear God as her Son! Mary is not "the mother of God" but "the mother of my lord" (Luke 1:43). Elizabeth so designates Mary, employing the critically significant Messianic title of Psalm 110:1 where the Messiah is indeed "my lord" (*adoni*). To call Mary "mother of God" would make a nonsense of the Bible's birth narratives. It would also overthrow monotheism. Gabriel's visit to Mary in Luke 1:26-38 is designed to lay a clear and simple foundation for our understanding of who God is and who Jesus, the Son of God is in relation to the God of Israel. Mary is informed that her son is to be the Son of the Most High, that is, of course the Son of God. Critically important is Gabriel's revelation as to how the Son of God is to come into existence.

Joseph Fitzmyer comments on Luke 1:35:

> [Holy spirit] is understood in the OT sense of God's creative and active power present to human beings...Later church

tradition made something quite other out of this verse. Justin Martyr wrote, "It is not right, therefore, to understand the Spirit and the power of God as anything else than the Word, who is also the First-begotten of God" (*Apology* 1.33). In this interpretation the two expressions [spirit and power] are being understood of the Second Person of the Trinity. It was, however, scarcely before the fourth century that the "holy Spirit" was understood as the Third Person...*There is no evidence here in the Lucan infancy narrative of Jesus' preexistence or incarnation.* Luke's sole concern is to assert that the origin of God's Messiah is the effect of his creative Spirit on Mary.[20]

Protestant evangelical commentator Frederic Godet observed:

By the word "therefore" the angel alludes to his preceding words: he will be called the Son of the Highest. We might paraphrase it: "And it is precisely for this reason that I said to you..." We have then here, from the mouth of the angel himself, an authentic explanation of the term Son of God, in the former part of his message. After this explanation Mary could only understand the title in this sense: a human being of whose existence God Himself is the immediate author. It does not convey the idea of preexistence.[21]

Godet admits that "The Trinitarian sense should not be here applied to the term Son of God. The notion of the preexistence of Jesus Christ as the eternal Son of God is quite foreign to the context."[22]

Luke therefore was certainly not a believer in the Trinity or God the Son. Justin Martyr and later tradition did, as Fitzmyer said, indeed make "something quite other" out of Luke 1:35. By 150 AD Justin believed that the preexisting Son of God was the power and spirit who overshadowed Mary. This would mean that the Son engineered his own conception in his mother![23] The story had become hopelessly

---

[20]*Gospel According to Luke I-IX,* 350-351, emphasis added. Fitzmyer says that the elements of the Trinity but not the doctrine itself are found elsewhere in Luke.

[21]*Commentary on St. Luke's Gospel,* I.K. Funk & Co., 1881, 58.

[22]Ibid., 56.

[23]For the evidence of the switch from the biblical view of the origin of the Son to a prehistorical origin, see Ignatius, *Ephesians,* 7, 2; *Smyrneans,* 1, 1;

garbled, and it led eventually to an entrenched dogmatic view that the Son was eternally existing and could thus not truly be David's descendant through Mary, but merely a visitor from outside Mary, passing *through* her, instead of being born, brought into existence "from" her. God the Son of later tradition is not really the promised descendant of David. Once given an a-historical origin, his relationship to David was severed. A prehistorical person cannot also be the direct biological descendant of the historical figure David.

The lengths to which some standard works on the Trinity go, to negate Gabriel's brilliant theological insight, are quite remarkable. Hastings' *Dictionary of the Bible* proposes the exact opposite of Luke's grounding of Jesus' Sonship in the virginal conception: "It was to bring out the truth that it was not the *Sonship* but His *holiness* from His very birth which was secured by the miraculous conception,"[24] that the revisers (of the RV, 1881) were so careful to correct the translation here.

Had the lucidly simple description of the Son of God proposed by Luke been allowed to stand as the official doctrine of the Son of God, the course of the Christian faith and of church history would have been vastly different: "the holy thing begotten in you will be called the Son of God" (Luke 1:35) was easy enough. But when evangelicals rewrite the biblical story and read into it an eternal Son of God, this is the result. Charles Swindoll, chancellor of Dallas Theological Seminary, writes:

> On December 25th shops shut their doors, families gather together and people all over the world remember the birth of Jesus of Nazareth…Many people assume that Jesus' existence began like ours, in the womb of his mother. But is that true? Did life begin for him with that first breath of Judean air? Can a day in December truly mark the beginning of the Son of God? Unlike us, Jesus existed before his birth, long before there was air to breathe…long before the world was born.[25]

Swindoll goes on to explain:

Magnesians 8, 2; also Aristides, *Apology* 15, 1; Justin Martyr, *Apology* 1, 21 and 33; Melito, *Discourse on Faith*, 4.

[24]Hastings, *A Dictionary of the Bible*, extra vol., 309.

[25]*Jesus: When God Became a Man*, W Publishing Group, 1993, 1-2.

John the Baptist came into being at his birth — he had a birthday. *Jesus never came into being*; at his earthly birth he merely took on human form...Here's an amazing thought: the baby that Mary held in her arms was holding the universe in place! The little newborn lips that cooed and cried once formed the dynamic words of creation. Those tiny clutching fists once flung stars into space and planets into orbit. That infant flesh so fair once housed the Almighty God...As an ordinary baby, God had come to earth...Do you see the child *and* the glory of the infant-God? What you are seeing is the Incarnation — God dressed in diapers...See the baby as John describes him "in the beginning" "with God." Imagine him in the misty pre-creation past, thinking of you and planning your redemption. Visualize this same Jesus, who wove your body's intricate patterns, *knitting a human garment for himself*...Long ago the Son of God dove headfirst into time and floated along with us for about 33 years...Imagine the Creator-God tightly wrapped in swaddling clothes.[26]

Dr. Swindoll then quotes Max Lucado who says of Jesus, "He left his home and entered the womb of a teenage girl...Angels watched as Mary changed God's diaper. The universe watched with wonder as the Almighty learned to walk. Children played in the street with him."[27]

Dr. Jim Packer is well known for his evangelical writings. In his widely read *Knowing God*, in a chapter on "God Incarnate," he says of the doctrine of the Trinity and the Incarnation:

Here are two mysteries for the price of one — the plurality of the persons within the unity of God, and the union of Godhead and manhood in the person of Jesus. It is here, in the thing that happened at the first Christmas, that the profoundest and the most unfathomable depths of the Christian revelation lie. "The Word was made flesh" (John 1:14); God became man; the divine Son became a Jew; the Almighty appeared on earth as a helpless baby, unable to do more than lie and stare and wriggle and make noises, needing to be fed and changed and taught to talk like any other child.

---

[26]Ibid., 3-8, emphasis added.
[27]Ibid., 10, quoting Max Lucado, *God Came Near.*

And there was no illusion or deception in this: the babyhood of the Son of God was a reality. The more you think about it, the more staggering it gets. *Nothing in fiction is so fantastic as is this truth of the Incarnation.* This is the real stumbling block in Christianity. It is here that the Jews, Muslims, Unitarians, Jehovah's Witnesses...have come to grief...If he was truly God the Son, it is much more startling that he should die than that he should rise again. "'Tis mystery all! The immortal dies," wrote [Charles] Wesley...and if the immortal Son of God really did submit to taste death, it is not strange that such a death should have saving significance for a doomed race. Once we grant that Jesus was divine, it becomes unreasonable to find difficulty in any of this; it is all of a piece and hangs together completely. The Incarnation is in itself an unfathomable mystery, but it makes sense of everything else that the New Testament contains.[28]

With the greatest respect for the sensibilities of our readers, we want to suggest that the above accounts of the pre-history and Incarnation of Jesus, the Son of God are severely mistaken. They are profoundly untrue to the Bible. The situation appears to us and many others in the history of Christianity to be akin to the story of the "Emperor's New Clothes." The fact that the emperor was naked was noticed by one small boy when the majority was tricked into thinking he was not. The mere fact of rehearsing, year after year, a story of "God being born as a baby" and the *immortal God, who thus cannot die,* later *dying* on a cross does not make it true. Far from being a "mystery" it is rather obviously a fairy-tale mystification. This results in a crucifixion of the fundamental Protestant principle that God has graciously *revealed His purposes to us in Scripture and, in order for His revelation to be successful He has spoken to us in language which conforms to the universally accepted meaning of words and of logic itself.* If that principle applies, then God cannot die. He is immortal (1 Tim. 6:16).[29]

---

[28] J.I. Packer, *Knowing God.* Intervarsity Press, 1998, 46, 47, emphasis added.

[29] It is a remarkable fact that the Koran states that Jesus did not die. Orthodox Christianity despite its claims is committed to the contradiction that the immortal God the Son died. One cannot die if one is immortal! So no Son of God died.

To speak of Jesus as God and God dying is to dissolve the most basic understanding of the nature of Scripture as revelation to man. It is to utter illogical impossibilities. Surely we must plant ourselves on the famous maxim about how to read the Bible:

> I hold for a most infallible rule in expositions of the Sacred Scriptures, that where a literal construction will stand, the furthest from the letter is commonly the worst. There is nothing more dangerous than this licentious and deluding art, which changes the meaning of words, as alchemy doth, or would do, the substance of metals, making of anything what it pleases, and bringing in the end all truth to nothing.[30]

We may say that if God has really intended to make His will known to us humans, it must follow that He has conveyed His truth to us in harmony with the well-known rules of language and meaning. As a nineteenth-century theologian wrote:

> If [God's] words were given to be understood, it follows that He must have employed language to convey the sense intended, [in agreement with] the laws...controlling all language...We are primarily to obtain the sense which the words obviously embrace, making due allowance for the existence of figures of speech.[31]

Churchgoers seem to reflect little on the extreme illogicality of a virginal begetting which does *not* bring the person of the Son into existence, because according to "orthodoxy" that same person already exists! James Mackey alerts us to the acute logical problem involved in the whole idea that one can exist before one exists:

> It is best to begin with [the problem of preexistence], not only because there are linguistic difficulties here...but because it leads directly into the main difficulties encountered in all incarnational and trinitarian theology...As soon as we recoil from the suggestion that something can pre-exist itself we must wonder what exactly...pre-exists what else, and in what sense it does so...It does not take a systematician of any extraordinary degree of perspicacity to notice how exegetes themselves are often the unconscious victims in the course of

---

[30]Richard Hooker (1554-1600), cited in George N.H. Peters, *The Theocratic Kingdom of Our Lord and Savior*, rep. Kregel, 1952, 1:47.
[31]Ibid.

their most professional work of quite dogmatic (that is, uncritical) systematic assumptions.[32]

Church creeds deny that the Son of God had a beginning of existence! Luke and Matthew say emphatically that he did. According to Trinitarianism the Son of God was begotten in eternity and as Son of God he had no beginning in time. Such language about "eternal begetting" is totally foreign to the Bible and as baffling to the ordinary reader or churchgoer as to the in-depth student of the meaning of words. To "beget" means in English to bring into existence, to cause to come into existence. The word is used countless times in the Old and New Testaments to describe the begetting of sons by fathers or their birth to mothers. No one should have any difficulty understanding its meaning. They don't, until they fall under the spell of "churchspeak," which invented unheard of meanings for ordinary words and erected a whole theological system on those novel definitions which no lexicon will support. The very fact that the Son of God is said to be *begotten* — and "begotten in" Mary as Matthew 1:20 says[33] — should eliminate with one blow any possibility that he is an eternal God the Son without beginning. All that is required is that we let the Bible speak and stop allowing the "church fathers" or creeds to drown out the simple teaching about the origin of the Son of God. The Son was not just "born of the virgin Mary," he was brought into existence as the Son of God by the direct intervention of his creator, using the human biological chain.

The crowning insult to the text of Scripture occurred when later church councils pronounced an anathema on anyone daring to challenge the notion that the Son of God did not exist literally from eternity! Gabriel, Mary and Luke would have come under that ban. The angel announced the begetting, the *coming into existence* of the Son of God.

It should be obvious that if God is a single Lord (Deut. 6:4; Mark 12:29), there cannot be another God alongside Him who is coeternally also Lord. It is equally clear that if the Son of God is caused to come

---

[32]*The Christian Experience of God as Trinity*, SCM Press, 1983, 51.
[33]The Greek word in Matt. 1:20 is the passive participle of *gennao*, and means here "begotten" in her. The action is that of the father. It was also of course a conception for Mary, but the full force of Matthew's words is lost when the word is mistranslated as "conceived." The RV of 1881 noted the literal Greek meaning in its margin.

into existence (begotten) he cannot have always existed! This simple fact destroys the ancient creeds, which were enforced sometimes with threats of punishment or even death, compelling belief that Jesus was the uncreated God the Son, coequal with his Father from eternity. The anathema later appended to the creeds banished from fellowship anyone bold enough to declare that "there was a time when the Son did not exist." Ironically, Luke and Matthew would have been among the first to have been dismissed from fellowship. And would Jesus have been unfit for church membership?

Gabriel's concise teaching about who Jesus is appears to be one of the most amazingly neglected sections of Scripture. No wonder. It is a considerable embarrassment to the traditional view of Jesus as God the Son. First we learn that Mary is to have a son who is to inherit the long-promised throne of David. The promise was based on the celebrated and treasured covenant made with David, recorded in 2 Samuel 7, 1 Chronicles 17, and Psalms 2, 72, 89 and 132. In those remarkable passages the God of Israel announced His intention to become, in the future, the father of a biological descendant of King David. That Son was to be God's "firstborn, the highest of the kings of the earth" (Ps. 89:27). It is exactly this promise which Luke and Matthew explain as historically fulfilled in Jesus. God's Messianic promise became reality some two thousand years ago, as the most astonishingly significant event of the world's entire history. God became the father of his son *in time, in Israel, and according to promise.*

Upon learning that she is the favored young Jewess who is to be mother of the long-promised Messiah, heir to the throne of David, Mary very reasonably asks the angel, "How can all this be, since I am a virgin?" (Luke 1:34). Her request was for further information about the fulfillment of the divine plan, and Gabriel explained, "Holy spirit will come over you and the power of the Most High will overshadow you. For that reason precisely the one being begotten [or possibly, 'to be begotten'] will be called the Son of God" (Luke 1:35).

When this biblical passage is taken seriously it will cause a revision of nearly two thousand years of distorted thinking about what it means for Jesus to be the Son of God. Could this portion of Scripture possibly be understood to teach that an eternally existing Son of God was to leave his heavenly status and be introduced into the womb of Mary, reducing himself in some mysterious way to a fetus and emerging as one who is fully God and fully man?

It would be preposterous to suggest that Gabriel intended any such idea. Rather he states that the power of the One God, the Most High, will cause a biological and creative miracle in Mary. The facts are straightforward. The Most High, working through His own personal creative spirit, will cause the conception of the baby, without the benefit of a human father. The child thus miraculously brought into existence, begotten, will rightly be called God's Son.[34] The event will be a repeat, with some differences, of God's initial creation of Adam whom Luke also calls "son of God" (3:38). Since God intervenes in the human biological chain and personally brings about the begetting or conception of Jesus, he is very properly and reasonably the Son of God, God's Son in a unique sense as being the direct creation of the One God. He is God's own Son. But he is not God Himself.

One fact is clear beyond dispute. The Son of God is a creature, one procreated miraculously by a marvelous intervention of God Himself, begetting His Son in Mary. This simple truth requires no more than a handful of well-chosen words, certainly not centuries of disputatious theologizing. "The power of the Most High will overshadow you, Mary, and for that reason precisely the one begotten will be the Son of God." The miracle, then, is the basis for Jesus being the Son of God. This is the explanation of what it means to call Jesus the Son of God. The theological basis for his Sonship is the miracle performed by the One God, his Father. No further explanation is needed. Indeed any speculation about Jesus being Son of God for some *other* reason[35] interferes disastrously with the biblical account.

---

[34]In desperation some commentators, finding Gabriel disastrously unorthodox, attempt an evasion. They think that to "be called Son of God" does not mean that he is Son only from that moment on. However "to be called" is precisely the same as "to be." Raymond Brown says helpfully, "'Calling' brings to expression what one is, so that it means no less than 'he will be'" (*The Birth of the Messiah*, 289).
[35]The KJV is misleading with its "therefore *also*..." suggesting that there might be another reason for the Son being the Son of God! It tends to distract the mind from the one and only reason for the coming into existence of the Son. If the miracle in Mary is *also* a reason for his Sonship one might be able cleverly to imagine there was another, prior, reason for his sonship — in

There is one explanation and one reason for Jesus' Sonship: It is the historical miracle executed in the womb of Mary. Very few Bible verses contain their own theological definitions. But Luke 1:35 provides the biblical definition of Jesus as Son of God.

The story-line provided by Luke and Gabriel is the climax of the age-old promises of God given to mankind, to Abraham and David. The story is drastically undermined and altered if suddenly, with no warning, the Son of God, far from being the descendant of David, is actually an already existing Son!

Mary conceived the Son of God. God the Father begat him. There is no visitor from outer space. Such a figure would be an intruder turning the biblical history into mythology.

It will be perfectly obvious that the creation or procreation of the Son poses not the slightest threat to the Jewish unitary monotheism which pervades the New Testament. The Son of God is not a second God arriving from heaven, metamorphosed into a fetus. The Son of God is the miraculous result of God's act of creation and begetting. The Son is a creature, a member of the human race, divinely brought into existence.

This account, if believed, could have saved the Church centuries of pointless and angry dispute about what it means for Jesus to be the Son of God and how we are to think of his relationship with God. There is no abstruse "problem" to be solved here. The account is lucidly simple. The story is about the One God sovereignly choosing to beget a unique Son in human history in a Jewish female. That miraculous progeny would for that reason logically enough be called the Son of God (Luke 1:35).

Luke wrote more of the New Testament than any other writer. Paul wrote a lot of it, but if we exclude Hebrews, he wrote less than Luke. Luke wrote about Jesus before and after the cross. He is a major witness to Christianity in its pristine days. What did Luke believe about Jesus? "For Luke, Jesus is above all Messiah, Lord, and Son of God, and he is such from the virginal conception onwards."[36]

---

eternity! This would however be to destroy Luke's straightforward record. *Dio kai* means "for this reason indeed, or exactly." The KJV also curiously avoids telling us that the Son was "begotten" in Mary (Matt. 1:20). It was certainly also a conception on the part of Mary, but "begotten" points to the activity of the Father in His creative act bringing the Son into existence.

[36]John P. Meier, *A Marginal Jew*, Doubleday, 1994, 2:796.

Simple and clear. "The infancy narratives do not seem to have any contact with traditions of preexistence and incarnation."[37] No hint of any Trinitarian Jesus here. Luke also calls Jesus before his crucifixion "lord," more than any other writer. This simply proves that for Luke Jesus is the Lord Messiah. How he is Son of God, Messiah and Lord is explained very clearly by Luke 1:35, probably the most bypassed verse in the entire New Testament.

The original New Testament documents do not produce a doctrine of God as Trinity. The best that can be pleaded for Trinitarianism is that it appeals to a few "triadic" statements which coordinate God, Jesus and the Holy Spirit. But these verses, which do not address the question of creed or confession directly, do not arrive at the conclusion later taught as "orthodoxy" that the three amount to the One God.

The New International Dictionary of New Testament Theology reports these facts:

> Jesus Christ does not usurp the place of God. His oneness with the Father does not mean absolute identity of being...After the completion of his work on earth he has indeed been raised to the right hand of God and invested with the honour of the heavenly Lord. But he is still not made equal to God. Although completely co-ordinated with God, he remains subordinate to him (cf. 1 Cor. 15:28). This is true also of his position as eternal high priest in the heavenly sanctuary according to Hebrews (cf. Ps. 110:1).[38]

The same authority notes that texts which are often claimed as references to Christ as "God," like Romans 9:5, "are disputed." He says that the "much more probable explanation is that the reference is to the Father" in that verse.[39] Titus 2:13 may speak of "the glory of the great God and our Savior Jesus Christ," thus not equating Jesus with God. The text cannot be relied on as a proof of the Deity of Jesus since translations vary because of grammatical ambiguity in the Greek.

The direct evidence for the answer to our question about how many God is, is not decided by a handful of grammatically

---

[37]Ibid., 236.
[38]Colin Brown, ed., *The New International Dictionary of New Testament Theology*, Paternoster Press, 1976, 2:80.
[39] Ibid., 80.

ambiguous verses, but by those texts which brilliantly and directly define the creed of Jesus, by which he displays his unchanging Jewishness: God is a single Person, his Father, and Jesus is the supremely elevated human agent of that One God. Thus the creed of the Hebrew Bible and of Jesus is maintained, not assaulted by alien Gentile conceptions of God.

Jesus the Messiah, "Lord, son of David" (Matt. 15:22; 20:31)

"Jesus is God" has become for many the badge of correct understanding about who Jesus is. In the context of the first-century New Testament, however, it would have been heard as "Jesus is the One God of Israel." Since that one God was known to be not a man, anyone one about six feet tall walking around Palestine could not have claimed to be GOD without appearing to have become deranged. The worst they could say of Jesus at his trial was not that he claimed to be the Creator of heaven and earth, but the Son of God (John 19:7). And in those days, unlike ours, no one thought that Son of God = God Himself!

Those trusting blind men who appealed to Jesus to restore their sight knew who the Messiah was. They addressed him not as the Lord God, but as "Lord, son of David" (Matt. 20:31). They knew that God was not a man. They knew that the Messiah was both the descendant of David and their Messianic Lord. Everyone in Israel knew that the One God was in heaven ruling the universe. He was not confined to a Jewish human frame — having abdicated His position in the universe (letting it control itself?). They had never heard about the later doctrine of the Incarnation.

Jesus never once said anything as mad as "I am the one God." He claimed always to be the Messiah and everyone knew that the Messiah was the promised anointed king of Israel, not God but the Son of God. Happily in our day, the clouds of confusion are rolling back and the sunshine of truth is once again emerging. Not that this truth has not been known before, but it is largely lost in dusty libraries or learned tomes.

At the very famous Fuller Theological Seminary in California the distinguished professor of systematic theology has written, "To be a 'Son of God' one has to be a being who is *not* God! It is a designation for a creature indicating a special relationship with God."[40] With that simple statement the world of Bible study is dramatically advanced. Dr. Colin Brown has merely been good enough to show us what we can all check for ourselves, that "Son of God" in the Bible means a creature, either Israel the nation, an angel, Adam, or supremely Jesus, the Son of God and son of David. The Messiah (Christ) is the Son of God and on that rock foundational proposition (certainly not on the proposition that Jesus is God!) the Church of Jesus Christ is to be stably founded (Matt. 16:16-18).

How is Jesus the Son of God? When did he become Son of God? This is an easy question, but it is not answered well by church tradition. Try it out on your friends, for a lively conversation. Luke has answered the question in a way which should silence all objections (though in practice you may find that it may not!).

It was the mission of the mighty angel Gabriel to inform us, through a conversation with the young Jewess Mary, about how Jesus is the Son of God. What a joy and blessing that we can be party to that conversation, recorded, copied and preserved so meticulously over these many years. We can listen in as Gabriel engaged Mary in a brief dialogue, revealing the secrets of the universe.

We must be ready, however, for some real shocks. The theology of Gabriel and of Luke and Matthew about the Son of God is far removed from the later traditional Trinitarian teaching about an "eternal Son" who had no beginning!

The biblical Son of God and of David is the head of the New Creation. He is the firstborn, we are delighted to report, among many brothers and sisters (Rom. 8:29). Thus his vital importance for all of us interested in the pursuit of immortality.

Jesus is the Son of God and son of Mary in this way: "Holy spirit will come over you, Mary, and the power of the Highest One will overshadow you, and that is precisely why he will be called Son of God" (Luke 1:35). Is that clear? The *reason* and basis for the title Son of God is the miracle in Mary. It is that creative miracle which, marking the greatest event of human history thus far (besides the Genesis creation itself), brings into existence (that is what "beget" means) the Son of God.

---

[40]Colin Brown, "Trinity and Incarnation: In Search of Contemporary Orthodoxy," *Ex Auditu* 7, 1991, 88.

Now note what happened three centuries later when church councils (Nicea, 325; Constantinople, 381; Chalcedon, 451), thinking no doubt that they were "doing God a service" (John 16:2), decided formally to anathematize anyone who dared to say "there was a time when the Son did *not* exist." Gabriel and Mary would have been in dire trouble in those days! They would have been excommunicated for being anti-Christian. The cult label would no doubt have been applied. But did Mary and Gabriel really deserve the cult sticker, or had the Church long lost its pristine understanding of who the real Jesus was and is?

The Son of God was produced without the benefit of a human father. That insight was enough to provide a clear theology of the Son of God, an indispensable Christology. But man being man, and the Devil being subtle, managed to wreck that simple story of God's wonderful creative act. The notion was cleverly advanced that Jesus had preexisted. Preexisted? You mean, he existed before he existed? He *was* before he was? Explain that, if you can, to your friends, or to your children. The attempt to explain it will probably leave you baffled and hopefully driven back to the biblical drawing board. You cannot come into existence if you are already in existence. You cannot be human and pre-human. So, under the guise of the very misleading term "preexistent Christ," another *pre-historical* Christ was added to the biblical story, affecting it adversely at its very heart. The *origin* of the Christ, the Son of God, in Mary was thrown into confusion.

Once there was a *pre-existing* and a post-existing Jesus, a "before and after Jesus," it was impossible for him to have a *beginning* in Mary. But to be *begotten* one must be brought into existence. That is the case with all human beings. That is what begotten means: to be brought into existence.

Thus, ingeniously, the Jesus who was descended from David and brought into existence as God's Son in Mary according to God's oathbound promises to Abraham and David (Gen. 12; 13; 15; 17; 2 Sam. 7), was really eliminated. There could be no real lineal descendant of David as the Messiah if that Son of God was *already alive*.

This may take some careful pondering (even Mary "pondered all these things in her heart," Luke 2:19), but you cannot preexist yourself. You cannot be before you are. A "preexisting" Jesus appears to be "another Jesus" altogether, one who cannot by definition be the lineal and biological descendant of David (which he must be to qualify as the Messiah). He must of course be the Son of God Himself, and this truth is secured by and rooted in the virginal conception. Thus a denial of the miraculous conception/begetting in Mary also disfigures the identity of the true Jesus. Christology is indeed important and is not some abstruse doctrinal concern for learned and remote theologians! Knowing the Jesus of the Bible is important for the life of the age to come. Jesus said this in John 17:3.

If you preexist your birth, you are not begotten as a human being; you are metamorphosed from one existence to another. Preexistence makes begetting impossible. Or as "prince of church history" Adolf Harnack and others long ago protested, virginal begetting and birth contradict the idea of literal preexistence. Churches have managed to muddle the two contradictory ideas together and seem to hope that you will not think long enough about them to see that they cancel each other out.

A Textual Framework

Here is the biblical scheme for identifying the real Messiah in the considerable confusion which plagues our religious scene today after many years of dispute and disagreement. The backbone of Scripture and its Messianic story-line is provided by the marvelous promise that the God of Israel would one day become the father of a unique son, the last Adam and son of David. The revelation granted to David is unmistakably clear:

2 Samuel 7:12-14: Messiah will be the descendant of David. God will be his father. He will be God's son. He will have the throne of David forever.

Isaiah 49:5: "And now the LORD says, he who formed me *from the womb* to be his servant, to bring Jacob back to him, and that Israel might be gathered to him (for I am honored in the eyes of the LORD, and my God has become my strength)...."

Luke 1:32, 33, 35: Mary's supernaturally begotten child will be the Son of God. His father is David. He will have the throne of his father David forever.

Matthew 1:18, 20: The *genesis* of Jesus results in Mary's baby being "the one begotten in her."

Romans 1:1-4: The Gospel of God was promised in the prophets. God's Son came into existence (*egeneto*) as a descendant of David. He was declared Son *in power* later by the powerful act of God which brought about his resurrection.

Hebrews 1:5: The Son of God is the one prophesied in **Psalm 2:7** and **2 Samuel 7:14.**

Psalm 2:7: God begat him: "Today I have begotten you."

Psalm 110:3 (LXX): "From the womb before the morning star I begat you."

Psalm 89:26, 27: He will call Me Father. "I will make him My firstborn, the highest of the kings of the earth."

Hebrews 1:6: God brought him into the world: "When He brings the firstborn into the world."

Hebrews 7:14: Our Lord is a descendant of Judah.

Revelation 22:16: The Messiah is the offspring and descendant of David.

2 Timothy 2:8: Jesus is the lineal descendant of David according to Paul's gospel.

1 John 5:18: Jesus "was begotten."

Acts 13:33: God raised up, produced, Jesus by begetting him (**Ps. 2:7**), and later raised him *from the dead* (**Acts 13:34**).

Psalms of Solomon 17:23: "O Lord, raise up for them their king, the son of David at the time in which you, O God, see that he may reign over Israel your servant."

How beautifully the plan of God for His Messianic Son unfolds. God is really one, and His Son is the pinnacle of His amazing creation and purpose for us all.

The backbone of the unfolding Divine Plan revealed in Scripture is provided by the marvelous promise that the God of Israel would one day become the father of a unique son. The revelation granted to David is unmistakably clear in 2 Samuel 7:14. Indeed the whole of the divine future, which is the basis of the New Testament also, lies in the promise that it is God's unshakeable intention to rule the world through David and his family:

> Behold, days are coming, declares the LORD, when I will fulfill the good word which I have spoken concerning the house of Israel and the house of Judah. In those days and at that time I will cause a righteous branch of David to spring forth; and he shall execute justice and righteousness on the

earth. In those days Judah will be saved and Jerusalem will dwell in safety; and this is the name by which she will be called: the LORD is our righteousness. For thus says the LORD, David shall never lack a man to sit on the throne of the house of Israel; and the Levitical priests shall never lack a man before Me to offer burnt offerings, to burn grain offerings and to prepare sacrifices continually. The word of the LORD came to Jeremiah, saying, Thus says the LORD, If you can break My covenant for the day and My covenant for the night, so that day and night will not be at their appointed time, then My covenant may also be broken with David My servant so that he will not have a son to reign on his throne, and with the Levitical priests, My ministers. As the host of heaven cannot be counted and the sand of the sea cannot be measured, so I will multiply the descendants of David My servant and the Levites who minister to Me (Jer. 33:14-21).

Jeremiah 30:9: "They shall serve the LORD their God and David their king, whom I will raise up for them."

From the Dead Sea Scrolls: "When God will have begotten the Messiah among them" (1 QSa. 2:11). The hoped for Davidic Messiah is described in the language of 2 Samuel 7, associated with Psalm 2:7 (4QFlor. 1:10). A mighty king will be hailed as the Son of God and they shall call him Son of the Most High (4QpsDan A; cf. Testament of Levi 4:2).

This simple story is severely complicated and altered if one superimposes upon it the idea that the Son of God was begotten (came into existence) billions of years earlier and was thus not a biological descendant of David, but David's predecessor in another realm. The Trinitarian concept in fact obliterates the actual descendant of David who is the Messiah supernaturally begotten in history. One cannot be both the ancestor and the descendant of David.

The Church spent centuries trying to construct an intelligible account of the new story of Jesus which they had invented. The attempt was a failure and the Messianic son of David and God was obscured. The Jewish Jesus is the promised descendant of Eve, of Abraham, Judah and of David. He is heir to that permanent throne of David to be restored in a renewed land of Israel. This event is promised for the future when Jesus comes back. It is also a critical element in Jesus' saving Gospel about the Kingdom.

The simple truth about Jesus' origin, preserved in Luke's account of Gabriel's visit to Mary, is thankfully fully confirmed by the massive *Theological Dictionary of the New Testament:* "[Christ's] existence is peculiarly determined by the power of God. This is the most important feature in the Lucan infancy story...[Luke] perceives at *the beginning of His existence* a special and unique act of divine power which gives Him the title *Son of God.*"[41]

The same individual does not come into existence twice! The begetting of the Son in Mary is defined as the beginning of the Son's existence. His origin is properly within the human biological chain. Otherwise he cannot be from the line of David. He must be this, in order to make good his claim to be the promised Messiah.

This fundamental fact about the New Testament's testimony to the Sonship of Jesus, so drastically obscured by *later* theological argumentation, was stated by the noted Swiss theologian Oscar Cullmann, who wrote: "Matthew and Luke...try by means of the infancy narratives to *explain* Jesus' sonship, and to lift the veil from the question 'how' the Father begets the Son...With their completely philosophical approach the later Christological speculations tried to explain this 'how' in a different way."[42]

Here we have the good news and the bad news set side by side. Unfortunately scholarship is anemic in its failure to warn us of the dangers of redefining Sonship *later* in "different" terms. That difference was unfortunately not just a pleasing alternative but a rejection of Scripture and in particular of the birth narratives of Matthew and Luke who knew nothing at all of an Incarnation of a previously existing Son. Incarnation later imposed its own narrative by describing not a begetting of the Son but his transformation from one form of existence to another. This contradicts the Bible.

Protesting Voices
Various voices have been raised in protest against what later became the Church's official version of the origins of the Son of God. His beginning was supposed to have been in pre-history. He was presented as an apparent rival to the One God, coequal with Him in every way, even self-existent. Because the language of begetting was

---

[41]2:300.
[42]*The Christology of the New Testament*, SCM Press, 1963, 294.

biblical it was maintained but emptied of recognizable meaning. Commentator Adam Clarke was one of many who protested about the garbled language attributing a non-biblical Sonship to Jesus:

> With all due respect for those who differ, I must say that the doctrine of the eternal Sonship of Christ is antiscriptural and highly dangerous. This doctrine I reject for the following reasons: I have not been able to find any express declaration in the Scriptures concerning it...To say that the Son was begotten from all eternity is in my opinion absurd. And the phrase "eternal Son" is a positive self-contradiction. "Eternity" is that which has had no beginning, nor stands in any reference to time. "Son" supposes time, generation, and father and time also antecedent to such generation. Therefore the conjunction of these two terms "Son" and "eternity" is absolutely impossible as they imply essentially different and opposite ideas.[43]

Equally outspoken was the protest of the British poet, politician and theologian John Milton. Reflecting on the "orthodox" creeds of the Church he remarked:

> It is wonderful with what futile subtleties, or rather with what juggling artifices, certain individuals have endeavoured to elude or obscure the plain meaning of these passages...They hold that the Son is also co-essential with the Father, and generated from all eternity...It is impossible to find a single text in all Scripture to prove the eternal generation of the Son.[44]

J.O. Buswell, who was formerly Dean of the Graduate School, Covenant College, St. Louis, Missouri, examined the issue of the begetting of the Son in the Bible and concluded with these words. He wrote as a Trinitarian:

> The notion that the Son was begotten by the Father in eternity past, not as an event, but as an inexplicable relationship, has been accepted and carried along in the Christian theology since the fourth century...We have examined all the instances in which "begotten" or "born" or related words are applied to Christ, and we can say with confidence that the *Bible has*

---

[43]*Commentary,* on Luke 1:35.
[44]John Milton, "On the Son of God and the Holy Spirit," 60, 51.

nothing whatsoever to say about "begetting" as an eternal relationship between the Father and the Son.[45]

No less strong was the exclamation of Professor Nathaniel Emmons of Yale (1745-1850) that "eternal generation" is "eternal nonsense."[46] Emmons was a keen logician with a terse and lucid theological style. It is doubtful if the critically important Trinitarian phrase "eternal generation" should be ranked as any more intelligible than "hot ice cubes," "married bachelors" or "square circles."

Had *The New Schaff-Herzog Encyclopedia of Religious Knowledge* been consulted, Bible readers would have been warned against the concept underlying the Trinity that the Son was "eternally generated." "Thus the doctrine of eternal generation as a basis for the preexistence lacks support in the Bible."[47] Protestants taking their "sola scriptura" slogan seriously could have safely dropped the idea of eternal generation and returned to belief in the One God and Jesus as the human Messiah.

It is only by reading certain verses in John, and a very few in Paul and Hebrews, *through Trinitarian lenses* that the unitarian creed of Jesus is avoided and obscured. Starting with the Hebrew Bible and taking seriously the New Testament's own accounts of Jesus' origin and his own creedal unitarianism will provide the necessary and illuminating corrective.

Alexander Campbell, Barton Stone and the Church of Christ

Of the same mind on this crucial question of the origin of the Son of God was the founder of the denomination the Church of Christ. Barton Stone was outspoken in his denunciation of one of the main pillars of Trinitarianism:

> On this doctrine [of the Trinity] many things are said, which are dark, unintelligible, unscriptural and too mysterious for comprehension. Many of these expressions we have rejected; and for this reason we are charged with denying the doctrine itself. I shall…give my reasons why I cannot receive it…I am

---

[45] *A Systematic Theology of the Christian Religion*, Zondervan, 1962, 110.
[46] L.L. Paine, *A Critical History of the Evolution of Trinitarianism*, 104.
[47] 12:21. Otto Kirn adds most helpfully, "'Only begotten' of John 1:14, 3:16 expresses the close relation between Father and Son in regard to its stability, not its origin; and 'the firstborn of every creature' of Col. 1:15 alludes to the preeminence of the author of salvation over creation, not to his origin."

confident that mystery will be urged as the great argument to refute and cover these difficulties. But shall we cover ourselves in the mantle of mystery, woven by our own hands?...A mystery which destroys the efficacy of his blood...and involves so many absurdities and contradictions? Mystery is one of names of the whore of Babylon, written in large letters on her forehead. Her daughters have the same mark (Rev. 17)…When they so unequivocally express "That there is but one only living and true God without parts," I thence conclude that they do not believe that *another* real and eternal God was begotten from eternity, and sent down from heaven into the world. If they do, there is a pointed contradiction…

Church of Christ theologian Alexander Campbell wrote:

The names Jesus, Christ, or Messiah, only-begotten Son, Son of God belong to the Founder of the Christian religion, and to none else. They express not a relation existing before the Christian era, but relations which commenced at that time...There was no Jesus, no Messiah, no Christ, no Son of God, no Only-begotten before the reign of Augustus Caesar...I have held the idea for sixteen years that Jesus is called the Son of God, not because of an "eternal generation" (which I conceive to be nonsense), but because he was born as the angel described to Mary.[48]

Dave Hunt and Incarnation

The attempt to remain loyal to what is no more than a post-biblical portrait of Jesus as arriving from outside of history leads some modern commentators to a bizarre concept of the Jesus they so ardently support. Dave Hunt, well known for his fine exposure of some of the obvious paganism of the Roman Catholic faith and the fatalism of the hyper-Calvinist doctrine of double predestination, has this to say about who Jesus is:

Even though Jesus is God and Mary is the mother of Jesus, that does not make her the mother of God as Catholicism teaches. The birth of her *firstborn* Son (Matt. 1:25) in

---

[48]Greg Demmitt, "The Christologies of Barton Stone and Alexander Campbell, and their Disagreement Concerning the Preexistence of Christ," *A Journal from the Radical Reformation*, 12:2.

Bethlehem was not the birth of Christ *as God*, but of his human body, soul and spirit — "a body you have prepared me" (Heb. 10:5). She was the honored mother of the *man* Christ Jesus. But she was not the mother of the eternal Son of God, who created this universe...Mary had the unique honor of being the means by which the Son of God became man — but she was not the mother of the Eternal One...She wasn't the mother of the Son of God. To call Mary the mother of God, as official Catholic doctrine teaches, is the worst blasphemy possible. Although the eternal Son of God through virgin birth became fully man, He remained fully God...Even as a fetus in Mary's womb, He did not cease to be the One who said, "I am the Lord, I change not" (Mal. 3:6).[49]

Dave Hunt's Jesus is a bizarre figure, apparently a bi-person. There is an eternal Son of God (Dave does not explain how since the Father is also the "Eternal One" this does not make two Eternal Ones), and Mary then bears Christ who has "body, soul and spirit." So Mary's Son is now two persons, a preexisting eternal Son added to a fully human person Jesus. This is not even "orthodox" Christianity. Trinitarians were aware that a single person cannot be two persons at the same time. This heresy called Nestorianism was rejected. Instead the official portrait of Jesus declared him to be fully God as to his essential ego, but "man," *not* "*a man*," relative to his humanity. Mary on this theory bore "human nature," but not a fully human person. But what happens to the lineal descendant of David who the Messiah must be to qualify as Messiah?

Dave Hunt's loyalty, as he thinks, to the "orthodoxy" of which he is otherwise quite critical, drives him to contradict Luke.[50] Gabriel explained that Mary's son was to be Son of God precisely because of the divine miracle performed by God in her. She was indeed the "mother of the Son of God." Dave Hunt, believing in Jesus as eternal Son, says (above) that she was not. "For this reason precisely [the

[49]*Berean Call*, Dec., 2006.
[50]Equally astonishing is this assertion: "When the title 'Son of God' is used of Christ, it has nothing to do with His birth to Mary. As the Son of God, He was not born; He was given" (Charles Swindoll and Roy Zuck, eds., *Understanding Christian Theology*, Thomas Nelson, 2003, 570). It would be hard to imagine a more blatant rejection of the words of Gabriel in Luke 1:35.

miraculous generation in Mary] the holy child will be called the Son of God" (Luke 1:35). Because Hunt is burdened with a preexisting personality, the eternal Son of God (he makes no attempt to explain "eternal begetting"), Mary's son, who is also God's Son, cannot for him be "the Son of God." There are two theories in conflict here. Either Gabriel is right or "orthodox" definitions are right. They cannot be harmonized. You cannot come into existence as Son if you are already in existence as the Son.

Underlying this perplexing doctrinal impasse is the need, stated as an unquestionable dogma, for "God to die" as an adequate atonement for human sin. But God "dying" is itself a blasphemous concept. The God who cannot lie expressly states that He cannot die (1 Tim. 6:16). Once that element of God's constitution is believed and clung to, it becomes obvious that the Son of God is not God. He is the selected sacrifice for sin, the sinless human being, the "lamb crucified [in God's plan] before the foundation of the world" (Rev. 13:8). When Scripture was abandoned in relation to the immortality of God then the floodgates were opened to the notion of a member of the Godhead dying.

The acute problem remains in need of a radical solution. How can God be one, if one of the Godhead leaves heaven for earth and functions as fully God on earth? How do you distinguish between the God who did *not* become man and the God who did without destroying the precious doctrine of the unity of God? It is a feat which cannot be done and the whole attempt would be much better abandoned. It is by the teaching of Jesus that we are to be judged. His publicly proclaimed creed provides an indispensable foundation for the Christian faith. Tradition, however long held, cannot be pleaded against the Bible.

Chapter 8

Church Councils, *The Da Vinci Code* and Modern Scholarship

"Christian faith has not centered on the historical Jesus. The Apostles' Creed...moves from 'born of the Virgin Mary' to 'crucified under Pontius Pilate.' The Creed's omission suggests that the intervening years and activities of Jesus were of no real consequence to faith."[1]

"The official line taken by Christianity...was not directly tied to the actual words and deeds of the historical Jesus."[2]

Christology, the study of who Jesus is in relationship to God, has entered the public domain in recent days with a vengeance. The occasion was the appearance of the best-selling book and movie by Dan Brown, *The Da Vinci Code*. The plot is mostly fantasy (although I am not sure that some audiences would know the difference between religious fact and fiction). Interestingly, a number of remarks are made by the "expert" on the development of belief in Jesus which bear directly on the definition of God and Jesus. They cry out for comment and clarification. They might stimulate public interest in a quest for the origins of their beliefs about God and Jesus.

The character Sir Leigh Teabing reports that it was the emperor Constantine who deified Jesus and then suppressed earlier documents which had stressed the humanity of Jesus. In this way Jesus became

---

[1] R. David Kaylor, *Jesus the Prophet: His Vision of the Kingdom on Earth*, 212.

[2] Bart D. Ehrman, *Jesus: Apocalyptic Prophet of the New Millennium*, Oxford University Press, 1999, 241.

God. In fact, Constantine did not in any way *initiate* the idea that Jesus was God. He did of course convene and approve the church council which fixed permanently the idea that Jesus was God, as they said at the Council of Nicea, "Very God of very God."[3]

Tabloid religion is nothing new. From the early days of Christianity there were apocryphal, fantasy gospels which had a powerful public appeal. The idea that Jesus was married to Mary Magdalene is just such an imaginative tale. Books which did not qualify as Christian Scripture propagated a variety of fanciful legends.

In the Acts of Thomas Jesus appeared in the form of Thomas exhorting a young couple to dedicate themselves to virginity. Sexual abstinence was a dominant theme, reflecting Platonic ideas, which have affected orthodox Christianity in different ways. One was a tendency to disparage the physical body.

The apocryphal Gospel of Peter disrupts the New Testament program for resurrection: those who belong to Christ will be made alive in resurrection at Christ's future coming (1 Cor. 15:23). The apocryphal Gospel of Peter describes Jesus as overruling the biblical scheme and bringing the dead to life *before* the resurrection. The same interference with Christian hope is popular today when the grieving are assured that their relatives have become alive in another spirit world —"heaven" — but apart from the resurrection promised when Jesus returns.

Apocryphal gospels supplied the reader with material supposed to be fact. In one Jesus is accused of breaking the Sabbath and when challenged by Joseph he claps his hands and clay sparrows fly off. *The Da Vinci Code* allows itself similar liberties.

Apocryphal gospels did not make it into the canon of Scripture, but the question is how far apocryphal, philosophically tainted ideas about God and the Son of God continue to affect the way churchgoers read the Bible. Mysterious doctrines can obviously enter the public religious consciousness from paganism. Today the public may not be able to tell the difference. There is a classic moment in *The Da Vinci Code* movie when a mother and child picture is presented to an audience who confidently identify the figures as belonging to

---

[3] "God of God" can of course imply some subordination, undefined, for the Son.

Christianity. The lecturer corrects them by pointing out that the so-called "Christian" heroes are the pagan Isis nursing Horus! Mother and Son appear in lots of pagan religious systems and so the danger of counterfeit is very real. It threatens to confuse churchgoers and make it impossible for them to read the Bible with intelligence and understanding.

Confusion over the identity of Jesus has been a feature of Christianity's long and often tangled history. The debate about who Jesus was had been going on for over two hundred years before the major council at Nicea in 325 fixed on a "solution" deemed final. It was during that period that the New Testament's unitary monotheism — belief that God the Father alone is truly God (John 17:3) — was gradually, not overnight, abandoned and replaced eventually by the doctrine of the triune God.[4] The process by which "Jesus became God" was prolonged and represented the victory of one of the parties to the argument. It is a great mistake to assume, merely on the strength of a majority opinion, that it was truth which won the day. Nor necessarily that *either* party, Arian or Athanasian, was working within legitimate biblical categories. It may be that the terms of the discussion had already excluded a biblical solution.

The decision about the Deity of Jesus was certainly not just a political one on the part of the emperor. As far as Constantine had a hand in the confirmation of the canon of the New Testament, rather than excluding all references to the *humanity* of Jesus, as Teabing said mistakenly in *The Da Vinci Code* movie, the emperor helped to *exclude* books which made Jesus barely human at all. The New Testament as it has been handed down to us provides the strongest evidence that the earliest followers of Jesus believed him to be a human being, supernaturally begotten, a member of the human race — certainly not a second God, part of a Trinity.

The dialogue in *The Da Vinci Code* goes like this:

> "My dear," Teabing said, "until that moment in history [the Council of Nicea presided over by Constantine], Jesus was viewed by his followers as a mortal prophet...a great and powerful man, but a man nonetheless. A mortal."
>
> "Not the Son of God?"

---

[4]An official decision about the status of the Holy Spirit, as distinct from the decision about the Father and Son, was not achieved even in 325 at Nicea. The bishops decided to say no more than "we believe in the Holy Spirit."

"Right," Teabing said, "Jesus' establishment as 'the Son of God' was officially proposed and voted on by the Council of Nicea."

"Hold on. You're saying Jesus' divinity was the result of a *vote?*"

"A relatively close vote at that," Teabing added. "...By officially endorsing Jesus as the Son of God, Constantine turned Jesus into a deity who existed beyond the scope of the human world, an entity whose power was unchallengeable."[5]

Though there are elements of truth here about what the bishops decided at Nicea, the interchange introduces a fatal confusion by using the term "Son of God" in a sense unknown to the Bible. If we are to sort out the significance of Jesus as Son of God *within the pages of the New Testament*, it is necessary to show how confusingly "Son of God" is being used in this conversation. The term Son of God is used by *The Da Vinci Code*, as so often today, in a *post*-biblical and not a biblical sense. In the Bible, as we have seen, Son of God designates a member of the human race, a mortal. It denotes a human person with a special relationship to God. Sons of God are created human beings (the term is also applied to angels, who are classified as created beings, but, in the case of *holy* angels, endowed with permanent life). Israel is called collectively the son of God (Exod. 4:22). Adam was also God's son: Luke 3:38). Jesus is said to be "God's only Son" and "God's own Son," His "beloved Son." By the time we arrive at the Council of Nicea in 325 AD, however, the term "Son of God" as applied to Jesus has come to mean *God the Son*, a "deity who existed beyond the scope of the human world."

How historically accurate is this dialogue in *The Da Vinci Code?* It is quite untrue to say that believers right up to the time of the Council of Nicea thought of Jesus as just "a mortal," and not God the Son. The Council of Nicea was convened to settle the major controversy about the identity of Jesus, between two major rival opinions. Athanasius claimed full and eternal Deity for the Son. Arius saw him as definitely subordinate to the One God as a person created before Genesis. The council did indeed confirm by an overwhelming, not a narrow majority, that Jesus was fully Deity. This was in opposition to the rival view, held by many, that he was not on a par

---

[5]Dan Brown, *The Da Vinci Code*, Doubleday, 2003, 233.

with God, but had been created as God's Son *before the Genesis creation.* This latter view, known as the Arian view (after Bishop Arius), was roundly defeated at Nicea in 325 AD, leaving the creedal statement that Jesus must be considered "God from God," i.e. as Deity.

That view of Jesus as "God the Son" has remained the dominant definition of Jesus ever since that time, despite strong protests from minorities throughout all of church history. The council of bishops at Nicea, presided over by Emperor Constantine, was responsible for establishing that dominant view as the official orthodox understanding of Jesus binding upon all members of the Church. The victory of the Trinitarian idea was again challenged by the Arians after Nicea and it took a further sixty years before Arian opposition was defeated. The council in 325 AD did not deal with the question of how Jesus was also, obviously, a human being. Since it was clear that Jesus was also a man, a subsequent council was convened at Chalcedon in 451 AD to settle the question as to how the single person Jesus could be fully God and fully man. Without explaining how it is possible to be 100% man and 100% God, that council declared that it simply is so, and that is what Christians are to believe. The decision was backed and enforced by both church and secular authorities. Dissenters were punished and banned from membership in the Christian Church.

The question that remained unsettled was, as Bart Ehrman says, "How could both Jesus and God be God if there is only one God?"[6] And how could one think of "God" who remained in heaven and "God" who came to earth, without falling into bitheism, belief in two Gods?

The Artificial Jesus of the Councils

It was not until 451 AD that the Council of Chalcedon tackled the question of Jesus' "two natures," based on the supposition that he was "of the same substance" as God. Writers on the "problem" of the "two natures" in Christ have sometimes shown an admirable candor in admitting what a tangle theology got itself into trying to describe intelligibly a person who is "fully God and fully man."

---

[6]*Truth and Fiction in The Da Vinci Code*, Oxford University Press, 2004, 14-15.

T.B. Kilpatrick, D.D. was writing on "Incarnation" in the *Dictionary of Christ and the Gospels* in 1906:
> However remarkable these schemes [for describing the person of Jesus at Chalcedon] may be as intellectual efforts, and whatever value they may have in directing attention to one or another element in the complex fact [of the so-called dual nature of Jesus], it is certain that they all fall under *a threefold condemnation*: (1) They are dominated by metaphysical conceptions which are profoundly opposed to the ideas which prevail throughout Scripture; being dualistic to the core, whereas the ruling ideas of Scripture are synthetic, and are far removed from the distinctions which mark the achievements of the Greek mind.[7]

The professor exposes the popular false argument that Jesus died as a man and not as God, that he was tempted as a man and not as God, and that as a man he did not know the day of his return, but as God he did! The whole conception of Jesus as possessing two mutually incompatible natures leads to nonsense. The biblical Jesus is a unified personality. Jesus declared clearly that "no one knows the day or the hour, neither the angels in heaven, nor the Son, but only the Father" (Mark 13:32). This is a plain statement that Jesus the Son is not omniscient Deity. The artificial attempts to avoid the obvious are completely unconvincing and point to the laborious struggles of those intent on reading the Trinity into the Bible. Jesus, the Son of God, did not know the day of his return. Church fathers produced implausible excuses for not believing what they read in this passage. The Son really did know, but was not permitted to say! It would be like a person replying "no" to the question whether he has any money. He does not have money in one pocket but he does in the other. Or a person who says he is blind, when he can see with one eye and not the other.

The professor who is critical of the Incarnation continued:
> 2) [Attempts to describe "two natures" in Christ] do not correspond with or do justice to the knowledge which faith has of the personal Christ, separating as they do what faith grasps as a unity, while their attempted harmonies are artificial and not vital.

---

[7] 1:812, emphasis added.

3) They fail to reproduce the portrait of Christ presented in the gospels; they utterly fail to give adequate utterance to the impression which the Christ of the gospels makes upon the minds which contemplate him. This is true even of the Chalcedonian scheme which in substance is repeated in many modern creeds and confessions. They describe "A being who combines in an inscrutable fashion Divine with human properties, and of whom, consequently, *contradictory* assertions may be made while his dual natures hold an undefined relation to one another. This is not a scheme to satisfy head or heart."[8]

The problem was that the council's "Jesus" was a self-contradiction. He did not know and yet really knew the day of his return. Not only that. It remained a puzzling issue, as it still is today, how, if there is only one God, Jesus could be God in addition to his Father being God. Does that not make two Gods? "The Father is God; Jesus is God; the Holy Spirit is God; and yet there is only one God" exposes for every unprejudiced reader the fundamental mistake of the Trinity. The problem is insoluble, but the problem is the creation of the Church itself, which gave up belief in Jesus as the Davidic Lord Messiah (Luke 2:11), God's Messiah (Luke 2:26), not another person who is equally God!

Covering up that error — the declaration that two Persons, each of whom is God, makes one God — has been the work of learned theologians. Most church members have not challenged the obvious illogicality of saying that 2x equals 1x! Many have harbored the strongest doubts, yet seem cowed into silence and compliance. Since sermons are very seldom preached on the Trinity, the whole issue tends not to be a subject of public discussion. Nevertheless, that extraordinary proposition that "there is one God, yet both Jesus and the Father are God," exercises, often silently, an iron control over the churches in which millions gather every Sunday. The question is whether it is honest to saddle churchgoers with a creed about God which cannot be found in the teaching of Jesus himself — one which thus erects a confusing barrier between them and the Scriptures which belong to all mankind. "Being like Jesus" is very much more feasible

---

[8]Ibid., quoting J. Oswald Dykes, "The Person of our Lord," *Expository Times* 17, 1905, emphasis added.

if one is allowed to think like Jesus! Thinking like Jesus begins with listening to his marvelous teaching.

The noble principle that each believer exercises his own right to determine what he is to believe is hopelessly frustrated by the imposition of an unexplained and often uninvestigated dogma — one which dramatically affects the heart of all religion and theology.

The Church attempted to resolve this problem of how two Persons, each of whom is fully God, can amount to one God, by *shifting* the notion of God's oneness to one "essence" shared equally by two (and later three) members of the one Godhead. *It was this fatal step which set the Church's doctrine of God in direct opposition to Jesus' and the Hebrew Bible's picture of God as a single divine Person.* When the Holy Spirit was later given the status of "third Person" (though at Nicea in 325 AD no attempt was made to define the status of the Spirit), the doctrine of the Trinity became the permanently official, orthodox description of God. Dissenters were to be stigmatized as unbelievers.

The legacy of those councils ought not to be accepted uncritically:

> The great ecumenical councils that formulated the old theology were the scene of unchristian antagonisms, and bitter strife and fightings that were never rivaled in the history of any other religion, and no religion of which history has a record was ever guilty of such cruel persecutions as Christianity, whose founder was the meek and lowly Jesus of Nazareth...The history of Christianity's so-called disciples, from the fourth century down to recent times, has been one to make men often blush, and the story of many of the practical fruits of the old theology is one of the saddest chapters in human annals.[9]

The biblical God, who is defined as single by every form of words available to language, was supplanted by a tri-personal "one God essence." But an "essence" is a disappointing and feeble substitute for the vigorous and dynamic Person revealing Himself as the true God of the Bible. It is to treat the public as terribly gullible to

---

[9]L.L. Paine, *A Critical History of the Evolution of Trinitarianism,* 262.

offer them the teaching that God is "One What in three Who's." God is "one What"! Which verse tells us that?[10]

Back to *The Da Vinci Code.* This point needs to be repeated: Teabing's account of the development of the Trinity is inconsistent and confusing in another matter of fact. He maintains that Constantine at the time of Nicea accepted in the canon of Scripture only those gospels which taught the Deity of Jesus, and that the emperor and the council banned gospels which saw Jesus only as human. Quite the opposite is true, because the gospels which the council did *not* allow were those which made most of the Deity of Jesus and allowed very little room for his humanity! Certainly Constantine, with the council, believed that the Deity of the Son in the Trinitarian sense was found in the canonical works to be known as Scripture, but no effort was made to suppress documents which portrayed Jesus as essentially mortal.

Despite the confusion in terminology and errors of historical fact presented by the "expert" in *The Da Vinci Code* movie and book, they do in fact raise the basic question of how the human being Jesus came to be viewed as God, the second member of the Trinity. Merely stating the fact that this has happened should strike the reader as bizarre in the extreme, since, as we have seen, Jesus himself, *as a Jew loyal to the unitarian creed of Judaism*, could hardly have imagined that he had personally preexisted as God for eternity!

There is not a shred of clear evidence that Jesus ever said "I am God." When challenged, he constantly protested that he was entirely dependent on his Father and could do nothing by himself. These are hardly the words of a person who is trying to convince his audience that he is an eternal being, a second God in addition to the Father, overthrowing his own Jewish heritage which he so stalwartly proclaimed as the basis of true religion.

Jesus never said he was God. The churches after Bible times gradually developed this novel concept. Jesus knew nothing of such a claim. The claim of the Deity of Jesus cannot be based on his own words, and should be discarded for that good reason, unless of course even Jesus did not know who he was! Such a counsel of despair is however quite unnecessary, since our New Testament documents

---

[10]God is defined as "one what" by James White in his apology for the Trinity, *The Forgotten Trinity* (27). Hank Hanegraaff offers the same definition on radio.

repeatedly tell us that Jesus believed with his Jewish compatriots that God was a single Person, his Father, and that he, Jesus, was the promised Messiah of Israel. That creed is extremely simple and clear and springs off the pages of the New Testament from beginning to end.

Modern Scholars and Jesus

Confirmation of these facts about Jesus' own belief is provided by a leading Roman Catholic theologian and provides the clearest evidence of how far we have strayed from the faith of Jesus as recorded in the Bible. Joseph Fitzmyer writes:

A second theme of Jesus' preaching was the fundamental validity of what scripture and tradition of old had taught. Jesus repeated the *Shema* (Deut. 6:4, quoted in Mk. 12:29) and acknowledged the law in the Old Testament as the source of God's will for human conduct...A third theme of Jesus' preaching was a special emphasis on God as Father [a purely unitarian emphasis]. His preaching reinforced the traditional Israelite view of God...Yahweh was still the sole divine being who chose Israel.[11]

Fitzmyer lists another main theme of Jesus' preaching: he claimed to be an agent of God. He then answers the question "Did Jesus clearly claim to be God?" with this candid reply: "If the question is meant to stress a 'clear claim,' we can answer it in two ways: If the Jesus of history ever explicitly claimed to be God, the gospels have not so presented that claim. They never put on his lips *ego eimi theos,* 'I am God.'"[12] Fitzmyer shows how unintelligible the words "I am God" would have been:

Would it have been possible in the monotheistic setting of pre-Christian Palestine for a Jew like Jesus to claim openly, *anah elaha* (in Aramaic) or *ego eimi theos* (in Greek), "I am God"?...It is impossible to imagine how such a statement would have been understood, given the fact that 'God' would have meant the 'one God' of Israel, Yahweh...the one whom Jesus himself called *abba.*[13]

---

[11]*A Christological Catechism,* Paulist Press, 1991, 46-47.
[12]Ibid., 97.
[13]Ibid., 98-99.

This of course is to concede the obvious unitarianism of the first century, of Jesus himself, and of biblical times. No Jew, basing himself on the divine revelation provided by his Hebrew Bible, would possibly have imagined the Messiah to be other than a lineal descendant of Eve and of Abraham and David, supernaturally generated[14] by God (Ps. 2:7) and empowered as God's anointed Son. Jews knew well, as we all ought to, that *descendants* of David cannot at the same time pre-date their own ancestor! The Church, however, committed itself in perpetuity to the amazing idea that the Son of God was at the same time both older and younger than David. He was both God who had existed from eternity, and a man conceived and born of a woman. The hairsplitting arguments which followed from this mistaken concept fill the pages of church history for centuries and the decision to call God triune rules to this day.

The Da Vinci Code introduces vocabulary about Jesus and his so-called Deity as "Son of God," which conveniently brings to public attention the immense muddle over terminology and simple logic which often blights the whole discussion about who Jesus is. Only when terms are calmly defined can we make any progress.

It has to be emphasized that "Son of God" when read in the pages of the Bible is in no way the equivalent of Son of God as *later* meaning God the Son. The facts are not complex. If we stay within the bounds of Scripture, "Son of God" refers always to created persons, never to God. Jesus claimed the title for himself (John 10:36). He did so in an important passage in which he rebuffed the accusations of his opponents that he was claiming to be "[a] god" (John 10:33). Jesus argued brilliantly that even the judges of Israel, as God's human representatives, had been entitled to the designation "gods" (John 10:34-36; Ps. 82:6; see also John 5:18-19). The term Son of God in the Bible identifies a created person or persons. The One God, however, is of course uncreated. A firm line is thus established between the one uncreated Creator and His various created beings and representatives.

Son of God is a fixed term in Scripture for a person who is *not* God. If biblical terminology is to teach us how to think of Jesus, then we must understand that "Son of God" is the title which establishes that Jesus is not God, but a human creature. This point is at the root of

---

[14]The exact sense of such generation was clarified in the birth narratives.

our whole discussion. The truth about the biblical meaning of "Son of God" is available to the public as stated by leading experts of our day. Professor Colin Brown, systematic theologian at Fuller Theological Seminary, says, along with scores of other authorities, "To be a 'Son of God' one has to be a being who is *not* God!"[15]

The truth of that proposition can be established by any reader of Scripture. One may also consult any good Bible dictionary. One will search in vain for any hint that "Son of God" describes an uncreated second member of the Godhead. The peril of adding "Gods" to the One God of Jesus' and Israel's creed is extreme. The addition of "gods" of any description to the One God of the Bible is in fact the ultimate crime against God. Readers should inspect their own thinking on this point with urgency and care. Did not Paul warn that amongst the follies committed by humankind was that of worshipping the created being in place of the Creator? (Rom. 1:25).

Two thousand years later the precious biblical term "Son of God" has suffered severe confusion. This is because Jesus' identity has been revised by the Church and its creeds to mean "God the Son." Jesus' biblical title "Son of God" has at the same time been retained, but given a new non-biblical meaning. Son of God in other words has been removed from its biblical context, severed from its Hebrew roots and made to express the idea of a second uncreated Person, "God the Son." Where terminology has been altered, a difference of meaning has naturally occurred. There has been a subtle and significant change of identity. Detective work is needed to expose and clear up the shift in the title given to Jesus. It was a shift so monumental that it actually led to the disturbance of the most central of all biblical truths that the Father is "the only one who is truly God" (John 17:3).

The subtle switch of identity as between "the Messiah, Son of God" and "God the Son," the creation of post-biblical theologians, calls for a public investigation since it continues to affect the thinking and spirituality of massive numbers of persons desiring to make a relationship with God "in spirit and truth" (John 4:24).

---

[15]"Trinity and Incarnation: In Search of Contemporary Orthodoxy," *Ex Auditu* 7, 1991, 88.

One Single Person Is the God of the Bible

We have seen that the personal God of Israel and the Hebrew Bible is known by various titles. He is first of all the God (*Elohim*) who created the heavens and earth, an activity in which He was entirely unaccompanied. Speaking of Himself by His personal name YHVH, He announced this fact in Isaiah 44:24 in terms which really cannot be misunderstood (I have emphasized the singular pronouns): "*I* YHVH created all things by *Myself…*Who was with *Me*?" Some seven thousand times this same YHVH, the God of Israel's creed, introduces Himself as the one and only God. The seven thousand appearances of the so-called tetragrammaton YHVH (four-letter word rendered LORD in many translations) are accompanied invariably by *singular personal pronouns* and by verbs in the *singular.* The same God speaks of Himself as "all alone," and adds that "no one is beside Me." "There is no other God."

Every form of language available which denotes *exclusive singular personality* is employed in the Old Testament to describe the true God. This language is meant to fend off the idea that there could be *more than one* Person as Deity. Jewish monotheism has justly been called "strict" and "uncompromising." It is strictly unitary. For this conviction Jews were prepared to die, as were some Christians. Language has no other means of describing a single and sole Person totally alone and unique in His class, without rival or competitor. All this can be discovered by reading the Old Testament in any translation. Historians of Judaism, both Jewish and non-Jewish, will confirm this very simple fact. "God is one, and there is no one else besides Him." "Yahweh is our God," "Yahweh is One Lord." "Yahweh alone."

I am not *assuming* that monotheism is unitarianism. I am pointing to the thousands and thousands of texts which present us with a unitary monotheistic theology, by equating the only God with the Father. It would seem to be a sort of dicing with theological confusion to interfere with this primary theological and biblical data. It is time for the Church to retrace her steps to Jesus, the master who declared, in agreement with the Jewish scribe, that God is a single Person, his God and the God of Abraham, Isaac and Jacob.

The proposition about God's unity was simple and clear enough. Young Jewish children were taught to memorize and recite the central and primary fact of true religion. It is the Shema — the "Hear, O

Israel" of the Bible (Deut. 6:4) — repeated by Jesus as the source of the Christian faith (Mark 12:28-34), yet curiously relegated to a pre-Christian status by commentary. Jesus himself on that argument would be "pre-Christian" and deprived of his claim to authority over the Church. By Jesus' words we are to be judged. Compliance with his mind and teachings would seem to be the only safe policy.

Jesus as a Jew never hinted that his native creed was to be interfered with in any way. When challenged about his enormous claims as God's unique, special agent, empowered to be even "Lord of the Sabbath" (Mark 2:28; cf. John 5:18), Jesus replied that he could "do nothing of himself, but only what he understood his Father to be doing" (John 5:19). He and his Father were working in complete and utter harmony, as Jesus carried out the will of his Father, the One God of Israel. "I and the Father are one" (John 10:30) was clearly meant to describe the perfect unity of purpose and action possible between God and himself as the human Messiah. We know that this is the meaning Jesus intended, because only a few chapters later, in the same gospel of John, Jesus desires the same unity to be realized between God and Christians. "Just as the Father and I are one, so you and God are to be one" (see John 17:11, 22).

Any argument, therefore, that forces "I and the Father are one" to mean "I and the Father are both God" collapses immediately on the patent evidence that Jesus describes the unity between disciples and God in exactly the same language as his own unity with God. This fact leads to this conclusion: Since the disciples and God can be "one," and we know that the disciples are not God, "Jesus and the Father are one" would prove likewise that Jesus is *not* God. He must be the ideal of a human being in perfect relation to his Creator. And as such, enjoying that unity with God, he wishes this also for his followers. Just as he was "sent," so he sent his disciples (John 20:21). That saying should remove all substance from the frequent claim that Jesus' being sent means that he was conscious before he was born. John the Baptist was "a man sent from God" (John 1:6) but this does not mean he preexisted his birth!

What distinguishes Jesus is his complete reliance on and subordination to his Father who has commissioned him as His agent. "The Father is greater than I" (John 14:28); "I can do nothing by myself" (John 5:19) sum up Jesus' uninterrupted sense of dependence on the One God. That biblical model of who Jesus is has the enormous advantage of showing what marvelous things the Creator can perform through a *perfectly dedicated human person.* If Jesus is God, not only is Jewish and Christian monotheism subverted and thousands of references to God as a single Person overthrown — worse still, Jesus' amazing accomplishment on our behalf becomes an empty charade. If he is God he cannot be tempted, because God cannot be tempted with evil (James 1:13). And because God is immortal according to the plain statement of 1 Timothy 6:16, the Son of God, if he is God as orthodoxy holds, cannot by definition die. Yet Paul, unaware of any difficulty, writes that the Son of God died (Rom. 5:10). The best that Christian hymnology could do was to write nonsense: "'Tis mystery all: the immortal dies."[16] But on what authority are intellect, logic and the precious gift of words to be crucified in the interest of "mystery," or rather "mystification"? The destruction of the meaning of words means the destruction of information and in this case the destruction of Truth. God cannot die. The Son of God died. A world of understanding is to be drawn from these basic propositions.

The falsehood that Jesus being called "lord" proves that he is the One Lord God needs to be challenged and dismissed. Yes, there are some Old Testament "Yahweh verses" fulfilled by Jesus as Yahweh's unique representative in the New Testament, but this no more makes Jesus identical in person with Yahweh, than the angel of the Lord is identical with the Lord God. The angel could bear the divine name without actually being God. "An agent is as his master's person" is the well-established principle known to Judaism and so obviously true of Jesus in relation to God. Jesus spoke of the persecution of Christians as the persecution of himself (Acts 9:4; 22:7; 26:14). This does not make Jesus and the Church identical.

The critically important Psalm 110:1 comes into play here, and it needs massive publicity in church circles and outside. No sooner had Jesus declared the Shema to be the heart of good theology (Mark 12:28-34), than he raises the issue about himself, with a question based on Psalm 110:1 and his own position in that oracle: "The Lord [Yahweh] says to my lord..." Both Jesus and his opponents recognized this Psalm as Messianic. The question is, Who is this

---

[16] Charles Wesley, "And Can It Be That I Should Gain."

second "lord," and how can he be David's son and also his lord? Above all, what is the status of the second lord?

The answer to the puzzle presented by Jesus is not difficult. Jesus is firstly born the son of David, from Mary, and later elevated to the supreme position as the man Messiah at God's right hand, where he arrives in Acts 2:34-36.

The application of Psalm 110 to our Lord is one of the most outstanding features of the apologetics and theology of the earliest Church. In Acts 2:34 Peter regards Psalm 110:1 as prophetic of Jesus' ascension. It demonstrates the fact that the Lord Messiah has now been exalted to the Father's right hand. In Hebrews 10:12-13 Psalm 110:1 describes Jesus' continuing session at the "right hand" of the Father, and in Hebrews 6:20; 7:17, 21 verse 4 of the same Psalm describes Jesus' eternal High Priesthood "after the order of Melchizedek." In Mark 12:35-37 Psalm 110:1 is the evangelist's definitive testimony to Jesus' exaltation, justifying from Scripture the use of the title "Lord" for him — a title which from the start (Luke 2:11) was the characteristic description of Jesus. The use of the title did not originate in Greek-speaking Christianity, as is obvious from the Aramaic *Maranatha* ("Our Lord come," 1 Cor. 16:22). It is certain that the original and enduring basis for the title Lord as applied to Jesus was Psalm 110:1.

Everyone knew, who read the Hebrew or Greek of that verse, that "my lord" (*adoni*) was a designation of non-Deity, a human superior, in the case of Jesus a human being supremely and uniquely elevated. Mark, then, in his twelfth chapter has portrayed Jesus as summarizing Israel's religion by quoting the Shema as the most important of all truths, and then defining his own position in relation to that One God as the *adoni*, my lord, of the famous Messianic Psalm 110:1. The creed of Israel is revealed not only as belonging to the nation but to Jesus Christ, the ultimate Christian theologian and author of the original and authentic Christian faith (Heb. 2:3). The importance of Psalm 110:1 as defining who Jesus is cannot be overemphasized.

It is indicative of Christianity's reluctance to see Jesus as the Messianic Lord of Psalm 110:1 that Oscar Cullmann remarks:

> All the numerous New Testament passages which mention that Jesus "sits at the right hand of God"…come into consideration with regard to the "lordship of Christ."…These ideas are a messianic application of Ps. 110. Scholars do not

usually attribute sufficient importance to the fact that statements about the exaltation of Christ to the right hand of God (which were very early included in the creed) *formally go back to this psalm.*[17]

This is profoundly true.

The failure to understand what is meant by the *lordship* of Jesus underlies the whole effort of Trinitarians to complicate the oneness of God. Professor Gregory Boyd in his *Oneness Pentecostals and the Trinity* begins with a lucid statement about monotheism:

> The Bible uniformly and unequivocally teaches that there is only one God. Certainly it was the proclamation, "Hear, O Israel, The Lord our God, the Lord is One," that formed the cornerstone for everything that was distinctive about the faith of God's people in the Old Testament. The message of God's uniqueness and singularity is driven home literally hundreds of times throughout the pages of the Old Testament (e.g., Isa. 42:8; 43:10b-11; 44:6). This strict monotheism is by no means forgotten when we enter the New Testament era. Rather, it forms the presupposition of the Christ-centered faith articulated in the New Testament (e.g., Mark 12:29; 1 Cor. 8:4b-6; Eph. 4:4, 6; 1 Tim. 2:5). It is therefore an incontestable fact that the Bible is monotheistic through and through...No biblical author would have ever entertained the notion that there could be more than one supreme being. This is the cornerstone to ancient and contemporary Judaism and the first foundational stone to Oneness theology [Modalism].[18]

But if the strict monotheism of God's ancient people is "by no means forgotten" in the New Testament, how is it that the Church has in fact forgotten it by changing it radically? If that same strict monotheism was the hallmark of Jesus' theology, why do his followers not adopt it as the centerpiece of their own confession?

We remind readers of the admission of *The New Bible Dictionary* in its article on "Trinity":

> The Old Testament witness is fundamentally to the oneness of God. In their daily prayer, Jews repeated the Shema of

---

[17]Cullmann, *Christology of the New Testament*, 222-223.
[18]Gregory Boyd, *Oneness Pentecostals and the Trinity*, Baker, 1992, 26-27.

Deuteronomy 6:4, 5, "The Lord our God the Lord is one." In this they confessed the God of Israel to be the transcendent creator without peer or rival. Without the titanic disclosure of the Christ event *no one would have taken the Old Testament to affirm anything but the exclusive, i.e., unipersonal monotheism* that is the hallmark of Judaism and Islam.[19]

Yes, indeed. But the "titanic Christ event" does not apparently include the stunningly authoritative teaching of Jesus himself, the rabbi who spoke uniquely with the authority of the One God who commissioned him! It was God who said "Listen to my Son" (Mark 9:7), and it was Jesus who constantly and repeatedly insisted that we are to be judged by our conformity to his words, which were the very words of his Father (John's gospel says little else than that adherence to what Jesus taught is the criterion by which we will all be assessed). How is it then that the Bible dictionary, paralyzed by its own tradition, can conclude that somehow the creed of Jesus justifies a titanic departure from that creed?

James Dunn

With the arrival of the universally acclaimed scholarly work of James Dunn we might expect that the Christian world would be propelled into a re-investigation of its long-cherished doctrines of God and His Son.

In his widely acclaimed *Christology in the Making* Professor Dunn writes:

> The confession that God is one is clearly Jewish (cf. particularly Deut. 6:4; James 2:19)...[Paul] starts from the common ground of the basic monotheistic faith ("There is one God, the Father")...Paul may intend 1 Corinthians 8:6b to be a statement about Christ's present Lordship...[Lord] was a title Jesus received on his exaltation, by virtue of his resurrection (Acts 2:36; Phil. 2:9-11; cf. Rom. 10:9; 1 Cor. 16:22): it was the exalted Lord who had supplanted all other "lords" and absorbed their significance and rule in regard both to the cosmos and to redemption (1 Cor. 8:5-6). Likewise the addition of "we" to both lines of v. 8 may well indicate that Paul is speaking primarily about the new

---

[19]"Trinity," *New Bible Dictionary*, Intervarsity Press, 1962, 1209.

understanding and the new state of affairs brought about for believers by Christ's Lordship [which would be nothing new if Jesus was already Lord in Genesis!], about the relations between God, Christ, believers and created things that now pertains...In other words, we may have to recognize that Paul is not making a statement about the act of creation in the *past*, but rather about creation as believers see it *now* — that just as they have found their *own* true being and meaning through Christ, so faith has enabled them to see that *all things* find their true being and meaning through Christ.[20]

Dunn continues:

Paul is not thereby abandoning his monotheism (and he seems to recognize no such tension in his affirmation of Jesus' lordship elsewhere – Rom. 15:6; 1 Cor. 15:24-28; 2 Cor. 1:3; 11:31; Eph. 1:3, 17; Col. 1:3; even Phil. 2:11, "Jesus Christ is Lord to the glory of God the Father")...Certainly his splitting of the creative power of God between God the Father and Christ the Lord is precisely what we find in the Wisdom writings of pre-Christian Judaism...1 Corinthians 8:6b *is not in fact a departure from Jewish monotheism*, but asserts simply that Christ is the action of God, Christ embodies the creative power of God.[21]

From the beginning of his existence Jesus was evidence of the creative power of God, reminding us of Psalm 104:30: "When you send forth your spirit they are created, and you renew the face of the earth." The procreation of the Son of God as described in detail by Matthew and Luke marks the beginning of a grand renewal still in progress.

Paul did not give up for one moment the strict monotheism of his Jewish heritage. So says one of the world's top experts on who Christ is in the New Testament. Paul, indeed, is a superb New Testament theologian, as was Jesus before him. Paul had been trained as a Jew in the top school of the day. Despite his dramatic conversion from persecutor of Jesus and murderer of Christians to passionate protagonist of Jesus, one conviction of Paul never changed. He believed to his dying day in the non-Trinitarian creed of his Jewish

---

[20]*Christology in the Making,* 179-182.
[21]Ibid., 182.

heritage. For Paul, indeed, the creed of the Hebrew Bible, the creed affirmed by Jesus Christ, was, logically enough, the *Christian* creed. Dunn expressed the point concisely: "The Jewish Scriptures were fundamental to the self-understanding of every first-century Christian church, but the focus of revelatory significance lay in the whole 'event of Christ.'"[22]

It is obvious, however, that churches are not measuring up to their cherished claim to be "going by the Bible," the principle of *sola scriptura.* They are evidently failing to meet the claim that biblical theology must "expound the theology found in the Bible in its own historical setting, and its own terms, categories and thought forms."[23] And they are failing to do this at the most fundamental level. They are not reciting and following the creed of Jesus or of Paul. Dunn says, "Traditional Christianity wants to say much more about Christ than merely to affirm the unity between the earthly Jesus and the exalted Christ."[24] Affirming that the risen Christ was first the Jesus who walked the earth hardly needs to be said, unless one balks at the New Testament accounts. It is patently obvious that the writers of the New Testament think that the risen Jesus is the Jesus who first lived on earth.

But what is this "much more" which the churches want to say about Jesus? Dunn says:

> The Church wants to say that he is "divine, the second person of the Trinity, the God-Man." A striking expression of this is the simple statement adopted by the World Council of Churches: for the participating churches the minimal Christian confession meant accepting "our Lord Jesus Christ as God and Savior."[25]

But have churches faced the fact that *Jesus* did not believe himself to be part of the Godhead? That he recited the unitarian creed of his Jewish heritage? And that he said that this was the most important key to all sound theology? Jesus summarized the attainment of eternal life as coming to know the Father as "the only one who is truly God" (John 17:3). The Father is here said to be a single Person as well as the one Person who is truly God. And this is reported by

---

[22]*Unity and Diversity in the New Testament,* SCM Press, 1977, 203.
[23]George Ladd, *A Theology of the New Testament,* Eerdmans, 1974, 25.
[24]Dunn, *Unity and Diversity,* 204.
[25]Ibid.

246 Church Councils, The Da Vinci Code and Modern Scholarship

John writing *late* in the New Testament period. Jesus' unitary statement is directly contradicted by the Trinity which states that God is three Persons in one Essence.

Have those clergy who assemble as the World Council of Churches faced the fact that Paul was as strictly monotheistic as Jesus? Well may Professor Dunn say, "It is not clear whether traditional Christology has firm roots in earliest Christianity."[26] I think the evidence is simple and overwhelming that in respect of the creed, it does not.

Dunn issues a salutary warning about reading the later creed back into the Bible in order to provide reassurance that we are following Jesus:

> We should perhaps repeat the warning given at the beginning of chapter 3 — that in trying to reach back to the beginnings of Christological thought in the first century we must *not read back the later conclusions of the classic Christological debates*; we must not assume that everywhere we will find a latent orthodoxy waiting to be brought to light; otherwise we cannot handle the New Testament material without prejudice.[27]

But just that mishandling of the New Testament goes on day after day, and has for centuries, when earnest evangelicals ransack the Bible for isolated texts (often only from John), ignoring John 17:3, to produce the "God Jesus," second member of the Trinity. It does not seem to occur to them that the creed recited and affirmed by Jesus, the creed of Israel, ought to have put to an end this exhausting and tedious effort to make Jesus believe what he did not believe — and what God Himself does not believe, that He is three Persons, nor that His uniquely begotten Son is coequally and coeternally God. God Himself has never been a Trinitarian.

Dunn's warning is particularly telling:

> He who enters the period of Christian beginnings with the classic formulations of Christian orthodoxy ringing in his ears is hardly in a position to catch the authentic tones of first-century Christian thought (should they be different). We must rather put ourselves as best we can in the position of first-

---

[26]Ibid., 205.
[27]Ibid.

century Jews with their strong tradition of monotheism and try to hear with their ears the claims of Jesus and of the first Christians.[28]

A good place to start would be to hear the "Hear, O Israel," of Jesus' own faith. Commentaries on Mark's gospel find themselves in a strange state of uncertainty and confusion when dealing with the embarrassing fact that Jesus "in his statement of the first commandment stands foursquare within the orbit of Jewish piety."[29] But why do Jesus' followers not stand in that same grand tradition of unitary monotheism modeled by Jesus? Hugh Anderson seems to make nothing of the importance of Jesus' confession here. He adds that Mark's reporting of Jesus' saying here "goes back to oral tradition passed on by a Church *that did not any longer recite the Shema.*"[30] But who said that the New Testament Church no longer recited the Shema? Anderson points out that Jesus gives us "an almost word-for-word citation of *two* Old Testament texts (Deut. 6:4-5 and Lev. 19:18)." He then says that the former text — Deuteronomy 6:4-5 defining the true God — was "at the heart of Jewish piety," and that both texts, about God and loving one's neighbor, were "much canvassed by the rabbis."[31]

On what basis can commentary declare that Mark's Church had given up on the creed of Jesus? Was not Mark an evangelist for the faith as having its source in Jesus? Can the Church afford to disregard what Jesus announced as the greatest of all the commandments? The early Church was deeply impressed by and devoted to Jesus, the rabbi and lord of the Christians. Later as the Church became loosed from its moorings in the Jewish atmosphere of Jesus, the creed of Israel was abandoned. Anderson helpfully points out that "the scribe wholly endorses what Jesus has said and adds that faithfulness to the twofold commandment 'is much more than all burnt offerings and sacrifices.'"[32]

What can be said about Paul? Did he advance beyond the precious creed of Jesus? Did Paul lead the Christian faith away from

---

[28]Ibid., 205.
[29]Hugh Anderson, *The Gospel of Mark (New Century Bible Commentary),* 280.
[30]Ibid., 280.
[31]Ibid., 281.
[32]Ibid., 282.

Jesus into belief in a God Jesus did not know? Professor Dunn was asking *the* question in 1977: "Should we then say that Jesus was confessed as *God* from earliest days in Hellenistic Christianity? That would be to claim too much."[33] Those early Christians did not teach that Jesus was God Himself, as is now required of members in Christian churches. Dunn explains:

> The emergence of a confession of Jesus in terms of divinity [he does not mean here Deity as we shall see] was largely facilitated by the extensive use of Psalm 110:1 from very early on (most clearly in Mark 12:36; Acts 2:34ff; 1 Cor. 15:25; Heb. 1:13), "The Lord says to my lord [note the lower case 'l' on lord as correctly rendering the Hebrew *adoni*], 'Sit at my right hand till I make your enemies your footstool.'"[34]

Dunn's comment is precisely to the point: "The importance of this Psalm lies in the double use of *kurios* [lord]. The one is clearly Yahweh, but who is the other?"[35] That question when answered properly will lead to a revolution in the Christian faith as we know it. So who is this at the right hand of Yahweh? "Clearly not Yahweh, but an exalted being whom the psalmist calls *kurios*. Paul calls Jesus *kurios* but seems to have marked reservations about actually calling Jesus 'God.'"[36] Reservations? How could Paul possibly imagine two Persons, both of whom are equally God?

We note now the further conclusion of Dunn about Paul's view of who Jesus was. It is likely to be embarrassing to the "received" view of Jesus as fully God. "Paul refrains from praying to Jesus. More typical of his attitude is that he prays to *God through* Christ (Rom. 1:8; 7:25; 2 Cor. 1:20; Col. 3:17). For at the same time as he affirms that 'Jesus is Lord' he also affirms 'God is one' (1 Cor. 8:4-6; Eph.

---

[33]Dunn, *Unity and Diversity*, 53.
[34]Ibid., 53.
[35]Ibid., 53.
[36]Ibid., 53. Dunn goes on to say that Rom. 9:5 is the only real candidate for the claim that Paul calls Jesus God, and even there the text is unclear. In a later work Dunn discusses this text in more detail and concludes that Paul did not call Jesus God here. The issue is one of ambiguous syntax and no certain conclusion should ever be drawn, where the text is not explicit and clear.

4:5-6)."[37] Dunn's point is straightforward, but with explosive potential to change the face of the traditional creed. Dunn goes on:
Here [in Paul] Christianity shows itself as a developed form of Judaism, with its monotheistic confession as one of the most important parts of its Jewish inheritance; for in Judaism the most fundamental confession is "God is one," "There is only one God" (Deut. 6:4). Hence also Rom. 3:30, Gal. 3:20, 1 Tim. 2:5 (cf. James 2:19). Within Palestine and the Jewish mission such an affirmation would have been unnecessary — Jew and Christian shared a belief in God's oneness. But in the Gentile mission this Jewish presupposition within Christianity would have emerged to prominence, in the face of the wider belief in "gods many." The point for us to note is that *Paul can hail Jesus as Lord, not in order to identify him with God, but rather if anything to distinguish him from the one God.*[38]

Dunn then strengthens his point by referring to another statement of Paul in 1 Corinthians 15:24-28 where Jesus is subjected to the One God. He is certainly not seen as "coequal God" as required by the traditional creed.

Dunn is quite clear that Jesus was no believer in the Trinity. "There is no good evidence that Jesus thought of himself as a preexistent being."[39] No evidence thus of Jesus making any claim to "be God." But woe betide the church member who expresses his doubt about the Deity of Jesus! How far we have come from the first-century faith of Jesus and Paul. But is anyone in the pews in any way exercised by this amazing discrepancy over the creed?

In a much later writing (1998), discussing the full range of Paul's theology, Professor Dunn concludes: "The christological reflection evident within Paul's theology is held within the bounds of his inherited monotheism. Jesus as Lord does not infringe on God as one, and even the highest accolade given to the exalted Christ is 'to the glory of God the Father'" (Phil. 2:11).[40]

---

[37]Ibid., 53.
[38]Ibid., emphasis his.
[39]Ibid., 225.
[40]*The Theology of Paul the Apostle*, Eerdmans, 1998, 265.

In a section invitingly entitled "Jesus as God?" Dunn discusses Paul's deliberate teaching about Christian monotheism as distinct from pagan belief in many gods:

> In an astonishing adaptation of the *Shema* (Deut. 6:4), Paul attributes the lordship of the one God to Jesus Christ. And yet his confession of God as one is still affirmed. Evidently the lordship of Christ was not thought of as any usurpation or replacement of God's authority, but expressive of it.[41]

Paul in fact has not given up Jewish-Christian monotheism. He has not revised it in any way. He has not contradicted or expanded the creed of Jesus himself. To have done so would have thrown his readers into hopeless confusion about who God is. Paul consistently thinks of Jesus as the Lord *Messiah,* the Lord Jesus *Christ* (Messiah), and he is the *one* Lord Jesus Messiah (1 Cor. 8:6), head of the new humanity in Christ, the firstborn of the new creation, who is kept quite distinct from the One God, the Father of monotheism.

The amazing new thing that has happened is not that the Jewish creed has been expanded to include a second Person as Deity, but that God has elevated a unique man, His Son, to the position of honor at God's right hand. God has thus demonstrated His purpose for the man Messiah, as head of the *new* creation. Jesus is still a man, however elevated. The full glory of the position of the Messiah is the theme of Paul's writing, but his theology is collapsed if it is suggested that elevating the Messiah means compromising the unique Deity of the Father — and if, after all, Jesus was from the beginning God Himself!

The glory of Paul's faith is that the Messiahship of Jesus is given its full dimensions, while the position of the One God who planned it all remains, thankfully, intact. Paul really could not have asserted his unitary monotheism more clearly: "For us there is no God but the one God, the Father" (combining 1 Cor. 8:4, 6). Jesus is God's chief agent now coordinated with the Father. Jesus is directly involved in the new creation in preparation for his coming rule in the Kingdom of God on earth.

Certainly Jesus the Messiah is uniquely associated in heaven with the Father. But the Father is still the One God, besides whom there is no other. The astounding truth to be noted is that there is now an exalted *human being* intimately associated with the One God, his

---

[41]Ibid., 253.

Father. The biblical story is thus about the staggering destiny of the virginally begotten *Son of God* and his meteoric exaltation to the second place in the universe beside the One God of Judaism and original Christianity. On the other hand, to have *God* exalted to the place of God, one God beside a second God, ruins the point of the New Testament, and deprives Jesus of his extraordinary achievement, and God of His magnificent plan to immortalize Jesus as a human, as the forerunner and pioneer of many other sons currently in process and awaiting immortality at the resurrection (not before). Jesus is indeed the firstborn amongst many brothers and sisters (Rom. 8:29). He shares with them membership of the human race.

There is a repeated formula about God and Jesus which occurs in the letters of Paul. The Apostle defines God, in strict monotheistic fashion, as "the God and Father of our Lord Jesus Christ." God is not the Father of God! God is the Father of the Lord Messiah, as the rest of the New Testament declares. Dunn points out that "even as Lord, Jesus acknowledges his Father as his God. Here it becomes plain that *kurios* [lord] is not so much a way of *identifying* Jesus with God but if anything more a way of *distinguishing* Jesus from God."[42] This truth needs to ring out amongst Bible readers and churchgoers. May the day come when the normal way of identifying the followers of Jesus will be by their deliberate distinguishing Jesus from God. Paul set the example, following Jesus and his creed. "God is the head of Christ" (1 Cor. 11:3). In 1 Corinthians 15:28 the Lord of all, the Messiah, has been *given* his lordship by God. Imagine how destructive of this amazing truth would be the idea that Jesus already had a coequal lordship with his Father from eternity. The biblical story would lose its gripping point, the dramatic career of a uniquely begotten human creature on his way to supreme exaltation at the right hand of the One God.

The Pauline teaching is that Jesus is the *man* who fulfilled the destiny originally assigned to Adam, that of ruling the world as the One God's vice-regent. This is the overarching point of New Testament Christianity, promising to other human beings the prospect of following Jesus, the pioneer human being, to glory as rulers of the future Kingdom on earth (Matt. 19:28; 1 Cor. 6:2; Rev. 2:26; 3:21, etc.). This is the theme of the much neglected Christian Gospel *of the*

---

[42]Dunn, *Unity and Diversity*, 53.

Kingdom of God, preached as the central saving message by Jesus, and by Paul following the orders of Jesus in the Great Commission (Luke 4:43; 8:1; Acts 19:8; 20:24-25; 28:23, 31, etc.)

What then of the Yahweh texts applied to Jesus? Dunn has the obvious answer:

> The only obvious resolution of the tension set up by Paul's talk of Jesus as Lord [Is there in fact any tension here, except the problem caused by the confusing *later* views of Jesus as Lord *God*?] is to follow the logic suggested by his reference to Yahweh texts to Jesus. That is, that Jesus' lordship is a status granted by God, a sharing in his authority. It is not that God has stepped aside and Jesus has taken over. It is rather that God shared His lordship with Christ, without it ceasing to be God's alone.[43]

The marvelous truth of the Bible's story is the sharing of the glory of the One God with His chosen creature and creatures. Not the sharing of God with God, which would cause a breach in the fundamental monotheism of the Bible, so evidently held to by Jesus and Paul.

To make Paul the proponent of a revision of the creed of Israel is to pit Paul against Jesus and both against the creed of Israel. No such suggestion is in the minds of the canonical writers. No theory of progressive revelation as might be applied to the issue of the works of the law under the New Covenant, is thinkable in the case of the definition of God. Paul is from start to finish a unitary monotheist, just as Jesus was. God is "the God of our fathers" (Acts 24:14), and the same God of the Jews is the God of the Gentiles (Rom. 3:29).

---

[43]Dunn, *Theology of Paul,* 254.

Chapter 9

Detective Work
and Word Tricks

"It might tend to promote moderation, and, in the end, agreement, if we were industrious on all occasions to represent our own doctrine [the Trinity] as *wholly unintelligible*."[1]

"In the first place it should be noted that John is as undeviating a witness as any in the New Testament to the fundamental tenet of Judaism, of unitary monotheism (cf. Rom. 3:30; James 2:19). There is the one, true and only God (John 5:44; 17:3): everything else is idols (1 John 5:21). In fact nowhere is the Jewishness of John, which has emerged in all recent study, more clear."[2]

The Bible should be thought of in some sense as a crime scene. Unknown to much of the churchgoing public, who generally do not read the documents in their original Hebrew and Greek, a powerful and unfair bias is at work in some translations. (We provided an example in our discussion of the word "worship" in chapter five). Translation can be the subtlest form of interpretation. The text has sometimes been made to say what — according to "orthodox" views of God and Jesus and salvation — it *ought* to say in the light of *later* theology. There has been an unconscious attempt by those holding the majority opinion to buttress the text of Scripture with supports for "correct" doctrines. But there has been also a steady barrage of

---

[1]Dr. John Hey, cited in John Wilson, *Unitarian Principles Confirmed,* 322.
[2]J.A.T Robinson, "The Fourth Gospel and the Church's Doctrine of the Trinity," in *Twelve More New Testament Studies*, 175.

challenges from opponents that in fact "orthodoxy" may not be quite what it claims. The objections raised against the majority opinions have a long history. Complaint that the New Testament is misrepresented in church is nothing new.[3]

The sophistication of modern Bible study and the flood of easily obtainable information via Internet help inquirers discover the clear tendency for the "orthodox" to make the Bible, wherever possible, conform to post-biblical theology.[4] Rather than admit that the faith from the second century took a turn for the worse, as philosophically trained Greeks became in some sense Christian, bringing with them their philosophical presuppositions, the "orthodox" insist on tracing the "right views" through a continuous line back to the Bible itself.

A little detective work will reveal some startling facts about what has been going on. John's gospel has been used to force the rest of the Bible, against the grain of the Scripture taken as a whole, into the later theology of the church councils. John 8:58,[5] for example, has been used to promote the idea, absent from the rest of the New Testament, that Jesus is equal in every sense with God and preexisted as the "eternal God the Son." A heavy concentration on John is then supported by a few verses in Paul. The synoptic gospels — Matthew, Mark and Luke — are not treated as primary data for finding out

---

[3]Desmond Ford in his extensive inquiry into Jesus' Olivet Discourse noted that "F.W. Farrar has written at length to prove that the history of exegesis is a history of error, and if black and white really mean different things, then the statistics are in favor of the one-time dean of Canterbury" (*The Abomination of Desolation in Biblical Eschatology*, University Press of America, 1979, 6).
[4]For a penetrating account of how the Greek manuscripts were manipulated, in some verses, to suit the needs of later orthodoxy, we recommend Bart Ehrman's *The Orthodox Corruption of Scripture*.
[5]Where Jesus states that "I am he [the Messiah] before Abraham came to be," or as it reads equally well in the Greek "before Abraham comes to be." If so translated (the Greek is ambiguous) Jesus makes the claim to be prior to Abraham in the resurrection. If Jesus means before Abraham's birth he is the Messiah, this would be very similar to the text in Rev. 13:8 that Jesus was crucified before the foundation of the world, that is, in God's foreordained purpose (see 1 Pet. 1:20). Jesus is indeed prior to Abraham in the resurrection. Job expected to come into existence again in the resurrection (Job 14:14: "If a man dies will he live again? I will wait until I begin to exist again," *palin genomai*, LXX).

about God and Jesus. John is twisted and a distorted version of John is then read back into the rest of the Bible. John has been made the main support for the later theology of God as more than one Person, and Jesus as not originally human.

What gets forgotten in all the quotations from John is that "John is as undeviating a witness as any in the New Testament to the fundamental tenet of Judaism, of unitary monotheism...(John 5:44; 17:3)."[6] These texts in John ought to have provided a solid barrier against any watering down, modification, or "expansion" of Jesus' own creedal statements. Unfortunately John's and Jesus' unitary monotheism has been swamped by texts marshaled from the same John and used against him, to contradict him and Jesus — and to contradict the lucidly straightforward and detailed account of Jesus the Son of God's origin and thus who he really is.

The Accumulative Effect of Language About God

It is an uphill struggle indeed to find in Scripture the doctrine that both "Jesus is God" and "the Father is God" when God is thousands and thousands of times defined by singular personal pronouns (I, You singular, Me, He, and Him). Single personal pronouns, if one is following the historical grammatical method of interpretation claimed by evangelicals, or indeed if one is using normal common sense, denote a single Person. The word "I" used constantly for God means a single, distinct personal self. God is so described constantly. Jesus is equally "I" as a separate and distinct personality,[7] as are all sons in relation to their fathers. Jesus speaks of his Father and himself

---

[6]J.A.T. Robinson, "The Fourth Gospel and the Church's Doctrine of the Trinity," in *Twelve More New Testament Studies*, 175.
[7]The idea that the Father and the Son are the *same person* (held by Oneness Pentecostals) would equally overthrow the use of singular pronouns for the Father and the Son, who speak to each other as "I" and "You," and who are collectively known as "we" and "us." The Oneness Pentecostal position is expressed like this: "If there is only one God and that God is the Father (Mal. 2:10), and if Jesus is God, then it logically follows that Jesus is the Father" (David Bernard, *The Oneness of God*, cited by Gregory Boyd, *Oneness Pentecostals and the Trinity*, 28). The "logic" fails because Jesus is never said to be the one and only God, or "the true God." And it really ought to be obvious that a father and a son are not the same person. The power of denominational dogma to befuddle its adherents at the most elementary level is truly amazing.

together as "we" and "us" (John 14:23; 17:21). His Father is an additional individual witness to what he, Jesus, says (John 8:17-18).

The emphatic assertions of God in the Bible, that He is one single Person claiming the unique position of Deity, constantly rule out all contrary views which might make Him more than One: "I am the LORD and there is no other; there is no God besides Me" (Isa. 45:5). "You alone are God" (Isa. 37:16; Ps. 86:10). "I am the Lord, and there is no other" (Isa. 45:6). "I, the LORD, besides whom there is no other God. There is no just and saving God but Me" (Isa. 45:21). "You are the only true God" (John 17:3). The Bible exhausts language in its effort to inform the reader that there is one single God and that He is a single divine individual. No one has any difficulty identifying Elijah as a single human person: "I, even I only, am left" (1 Kings 19:14). Precisely the same language presents God as a single individual. But the simplicity of the Bible's unitarian theology has become a nightmare of complexity under the pressure of later Greek philosophically driven theology.

Not one of the twelve thousand appearances of the words for God in the Bible can be shown to mean a triune God, or a tri-personal God. The Trinity as "God" is never so named in the Bible. Neither the word Trinity, nor the slightest hint that God is three equal, eternal Persons appears in any of Scripture's thirty-one thousand verses. Father, Son and their holy spirit are mentioned together frequently in the New Testament. Only indoctrination from later times compels readers to leap to the assumption that all "three" compose the One God. Paul, when he makes creedal statements, associates God and Jesus in a relationship of God and man. "There is one God and one mediator between God and men, *the man* Messiah Jesus" (1 Tim. 2:5). The Lord Messiah is still a human person as distinct from the One God, his Father.

The obvious fact that New Testament writers mean the Father when they say God (over 1300 times) has forced some commentators into the strange position of claiming that "Father" sometimes refers to the whole Trinity! Each of the more than 1300 references to God (*theos*) as Father is a testimony to the unitarian creed of Scripture. This has been a problem for commentators who expect to find the theology of church councils in Scripture.

Forcing the Trinity on the Biblical Text

Thus Stuart Olyott in *The Three Are One* cites Paul's unitarian statement, "But to us there is but one God, the Father" (1 Cor. 8:6). He comments, "Here the word 'Father' equals the words 'one God.' Paul is saying that there is but one God, and is not thinking of the Persons of the Godhead at all...The title 'Father' is used of God, *but not of a distinct Person in the Godhead*."[8] His desire to justify his Trinitarianism in Scripture forces him to read "Father" as not one of the Persons, but as the whole triune Godhead. Apparently the constant equation in the New Testament of God with the Father does not convince him of the Bible's unitary monotheism. The pressure of loyalty to "the system" makes objectivity impossible.

With the enormous evidence for Jewish-Christian monotheism against them, Trinitarians have been driven to assemble whatever "proof-texts" they can to support them. Sometimes they are assisted by texts which have been manipulated, in the original Greek, in favor of the Trinity. The history of the transmission of the Greek manuscripts from early centuries to our present time is most revealing. It shows some blatant cases of "fiddling" the Greek text to insert the idea that God is three and that the Son of God is actually God.

The King James Version of the Bible contains a passage in 1 John 5:7 which is now universally recognized as a forgery. It was added to the manuscripts as a Trinitarian proof text and was included almost as an accident in the Authorized Version of 1611. The notes in any modern study Bible will provide the reader with the necessary information about its absence from the original. Bruce Metzger concluded, "That these words are spurious and have no right to stand in the New Testament is certain."[9] Another example of a text which was altered is 1 Timothy 3:16. This verse reads in the KJV: "*God* was manifested in the flesh." Modern versions have corrected the word "God" to "He who." The alteration of an original "He who" (in Greek Ος) was very sneakily accomplished when some scribes changed the Ο (omicron) into a θ (theta) giving θς (theta sigma). The reading THS was an abbreviated form of the Greek word *theos*, God. All that had

---

[8]Stuart Olyott, *The Three Are One*, Evangelical Press, 1979, 29.
[9]*A Textual Commentary on the Greek New Testament*, United Bible Societies, 1971, 715.

to be done was to draw a little line across the middle of the O to produce the Greek letter theta (θ). Then the text was made to sound Trinitarian and to support the Incarnation: *"God* was manifested in the flesh." "He who" (Ος) was made to read "God" (θς).

1 John 5:20 ("And we are in Him who is true, in His Son Jesus Christ. This is the true God and eternal life") is held by some commentators to be an indication that Jesus is God. Since this would overthrow the unitarian creed of Jesus, many other commentators, both evangelicals and liberals, recognize the reference to "the true God" as a title for the Father of Jesus. The verse is then an echo of John 17:3 where Jesus carefully distinguishes the "only true God" (the Father) from himself the Messiah. In 1 John 5:20 we are in Him who is true by being in His Son Jesus Christ. It is the Father who is this one true God, as Jesus had said in John 17:3.[10] We are in union with the one God, the Father, by being in harmony with His unique and human Son.

An attempt was made by copyists to obscure the begetting (coming into existence) of the Son of God in 1 John 5:18. John speaks of Jesus as "the one who was begotten," using the aorist tense of the verb which indicates a point of time in the past. The begetting of the Son would be an obvious contradiction of the Trinitarian concept that the Son has always existed. Some Greek manuscripts reflect an attempt to evade the origin of the Son as begotten in time. They changed the "him" in the sentence "the one begotten from God keeps *him,*" to "himself," thus avoiding the reference to *Jesus* as the one "begotten" and who now preserves the Christian. The text was manipulated to give the odd sense that the Christian preserves *himself.* Again, Metzger prefers the more obvious reading: "The committee understood 'the one begotten' to refer to Christ."[11] This verse is particularly important, since it shows John to be in perfect agreement with Luke and Matthew who likewise speak of the begetting of the Son in history, in the womb of his mother (Luke 1:35; Matt. 1:1, 18, 20).

---

[10]The pronoun "this" in John's epistle does not always refer to the nearest noun, for example see 1 John 2:22; 2 John 7. See the strong confirmation of our point of view candidly admitted by Trinitarian expositor Henry Alford in his commentary on the Greek Testament. See also his good analysis of the corruption of 1 Tim. 3:16.

[11]*A Textual Commentary on the Greek New Testament,* 718.

John knew the synoptic gospels and very probably referred to the virgin birth in John 1:13, where there is very ancient and widespread evidence that the verb "begotten" should be *singular* as a reference to *Jesus* who was not begotten of "bloods nor the will of the flesh nor the will of a man." The Jerusalem Bible of 1968 chooses this version of John 1:12-13: "But to all who did accept him [Jesus] he gave power to become the children of God, to all who believe in the name of him, who was not born out of human stock or urge of the flesh or the will of man, but of God Himself." Jesus was of course born from Mary and so in this sense was very much of human stock, being the direct descendant of David. He was not however born of "bloods" (as the Greek reads), the mixing of the blood of two human parents. He was not born of the will of man or urge of the flesh, but directly by God's intervention.

Tertullian accused the Gnostics of having altered the Greek text to avoid a reference to the virgin birth in John 1:13, and this may well be so. Even if the verb is taken as plural ("who were born"), referring to Christian rebirth, there is a parallel between our rebirth and the miraculous begetting of Jesus the Son.

There are one or two further verses where Trinitarians think they have found references to Jesus as God. The 1317 references to the Father of Jesus as "God" seem not to persuade them that the Father alone is God. In the very few verses alleged to be references to Jesus as "God," there is a grammatical ambiguity which makes a decision about who is being called God quite uncertain. An occasional use of "God" for Jesus, in a secondary sense, would anyway not overthrow the massive and consistent biblical use of "God" for the Father alone.

Certainly the creed should be established on the overwhelming and unambiguous evidence for God as a single Person *across the whole range of Scripture*. To base creeds on grammatically ambiguous texts is very unwise. We may say with certainty that Jesus is called "God" twice, in Hebrews 1:8 and John 20:28. The few other passages cannot be produced as firm evidence. Titus 2:13 is an example of a text often advanced by evangelicals as clear, when in fact translations differ in a striking way. The translation of the KJV may well be correct: Christians are "looking for that blessed hope, and the glorious appearing of the great God and our Savior Jesus Christ."[12]

Jesus is not called "God" here. As Nigel Turner remarked, "Sometimes the definite article is not repeated even when there is clearly a separation of idea."[13] In this verse God and Jesus are clearly separated and there was no need for the definite article to be repeated to ensure that separation.

There is certainly no Trinity in Isaiah 48:14-16. Note the punctuation in the RSV:

> "Assemble, all of you, and hear! Who among them has declared these things? The LORD loves him; he shall perform his purpose on Babylon, and his arm shall be against the Chaldeans. I, even I [the LORD God], have spoken and called him, I have brought him [the Messiah], and he will prosper in his way. Draw near to me, hear this: from the beginning I have not spoken in secret, from the time it came to be I have been there." And now the Lord GOD has sent me and his Spirit.

Note carefully that the RSV closes the quotation marks after "I have been there." A new speaker then says, "And now the Lord GOD has sent me and his Spirit." The Messiah, or perhaps the prophet, is here represented as being sent by the LORD (God). The vast majority of Trinitarian scholars would never advance this passage as any evidence for the Trinity. It is incredible that our understanding of who God is should be based on a grammatical quibble.

Beget Means Beget

Evidence for the extraordinary lengths Trinitarians have gone to justify a post-biblical creed is seen when the word "beget" is deprived of its actual meaning and given a new "theological" meaning not recognized by any lexicon.[14] This expedient shows how persistently

---

[12]Cf. Matt. 16:27, where Jesus comes in the glory of his Father.

[13]*Grammatical Insights into the New Testament*, T & T Clark, 1965, 16. Note the typo in the text: the word "not" was omitted in the edition of 1965. Famous Trinitarian commentator Henry Alford also does not think that Jesus is called "God" in this verse.

[14]In genealogies it is possible for "beget" occasionally to be equivalent of "to become the father of" in a *legal* rather than biological sense. Matt. 1:12 speaks of Shealtiel as begetting Zerubbabel. In fact Shealtiel was his uncle.

tradition tries to overwhelm and suppress the sense of simple biblical terminology. Psalm 2:7 declares that God has begotten His Son: "You are My Son; today I have begotten you." It is a divine oracle pointing us to the subsequent appearance of His unique Son, the Messiah. Since to beget means to bring into existence, to originate,[15] how is this to be reconciled with the dogmatic view that the Son has no beginning and is eternal? The problem was acute since in this text not only is the Son begotten, he is begotten "today." This verse was applied to Jesus' birth in Acts 13:33: God "raised up Jesus."[16] Acts 13:34 by contrast refers to the resurrection (see also Heb. 1:5; 5:5; cf. 1 John 5:18, not KJV).

The architects of the Trinity showed extraordinary ingenuity as they worked their way around the "problem." It was argued that when God "begets" it must be an event outside time, since God is eternal. Furthermore, with God all time is the same, so when He says "today," He must mean "the eternal day which has no beginning nor end." But this is to engage in the demolition of words and communication. Olyott whom we cited earlier writes, "The Son owes His generation to the Father," and then, destroying the word "generate," states, "This relationship of the Son to the Father did not have a beginning."[17]

The point we are making in this book revolves around how many uncreated eternal Persons there are in the universe. Since the post-biblical Church decided on three Persons in the Godhead, the origin of the person of Jesus was an embarrassment. The Son after all was begotten. The word beget had a perfectly easy meaning: to originate, to procreate, to cause to come into existence. Moreover the Son was

---

Zerubbabel was considered his son legally. But "beget" used of Jesus does not appear in that sense, of course. And one who is begotten is by definition not as old as the one who begets him!

[15]The word retains its meaning as originate, produce, whether used literally of persons being begotten, or in metaphorical ways such as a prophet "producing children" as disciples.

[16]Not "raised up Jesus *again*," as mistranslated in the KJV. The error was corrected by the RV of 1881. The KJV prevents us from seeing that the *begetting* of Jesus as Son was at his birth, as Luke 1:35 and Matt. 1:18, 20 say. F.F. Bruce emphasizes the fact that the "raising up" of verse 33 refers not to the resurrection of Jesus but to his origin at birth (*Commentary on the Greek Text of the Acts of the Apostles*, Eerdmans, 1975, 269, 270.)

[17]*The Three Are One*, 65, 67.

clearly begotten *in time* and on a specific day: "You are My Son: *Today* I have begotten you" (Ps. 2:7). Christianity is firstly a religion rooted in history. The Jesus story is both God's and ours, and it is set within time. Its major events occur on specific days and at specified times. In Old Testament Scripture, the Son was *promised* for a time in the future, meaning that he was not yet in existence. The coming of the Son, as a descendant of King David, was guaranteed in God's program and according to His own timing. But this is untrue of the very philosophically oriented doctrine of God and of the Son inherited from the church councils.

The critically important biblical statements about how and when God begat, i.e., brought into existence, His own Son, cannot be reconciled with a Son of God who had no beginning. But without such an eternal, "beginningless" Son there can be no Trinity as handed down from Nicea.

What was to be done? "Church-speak" came to the rescue and the "offensive" words were given new definitions unknown to dictionaries or lexicons. The words of the Bible relevant to the origin of the Son of God were simply emptied of their actual significance. The task of explaining the novel meanings for biblical words and giving them a theological "spin" was assigned to the learned clergy. They became guardians of these esoteric, non-normal meanings. The ordinary public, understanding words in their dictionary sense, was thought to be incompetent to judge the "higher sense" conferred on words by the educated ecclesiastical leaders. And the results of this obfuscation of plain words remain with us to this day. Sometimes enquiring church-members are urged not to trouble their heads with "theological" issues best left to the "experts."

In contradiction to their claim that in the case of the Son of God "beget cannot mean beget," the same scholars inconsistently continued to say that they believed in the grammatical method of interpretation, by which words are to be given their normal lexical meaning. But what lexicon or dictionary will support the claim that "beget" does not mean "to cause to exist, to produce" or that "today" means "in a timeless eternity"? The evidence for this sabotaging of the Bible in the name of Christianity is available for all to inspect.

The point is exposed clearly in Professor Donald Macleod's work on *The Person of Christ*. In his section on "Eternal Generation," he tells us that this idea "figures prominently in the statements of the

Nicene fathers and their successors."[18] Then this amazing admission: "But it is far from clear what content, if any, we can impart to the concept."[19] There may then be no meaning to the phrase which dominates so much discussion of the Trinity — no meaning indeed to the term on which the Trinity is so largely dependent.

Macleod feels the need to cover his uncertainty. Eternal generation:

> is revealed, but it is revealed as a mystery, and the writings of the fathers abound with protestations of inevitable ignorance on the matter. Athanasius, for example, writes: "nor again is it right to seek...how God begets, and what is the manner of his begetting. For a man must be beside himself to venture on such points; since a thing ineffable and proper to God's nature, and known to him alone and the Son, this he demands to be explained in words...It is better in perplexity to be silent and believe, than to disbelieve on account of perplexity."[20]

This is a sort of "no-go" warning, a "hands off" admonition. Don't look too carefully at the word "beget." It has a special non-meaning when applied to the mysterious workings of the Deity and the Trinity. Such was the impression conveyed to the laity. While the Trinity was required as a necessary belief for salvation, its meaning could not and should not be probed in detail, since it was declared to be a "mystery." It required unrecognizable meanings for key words. According to one popular source it can be apprehended but not comprehended.

Some modern examinations of the Trinity are refreshingly candid. One has to read them carefully to see how in fact they really undermine the tradition they hope to support. Millard Erickson almost gives up the unequal struggle over the impossible notion of "eternal begetting" when he concedes: "The begetting passages [in the New Testament] should be seen as referring to the earthly residence of Jesus, rather than some continuous generation by the Father."[21]

---

[18]Donald Macleod, *The Person of Christ*, Intervarsity Press, 1998, 131.
[19]Ibid., 131. Leonard Hodgson lecturing on the Trinity noted that Augustine's "repeated assertion that in God each attribute *is* all the others, I find quite unintelligible" (*The Doctrine of the Trinity*, Charles Scribner's Sons, 1944, 151).
[20]Macleod, *Person of Christ*, 131.
[21]*Making Sense of the Trinity*, Baker Books, 2000, 86.

Without the doctrine of the "eternal begetting" of the Son, the Trinity collapses. A strong protest must be raised on the basis of Scripture and the grammatical historical method by which it is to be read. Athanasius' and Gregory Nazianzen's argument for "eternal generation" is founded on a completely unknown sense of a well-defined Greek word. Macleod ventures to explain the church fathers' point of view with this astonishing sentence: He says that for the architects of the dogma about the Son, "To beget does not mean to originate."[22]

I suggest that all the confusion over who God and Jesus are is derived from that amazing proposition. A "Humpty Dumpty" approach to words has taken over, and deprived us of access to precious truth. It was Humpty Dumpty who declared that words mean exactly what he chooses them to mean.[23]

In any dictionary of Greek or English one finds immediately that to "originate" means to "generate" and to "generate" is to "beget," to "bring into existence." But the meaning of the word "beget" had to be disposed of, lest the *origin* of the Son of God become clear. A later Catholic spokesman for the Church, John of Damascus, spoke of the everlasting God who "generates...without beginning...that God, Whose nature and existence are above time, *may not engender* in time."[24] But this is to tell God what He may not do. On this argument the Son simply *is*, without any hint of becoming. In the words of church father Gregory Nazianzen, the Son is "unoriginatedly begotten."[25] The Son, then, in view of the actual meaning of these words, has a "beginningless beginning." No wonder, as Macleod comments, "That question [about generation] drove Gregory of Nazianzen almost to apoplexy. The truth is, we are lost. We know that the Son is distinguished by the fact that he is begotten, but we do not know what *begotten* is."[26]

But we do! Matthew and Luke explained it very adequately. And we can find our way again when we abandon the maze of confusing

---

[22]Macleod, *Person of Christ*, 132.
[23]"'When *I* use a word,' Humpty Dumpty said in rather a scornful tone, 'it means just what I choose it to mean — neither more nor less'" (Lewis Carroll, *Through the Looking-Glass*, HarperCollins, 2003, 88).
[24]Cited in Macleod, *Person of Christ*, 133.
[25]Ibid., 133.
[26]Ibid., 137-138.

terminology[27] which swamped the plain use of "beget" in Scripture. Once we acknowledge the revealed words of Scripture and cease trying to get rid of them, all will be clear. Luke and Matthew take the greatest trouble to tell us in detail about the begetting of the Son. The Son is linked, step by step, by a 42-stage process of generation or lineal descent from Abraham through David.[28] Matthew tells us that he is giving us the facts about "the *genesis* of Jesus Christ" (Matt. 1:1). The central hero of the Christian faith is introduced by the opening verse of the New Testament as "Jesus Christ, son of David and Abraham." 1 John 5:18 also speaks of Jesus as "the one who was begotten" — the aorist indicates a point of time in the past — and there is not a hint that John was perplexed about the meaning of the word "beget." It means that the Son was brought into existence, not transferred from one form of existence to another. The Son is according to John the uniquely-begotten Son. His origin is one of a kind. It was a begetting or procreation derived directly from the Father's intervention.

The whole problem can be reduced to this: According to the church fathers generation cannot mean origination. Macleod admits the obvious, that "in human generation, of course, it does, but in *divine* generation it does not."[29] But what is this arbitrary disallowing of plain language? Is God not able to work in His own creation and by biological miracle procreate, beget, engender through His Spirit the second Adam, the head of the new creation, the Son of God? Did not Paul speak of Adam as the "type" of the one to come? (Rom. 5:14). The whole concept of "eternal generation," "beginningless beginning" is a mythical construct unwarranted by the text of the Bible or by any lexical definition of words. It involves hijacking the proper meaning of words. Language has been bludgeoned to death. The results suffered by church members and their leaders have been chaotic and confusing.

---

[27]Some Trinitarian church fathers were nervous about the introduction of the word *homoousios*, "of the same essence." They recognized the dangers of importing unbiblical terminology.
[28]See Matt. 1:17.
[29]Macleod, *Person of Christ,* 132.

Dr. John MacArthur

An unfortunate retreat into misunderstanding of the word "beget" occurred when commentator and evangelist John MacArthur decided to adopt a view of generation which in earlier years he had seen as impossible. MacArthur had agreed with a number of prominent Protestants that "beget" means to bring into existence and that "eternal begetting" was a simple contradiction. In his commentary on Hebrews, written in 1983, he had supported the view that there was no Son of God until the birth of Jesus.[30] Abandoning his earlier realistic view of the meaning of words, MacArthur later wrote:

> It is now my conviction that the begetting spoken of in Psalm 2 and Hebrews 1 is not an event that takes place in time...[Christ] had no beginning but is as timeless as God Himself. Therefore, the "begetting" mentioned in Psalm 2 and its cross-references has nothing to do with his *origin*.[31]

The word "beget" has been conveniently dissolved into nothing, under the pressure of "orthodoxy." "Beget" is one of those fixed terms which point to the beginning of existence. The Bible was tragically overwhelmed by philosophy and the grammatical method had to be abandoned. The human Jesus was obscured.

Amazing Attempts to Avoid a Begetting of the Son in Time

This issue of "eternal generation" drove some evangelicals to extraordinary lengths. George Zeller and Renald Showers in *The Eternal Sonship of Christ: A Timely Defense of This Vital Biblical Doctrine* admit that the word "beget" is used a great number of times in the Old Testament, "both in the simple (*qal*) and in the causative (*hiphil*) conjugations in the ordinary sense of to generate, or to beget, just as anyone familiar with the content of the Old Testament would expect. It appears twenty-eight times in the fifth chapter of Genesis alone in this ordinary sense."[32]

At this point in their discussion a remarkable example of "unfair play" occurs. The authors would prefer that the *causative* form of the verb appear in the text of Psalm 2:7 ("This day I have begotten you").

---

[30]He wrote that the "today" of Hebrews 1:5 "shows that His sonship began in a point of time, not in eternity. His life as Son began in this world" (*The MacArthur New Testament Commentary: Hebrews*, Moody, 1983, 28).
[31]"Reexamining the Eternal Sonship of Christ," www.gty.org/resources.php
[32]Loizeaux Brothers, 1993, 106.

It would be easier, in other words, for them to dispense with its obvious meaning by claiming that in the causative form, it might just mean "to *declare* sonship" rather than to bring it into existence. The problem for these Trinitarian authors was that allowing for a *beginning* of Sonship would destroy at a stroke the doctrine of the eternal Son and thus the Trinity. If we could simply render the text in Psalm 2:7, "I have *declared* your sonship," this would "remove [from the verb], of course, any necessary reference to beginnings."[33]

They then make a curious technical blunder. They say that one could change the verb from the simple to the causative form *without changing any of the Hebrew consonants*, just altering the vowels. The facts are wrong. The causative form of the verb would indeed require a consonantal alteration, not only just a change of the vowels. In either case the sacred text would have to be tampered with. Undaunted, the authors, after much struggle, conclude that "begotten" in the case of Jesus means that he is the *ungenerated*, cocqual Son of the Father. "To generate," in other words, does not mean to generate. It means "not to generate"!

What is most remarkable about this attempt to get rid of unwanted information is that even if one changes the Hebrew verb from one form to another, it *does not* alter the plain sense of "beget" in Hebrew. If one altered the text to a *hiphil* form of "beget," the meaning of the verb is still "to beget," to "bring into existence," which on the Trinitarian theory of the "eternal Son" is impossible. Both the *qal* and *hiphil* forms of *yalad* in the Hebrew Bible mean to beget.

I cite this example merely to show how, rather than releasing a cherished traditional theory about an unoriginated Son, scholars who otherwise hold Scripture in high regard would rather sacrifice principles of integrity than abandon what is only a tradition. It is refreshing to return to the work of other modern scholars who are not resisting the text in support of a long-held dogma originating in the centuries following the writing of the New Testament.

James Dunn brings us back to reality and plain good sense with his observation that Matthew's and Luke's birth narratives portray the virginal conception as:

---

[33]Ibid., 107.

Jesus' *origin*, as the *begetting* (= becoming) of Jesus to be
God's Son...It is a begetting, a becoming which is in view,
the coming into existence of one who will be called, and will
in fact be the Son of God, not the transition of a pre-existent
being to become the soul of a human baby or the
metamorphosis of a divine being into a human fetus.[34]
"Orthodoxy" leaves us bewildered when we are told that
"Christ's birth is *not* the origin of his personality, but only its entrance
in the conditions of human life." This leads to the strange idea that
Christ "could not be quite passive in the moment of conception as we
are...he could not come in this way into existence, but because he
previously existed, *his conception was his own deed*. He assumed
consciously and freely our human nature."[35]

But the biblical accounts of the origin of Jesus leave no room at
all for this extraordinary teaching that Jesus was responsible for his
own conception. Fortunately the same authority admits that Matthew
and Luke "say nothing about Christ's preexistence, but speak *as if* he
first began to be at his birth in Bethlehem."[36] That is exactly right. But
they do not just speak "as if" these are the facts. They declare the
actual facts about the all-important origin of Jesus. They provide thus
a plain definition of who he is. The beginning of the Son's existence
is an historical event marked by his conception/begetting. And
Matthew and Luke composed their gospels *after* Paul wrote his
epistles. This is very strong evidence that neither the gospels nor Paul
thought of Jesus as alive before his birth. The New Testament is
unified in its testimony to the human Messiah. It is in the highest
degree improbable that Luke and Paul did not agree on who Jesus
was.

---

[34]*Christology in the Making*, 50-51. Raymond Brown is equally candid and
fair in his treatment of the birth narratives of Matthew and Luke. He makes
no attempt to equate "orthodoxy" with the views of these writers of
Scripture. See his *The Birth of the Messiah*. He repeatedly tells us that
Matthew and Luke have no doctrine of Incarnation.
[35]James Orr, D.D., *The Virgin Birth of Christ*, Charles Scribner's Sons, 1912,
215, 278.
[36]Ibid., 208, 209.

Getting Rid of Unwanted Biblical Words

The begetting of the Son was the subject of a grand prophetic utterance in Psalm 2:7. For what later became "orthodoxy" the begetting of the Son was an impossible concept. The word "beget" had to be eliminated by a drastic denial of its actual meaning. The begetting of the Son was pronounced by the "fathers" to be timeless. But far from being a timeless event, which is anyway impossible if the word "beget" is to retain its meaning, God's action in Psalm 2:7 was to happen "today." The church fathers and later Luther, and many who have followed him, seemed to have no qualms about voiding the term "today" and "beget" of their clear import.

Celebrated church father Origen disposed of the awkward information about the origin of the Son of God:

"You are My Son; this day I have begotten you." This is spoken to him by God with whom all time is today, for there is no evening with God, as I consider, and there is no morning, nothing but time that stretches out, along with His unbeginning and unseen life. The day is today with Him [God] in which the Son was begotten and thus the beginning of his birth is not found, as neither is the day of it.[37]

Augustine, on whom much of our Western theology is built, gets rid of the concept of the begetting or coming into existence of the Son with the same arbitrary treatment of the biblical text. What is he to do with the awkward fact that the Son of God begins to exist on a certain day? He comments on Psalm 2:7:

Although that day may also seem to be prophetically spoken of, on which Jesus Christ was born according to the flesh; and in eternity there is nothing past as if it had ceased to be, nor future as if it were not yet, but present only, since whatever is eternal, always is; yet as "today" intimates presentiality, a divine interpretation is given to that expression, "Today I have begotten you," whereby the uncorrupt and Catholic faith proclaims the eternal generation of the power and Wisdom of God, who is the only-begotten Son.[38]

The Protestant Smith's *Bible Dictionary* under "Son of God" asks us to believe, after correctly defining Son of God as Messiah, that:

---

[37]*Commentary on John*, 1. 32.
[38]*Expositions on the Psalms.*

in *a still higher sense,* that title is applied by God to His only Son, begotten by eternal generation (see Ps. 2:7), as interpreted in the Epistle to the Hebrews (1:5; 5:5), the word 'today,' in that passage, being expressive of the act of God, *with whom is no yesterday, nor tomorrow.*[39]

Luther is quoted in support: "In eternity, there is no past and no future, but a perpetual today." Luther's uncritical copying of the church fathers, especially Origen, on this doctrine points to how far the Reformation was merely partial.

In the third century Origen had claimed that God begat His Son by an "eternal generation." He warns us against any ordinary understanding of the word "beget." Human thought cannot apprehend how the unbegotten God becomes the Father of the only-begotten Son. He calls the generation of the Son "eternal" and "endless."

Other church fathers remain agnostic about the generation of the Son. Irenaeus "admits he does not understand how the Son is 'produced' from the Father."[40] He speaks of the event being "ineffable" and reduces the word "beget" to the existence of an attribute of God. Or perhaps the begetting of the Son is an "emitting of a material substance." Later theologians shied away from this model as suggesting, as it obviously does, a beginning in time.

The Hebrew for "today" occurs some 350 times in the Old Testament and has nothing to do with eternity. The precious text "Today I have caused you to come into existence as Son" (Ps. 2:7) has been sacrificed to the requirements of a post-biblical dogma which denied that the Son of God had a beginning in time. Thus the Messianic son of David and of God (Luke 1:32-35) was turned into a second member of an eternal Godhead. The Messiah of Scripture promised as the offspring of David and thus of the tribe of Judah was replaced by a strange visitor from outside the human race.

C.S. Lewis

As for "the eternal begetting of the Son," in our own time theology has had to indulge in much "waffly" language to avoid the obvious fact that in the Bible the Son is begotten by a miracle in Mary. "Imagine," says C.S. Lewis, "two books lying on a table one

---

[39]London: John Murray, 1893, 3:1355.
[40]Roger Olson and Christopher Hall, *The Trinity,* Eerdmans, 2002, 27.

on top of the other...for ever and ever."[41] Such, he says, is the "eternal begetting" of the Son. There has been an everlasting *relationship* between the two. By this learned "spin" Lewis avoided the word "beget":

Lewis also tackled an explanation of what is commonly called "the eternal generation of the Son." He wrote: "One of the creeds says that Christ is the Son of God 'begotten, not created'...[which] has nothing to do with the fact that when Christ was born on earth as a man, that man was the son of a virgin." Rather, "what God begets is God." This negative explanation clarifies somewhat but is not overly helpful. Elsewhere he penned that "the one begets and the other is begotten. The Father's relation to the Son is not the same as the Son's relation to the Father." Christ as "Son," Lewis observed, "cannot mean that he stands to God [the Father] in the very same physical and temporal relation which exists between offspring and male parent in the animal world"; this doctrine involves "a harmonious relation involving homogeneity." The normally ingenious and down-to-earth Lewis left his readers in the complicated and heady realms of theological disquisition on this doctrine, but (let's face it) who has ever heard a clearly illustrated exposition of it from the pulpit? In one more attempt Lewis declared: "The Son exists because the Father exists; but there never was a time before the Father produced the Son." Lewis would probably have done better to steer clear of this subject altogether.[42]

The Church would have done immeasurably better to leave all this anti-biblical speculation alone and stay with Matthew and Luke as a basis for their definition of God and Jesus. Lewis was surely out of his depth, gallantly trying to defend his "orthodoxy," but having abandoned the New Testament creed of Jesus and the accounts of the origin of the Son of God. To beget does not mean just to have "a harmonious relation involving homogeneity"!

One book resting on another has nothing to do with one book begetting the other. The analogy fails to convince. To beget is much

---

[41]*Mere Christianity*, 172.
[42]James Townsend, "C.S. Lewis's Theology: Somewhere Between Ransom and Reepicheep," *Journal of the Grace Evangelical Society*, 13:24, spring 2000.

more than having a relationship; it means to cause someone to come into being. Begetting initiates a new person. The Bible in Basic English captures the sense of Psalm 2:7 well: "You are My Son; this day I have *given you being*." That verse lies behind the accounts of Jesus' origin in Mary in Matthew and Luke and Paul applies it to the beginning of the Son's life in Acts 13:33.[43] Hebrews 1:5 and 5:5 likewise explain the begetting of the Son as the fulfillment of the promise that God would be father of the son of David (Heb. 1:5, combining Ps. 2:7 and 2 Sam. 7:14 to make the same point).[44]

John who is supposed to be the chief witness of an eternal Son of God speaks of Jesus as the "the one who was begotten" (1 John 5:18): "He who was begotten preserves [the believer]." As we saw in some manuscripts attempts were made to get rid of this embarrassing verse, by avoiding the word "begotten" as descriptive of Jesus, but the reference to the Son who *was begotten* survives clearly in modern translations based on a more secure manuscript reading.

Prodigious displays of verbal dexterity characterize the attempts of writers seeking to justify the non-biblical creed which includes an "eternally begotten" Son. Once the plain meaning of words is jettisoned, the Bible could be made to say almost anything. In the case of God begetting His Son Jesus, the plain sense *had* to be replaced, if the Son was to be made coeternal with the Father. Luke was lucidly clear. His nativity account explains the begetting of the Son, how this happened by a divine biological miracle. Equally obvious is Luke's mention of the holy spirit as the instrument of God's creative miracle performed in Mary. The holy spirit causes the reader to think immediately of the creative activity of the spirit in Genesis, excluding any thought of an uncreated Son!

---

[43]Note F.F. Bruce's important comment: "The promise of Acts 13:23 finds fulfillment in v. 33...It has to do with the sending of the Messiah, not his resurrection (for which see v. 34)" (*The Acts of the Apostles*, 269).
[44]And confirming the event as the birth of Jesus by adding a third supporting quotation: "When he brings the firstborn into the world..." (Heb. 1:6). Wilhelm Michaelis finds "brings the firstborn into the world" as suitable for the birth of the Son (*Theological Dictionary of the New Testament*, 6:880, n. 58). In earlier writings I had favored a reference to the second coming, but on balance I think that the three OT quotations make the same point, as in Heb. 2:12, 13.

John Chapter 1

Less obvious than the attempt to avoid the word "beget" was the intrusive capital "W" put on the word "word" in John 1:1, creating the impression that there are two Persons in the Godhead. But John did not write "in the beginning was *the Son*," and it is proper to render John 1:3 as "all things were made through *it*," the word.[45] In addition, and in the interests of "pushing" the text in favor of the traditional Jesus, the NIV seemed determined to leave the reader with the wrong impression when it made Jesus say he was "returning" or "going back" to God (John 13:3; 16:28; 20:17). What in fact Jesus said was that he was *going* to God, not going *back* or *returning* to Him. He could not be returning since he had not yet been in heaven with the Father. He achieved this only at the ascension. Readers of the NIV, NAB and NLT are made to think that Jesus went *back* to the Father. This, however, is not what the Greek says.

The Jesus of John is the new Moses. Only by putting a capital "W" on the word "word" in John 1:1 is any difficulty produced. When a second preexisting Person is forced into John, the testimony of Matthew and Luke about the real beginning of Jesus is contradicted. John begins by referring to the creative activity of the One God. His word or wisdom is His divine intention and mind. God's plans and purposes are in Jewish thinking said to be "with God." John later wrote in his epistle (1 John 1:1-2), in clarification of the opening of his gospel, that "life was *with* the Father."[46] Jesus is

---

[45]All eight English versions before the KJV, starting with Tyndale's translation, read "all things were made through it." In the KJV this was altered to "by him." Many translations in other languages read "the word" as "purpose" or "intention" and thus describe it as "it," not "him". John speaks of the neuter "light" as "him" in 1:10, and he is thinking of the Son as then in existence, but not before his birth. Jesus is what the word/wisdom *became,* not one-to-one equivalent to "the word," which never in the Hebrew Bible means "spokesman." "The word" did not *assume* flesh, as in orthodoxy; it became flesh, a human person. God's wisdom was expressed in a perfect human being whose origin was carefully described in Matthew and Luke and whom John recognized as "uniquely begotten," *monogenes.* The root of that word is *ginomai* which means to become or come into existence. See further our article "John 1:1: *Caveat Lector* (Reader Beware)" at www.restorationfellowship.org.

[46]"The word was with [*pros*] God" just as "life was with [*pros*] the Father" in 1 John 1:2. See Job 10:13 and 23:14 for God's intent being "with" Him.

that life become flesh, the divine program for immortality unveiled to us. The mind of God is uniquely expressed in the man Jesus. Jesus is "walking wisdom." Paul calls him "the wisdom of God" (1 Cor. 1:24).

Jews like Philo could speak of Moses as "according to God's forethought the logical and animated Law."[47] When the word became flesh in Jesus, this was equivalent, as John writes, to "grace and truth" coming by Jesus (John 1:17). Jesus is the embodiment of God's gracious purpose, just as Moses was earlier the embodiment of the Law (Torah). In neither case is it necessary to suppose that these pillars of God's plan were alive before their birth, creating a complexity which led to centuries of unresolved dispute.[48]

The concept of a preexisting purpose is well understood by some leading scholars. C.B. Caird in his "The Development of Christ in the New Testament" reflects on the Jewish background to John 1: "The Jews had believed only in the preexistence of a personification, either of a divine attribute or of a divine purpose, but never a person."[49] It is quite unnecessary to turn the purpose of God into a second Person existing from eternity. The Son is the human being promised as the descendant of David, and as such he is the covenant-bound purpose of God "foreknown...and then manifested" (1 Pet. 1:20). There is no eternal Son who "assumes" or "puts on" flesh. Rather the word "comes into existence, flesh,"[50] a human person begotten in Mary as "the uniquely begotten Son full of grace and truth" (John 1:14), a man who perfectly expresses God's will for us all.

At Qumran contemporaries of John were using almost the same language as John to describe God's eternal purpose. John shares the thought-world of the Dead Sea Scrolls documents. "All things came into being through it [the *logos*, word], and apart from it nothing came into being that has come into being" writes John (1:3). Compare with this verse the statement in 1 QS xi 11: "By His knowledge everything has been brought into being, and everything that is He established by His purpose, and apart from Him nothing is done."

---

[47] *Life of Moses* 1:28.
[48] Jewish writings spoke of Moses as foreknown, that is, planned in God's purpose.
[49] *Christ for Us Today*, SCM Press, 1968, 66-80.
[50] *Egeneto*, became, come to exist, in John 1:14. The same word describes the appearance of John the Baptist.

John and the Qumran writers worked out of a common Hebrew heritage, John of course telling us that God's great purpose had been "with" Him (John 1:1) from the beginning, and it became concrete reality in the man Messiah Jesus (John 1:14). Job had spoken of God's plans and purposes as being "with" Him, meaning that they were concealed in His heart: "These things You have concealed in Your heart; I know that this is *with* You" (Job 10:13). "He performs what is appointed for me, and many such decrees are *with* Him" (Job 23:14). "*With* Him are wisdom and might; to Him belong counsel and understanding...With Him are strength and sound wisdom" (Job 12:13, 16).

There is no need to capitalize "word" in John 1:1, forcing readers to suppose that a second Person has existed as God from eternity, thus shattering the first principle of sound theology that God is one Person, not two or three, as Jesus said so clearly in John 17:3.

John 1 introduces the word or wisdom of God as His self-expression and His creative activity. The Genesis account is recalled, and provides John with a way of introducing the *new* creation in Jesus. God's word is full of life and light and the darkness "did not overpower it" (not "him," v. 5). John then describes the historical event of the coming of John the Baptist who was "sent from God" (v. 6). He was a witness to the true light which when it comes into the world (v. 9) was the Son. John 1, from verse 6, describes the appearing of John and Jesus, the Son of God. The light coming into the world is now described as "him" (*auton*, v. 10), rather than "it" (*auto*, v. 5). Verse 14 resumes the description of the historical Son and introduces for the first time the title "uniquely begotten Son from the Father" (just as John was also "from God," v. 6). Verse 13 recalls the virginal begetting of the Son, probably, by comparing it with Christian rebirth. John has not overthrown the clear accounts of Matthew and Luke about the *genesis* (Matt. 1:1, 18) of the Son.

John 17:3: One and Only One God, the Father
The straightforward evidence that the God of Scripture is a single Person, so designated by repeated singular personal pronouns, has been discarded by theologians who desire a more philosophical view of God. This foray into the world of philosophy was undertaken with a price. It is hard to "kick against the goads" of singular personal pronouns and other equally simple and telling words describing God

and Jesus. I propose that what has happened is this: A brand new vocabulary, "church-speak," had to be invented to lend plausibility to the concept that going beyond the unitarian creed of Jesus is legitimate.

The revised vocabulary is as follows: God is not a Person. He is an essence or substance. He shares a unity of Essence eternally with two others in the Godhead. Jesus knew nothing of such a creed. The Church legitimizes this by calling it a shift "within biblical monotheism...from the unitary monotheism of Israel to the trinitarianism of the Council of Chalcedon."[51] But Jesus did not authorize this shift. Far from it. He solemnly declared that the essence of eternal life is that they should know "You [Father, v. 1] as the only one who is truly God, and Jesus Christ whom You sent" (John 17:3).

It is at this verse that one of the most startling manipulations of the text of Scripture has occurred. The celebrated Augustine, unable to find his beloved Trinity in Jesus' words, decided to rewrite the utterance of Jesus to accommodate a creed about which Jesus knew nothing. Here is how he deals with John 17:3 in his *Homilies on John*: "'And this,' He [Jesus] adds, 'is eternal life, that they may know You, the only true God, and Jesus Christ, whom You have sent.' The proper order of the words is, 'That they may know You and Jesus Christ, whom You have sent, as the only true God.'"[52]

In horror at what the church father had done here, fellow Trinitarian and distinguished commentator on the Greek New Testament Henry Alford wrote:

> The Latin fathers, Augustine, Ambrose, Hilary, anxious to avoid the inference unwarrantably drawn by some from this verse against the Godhead of Christ, read "that they may know You and Jesus Christ whom You sent, as the only true God." Others, Chrysostom, Euthymius...regarded Jesus Christ as included in the words "only true God." But all such violences to the text are unnecessary.[53]

---

[51]Harold O.J. Brown, *Heresies*, 431.

[52]*Tractates on the Gospel of John*, 105. Augustine was followed in this rewriting of John 17:3 by Beza, Aquinas, Aretius and several others. H.A.W Meyer refers to the alteration of the text as a "perversion, running counter to the strict monotheism of John" (*Commentary on the Gospel of John*, Funk and Wagnall, 1884, 462).

[53]*The Greek Testament*, Rivingtons, 1859, 1:823.

They are in fact assaults on Scripture. Alford then goes on to make the following extraordinary claim:

> The very juxtaposition of Jesus Christ here with the Father and the knowledge of *both* being defined to be eternal life is a proof by implication of the Godhead of Christ. The knowledge of God and a *creature* could not be eternal life and the juxtaposition of the two would not be conceivable.[54]

The same Henry Alford was forced from his usual straightforward honesty about biblical words, when dealing with the critical word "beget":

> In applying Psalm 2:7 to our Lord we want *another and higher sense* in both words, "begotten" and "today" which may be applicable to him, a sense in which I should be disposed to say the words must in the fullness of meaning be taken, *to the neglect and almost the obliteration of their supposed lower reference.*[55]

The reader will note the admission that the ordinary sense of "beget" has to be obliterated! A "higher" sense needed to be invented, to cover the traditional departure from the historically begotten Messiah of Scripture. But that "higher" sense eliminates the ordinary and actual reference of the word "beget." Such loose procedure in the matter of defining words is certainly not characteristic of Henry Alford. But "the system" drove him to it in the case of Psalm 2:7. A word does not receive a "higher" meaning when it is emptied of its actual significance.

Such was the grip of the orthodox definition of the Son of God on an otherwise clear-sighted commentator. God, he said, cannot be so coordinated with a *creature*. But who is to say what God may do? Is He not at liberty to provide as our Savior "the man Messiah" Jesus, and take him to be our mediator next to His throne, in a supreme position at the right hand of God? Paul had no difficulty with this, and as if to anticipate and ward off any confusion over God and Jesus wrote late in his career: "There is one God and one mediator between God and men, *the man* Messiah Jesus" (1 Tim. 2:5).[56] This is the

---

[54]Ibid.
[55]Ibid. on Heb. 1:5.
[56]When Jesus was promoted to being God, equal with the Father, Mary was elevated to the position of a human (and therefore more sympathetic?) mediatrix. One mistake led to another.

backbone of New Testament revelation. Even where Paul speaks of
the ascended Jesus as having conferred on him a supreme position or
"name" (Phil. 2:9), this is all "to the glory of *God, the Father*" (v. 11).
"In [rather than 'at'] the name of Jesus every knee will bow" (v. 10).
God is still the Father of Jesus. Far from modifying unitarianism in
Philippians 2:5-11 Paul concludes by affirming it.

Augustine's adherence to tradition led him to rewrite the words of
Jesus and of Scripture in John 17:3, and to the astonishing conclusion
that the "Son was sent by the Father *and the Son.*"[57] He described "the
mechanics" of the Incarnation: "Man was added to him [the
preexisting Son], God not lost to him...he emptied himself not by
losing what he was, but by taking to him what he was not."[58]

In this extraordinary picture of the Son, the Son was older than
himself! Jesus had two distinct "components" — he was a person who
antedated his own birth and then he added a new component to
himself. He added to himself what he was not! The Son who was born
to Mary arrived equipped with his own preexisting personality. Such
were the demands of the amazing system Augustine had inherited.
Augustine was notorious also for his arbitrary treatment of the words
of the Bible in connection with the millennium. He argued that the
thousand-year reign of Christ is an indefinite period starting at the
cross. The "first resurrection" was not a literal resurrection at all.
Peake's Commentary on the Bible properly refers to Augustine's
treatment of the words of Revelation 20 as "dishonest trifling,"
"simply playing with terms."[59]

The same must be said about the Trinitarian treatment of the very
common biblical word "beget." We dare not eradicate its meaning
and pretend that it just means to be in relationship with another. It
means "to bring into existence." In the case of the Son "to beget" was
connected with a definite moment in time, "today." That marvelous
moment arrived some two thousand years ago, as the fulfillment of
God's ancient promise to produce a Son in the house of David.

The Historical Facts about the Beginning (Begetting) of Jesus
Knowing the promises of the Hebrew Bible, Matthew speaks of
the begetting of the Son of God by direct intervention of God as His

[57]*On the Trinity*, Book II, ch. 5.
[58]*Tractates on the Gospel of John*, 8 and 17.
[59]941.

spirit performed a biological miracle in Mary. This Matthew calls the "origin" (*genesis*) of the Son (Matt. 1:18). It is the time when the Son began to exist. The angel speaks to Joseph and assures him that "what is *begotten* in her" (v. 20) is from holy spirit, divine operational presence and power. The Son so begotten is then appropriately called "My [God's] Son" who is brought into the land from Egypt just as Israel had been (2:15). Jesus is God's new "Israel" and he acts as the nation should have, shining the light of truth to the rest of the world.

Luke, as we have noted, keen to establish the facts about the faith in which Theophilus had been catechized, informs Mary that "what is begotten" is from the holy spirit (1:35). Based on the miracle in Mary, the holy child begotten, or possibly "to be begotten," is entitled, *"for that reason,"* to be called "Son of God." Paul in Romans 1:3-4 speaks of God's Son who "came into existence" from the seed of David as far as human lineage is concerned. He was later declared to be Son of God in a public display of power effected by his resurrection and ascension to the right hand of the Father. Paul preached the same fact in Acts 13:33 where his proof text is Psalm 2:7, "This day I have begotten you," to describe the raising up, i.e. the production of the Son as promised in Scripture (Acts 13:23). The writer to the Hebrews provides the same Psalm 2:7, "This day I have begotten you" as a second witness to the prediction and promise given by Nathan in 2 Samuel 7:14 (Heb. 1:5). God had assured David that He would be Father to the Messiah and the Messiah would be Son of God. In both Old Testament verses the precious truth about the origin of the Son at a specific moment in time, and as the direct descendant of a specific Jewish family, is guaranteed.

The origin of the Messiah as God's Son and the son of David, with Mary as his biological mother was meant to establish with complete clarity the beginning point and the nature of the one Son of God. The story was dealt a devastating blow when speculative, philosophically trained church fathers shifted the original begetting of the Son from known history back into prehistoric times, and eventually back into eternity. Hence the "eternally begotten" Son of the creeds was created as a mythological substitute for the historical Son of God and son of David. As Martin Werner complained, this was a move "behind which the historical Jesus completely disappeared."[60] He adds that the message of Jesus had been "falsified when it was interpreted in terms of the Church's later dogmas of the Trinity, the Two Natures...Thus was the 'Religion of Christ' set over against the 'Christian Religion' as something essentially different." Werner concluded:

> Whereas the relationship between Primitive Christianity and Early Catholicism had remained finally dark to Early Protestantism, historical research was now able to show the form of Early Church doctrine as an essential deviation from the content of the teaching of Jesus and the Primitive Christianity of the Apostles.[61]

Mary Conceived and Bore a Child

If Mary was taking into herself a being undergoing transformation from a spiritual being to a human person, Luke and Matthew have misled us. There is no room in the womb for two persons, one added to the other. Would this be a form of twins? Mary did not bear a person who is two "wholes," fully God and fully man. She did not bear a "double person," a preexisting spirit person adding to himself a human being. The biblical account of the genesis of Jesus is much simpler. Mary bore the blood descendant of David, one person, the promised Messiah whose coming into existence was promised for a definite moment in history. Mary conceived a child six months later than her relative Elizabeth. She did not take in and transform a person into a fetus.

By the time the church councils had finished with their new account of the origin of the Son of God, the Son had been cut in two. He was said to have had an existence before coming into existence. His real origin, it was said, was before Genesis. This was the view of Arius and the later neo-Arians Aetius and Eunomius.[62] What became the permanently orthodox view espoused by Athanasius held that Jesus was begotten in a timeless eternity. Both mistaken views battled it out for decades and the Church settled finally on the Jesus of Chalcedon in two natures, his real ego being that of the eternal second

---

[60]Werner, *Formation of Christian Dogma*, 298.
[61]Ibid., 320.
[62]For an account of the persistent non-Trinitarian spokesmen after Nicea, see Thomas Kopecek, *A History of Neo-Arianism*, Philadelphia Patristic Foundation, 1979.

member of the triune Godhead. But what became of the historical, lineal descendant of David who originated by miracle in Mary? What was left of the meticulously constructed accounts of Matthew and Luke about who Jesus really was?

No one seemed to notice that the virginal begetting, coming into existence of the Son of God should have blocked any suggestion of a double origin. The Son was not begotten (brought into existence) twice, once in eternity and then later in history. His historical origin as a descendant of David was completely sufficient to guarantee his claim to be the Messiah. A Son of God whose origin was removed from the biological chain was a stranger and unfit to qualify according to the divine promise guaranteeing the Messiah as the lineal descendant of David, as well as the procreated Son of God.

Dead Sea Scrolls

It is now well known that the Dead Sea Scrolls reflect many of the Messianic themes of the New Testament. The Qumran sect was expecting a coming Messiah. Texts such as the Patriarchal Blessings look forward to "the coming of the righteous Messiah, the sprout of David."[63] We read of "the coming of the Messiah of Aaron and Israel" in the Damascus Document.[64] Parallel to the Old Testament *Mashiach* (Messiah) is also expected as a prophet. The scrolls contain a variety of biblical titles for the expected Messiah: "branch of David," "scepter" and "star."

Most significantly we read in 1 QSa 2:11 (*The Rule of the Community*) of the time "when God will beget the Messiah" and of the Messiah as God's firstborn Son.[65] This Messiah is to have the power to raise the dead.[66] Nothing is said of a Son of God who has no beginning, or who is "eternally generated." The writer to the Hebrews likewise speaks of God bringing His firstborn into the inhabited earth (Heb. 1:6).

The New Testament is part of the intellectual world of the Jews. With the scrolls' mention of God's Son and his inheritance they "do help us understand why the evangelists Matthew and Luke would be

---

[63]See also 4QFlor 1-2. 2:11; 4QpIsa. 8-10:17.
[64]CD 19:10; 20:1.
[65]4Q369.
[66]4Q521, line 12.

interested in presenting Jesus' birth in such a light."[67] Once again the surrounding background of the New Testament demonstrates how first-century Christianity is a Messianic faith, holding in common with Jews the belief that God would bring into existence the Messiah, Son of God.

The Messiah who has come once is coming back to rule on earth in the Kingdom of God promised throughout Scripture and prayed for in the well-known petition "Thy Kingdom come." The same prayer is repeated in the request *maranatha*, "may our Lord come" (1 Cor. 16:22). "Our Lord" is the Lord Messiah, prophetically designated as "my lord" in Psalm 110:1. That precious verse is the master key to the identity of Jesus in relation to the One God.

More on Preexistence

When Psalm 110:1 was abandoned by the creeds, which could no longer recognize the distinction between the Lord God (Yahweh) and the Lord Messiah ("my lord," *adoni*), the figure of Jesus was severely obscured. The best that church members could do was to speak of the "preexistence" of Jesus. But what does that word "preexistence" mean?

As recently as 2003 a leading Roman Catholic scholar, Luke Timothy Johnson, asked in *The Creed: What Christians Believe and Why It Matters*: "How can someone exist before existing? How can 'Jesus Christ' exist before Jesus was born in Bethlehem?"[68]

That question ought to set off a mighty avalanche of questioning, reflection and rethinking among thoughtful churchgoers. The answer is that one cannot preexist oneself! Preexistence is a clever cover-up term for holding to "two existences," and thus two distinct persons. One has been added to the other and the blanket term "preexistence" is supposed to help us gloss over the fact that the first (preexisting) person cannot be the same as the second person. A single person cannot be older than himself. An individual cannot begin the same one journey at two different times. Since Jesus, the Son of God, came into existence, was *begotten*, in Mary, this marks the moment when he began to be. Matthew has expressly informed us about "the *genesis* of Jesus Christ" (1:1; 1:18). What preexisted him is someone else,

---

[67]Michael Wise, Martin Abegg, Jr., and Edward Cook, *The Dead Sea Scrolls: A New Translation*, HarperCollins, 1999, 329.
[68]Luke Timothy Johnson, *The Creed*, Doubleday, 2003, 108.

attempting to attach himself to the real Jesus. On that theory, the real Jesus comes into existence burdened by a strange other person who accompanies him and gets confused with him. "Preexistence" appears to be a way of papering over the obvious cracks in the theory that a single person can preexist himself. Luke 1:32 informs us that the make-up of the personality who is the Son of God is composed of two elements. He is both Son of God ("Son of the Highest") and son of David ("his father David"), and so constituted by miracle in the human biological chain. No further complication is needed.

Luke Timothy Johnson, rather than face the solution to his own excellent question about "preexistence," excuses the term on the plea that we humans are forced to talk about matters which are beyond us:

> "Preexistence" is an unfortunate term, but it is the understandable consequence of creatures who live in time trying to speak about God who dwells outside time...Such language seeks to express in ways we can understand that, somehow, God was in the one we call Jesus from beginning to end.[69]

Yes, but why does he start with the assumption, unwarranted by Scripture, that God begat a Son outside of time? Luke reports that Mary became pregnant six months later than Elizabeth.

Fortunately God is not so limited by language. He created language. He gives us a clear concept of time and speaks to us within those terms. He deliberately allowed historical time to elapse before He determined, according to His own promises, to bring into existence His own "dear Son" or "Son of His love" (Col. 1:13). He fixed that event for a specific geographical place at a definite moment of time. Moreover, He recorded meticulously the step-by-step genealogical line which links the ancestry of the Savior, not into timelessness, but back into the history of the Israelite people (in fact back to Adam, as Luke tells us, 3:38). Jesus the Son of God is thus happily a single person with a single origin in history, one effected by a biological miracle guaranteeing that God is uniquely his Father, while his ancestry is rooted in Israel. He is not older than himself or older as well as younger than his cousin John, born six months before him. There are no insoluble riddles and mysteries here, merely an historical account of the One God's determination to produce the

---

[69]Ibid., 108.

head of the New Creation, the second Adam and Messiah, Son of God. All this Luke had investigated carefully and describes as the core and foundation of the Christian faith he is recommending.

In modern times the extreme illogicality of "preexistence," the notion that one person can begin to exist when he already exists, was described as follows:

> The concept of pre-existence is an attempt to explain the (fundamentally irrational) relation between a being empirically known to exist, and another being who is in existence apart from and prior to the empirical and temporal world (a relation which is rationalized by the idea of incarnation)...Jesus' own conception was different. The idea of pre-existence was not in his thought. That idea puts a being, a life in (paradoxical) relation to a being which has always existed.[70]

It is important that Bible readers reflect on the precious teaching of Matthew and Luke about the *origin* (*genesis,* Matt. 1:1, 18) of the Son of God. That origin establishes who he is. As a French professor of the history of religion wrote:

> No thought either of pre-existence or of incarnation was associated in [Matthew and Luke's] minds [with the virginal begetting]. The fact is, that the two ideas cannot be reconciled. A pre-existent being who becomes man, reduces himself, if you will, to the state of a human embryo; but he is not conceived [as the birth narratives say he was] by action exterior to himself in the womb of a woman. Conception is the point at which an individual is formed *who did not exist before*, at least as an individual.[71]

When experts write about preexistence, without which there is no Trinity, they are faced with a perplexing difficulty. They admit that Old Testament expectation of the Messiah was "of a king of the line of David, born of the human stock (Jer. 30:21), though supernaturally endowed and blessed." They go on to say that a "higher conception"

---

[70]Rudolf Otto, *The Kingdom of God and the Son of Man*, Lutterworth Press, 1943, 175.
[71]Albert Réville, *History of the Dogma of the Deity of Jesus Christ*, Philip Green, 1905, 43, emphasis added.

is suggested by the "mighty God" and "Father of Eternity"[72] in Isaiah 9:6. The *Dictionary of Christ and the Gospels* can claim no certainty at all that the Hebrew Bible thought of the Messiah as existing literally in ancient times. It concedes that the prophets may have thought of the Messiah's existence only "in the eternal counsels of God." The dictionary is equally hesitant about any real preexistence in the synoptic gospels. There is is no firm ground for finding a preexistent Messiah. There are "but few hints." Psalm 110:1 "would seem to imply..." "A similar conclusion might be drawn..." "possibly..." It concedes also that the sermons in the book of Acts "confine themselves to the historical manifestation of Jesus Christ."[73]

"Pre-existence," says the *Dictionary of the Apostolic Church*, "does not belong to the primary data of Christian faith in the Historic and Exalted Jesus...It forms no element in the primitive doctrine recorded in the opening chapters of Acts."[74] The dictionary adds that "it is a necessary implicate of that faith." But there are difficulties:

> Here we are confronted with a problem. The thought of the Apostolic Church has advanced [in Paul] from the position reflected in the first chapters of Acts, in which there is no hint of a doctrine of pre-existence, to that presupposed even in the earlier Pauline Epistles, where its presence and activity are fully assumed.[75]

But how did this amazing transition take place? "A process of development so gradual, silent, and unconscious as to have left no trace, bridges the distance between the Pentecostal discourses and Colossians." But the dictionary admits that "little or no use is made of the conception of pre-existence in 1 Peter."[76] So Peter knows nothing of the extraordinary "new" view of Jesus as preexistent Son. Peter indeed speaks of Jesus as *foreknown* (1 Pet. 1:20),[77] which excludes preexistence.

---

[72] Jewish translators of the Septuagint (LXX) render this Messianic title as "father of the age to come." Jesus is indeed the supervisor and "parent" of the new order of the Kingdom of God.

[73] *A Dictionary of Christ and the Gospels*, 2:407.

[74] *Dictionary of the Apostolic Church*, 2:264.

[75] Ibid.

[76] Ibid., 264, 265.

[77] Jeremiah was foreknown but certainly not preexistent (Jer. 1:5).

The attempt of the dictionary to justify the *later* doctrine of a Son who did not begin in his mother's womb, finishes by speaking only of "an innate necessity of thought" as a basis for the "remarkable transition"[78] from the Jesus of Acts and Peter to what he supposes Paul in his later epistles says about Jesus as a preexisting Son. However, the transition is imagined. Paul knew of "the rock which followed" Israel (1 Cor. 10:4) as a *type* of Christ, not Christ himself preexisting literally (he uses the word "typically" twice in 1 Cor. 10:6, 11). Paul actually speaks of the Son as "coming into existence"[79] from a woman (Gal. 4:4) which excludes a prior existence. The fact that the Son was "sent" proves nothing about a previous life for the Son. All of God's prophets and agents were "sent."

If the Son of God comes into existence in history, as the gospels say, he cannot also exist before that. Talk of "preexistence" camouflages what is really the introduction of another Jesus who preexists the historical Jesus. Christians are urged in the New Testament to recognize, believe in and follow the actual Jesus of history, not another being who existed before the existence of the actual Son.

More on John's Gospel
Trinitarian argument makes its appeal very extensively from the fourth gospel. This in itself should raise suspicions. Was it only in the 90s AD that the beloved disciple felt the need to show how the creed of Israel had now been expanded to include two or three extra Persons? Was the affirmation of the creed of Israel by Jesus in Mark 12:28-34 (Mark writing probably around 65 AD) now to be superseded or shifted? Can the doctrine of God be so radically altered, without a huge treatment of this colossal change, if ever in fact it took place?

John, who was no doubt familiar with the work of Matthew, Mark and Luke, and certainly did not intend to contradict them, is as emphatically supportive of the Jewish view of Jesus that God is a single Person, as any New Testament writer. He wrote his whole book to convince us that Jesus is to be believed in as "Messiah, Son of

[78]*Dictionary of the Apostolic Church*, 2:264.
[79]Note Paul's special use of *ginomai*, to come into being, rather than the normal word to be born.

God" (20:31), thus registering his complete agreement with Peter's confession so strongly approved by Jesus in Matthew 16:16-18. During Jesus' extended discourses as recorded by John, Jesus constantly insists that he can act only in cooperation with and subordination to the Father who gives him his orders. The Jesus of John refers to God as "my God" (20:17) and declares emphatically that he can do nothing by himself (5:19), but only in response to the commands of his Father, who is the One God, "the only true God" (17:3).

John the Baptist pointed out that Jesus had moved ahead of him "because he was always my superior" (1:15, 30).[80] Jesus recognized that he had been seen in a vision as the Son of Man in Daniel 7, a human being alive with God and destined to receive the future Kingdom of God (6:62).[81] In John 17:3 Jesus makes belief in unitary monotheism the basis of true faith: The Father is "the only one who is truly God."[82] Any Jew would have approved this. Jesus associates himself with the One God who is the Father, but he is at the same time numerically distinct. In John 17.5 Jesus requests that he now receive as the reward of his ministry then accomplished, the glory "which I had with You [the Father] before the foundation of the world." This is glory in prospect, glory promised in advance. He says nothing about regaining glory, temporarily forsaken, but of winning that glory for the first time.

---

[80]Translations force preexistence into the text here. "Before me" can equally be translated "superior to me." Thus the Geneva Bible: "better than I." Rotherham: "my chief he was." C.H. Dodd translates: "There is a man in my following who has taken precedence of me, because he is and always has been essentially my superior" (cited by J.A.T Robinson in *The Priority of John*, SCM Press, 1985, 384). The *New International Commentary* on John has this note: "'A follower of mine has taken precedence of me, for he (always) was before me, my superior'...Some scholars take 'first' to mean not 'first in time,' 'before,' but 'first in importance'...'he was my Chief'" (Leon Morris, *The Gospel According to John*, Eerdmans, 1995, 96-97). Calvin says "more excellent than I." So also Barkar's Bible (1599), and many other commentators over the past 400 years.

[81]It is the human being, "Son of Man" who preexists here. He was of course there "before" in the vision of Daniel. Even Trinitarians do not think that the human Jesus was alive in the time of Daniel.

[82]Augustine recognized that this is the purest form of unitarian statement and avoided it only by restructuring the order of the words as we saw above.

In the very same context the same glory is promised by Jesus to disciples *not even alive* when Jesus spoke these words: I pray "for those who are to believe in me through their [the Apostles'] word" (v. 20). "I *have given* them the glory which You have given to me" (v. 22). It is glory promised but not yet conferred. In the New Testament rewards are regularly promised as existing now in heaven as treasure stored up for the future. If you "parade your uprightness in public to attract attention," Jesus said in Matthew 6:1 (NJB), "you *have*[83] no reward with your Father," i.e. stored up for the future with the Father. All the things of the future are laid up now with God. The glory Jesus requested for himself in John 17:5 was glory in prospect and promise. He possessed it in God's decrees and now it was time for it to be bestowed. The request reminds us of the statement "inherit the Kingdom prepared for you from the foundation of the world" (Matt. 25:34). The Kingdom itself lies in the future but it has been promised from the beginning. So too with the glory which Jesus asked to receive as a result of his completed work. The context of John 17:5 in verses 20 and 22 should not be overlooked.

Just as Paul was able to say that Christians "have" a body prepared in heaven (2 Cor. 5:1), though they do not actually have it yet, so too Jesus asked God to give him the glory which God had prepared for him, which he "had with" God, in God's intentions. There is no need for this one verse to pose the problem of a second eternal Person. Verses 22 and 24 of John's chapter 17 define glory as glory promised, glory in prospect, glory as future reward.

Distinguished Trinitarians Augustine and Calvin's colleague Theodore Beza understood John 17:5 as glory predestined before the world was, parallel to John's later statement that Jesus was "the lamb slain before the foundation of the world" (Rev. 13:8). German commentator J.G. Rosenmuller was convinced that the glory of John 17:5 was the same as Jesus would confer on his friends (v. 22). Anglican Bishop Samuel Parker (1640-1687) was amongst many who see that there is nothing in John 17:5 which would contradict the accounts of the origin of the Son of God:

> It was a proverbial form of speech among the Jews to express matters of great moment, resolved upon only in the divine decrees, as if they were really existing. Thus they say that the

---

[83]Note the present tense, though the reward is future.

Messiah is more ancient than the sun and the Mosaic order older than the world, not as if they understood them really as such, but only to express their absolute usefulness and necessity...The glory which Jesus prayed for in John 17:5...was that honor with which God had from all eternity designed to dignify the Messiah.[84]

Professor Wendt on John 8:58 and 17:5
There has been a steady protest against reading John in opposition to the other gospels and making him produce an essentially non-human Jesus. It is a false method which promotes one only of the four Gospels in support of a Jesus unknown to the synoptics or the preparation for the Messiah in the promises of the Hebrew Bible. What John has *not* done is to alter the unitarian creed of Jesus. John 17:3 is quite clear on this point. John 8:58 and 17:5 must be read in the light of John 17:3 and the rest of the Bible. Professor Wendt was writing in the late 1800s:

It is clear that John 8:58 and 17:5 do not speak of a real preexistence of Christ. We must not treat these verses in isolation, but understand them in their context. The saying in John 8:58, "Before Abraham came to be, I am" was prompted by the fact that Jesus' opponents had countered his remark in verse 51 by saying that Jesus was not greater than Abraham or the prophets (v. 53). As the Messiah commissioned by God Jesus is conscious of being in fact superior to Abraham and the prophets. For this reason he replies (according to the intervening words, v. 54ff) that Abraham had "seen his day," i.e. the entrance of Jesus on his historical ministry, and "had rejoiced to see" that day. And Jesus strengthens his argument by adding the statement, which sounded strange to the Jews, that he had even been "before Abraham" (v. 58).

This last saying must be understood in connection with verse 56. Jesus speaks in verses 55, 56 and 58 as if his present ministry on earth stretches back to the time of Abraham and even before. His sayings were perceived by the Jews in this sense and rejected as nonsense. But Jesus obviously did not

---

[84]Samuel Parker, *A Free and Impartial Censure of the Platonick Philosophie,* Oxford, 1667, 239, 240.

(in v. 56) mean that Abraham had actually experienced Jesus' appearance on earth and seen it literally. Jesus was referring to Abraham's *spiritual vision* of his appearance on earth, by which Abraham, at the birth of Isaac, had foreseen at the same time the promised Messiah, and had rejoiced at the future prospect of the greater one (the Messiah) who would be Israel's descendant. Jesus' reference to his existence before Abraham's birth must be understood in the same sense. There is no sudden heavenly preexistence of the Messiah here: the reference is again obviously to his earthly existence. And this earthly existence is precisely the existence of the Messiah. As such, it was not only present in Abraham's mind, but even before his time, as the subject of God's foreordination and foresight. The sort of preexistence Jesus has in mind is "ideal" [in the world of ideas and plans]. In accordance with this consciousness of being the Messiah preordained from the beginning, Jesus can indeed make the claim to be greater than Abraham and the prophets (John 8:58).

In John 17:5 Wendt caught the Hebrew flavor of Jesus' and John's words:

Jesus asks the Father to give him now the heavenly glory which he had with the Father before the world was. The conclusion that because Jesus possessed a preexistent glory in heaven he must also have preexisted personally in heaven is taken too hastily. This is proven by Matthew 6:20 ("Lay up for yourselves treasure in heaven"), 25:34 ("Come, you blessed by my Father, inherit the Kingdom prepared for you from the foundation of the world"), Colossians 1:5 ("the hope which is laid up for you in heaven about which you heard in the word of Truth, the Gospel"), and 1 Peter 1:4 ("an inheritance incorruptible, and undefiled, which does not fade away, reserved in heaven for you"). Thus a *reward* can also be thought of as preexistent in heaven. Such a reward is destined for human beings and already *held in store*, to be awarded to them at the end of their life. So it is with heavenly glory which Jesus requests. He is not asking for a *return*[85] to an earlier heavenly condition. Rather he asks God to give him now, at the end of his work as Messiah on earth (v. 4), the heavenly reward which God had appointed from eternity for him, as Messiah. As the Messiah and Son he knows he has been loved and foreordained by the Father from eternity (v. 24). Both John 8:58 and 17:5 are concerned with God's predetermination of the Messiah.[86]

The claim of Jesus is in all four of the gospels to be the Messiah of Israel and this claim is fully endorsed in John's specific purpose statement that his gospel is designed to bring about belief in Jesus as the Messiah, Son of God (20:31), certainly not in a second one who is God in an expanded Shema. The Messianic claim "I am he," "I am the one" runs like a golden thread throughout the narrative of John's gospel. Its basis is laid in the conversation with the woman at the well. "'I know that the Messiah is coming'...'I who speak to you am he'" ("*I am he*, namely the one speaking to you," 4:25, 26).

As Messiah, Jesus is the one we must not fail to believe in, lest we die in our sins (8:24), and in 8:56, the Messiahship of Jesus was foreseen by Abraham who looked forward to Jesus' day. Indeed even before Abraham was born, "I am he" (8:58).[87] The Greek here is identical with the phrase in 4:26 and 8:24 and is parallel to Jesus' grand statements, "I am the Good Shepherd" (10:11), "I am the way, the truth and the life" (14:6). He is the only way to the Father (14:6).

---

[85]Did Jesus ever say he was going to *return* to the Father? Or did he just say he was *going* to the Father? There is a big difference between going and returning! John 13:3, 16:28 and 20:17 should be carefully examined in the King James or RSV as well as in the NIV. You will find a startling difference of translation. Which is correct? You can look in a Greek-English interlinear or check the meaning of the words in *Strong's*. It is very illuminating. But remember that this is a rare case of poor translation in the NIV, to push an idea which is not there!

[86]H.H. Wendt, *System der Christlichen Lehre*, Vandenhoeck and Ruprecht, 1906, Part 2, 348, 349, translation mine. Cf. Wendt, *Teaching of Jesus*, 2:151-182.

[87]The Greek "I am he" is not the same as the declaration of God's name in Exodus 3:14, where God says "I am the one who exists" (*ego eimi 'o ohn*). This title is referred to the *Father*, never to the Son. It designates the Father not the Son in Rev. 1:8 (*'o ohn*).

The Messiah is the key to the creation of the world. His crucifixion "happened" in the counsels of God before the foundation of the world — he was the lamb already slaughtered "before the foundation of the world" (Rev. 13:8) — because "in him" (not "by him" as mistranslated in a number of versions) everything was made (Col. 1:16). All things are indeed "through" the Messiah and with him in view (Col. 1:16). But this preposition "through" does not warrant a contradiction of the multiple texts which say that God created the heavens and earth, unassisted (Isa. 44:24). The Christians of all the ages were indeed in Christ before the foundation of the world (Eph. 1:4), but this does not mean that they were then conscious and alive. It was usual for Jews to speak of the world having been made for the sake of Israel. It was made also with Jesus, the Son of God, in mind.

Jesus did indeed "come down from heaven" (John 6:38). But the Bible should be allowed to interpret its own sayings. James states that *every good gift* comes down from heaven and that true wisdom comes down from heaven (James 1:17; 3:15). Jesus also came down from heaven; that is, he is God's supreme gift to the world (John 3:16). We should observe that Jesus spoke of himself as bread which came down from heaven. No one thinks he was literally a loaf preexisting. Moreover that "bread" which came down is his "flesh" (John 6:51). It is the *human Jesus* who "descends from heaven," but that is not what the Trinity teaches. It maintains that the eternal Son of God existed in heaven before his birth. The descent of Jesus from heaven is simply a Jewish way of expressing the idea that Jesus is the expression of God's ultimate wisdom and the Son is the final gift of the One God for the salvation of mankind.

The Son as the Purpose for God's Creation
Paul's understanding of the destiny of the world is that all things are to be headed up in Jesus. He is the subject of the grand purpose planned long ago by the One God. "This was according to the eternal purpose that he has realized in Christ Jesus our Lord" (Eph. 3:11). For Paul Jesus is the wisdom of God (1 Cor. 1:24). He is what wisdom became, but wisdom itself is the wise thinking of the One God, and that wisdom or word (John 1:1) is eventually displayed in the procreated Son of God.

Neither Paul nor John contradict the Hebrew Bible's promise that a son is to be *born* in Israel (Isa. 9:6), a prophet from the family of

Israel like Moses (Deut. 18:15-19). Luke's and Matthew's accounts of the origin of the Son of God are designed to provide an impenetrable barrier to any speculation about another existence of the Son. John and Paul have unfortunately have been used and sometimes mistranslated to undermine, in fact to contradict, Matthew and Luke.

It is to accuse John of a kind of recklessness if he is supposed to have presented Jesus as God Himself. On the contrary the Jesus of John told his accusers that he was not God, but the duly authorized "Son of God," a supreme example of what God's agents may be. Had they not been called "gods" in the Old Testament period? How much more then is he, as the final and principal agent of God, entitled to be recognized as "Son of God," which is the equivalent of the Messiah throughout the New Testament? (John 10:34-36). And Jesus in John makes as strong a statement of the Shema as he does in Mark, when he defines the Christian God as the Father who is "the only one who is truly God" (17:3) and "the only God" (5:44).

The Constraints of Monotheism

Edith Schaeffer, wife of the celebrated Francis Schaeffer, makes a simple and unarguable point in her book *Christianity Is Jewish*.[88] It is a plain historical fact, which we should never forget, that the Christian faith has its roots in Judaism and in the Jewish people. With the possible exception of Luke, all the writers of the New Testament were Jews. Paul was a Jew. One may also say truthfully that the "one mediator between God and men, the man Messiah Jesus" (1 Tim. 2:5) is still a Jew. Since he was born a Jew that is still his identity. He is of course also the glorified head of the new race of human beings. All authority in heaven and earth has been vested in him by God, his Father (Matt. 28:18).

The concept of Jesus' sacrifice for sin is a Hebrew one and the whole concept of Jesus as Messiah, Son of God, is built on the Jewish definitions of those titles, derived from the royal Messianism of the Hebrew Bible, especially Psalm 2 which defines "the Lord's Messiah" (anointed) as the Son of God and King of God's coming Kingdom (vv. 2, 6, 7). He is to govern the world from Jerusalem. Psalm 2 is quoted some 18 times in the New Testament and the precious oracle found in Psalm 110:1 is referred to some 25 times by

---

[88]Tyndale House, 1975.

New Testament writers. The Gospel as Jesus preached it concerns the coming Kingdom of God. That, too, is a thoroughly Jewish Old Testament concept and must not be wrenched from its Hebrew context and made to serve modern theological interests.

The Church desperately needs reconnection to its Hebrew, Jewish roots.[89] The Church is currently drawing not from those Jewish roots, but from a massive Greek system of theology which makes our Bible reading confused and ineffective. E.F. Scott in a fine study of the Kingdom of God as the Christian Gospel complained about:

> the long and bitter controversy which led to the definition, in metaphysical terms, of the twofold nature of Christ. *Nothing seems to be more remote from the realities of the Christian faith than this dreary controversy*, but for the Greek mind everything was at stake in it...It is not surprising that modern writers have found a crucial proof that Christianity, in the course of the Gentile[90] mission, had changed into a new religion. The Church, *while still calling itself by the name of Jesus, had forgotten or refused to know what he had actually taught.*[91]

The Church has acted treacherously towards its mother in Judaism — in the matter of defining God. It has in some sense become a prostitute by allowing its belief system, at its heart, to be infected by an alien doctrine of God. In addition to entering into a "Constantinian concubinage," confusing the Church and the world, the Church has devised a view of God to which Jesus could not subscribe. "God is one Lord" (Mark 12:29) is not equivalent to "God is three Persons in one Essence." That difference needs to be

---

[89]This does not mean, however, a return to the Mosaic Judaism of the Old Covenant in terms of calendar and food laws, etc. Paul labored hard to proclaim the new freedom in Christ which is the heart of the New Covenant. Paul himself was "within the Torah of Messiah" (I Cor. 9:21), but not under the law of Moses. To make his point Paul spoke of Jesus who "abolished the law of commandments in ordinances" (Eph. 2:15) to create one new united "Israel of God" and spiritual circumcision (Gal. 6:16; Phil. 3:3) in which all nations in Christ are one in Christ.

[90]I.e. beyond the New Testament period.

[91]*The Kingdom of God in the New Testament*, Macmillan, 1931, 159, 160, 156, emphasis added.

recognized. The result of this recognition can have staggering effects for the future of world religion.

Christianity Lost its Identity
    The proper method for searching out the identity of the God of the Bible is to start with the "God" texts. It is wrong to begin with the Son of God texts and simply read them to mean God the Son. One can produce isolated texts from John's gospel which might imply indirectly that Jesus is God. But nothing should be concluded from these texts without first rooting one's thinking in the unitary monotheism of Jesus' own creed, restated in John also, in chapter 17:3. Here Jesus repeats the creed of Israel by referring to the Father as "the only one who is truly God." Jesus is never identified with God, though he functions as God's agent and perfectly obedient Son. Calling Jesus God promotes belief in *two* who are God and thus two Gods. Jesus is always distinct from the one he calls God and Father, the "only God" (John 5:44) and "the only one who is truly God" (John 17:3).That famous statement of Jesus merely confirms the clear fact that he believed in God as a single Person. John 17:3 states a pure unitarianism. Only the Father is God. No one else is the true God. The Father alone is God. This is the language of unitarianism. Using other much less clear statements to contradict it pits the Bible against itself. The secondary statements must be harmonized with the primary "God" texts which define Him expressly and thus provide the Christian creed. Across the pages of the New Testament the Father is the only one who is God. Jesus is never called "the only God" or "the only true God." And none of the thousands of "God" texts ever mean a Triune God. This argument ought surely to be decisive against a belief in the Trinity in the mind of the authors of the Bible.
    To make Jesus into a believer in himself as coequally God, a member of the Trinity, is impossible on the evidence both of the New Testament and Jewish history. Oxford theologian A.E. Harvey, delivering the Bampton Lectures in 1980, pointed out that Jesus was constrained by the unitarian theology of his Jewish heritage. Harvey says:

> I must now introduce one further instance of those historical constraints which, I have argued, give definition and content to the bare general statements which constitute the main part of our reliable information about Jesus. This is the constraint

of that instinctive and passionate monotheism which lay at the heart of all Jewish religion and (at least in the eyes of pagans) constituted a great part of its identity. "The Lord our God is one God": so begins the prayer (the *Shema*) which every Jew said, and still says, daily; "Thou shalt have no other gods besides me"; so began the Decalogue which, in the time of Jesus, was recited every day in public worship. The belief that there is only one God, and that he is Lord of all, was fundamental to the one religion in antiquity which offered determined and uncompromising opposition to the tolerant polytheism of the pagan world. It was within a culture indelibly marked by this monotheism that Jesus lived and died and was proclaimed. It was within this constraint that he had to convey his conviction of divine authorisation and that his followers had to find means of expressing his unique status and significance...

Within the Jewish community, the power of the monotheistic confession is seen perhaps most clearly in the criminal code: the most grievous offences were those which in any way diminished the unique majesty and honour of God...Moreover any intellectual or religious opinion which seemed to postulate a second celestial being independent of the one god was firmly anathematised...From the prophetic denunciation of idol-worship to the strident polemics of Hellenistic Judaism against any manifestation of paganism, faith in the exclusive oneness of God is felt to be totally incompatible with the recognition of any other divine being...

Jesus himself is recorded as having endorsed the standard Jewish confession of monotheism (Mark 12:29). (Justin [Martyr] cites Jesus as a teacher of traditional Jewish monotheism. 1 *Apol.* 13.) [Jesus] accepted the prohibition which this implied of any moral comparison between himself and God (Mark 10:18); moreover in the Fourth Gospel he is made to deny vigorously the accusation that he set himself up as a being equal to and independent of God. (Most explicitly at Jn. 10:33: Jesus' reply makes the semantic point that there is precedent in his own culture for using the word *theos* for beings who are other than the one God; but the main burden of his reply, as throughout the gospel, is that, far from being a

second or second rival god, he is totally dependent on and united with the Father.)[92]
And he calls "the one who alone is truly God" his Father (John 17:3).

Professor Harvey then says:

> The New Testament writers similarly are insistent about the absolute oneness of God, and show no tendency to describe Jesus in terms of divinity [Deity]: the few apparent exceptions are either grammatically and textually uncertain or have an explanation which...brings them within the constraint of Jewish monotheism. It was not until the new religion had spread well beyond the confines of its parent Judaism that it became possible to break the constraint and describe Jesus as divine. (The first unambiguous instances are in Ignatius of Antioch, writing c. 110 AD.) It is significant that Jewish Christian churches continued to exist for at least a century which refused to take this step...
>
> The immediate followers of Jesus were strictly bound by the constraint of that monotheism which, as Jews, they instinctively professed, and in their attempts to declare who Jesus was they stopped well short of describing him as "divine." But at the same time the importance they assigned to the title "Son of God" suggests that when it was accorded to such a person as Jesus was remembered to have been it was felt to imply the truth of those claims to divine authority which were characteristic of his whole style of action and utterance: Jesus had indeed shown that absolute obedience to God, had spoken of God with that intimate authority, and had acted with the unique authorisation which belonged to God's representative and agent on earth, which would be characteristic of one who was (in the senses usually ascribed to "sonship" in antiquity) in very truth "Son of God."[93]

I would add that that unique Sonship, marking him out as the head and in a sense progenitor of a brand new race of humans, was vindicated by the reversal effected by God, his Father — his resurrection from the dead.

---

[92]*Jesus and the Constraints of History,* Duckworth, 1982, 154, 155, 157.
[93]Ibid., 157, 158, 167.

Harvey notes that "There is no evidence whatever that [Jesus] spoke or acted as if he believed himself to be 'a god,' or 'divine.'" The attacks from the Jews are inferences which are "countered by showing that, far from usurping God's authority and power, Jesus was fully authorised to act as God's accredited agent."[94]

> He assumed an authority to declare the will of God for men, and to act in accordance with that will, such as had not been claimed by any previous figure in the religious history of the Jews...To describe himself...as "the Son of God" would have been a way...of claiming such unprecedented divine authorisation, at the same time as preserving intact that respect for the indivisible oneness of God which was the instinctive possession of any religious Jew.[95]

The Candid Admissions of Trinitarians and Church Fathers

History records some extraordinary admissions by churchmen that there is something radically amiss with the received doctrine of the Trinity:

> The Eastern theologian John of Damascus...replied to the criticism that icons are unscriptural by admitting the fact, and adding that you will not find in scripture the Trinity or the [one substance] or the two natures of Christ either. But we know *those* doctrines are true. And so, having acknowledged that icons, the Trinity and the incarnation are innovations, John goes on to urge his reader to hold fast to them as venerable traditions delivered to us by the fathers. If they were lost, the whole gospel would be threatened.[96]

Theodore the Studite (759-826) adopted the argument of John of Damascus that the Trinity should be accepted just as tradition. Professor Don Cupitt comments: "It brings out an odd feature of Christianity, its mutability and the speed with which innovations come to be vested with religious solemnity to such an extent that anyone who questions them finds *himself* regarded as the dangerous innovator and heretic."[97]

---

[94]Ibid, 168.
[95]Ibid.
[96]Don Cupitt, "The Christ of Christendom," in *The Myth of God Incarnate*, 133.
[97]Ibid.

One of the most influential architects of the Trinitarian doctrine, Gregory of Nyssa, admitted that the Trinity is in part a concession to paganism. The unitary monotheism of Jesus and Judaism he rejected as "Jewish heresy." Readers may find shocking this summary of Gregory of Nyssa's opinion of what he disparagingly calls "Jewish monotheism": "The mystery of the faith avoids equally the absurdity of Jewish monotheism, and that of heathen polytheism."[98] Another chief architect of Trinitarian dogma was Gregory of Nazianzus who says: "Into what were you baptized? The Father? Good but Jewish still. The Son?...good...but not yet perfect. The Holy Ghost?...Very good...this is perfect...And what was the common Name [of these]? Why, God."[99]

In *The Great Catechism*, Gregory of Nyssa wrote:

And so one who severely studies the depths of the mystery [of the Trinity] receives secretly in his spirit, indeed, a moderate amount of apprehension of the doctrine of God's nature, yet he is unable to explain clearly in words the ineffable depth of this mystery. As, for instance, how the same thing is capable of being numbered and yet rejects numeration, how it is observed with distinctions yet is apprehended as a monad, how it is separate as to personality yet is not divided as to subject matter. For, in personality, the Spirit is one thing and the Word another, and yet again that from which the Word and Spirit is, another. But when you have gained the conception of what the distinction is in these, the oneness, again, of the nature admits not division, so that the supremacy of the one First Cause is not split and cut up into differing Godships, *neither does the statement [of the Trinity] harmonize with the Jewish dogma*, but the truth passes in the mean between these two conceptions, destroying each heresy, and yet accepting what is needful for it from each. *The Jewish dogma is destroyed* by the acceptance of the Word, and by the belief in the Spirit; while the polytheistic error of the Greek school is made to vanish by the unity of the Nature abrogating this imagination of plurality. While yet again, of the Jewish conception, let the unity of the Nature

---

[98] *The Great Catechism*, ch. 1.
[99] Oration 33: "Against the Arians," XVII.

stand; and of the Hellenistic, only the distinction as to persons; the remedy against a profane view being thus applied, as required, on either side. For it is as if the number of the triad were a remedy in the case of those *who are in error as to the One*, and the assertion of the unity for those whose beliefs are dispersed among a number of divinities. [100]

Those who worked out the dogma of the Trinity apparently felt unembarrassed to speak of the destruction of "the Jewish dogma." But had not Jesus quoted that very "Jewish dogma"? Does not this hallowed church father condemn Jesus as one of those "who are in error as to the One"? The root of the church fathers' mistaken notion is that "we must be careful not to allow this term 'Begotten' to suggest to us any analogy with created things."[101] The word "beget" must be silenced by emptying it of its actual meaning.

But this is to deny God's activity in history, to keep Him out of His own creation. The whole method is ahistorical and Gnostic. Just as traditional Christianity has tended to describe the Christian future wrongly as "beyond time and space," instead of connecting it with the restoration of the earth in a new age of history on earth,[102] so the fathers de-historized the promise of the birth of the Messiah. They moved it back into invisible pre-history and obscured it. Henry Alford admits that the fathers had to "assign a fitting sense to the word 'today' in Psalm 2:7."[103] But that "fitting sense" was in fact the dissolving of the meaning of plain words and the rejection of prophetic Scripture in the interests of a mistaken view of the son of David. The whole Trinitarian project needs to be reexamined in the light of the biblical view of God's promises in history and within the human biological chain. Muslims are quite wrong to think of crude sexual begetting, but Christians undermine the historical biological miracle by which the Father procreated, and thus gave existence to, His unique Son.

No wonder then that Leonard Hodgson, Regius Professor of Divinity at Oxford, lecturing on the Trinity in 1943 admitted that unitarianism had a far firmer biblical basis. Speaking as a Trinitarian

---

[100]*The Great Catechism*, ch. 3.
[101]Gregory Nazianzen, Introduction to the Theological Orations.
[102]The promised Kingdom of God at the return of Jesus, which is the subject of the Christian Gospel.
[103]*The Greek Testament*, 4:16.

he said that in the debates in the 17th and 18th centuries "the unitarians as well as their opponents accepted the Bible as containing revelation given in the form of propositions...The impression which they leave on my mind is that on the basis of argument which both sides held in common, the unitarians had the better case."[104]

Professor Maurice Wiles of Cambridge noted in 1973 that "the Reformers, for all their recasting of the tradition and insistence on the New Testament as their sole authority, remained fully traditionalist in christological doctrine." He then reaffirms the words of Leonard Hodgson which we have just quoted. Unitarians had the Bible on their side, while the Christological doctrine of the official Church "has never in practice been derived simply by way of logical inference from the statements of Scripture." Calling for a large-scale reexamination of the Church's view of God and Jesus is the provocative conclusion of Maurice Wiles: "The church has not usually in practice (whatever it may have claimed to be doing in theory) based its christology exclusively on the witness of the New Testament."[105]

The reformers in fact did not fully examine the creeds which they inherited in the light of the Hebrew background of Jesus and the Apostles. Such historical sleuthing was left to later generations, and the results of close examination reveal a large gap between Jesus' and the later doctrine of God. Luther's exaggerated concern with Romans and his comparative neglect of the synoptic gospels was bound to result in an unbalanced view of the faith. When Jesus is not allowed to be the controlling factor in New Testament theology, we are in trouble. And Jesus makes that point, over and over again, as do the Apostles. He makes it repeatedly and emphatically in the gospel of John. Could anything be more shockingly clear than Peter's comment in Acts 3:23: "Everyone who does not listen to that prophet [the Messiah] will be cut off from the people," reflecting Jesus' own words in John 3:36: "Whoever disobeys the Son will not see life, but the wrath of God remains upon him."

---

[104]*The Doctrine of the Trinity*, 220, 223.
[105]*The Remaking of Christian Doctrine*, SCM Press, 1974, 54, 55.

The Bible Dictionary

Jesus' views of himself, of God and the spirit as the operational presence and power of God, not a third person, are made clear in the *Dictionary of Christ and Gospels*:

> The sphere of the revelation of Jesus was limited to the Fatherhood of God, and all His other references to the Divine Being are more or less incidental. They involve conceptions which He shared with OT prophets... He never sought to prove the existence or the personality of God. These were invariably assumed... To Jesus, as to His people through many centuries, God was one. *He did not modify this ancient belief.* To the scribe who asked which commandment was greatest, Jesus quoted the familiar confession from Deut. 6:4ff which begins with the words, "Jehovah our God is one Jehovah" (Mark 12:29); and the author of the Fourth Gospel represents Jesus as addressing these words of prayer to the Father — "This is life eternal, that they should know thee, the *only* true God" (Jn. 17:3)...
>
> The language of [Jesus' sayings on the spirit] does not appear to suggest a different view of the Spirit from that of the old prophets...It is obvious that we cannot draw any personal distinction between this Spirit and God...We conclude this paragraph with the statement that there is nothing in the narrative of the genuine teaching of Jesus which suggests a modification of the old prophetic conception of a pure monotheism.[106]

On what authority, we may well ask, has the Church broken trust with Jesus' central belief about God?

Other distinguished biblical authorities are just as candid. Hastings' *Dictionary of the Bible* in its long article on "God" says:

> The revelation God gives of Himself is a revelation of Himself as He is in truth, though it may be impossible to reveal Himself fully to men. The Old Testament conception of God is that *of a Person* with ethical attributes; it nowhere speculates on His physical essence. God is nowhere called spirit in the Old Testament; like men, He has a spirit; but spirit never denotes substance, but always connotes energy

---

[106]*A Dictionary of Christ and the Gospels*, 1:650, 651.

and power, especially life-giving power... From the earliest period when God is spoken of, He is regarded as a *Person*. The word Yahweh is a personal name...He is self-conscious, and swears "by his holiness" (Amos 4:2), that is by His Godhead (Gen. 22:16)...God is *fully personal* from the first, while His moral being becomes clearer and more elevated, or at least receives fuller expression...God's walking in the garden (Gen. 3:8) [and other such passages] are a testimony to the vividness with which God's personality was conceived.[107]

This fine statement seems so much more natural to the text of the Bible than that of some modern Trinitarians such as James White, who tries to persuade us that the biblical God is not a person but a Being, three persons in one *what*. White insists that "what 'person' means when we speak of [the three members of] the Trinity is quite different than when we speak of creatures such as ourselves." And "the one *what* is the Being or essence of God." Very confusingly, however, some pages later, White is defining the one Being as "the eternal God *who* created everything." For White "the word 'God' can refer to the Father, to the Son, to the Spirit, or to all three persons at once."[108] But no example of such a use of the word "God" can be found in Scripture.

---

[107]197, 198, emphasis added.
[108]*The Forgotten Trinity*, 27, 132, 71.

Chapter 10

Mathematical Marvels and the Obstruction of Monotheism

"We must never forget that Christianity was built upon the foundation of Jewish monotheism."[1]

"*Eis* [one] means 'single, unique, only, unitary, one of two.' Early Christianity has a comprehensive awareness of the astonishing import of the single and the unique."[2]

The idea that the God of the Hebrew Bible, who is a single divine Individual, reveals Himself as mysteriously three is contradicted by the New Testament from beginning to end. Jesus, as the center of the New Covenant, deliberately makes any change in the nature of God impossible. He insists on the unitarian Shema of his Jewish heritage (Mark 12:28-34). In John's gospel Jesus' unitarianism is equally patent. He sums up the Christian quest for eternal life as belief in "You [Father], the only one who is truly God, and in Jesus Christ whom You sent" (John 17:3). The Father, a single Person, is "the only God" (John 5:44). This is a transparently simple definition of the true God, uniting the Hebrew Bible and the Greek New Testament. If the Father is "the only one who is truly God" this means, of course, that no other person besides the Father is the true God. Jesus is never called "the only God," nor "the Almighty."[3]

---

[1]"Trinity," *A Dictionary of Christ and the Gospels*, 2:761.
[2]*Exegetical Dictionary of the New Testament,* Eerdmans, 1992, 2:434.
[3]Rev. 1:8 is no exception, though some red-letter Bibles wrongly ascribe this verse to Jesus. The Almighty in that verse is the Father as everywhere else in

Some modern exponents of religion are far removed from Jesus' concept of God. This is illustrated by the recent remark of Deepak Chopra in the *Atlanta Journal-Constitution*: "The most dangerous idea [in religion] is my God is the only true God and my religion is the only true religion."[4] Jesus would be judged guilty on both counts (John 17:3; 14:6).

As "the only true God" God is distinguished from the Messiah, His human agent. The Father is a single Person, and that single Person is defined as having "no others besides Him." This is pure unitarianism. It echoes the Hebrew Bible perfectly: "Do we not all have one Father? Has not one God created us?" (Mal. 2:10). There is nothing in John's account of Jesus' teaching, nor in any saying of Jesus, about the true God being one *substance* composed of two or three Persons. For Jesus, one single *Person*, the Father, constitutes the one true God. Jesus deliberately excludes all other persons from the Godhead. This is exactly what we expect in the context of the first century and from the Messiah, Son of God, who was a Jew as well as the founder of the Christian faith. Jesus affirmed this unitary view of God expressly in Matthew 19:17 where he says "only one is good." He was pointing to his Father. The unitarianism of Jesus is one of those immovable fixed pillars of biblical theology.

W.D. Davies, distinguished expert on the New Testament and its Jewishness, says helpfully that there are ways in which "the Old Testament and the New differ. But they constitute one book." Both Testaments present the same one God. "The God who speaks in Jesus Christ in the New Testament is the God of Abraham and Isaac and Jacob." The God who works in Christ as His final agent in the New is "the God who brought Israel out of the land of Egypt, who led her through the wilderness, spoke to her at Sinai, gave her the prophets, and brought her safely out of Babylon."[5]

The New Testament never doubts that the God of which it speaks is also the God of the Old Testament. The God who acted in creation in Genesis has acted also in Jesus Christ. As Paul puts it, "For it is the God who said, 'Let light shine out of darkness,' who has shone in our hearts to give the light of

---

the New Testament (10 times). "He who is, who was and is to come" is carefully distinguished from Jesus in v. 4 and 5.
[4]June 30, 2007.
[5]*Invitation to the New Testament*, SPCK, 1983, 6, 7.

the knowledge of the glory of God in the face of Christ" (2 Cor. 4:6). The God who spoke to Israel in diverse ways and manners also spoke in his son Jesus Christ (Heb. 1:1, 2).[6]

It would be to throw the biblical story into confusion and to contradict Hebrews 1:1-2, if one said that in fact God was working and speaking through an "eternal Son" from the beginning. This would destroy at a blow God's promise of and Israel's longing for the coming into existence of the Son of God, the descendant of King David. Just as in Jesus' parable God sent first a series of prophets and only finally his Son (Matt. 21:33-41), so the book of Hebrews tells us that God did *not* speak in a Son in Old Testament times.[7] That is because the Son was promised for the future and was not yet existing. He was to be "born" to Israel (Isa. 9:6), and the details of his birth in Bethlehem were predicted from ancient times (Mic. 5:2).

W.D. Davies has this also to say about the God of the Jews and thus of Jesus.

> A religious Jew in the first century...would begin by assuming that there was *One, Living, Personal God*, burning in his purpose, who gave meaning to life from outside life and demanded love of and obedience to himself. In other words, monotheism for first-century Judaism was an assumption...This One Holy God was the constant theme of the thinking of the Jew.[8]

That assumption is never challenged in the New Testament, and there is nothing complicated about this simple fact. It remains the potential center around which a rallying cry for faith in Jesus for all peoples may be issued worldwide. The irony is that Jewish alienation from Christianity as it has been presented to them in Trinitarian form,

---

[6]Ibid., 7.

[7]A.T. Hanson, professor of theology at the University of Hull, makes a point with which all unitarians will be delighted: "Hebrews 1:2 could be rendered: 'he has in the last days spoken to us in the mode of Son,' which would imply that the *sonship only began* at the incarnation" (*The Image of the Invisible God*, SCM Press, 1982, 83). The question is whether it is even fair to speak of Incarnation at all, if one believes, as we do, that the Son began to exist at his begetting. Hebrews has nothing to say about a non-human Son existing before his birth. Hebrews is contradicted if in fact the One God was speaking through His Son in Old Testament times.

[8]Davies, *Invitation to the New Testament*, 27, emphasis his.

may turn out to have been quite unnecessary! They could have come to Christ and rejoiced in the Messiah who like them quoted and never deviated one iota from the unitarian creed of Israel.

The great truth of unitary monotheism underlies the whole of our New Testament and is never called into question. As a Jewish unitarian, Jesus was passionately committed to the One God of his Jewish heritage. His own claims are unique, of course, and he is presented as the unparalleled human being, God's personal creation, and head of the new created race of humans, "the firstborn among many brethren" (Rom. 8:29), who are also products, as believers, of the same *new* (not the Genesis) creation. Jesus is the Son of God uniquely because of a miraculous creation in Mary. That fact is the demonstrable proposition of Luke 1:35. He comes before us as the perfect example of man in relation to his Creator. That he claimed to *be* the Creator himself is found nowhere in the New Testament. It would throw the entire Bible into confusion and result in a multiplying of God. The *whole point* of the promised Messiah is that he is the ultimate *human* representative of God, reflecting God as man was intended to do. As God's vice-regent he is man restored to the glory which Adam forfeited. To say that he is *himself* God, presents us immediately with *two* who are God, and biblical monotheism is threatened with collapse.

The Hebrew Word for One Means One

Faced with a traditional creed which contradicts the strict unitary monotheism of Jesus and of the Bible, some believers in Jesus as Messiah, even, remarkably, Messianic Jews, have felt compelled to find a way to justify their departure from Jesus' creedal monotheism. This has led to one of the most bizarre exercises in the distortion of simple words known, I suppose, to the history of ideas. It needs to be exposed as a bold venture in twisting the straightforward terminology by which the God of the Bible declares that He is one single Person.

The assault on common sense, simple language facts, and biblical authority we are speaking of has to do with the Hebrew word *echad*, which is the cardinal number "one." In counting in Hebrew one says *echad, sh'nayim, shalosh*: "one, two, three…"

Extraordinary verbal acrobatics have been performed with the word *echad* by some Trinitarians, in an effort to convince the public that the number one does not mean one. It is a tactic of desperation. It takes in only those who are not alert to the meaning of simple words. The obstruction of the straightforward meaning of the Hebrew *echad* (one) must rank amongst the most amazing pieces of bogus propaganda found in theological writing.

We cite some examples. Professor Boice attempted to find good reasons in the Hebrew Bible for believing that God is three in one. He wrote:

> It has been argued that because Deuteronomy 6:4 reads "Hear, O Israel: The LORD our God is one LORD" that the Trinity is excluded. But in this very verse the word for "one" is *echad* which means not one in isolation but one in unity. In fact, the word is never used in the Hebrew Bible of a stark singular entity. It is the word used in speaking of one bunch of grapes, for example, or in saying that the people of Israel responded as one people. After God has brought his wife to him, Adam says, "This at last is bone of my bones and flesh of my flesh; she shall be called Woman, because she was taken out of Man. Therefore a man leaves his father and mother and cleaves to his wife, and they become one flesh" (Gen. 2:23-24). Again the word is *echad*. It is not suggested that the man and woman were to become one person, but rather that in a divine way they do become one. In a similar but not identical way God is one God, but also existent in three "persons."[9]

The statement proposed by Professor Boice about the meaning of *echad* is completely untrue. *Echad* occurs 970 times in the Hebrew Bible and it is the number "one." It means "one single." It is a numeral adjective, the ordinary word for "one" functioning very much like our English number "one." The Hebrew for eleven is "one (*echad*) plus ten."

Lexicons of the Hebrew offer no support at all for any complication of the simple word "one."[10] Some unsuspecting readers

---

[9]J.M. Boice, *The Sovereign God,* Intervarsity Press, 1978, 1:139.

[10]Ernst Jenni and Claus Westermann, *Theological Lexicon of the Old Testament,* Brown, Driver and Briggs, *Hebrew and English Lexicon of the Old Testament,* Koehler and Baumgartner, *Lexicon of Biblical Hebrew.* The *Theological Wordbook of the Old Testament* speaks of diversity within unity, but states rightly that this sense is found in its plural form *achadim,* an adjective never used for the One God. Abraham was viewed as "the one"

have been bamboozled into the fraudulent argument that because "one" in English or Hebrew can *modify a compound noun*, then the word "one" itself must be "compound"! One can think of humorous ways of exposing this trick. Does the word "one" mean "black and white" in the phrase "one zebra"? Does "one" mean "one single" in the phrase "one loaf of bread" and yet *more than one* in the phrase "one loaf of *sliced* bread"? We trust that the point is clear. One tripod is still one tripod, despite the three legs on the tripod. It is the noun, in these examples, which contains the idea of plurality (three legs), while the word "one" maintains, thankfully, the stable meaning of "one single." One tripod is a single tripod. "One Lord" in the Bible does not mean two or three Lords. The meaning of "one" is precisely the same in "one rock" and "one family." The numeral adjective "one" is not affected in any way by the collective noun "family."

According to numerous popular websites and even a number of textbooks, the combination "one bunch," we are invited to think, shows that "one" means more than one, so-called "compound one" or "composite one." The mistake is quite obvious. One bunch is still in Hebrew and English *one* bunch and not two or more bunches! It is nonsense to suppose that the word "one" has altered its meaning when it modifies a compound noun. It is *the noun* which is compound and gives us the sense of plurality. The word "one" is fixed and unchanged in meaning in both "one pencil" and "one bunch." The numerical adjective, "one," retains its meaning always as "one single." When Adam and Eve are "one flesh," they are not two or more "fleshes"! One still means one. The combining of Adam and Eve as "one flesh" has not altered the meaning of "one" (*echad*).

On this amazing piece of verbal trickery Christians have been persuaded that in the phrase "one God" the word "one" imparts some sort of plurality to the word God. This is completely unfounded. It is

---

(*echad*) and "the one father." He was certainly not plural. The same work, however, curiously and without citing any examples, says that *echad* "recognizes diversity within that oneness." *Actual* definitions then follow: "one single blessing," "Solomon was alone," "uniqueness," "a single man," "one voice" (Moody Press, 1980, 1:30). The word "one" displays no sense of diversity. The complaint about the popular misuse of the Hebrew word for "one" is made well in Lindsey Killian and Dr. Emily Palik, *The God of the Hebrew Bible and His Relationship to Jesus*, Association for Christian Development, 2005, Appendix A, 35-37.

plainly false. Imagine the confusion which would ensue if when we present our one-dollar purchase at the check-out counter, we are told that "one" is really "compound one." Thus the item will cost three (or more) dollars! A compound noun is clearly made up of a number of items. But the word "one" which stands before it is not in any way changed by its proximity to the compound noun. However, the unwary have been taken in by the most amazing assertions that *echad* tells us that God is *more than one*!

Professor Boice's assertion that *echad* "in fact is never used in the Hebrew Bible of a stark singular entity" cannot possibly have been checked by that author. One suspects that it is a piece of misinformation passed on uncritically as dogma. It has, however, no basis in fact.

Equally unreasonable is the suggestion of Michael Brown on Zechariah 11:8, where the prophet speaks of one (*echad*) month. Brown asks, "What does that tell us about the essential nature of a month? Does it mean that a month does not have thirty days because it is one?"[11] The word "one" modifying "month" is not remotely connected to how many days there are in a month! On Brown's argument the word "one" loses its fixed sense as "one single." And the whole argument is then brought to bear on the central question of monotheism and is used to justify a plurality in the Godhead.

How would the proponents of one as "compound one" explain Nehemiah 11:1: "one [*echad*] out of ten"? Or Ezra 10:13: "one [*echad*] day or two"? "Two are better than one [*echad*]" (Ecc. 4:9). "If two lie down together they keep warm, but how can one alone [*echad*] keep warm?" (Ecc. 4:11). "Where a lone [*echad*] man may be overcome, two together may resist" (Ecc. 4:12). The rest of the 970 appearances of *echad* might be cited to make exactly the same point.

Ignoring this massive evidence for the meaning of the word "one" as "one single," "one alone," Robert Morey says that *echad* means "a compound of unified oneness...If the authors of the Bible were unitarians, we would not expect to find *echad* applied to God."[12] The facts are precisely the opposite. *Echad* always means "one single" and it is applied to God who is a single Person. Morey invites his readers to imagine that "one" means more than one. He cites six examples,

[11]*Answering Jewish Objections to Jesus*, Baker Books, 2000, 2:10.
[12]*The Trinity: Evidence and Issues*, World Publishing, 1996, 89.

including "one day" (Gen. 1:5). The word "one" refers to compound oneness, because the day combines morning and evening! The truth is that this means one day and not two or more days. The whole congregation from Dan to Beersheba can of course assemble "as one man" (Judges 20:1). But the word "one" means just as much "one and not more" as in every one of its occurrences.

In his long book on the Trinity Robert Morey claims that the Hebrew word "one" (*echad*) really means "more than one"! He claims support from a lexicon that "one" means "compound oneness." Morey includes a footnote to the standard Brown, Driver and Briggs *Lexicon of Biblical Hebrew* for support.[13] But the page he appeals to contains not a word of support for his theory that "one" really means "compound unity." The lexicons rightly define "one" as the cardinal number "one." *Echad is the word for "one" in counting.* Imagine the chaos of communication if "one" really means more than one. Ecclesiastes 4:9 speaks of two being better than one (*echad*). The use of "one" in the sentence "They shall become one flesh" (Gen. 2:24) does not mean that "one" is really plural. It means that two human beings in marriage become one (not two) things. The idea of plurality is not found in the word "one" at all. It is found in the context: male and female human persons.

The idea that the word *yachid* would be the only word suitable to describe a unitarian God is false. *Yachid* in Scripture is very rare and has associations like "lonely" or "solitary" which are not appropriate for God. *Echad* itself is the mathematical term meaning one and it is sometimes rendered properly as "unique" or "lone" (Ecc. 4:12, NAB) or even by the indefinite article "a." Professor Boice's extraordinary assertion that *echad* never means anything other than "compound one"[14] raises my suspicions as to how far people will go to force their view of God on to Scripture. When a contemporary author cited uncritically Boice's misinformation on the meaning of *echad*, I wrote to him and received the following gracious reply:

> Following our recent correspondence I have taken theological and academic advice, and it seems clear that...my comments on the Hebrew word *echad* are inaccurate. I am very grateful to you for pointing this out, and assure you that in the future

---

[13]Ibid., 104 referring to page 25f of Brown, Driver and Briggs.
[14]*The Sovereign God,* 1:139.

312 Mathematical Marvels and the Obstruction of Monotheism *Mathematical Marvels and the Obstruction of Monotheism*

printings of the book the paragraph will be replaced by one that uses other Old Testament arguments for the plurality of Yahweh's being. Thank you again for preventing that particular error being perpetuated in the book.[15]

This elementary information about the word "one" deserves the widest publicity. At present, the alleged "plurality" of the word "one" is being inadmissibly used to substantiate the completely unfounded idea that God in Scripture is composed of a plurality of Persons. In 2002 the Seventh-Day Adventists produced a complete book on the Trinity to reassure the religious world of their "orthodoxy." A team of their scholars argued for a personal tri-unity in God, and in support of this doctrine spoke of "the inherently plural word *echad*"[16] found in Israel's creed in Deuteronomy 6:4. If "one" is "inherently plural," then language has ceased to have stable meaning and (to quote Henry Alford from another context, Rev. 20:4-6) "there is an end to all significance in language, and Scripture is wiped out as a testimony to anything."[17]

For too long some systematic theologians have blithely inserted a post-biblical dogma into the pages of the Hebrew Bible. Gustav Oehler refers to the Shema as "the locus of the unity and Trinity of God."[18] Jesus, and many another rabbis, would feel strongly that this is to deface the sacred text.

One Lord God and the Hebrew Lexicons

"One Lord" in Israel's creed means one single Lord. Jesus said that God is one single Lord. He defined Him as the Father, as well as the God of Israel. He is "the only one who is truly God" (John 17:3). The number "one" is not in the slightest altered if the noun it modifies has different parts. This is as simple and true in Hebrew as it is in English. Thus "one family," though it has multiple members, is still one and not two families.

The fake argument is presented like this. One (*echad*) God can imply that God is more than one. This is untrue. One God or one Lord

---

[15]The reference is to John Blanchard, *Does God Believe in Atheists?* Evangelical Press, 2000, 450.
[16]Woodrow Whidden, Jerry Moon and John Reeve, *The Trinity*, Review and Herald, 2002, 76.
[17]*Greek Testament*, 4:726.
[18]*The Theology of the Old Testament*, Funk & Wagnalls, 1893, 30.

is still one single God or one single Lord. Jesus stated, agreeing with the constant reference to God as one Person in the Old Testament, that "the Lord our God is one Lord." If that statement is not clear, nothing is clear! Jesus was a unitary monotheist.

"Compound oneness" is a strange grammatical category and is certainly absent from the leading lexicons of biblical Hebrew. A glance at a reputable Bible Hebrew lexicon enables us to get our bearings. The following is the entry for the Hebrew number *echad*.

1. numeral one a)′אֶ מָקוֹם **one (single) place** Gn 1₉, בְּשָׁנָה אַחַת Ex 23₂₉,′אֶ בְּרָכָה Gn 27₃₈,′אֶ נֶפֶשׁ **one soul = one single person** Lv 4₂₇,′אֶ :: שְׁנֵי **two** :: **one** Lv 14₁₀;′אֶ מִשְׁפָּט **the same law** Nu 15₁₆, אֶ′דָתוֹ **the same law is in force** Est 4₁₁′אֶ מִדָּה **the same measure** Ex 26₂; אֶחָד ′ **Dt 6₄ Yahweh is one** (Sept., Pesh., Stade *Theologie* 1:84); alt.: the one Y, Y **alone**, Y **only;**′אֶ **one and only Zech 14₉**, the same (?) Jb 31₁₅ alt. one; → TWNT 3.1079f; vRad *Theologie* 2:226; Eichrodt *Theologie* 1:145, Labuschagne 137f; b) part. (VG 2:273a) אַחַד הָעָם **one of the people** 1S 26₁₅, הַנְּבָלִים אֶ′ 2S 13₁₃, אַחַת הַנְּבָלוֹת Jb 2₁₀′אֶ אֲחִיכֶם **one of you brothers** Gn 42₁₉, מִכֶּם אֶ′ אִישׁ **a single one of you** Jos 23₁₀, מִמֶּנּוּ אֶ′ (GK §130a) **one of us** Gn 3₂₂; c) negative form:′אֶ ...לֹא Ex 8₂₇ and לֹא אֶ′ עַד־אֶ (אַחַד abs., BL 622b) 2S 17₂₂ **not one,**′אֶ נַם ⌐yae **not even one** Ps 14₃′אֶ עַד ...לֹא. **not even one** Ex 14₂₈; d)′אֶ קוֹל **with one voice** Ex 24₃,′אֶ לֵב 1C 12₃₉ cj. Ps 83₆ (rd. וְ אֶחָד) unanimous,′אֶ שְׁכֶם **shoulder to shoulder** Zeph 3₉;′אֶ לְיוֹם **for a single day**, daily 1K 5₂, cj. Neh 5₁₅ for אַחַר;′אֶ יוֹם **never-ending day** Zech 14₇; אַחַת (sc.′אֶ פַּעַם) **once:** בַּשָׁנָה אֶ′ Ex 30₁₀ Lv 16₃₄;′אֶ :: שְׁתַּיִם **once ...twice** 2K 6₁₀ Ps 62₁₂ (?, → שְׁתַּיִם) Jb 40₅; בְּאַחַת Jr 10₈ and כְּאֶחָד Qoh 11₆ **in one and the same time;** (→ BArm. כַּחֲדָה, Aramaism Arm.lw. Wagner 124; Akk. *kīma ištēn*), אַחַת Ps 89₃₆ and בְּאַחַת Jb 33₁₄ **once and for all;** הוּא אֶ′ **only one** Gn 41₂₅ , אֶחָד... וַיְהִי **became one, a unit** Ex 36₁₃; אֶחָד הַמִּשְׁכָּן וְהָיָה **a single whole** Ex 26₆; in statistical records repeated after each name Jos 12₉₋ ₂₄ cj. 1K 4₈₋₁₈ (Sept.), Montgomery-G. 124; e) pl. יָמִים אֲ′אֶ אֲחָדִים **a few days** Gn 27₄₄ 29₂₀ Da 11₂₀ אֶ μyrlb;D" **the same (kind of)**

words Gn 11₁ Ezk 29₁₇ (:: Gordon UTGl. 126: like Ug. *aḥdm* du. "a pair")ʼ לְאֶ וִהְיוּ to become one Ezk 37₁₇.[19]

The unshakeable foundation of Jesus' theology is his rock-solid belief in the One God of Israel. The *Dictionary of Christ and the Gospels* calls us to a return to our Jewish-Christian roots:

> We must never forget that Christianity was built upon the foundation of Jewish monotheism. A long providential discipline had secured to the Jewish people their splendid heritage of faith in the One and Only God: "Hear, O Israel, Jehovah our God is one Jehovah..." This was the cornerstone of the religion of Israel. These were perhaps the most familiar of all sacred words to the ears of the pious Jew. They were recited continually. *Our Lord Himself had them frequently in His mind* (Matt. 22:37; Mark 12:29-30; Luke 10:27). That He thought of God always as the Supreme One is unquestionable.[20]

The non-Trinitarianism of Jesus is thus unquestionable. Jesus had the biblical definition of God always in mind and spoke of it as the most important of all truths. His followers today would honor him by thinking as he did about God.

God as One Person in the Greek New Testament

The New Testament not only defines God as the Father 1317 times, it also says expressly that God is one *Person*. Consider the following: In Galatians 3:20 (NLT) we read: "Now a mediator is helpful if more than one party must reach an agreement. But God, who is one, did not use a mediator when he gave his promise to Abraham." The same verse appears more literally in various versions: "Now there can be an intermediary only between two parties, yet God is one" (NJB). "A mediator, however, does not represent just one party; but God is one" (NIV). Tyndale translated: "A mediator is not a mediator of one. But God is one." The sense of the word *eis* (one) is "one person." So also in the creed: "Hear, O Israel, the Lord our God is one [*eis*] Lord." In Galatians 3:20 God, we might say, is a party of one. The Amplified Version captures the sense that God the Father is a single Person: "There can be no mediator with just one person. Yet

---

[19]Koehler and Baumgartner, *Lexicon of Biblical Hebrew.*
[20]"Trinity," *A Dictionary of Christ and the Gospels*, 2:761, emphasis added.

God is *only one person.*" What business then has the Church saying that God is three Persons? In so doing Jesus' creed has been replaced by a different definition of God.

A further examination of the word "one" is illuminating. In Mark 10:21 (BBE) Jesus remarked to the young man, "There is one thing [*en*] needed." The Greek here simply has the neuter form of the word one, with no noun added. "One is lacking." Translators correctly supply "thing": "One thing is lacking."

When it comes to the creed of Israel, the scribe's comment similarly provides no word after "one." But here the Greek word for "one" is masculine and carries the sense of "one person." Thus in Mark 12:32: "And the scribe said to him, 'Well spoken, teacher; you have rightly said that He is one Person, and there is no other besides Him." This is unitarian theology in its purest and simplest form. The scribe is in agreement with Jesus, the unitarian.

Similarly obvious examples of the word one are found in Mark. "One [*eis*] of the twelve" (Mark 14:20). The reference was to Judas who was one person. "This man is definitely one [*eis*] of them!" (Mark 14:69). So also in Romans 3:30: "For God is one, and will justify the circumcised on the basis of faith and the uncircumcised through faith." God here is one (*eis*), the masculine form of one. The sense is one Person, certainly not one thing — certainly not "one What."

Other passages follow the pattern of Galatians 3:20: "Now a go-between is not a go-between of one; but God is one." The sense again is that God is one Person. "Rebekah...when she had conceived twins by *one* man, our father Isaac" (Rom. 9:10). Here again we have the masculine form of the word "one." The sense of course is "one man," one person, exactly the language used of God, who as the Father is viewed as a single Individual. "Jesus said to him, 'Why do you call me good? No one is good but one [Person], that is, God'" (Mark 10:18).

The unitarian God appears when Paul makes a definitive creedal statement: "For there is one God and one mediator between God and men, *the man* Christ Jesus" (1 Tim. 2:5). James, the half-brother of Jesus, was a unitarian also: "You have the belief that God is one and you do well: the evil spirits have the same belief, shaking with fear" (James 2:19). The sense is, "You believe that God is one Person." "As

Scripture says: 'Not one of them is upright, not a single one'" (Rom. 3:10). Not a single person (*eis*) is upright.

In Romans 5:16-19, one individual is repeatedly described simply by the numeral adjective *eis* — one person:

Tthe free gift is not like the result of that one man's sin. For the judgment following one trespass brought condemnation, but the free gift following many trespasses brought justification. For if by the transgression of the one [*eis*], death reigned through the one [*eis*], much more those who receive the abundance of grace and of the gift of righteousness will reign in life through the one [*eis*], Jesus Christ...For as through the one man's disobedience the many were made sinners, even so through the obedience of the one [*eis*] the many will be made righteous (Rom. 5:16-19).

"The one" here is obviously one person, one individual. The same singular masculine word for one is used of God in the creedal statements we have examined.

The Loss of the Simple Numerical Concept "One"

The confusion over the simple concept of God as one Person, so unremittingly presented in Scripture, has led clergy to make extraordinary comments on the difficulty of their Trinitarian position: "It was our blessed Lord's Divinity which, we have seen, he studiously concealed, but wished all men to come to the knowledge of."[21]

Luther said of the Trinity that he did not so much believe it as find it true in experience...It was experience and not faith alone that made him a Trinitarian...Servetus, a Spanish physician, paid with his life at the hands of Calvin for disbelieving that three could simultaneously be one.[22]

J.H. Newman, who left the Church of England for the Roman Catholic Church, is hardly confident of the Trinitarian creed: "The mystery of the doctrine of the Holy Trinity is not merely a verbal contradiction, but an incompatibility in the human ideas

---

[21]Cited in John Wilson, *Unitarian Principles Confirmed by Trinitarian Testimonies*, 353.

[22]Jacques Barzun, *From Dawn to Decadence,* HarperCollins, 2000, 30-31.

conveyed...We can scarcely make a nearer approach to an exact enunciation of it, than that of saying that one thing is two things."[23]

Episcopal priest Dick Nolan remembers:

When I lectured "lightly" (meaning: as a novice scholar) along these [non-Trinitarian] lines in the 1970s at a Roman Catholic college in Connecticut, the chairman/priest of the theology department said right out that he didn't doubt what I was saying regarding Jesus and Scripture — *but* that the Roman Catholic Church teaches differently, *enriched* by the Greek philosophical heritage developing in the post-apostolic Church, period. Roman Catholics and many Anglicans place a great deal of confidence in their notion of Tradition apparently as authoritative as Scripture. This allows them to be dismissive of those of us who focus on Scripture as primary and do not accept the Councils as authoritative. I don't know how one responds to their epistemological assumptions, but to say that I disagree.[24]

Roman Catholic scholar Jules Lebreton, SJ, in his detailed study of the *History of the Dogma of the Trinity*, begins by speaking of the Jewish monotheistic faith as a creed Jews were willing to die for:

Jews recite every day at the beginning of their prayers: "Hear, O Israel, the Lord our God is one Lord." According to the Rabbinical tradition, the accent should be placed on the word "one," and it is said that, when Aqiba was put to death, he kept up his courage by the repetition of that sacred word, "one." This monotheistic faith was very inspiring and an efficacious preparation for Christianity. Similarly, when our Lord was asked which was the first Commandment, he replied: "Hear, O Israel, the Lord thy God is one God" (Mark 12:29). Unfortunately the Jews were soon to make an obstinate use of these holy words in their conflict with Christianity: in the Talmud, Trinitarian faith is refuted on the grounds of polytheism by this verse of Deuteronomy. At the date of which we are speaking, the decisive test has not yet been applied; Christ has not yet appeared, and the monotheism of the Jews is not yet in opposition to the dogma

---

[23]*Select Treatises of St. Athanasius*, 515.
[24]E-mail message, August 8, 2006.

of the Trinity; on the contrary, that Monotheism was a *preparation for belief in the Trinity* by widening the conception of God, and making it more universal and less national.[25]

What has happened here? With one hand Lebreton concedes that Jesus was an exponent of Jewish monotheism, and then he seems to reverse his own thinking. He speaks of the dogma of the Trinity as a legitimate universalizing of the idea of God. He relegates the teaching of Jesus about who God is to a mere "preparation for Christianity." Jesus therefore must have been a pre-Christian teacher. The Jews (wrongly as Lebreton thinks) stubbornly used the Shema against the later Christian dogma of the Trinity. But then Jesus was one of those stubborn unitarian Jews! Would he today be less at odds with the Christianity which bears his name?

Later church fathers admitted that their Trinitarian view of God was not found in Moses. Church father Epiphanius says: "The divine unity was first and foremost proclaimed by Moses, the duality (the distinction between Father and Son) was heavily stressed by the prophets, and the Trinity was clearly shown forth in the Gospel."[26] The affirmation of the Mosaic Shema by Jesus, however, prevents any such "enrichment" or expansion of the Godhead. The God of Jesus is the unchanging God of Moses and of Abraham, Isaac and Jacob — why not unanimously of the Christian followers of Jesus?

Epiphanius is quite mistaken to imagine that the prophets spoke of a duality of Father and Son in God. If, as Lebreton says, the Jews made "an obstinate use" of the Shema to counter the Christian Trinitarian creed, why does he not add that Jesus himself was an equally obstinate proponent of the unitary monotheistic creed of Israel? Jesus according to our records remains in opposition to the Church creed which has forgotten about his own teaching on the nature of God.

Surely it is time for the Church to become honest with the words of its founder and to admit that the appallingly complex notion of God as three-in-one is no part of the Bible, which is supposed to be the norm for Christian understanding, since at least Protestant Christians claim the *sola scriptura* slogan as the heart of their belief.

---

[25]*History of the Dogma of the Trinity*, Benziger Brothers, 1939, 1:76-77, emphasis added.
[26]Ibid., 416.

The words of a noted systematic theologian may encourage a return to Jesus as our theologian:

> The Church's doctrine of the Trinity would seem to be the furthest from the [New Testament writers'] minds, and today the reader may well wonder whether it is even helpful to refer to such a dogma in order to grasp the theology of the New Testament. When the Church speaks of the doctrine of the Trinity, it refers to the specific belief that God exists eternally in three distinct "persons," who are equal in Deity and one in substance. In this form the doctrine is not found anywhere in the New Testament; it was not so clearly articulated until the late fourth century.[27]

Modern Objectors to the Loss of Jesus' Creed

Other significant contemporary voices are being raised in protest against the obstruction of the teaching of Jesus about God. Professor of systematic theology Karl-Heinz Ohlig of Saarbruck concludes his magnificent study of the history of Trinitarianism by saying, "Jesus himself knew only of the God of Israel, whom he called Father...The Trinity...possesses no Biblical foundation whatsoever."[28]

Professor J. Harold Ellens pleads with the Church to speak with honesty:

> It should be candidly admitted by the Church, then, that its roots are *not in Jesus of Nazareth*...nor in the central tradition of Biblical Theology...Its roots are in Philonic Hellenistic Judaism and in the Christianized Neo-Platonism of the second through the fifth century.[29]

Professor Martin Werner had alerted the Church to its own early misdevelopment, complaining that the post-biblical Church achieved such a transformation in the identity of its Savior that it created "a myth, behind which the historical Jesus completely disappeared."

> The new interpretation of the concept "Son of God" did correspond to the mythological thought of Hellenistic folk-religion...The new interpretation had first appeared in the

---

[27]Christopher B. Kaiser, *The Doctrine of God: A Historical Survey*, Crossways, 1982, 23.
[28]*One or Three?* 129, 130.
[29]*The Ancient Library of Alexandria and Early Christian Theological Development*, Institute for Antiquity and Christianity, 1993, 39.

oldest form of Gnosticism...A Gnostic theory was rejected, but sooner or later *it was annexed by the Church to its own set of fundamental notions*...With what hopelessly confused formulae the Nicean party at first entered into the debate with the Arians[30]...Alexander of Alexandria [said that the Son] exists "independently of God (the Father), continually begotten, in a state of unbegottenness"...This theology no longer presented itself unequivocally as a monotheism...Judged by a rigorist monotheistic criterion, not only Gnosticism, but also the teaching of the Church's theologians was defective...For, according to the New Testament witnesses, in the teaching of Jesus and the Apostles, relative to the monotheism of the Old Testament and Judaism, there had been no element of change whatsoever. *Mk. 12:29 recorded the confirmation by Jesus himself, without any reservation, of the supreme monotheistic confession of faith of Israelite religion in its complete form.*[31]

How astonishing then that a contemporary apologist for the Trinity was able to pen these words in his discussion of the Shema:

The shadow of the *Shema*, "Hear O Israel: The Lord our God is one Lord" (Deut. 6:4), though *never quoted in the New Testament* (though alluded to in James 2:19), broods over its pages with all the weight it carried in Old Testament times, being the chief and holiest declaration of the Jewish religion.[32]

But it is indeed quoted in the New Testament, and by Jesus himself. One might wonder whether anyone is equipped to discuss the Trinity in the New Testament, if he is unaware that Jesus quoted the Shema in the New Testament!

Equally perplexing is the blatant contradiction of Luke 1:35 found in Hastings' *Dictionary of the Bible's* article on the Trinity. In its comment on Luke 1:35, which grounds the Sonship of Jesus in the

---

[30]Even at Nicea "person" (*hypostasis*) and "essence" (*ousia*) meant the same thing. Later a clear distinction between these terms formed the basis of the Trinity.

[31]Werner, *Formation of Christian Dogma*, 219, 221, 223, 233, 235, 241, emphasis added.

[32]E. Calvin Beisner, *God in Three Persons*, Tyndale House, 1984, 26, emphasis added.

miraculous begetting, the dictionary first quotes the RV: "that which is to be born [margin: or is begotten] shall be called holy, the Son of God," and then denies the obvious reason for Jesus' Sonship: "It was not the *Sonship* but his *holiness* from his very birth which was secured by the miraculous conception."[33] Luke makes no such distinction. Jesus is both the Son of God and holy *precisely because* he was supernaturally begotten in Mary. It is the miracle performed in his mother which constitutes Jesus Son of God. Jesus did not *become* a man after being an invisible spirit; he was a man from conception!

Jewish Opposition to the Trinity

We remind our readers again of Jewish commentary which is rightly offended by Christian attempts to interfere with the unitarian creed of Moses and Jesus. From an orthodox Jew comes this objection to the Christian departure from the creed of Israel:

As every Jewish child learns, "Shema Yisroel, HaShem Elokeynu, HaShem Echad" ("Hear O Israel, the Lord is G d, the Lord is One"). Deut. 6:4. This is a very simple and fundamental concept. G-d is one.

Christians give lip service to the Shema, but their theology says that there is a Trinity — G-d, Jesus (the "son of G-d") and the "Holy Ghost." They will try to teach you that this Trinity of three entities is really just one, like a "bunch of grapes" is one. But the Torah is very precise in its language...Christians cite Genesis 1:5 ("v'ai yehi erev, v'ai yehi boker, yom echad" — "...and there was evening and there was morning one day") to suggest that *echad* modifies morning and evening and puts them together into a "bunch." Clearly, it only modifies the word "day." Similarly, they quote Numbers 13:23 which describes how the Israeli spies cut down a branch with one (*echad*) cluster of grapes. But here, too, *echad* modifies the word "cluster" and not grapes. In the Shema, *echad* modifies the word "G-d" and means precisely what it says — "one." Moreover, if the Torah wanted us to know that G-d was more than One it would have

---

[33]Extra vol., 309.

told us then about the Trinity instead of making a specific point that there was only One G-d.[34]

[34]Bruce James (Baruch Gershom), "Why Can't a Jew Believe in Jesus?" http://judaism.about.com/od/jewishviewofjesus/a/jesus_onegod.htm

Chapter 11

An Introduction to Dissident Heroes

Friday, May 17th, 1527. Rottenburg, Germany.

The judges returned with a verdict of guilty and a sentence of horrifying and unmitigated savagery. "Michael Sattler shall be committed to the executioner, who shall convey him to the square and first cut out his tongue. Then he shall forge him fast to a wagon and thereon with glowing iron tongs twice tear pieces from his body, then on the way to the site of execution five times more in the same manner, and then burn his body to powder as an arch-heretic."

There was a moment of emotion. The prisoner's wife turned to her husband and, drawing him to her, embraced him in the sight of the entire crowd. It moved at least one member of the audience.

Sattler was remanded in custody for a further three days. Said a friend in a letter: "What fear, what conflict and struggle flesh and spirit must have undergone cannot be imagined."

There is a spot on the Tübingen road, about a mile out of Rottenburg, where men, following such dim light as they had, in the name of perverted justice, removed from their midst one more worthy than themselves. The cutting out of the tongue was bungled, allowing Michael to pray for his persecutors. As he was lashed to the ladder he spoke with concern to Halbmayer, urging him to have no part in the deed lest he also be condemned. The mayor answered defiantly that Sattler should concern himself only with God.

His last public words, uttered with difficulty, were a prayer for God's help to testify to the truth. The ladder was thrown on to the fire. As the fire burned through the ropes that bound his hands, he raised two fingers of his hand in a victory sign, a pre-arranged signal to his friends that he had been steadfast. He was thirty-seven...Eight days later [his wife] was thrown into the Neckar river and drowned.[1]

John Biddle (1615-1662) was a distinguished British academic, graduate of Oxford, and at the age of 26 elected headmaster of Crypt Grammar School in Gloucester, England. Since he was asked to teach Scripture, he began a painstaking examination of the Bible. He was supposed to teach his students according to the catechism of the Church of England but soon found this impossible. His relentless search for truth in Scripture produced in him an encyclopedic knowledge of the Bible. He knew the whole of the New Testament by heart in English *and* in Greek. He admitted that he had some difficulty in remembering the Greek text after Revelation 4!

He spoke against the spurious Trinitarian verse in 1 John 5:7 and explained the oneness of Jesus and the Father as "an union in consent and agreement...but never an union in essence."[2] He later debated with Bishop Ussher (of "Ussher's chronology" fame) and outwitted him, asserting that the Father is the only true God! He produced a pamphlet entitled "Twelve Arguments against the Deity of the Holy Spirit." Someone gave a copy to the magistrates and he was committed to jail.

In 1646 Biddle was summoned to London and confined in the Gatehouse at Westminster while his trial dragged on. He remained in prison for five years, mostly for his questioning of the Trinity. He spoke of the church fathers as those who "did in outward profession so put on Christ, as that in heart they did not put off Plato."[3] He alluded to Matthew 19:4 where he maintained that Jesus, in referring to "Him that made them in the beginning," attributed the creation to a Being other than himself. Deserted by his friends, he spent most of the rest of his life in prison.

The British Houses of Parliament passed the following law:

---

[1] Alan Eyre, *The Protesters*, The Christadelphian, 1975, 69-70. Sattler was convicted for his views on non-involvement in war.
[2] Ibid., 123-24.
[3] Ibid., 125.

Any who shall by preaching, printing or writing controvert the deity of the Son or the equality of Christ with the Father, shall suffer the pains of death, as in the case of felony, without benefit of clergy. Any who shall maintain that man hath by nature free will to turn to God; that the soul dieth after the body is dead;...that baptizing of infants is void and that such persons ought to be baptized again; that the use of arms is unlawful; that the churches of England are no more churches nor their ministers and ordinances true ministers and ordinances (shall be imprisoned).[4]

Biddle had single-handedly recovered central truths of the Bible. He claimed that he had read none of the (unitarian) Polish Brethren's literature (see below) before coming to his own conclusions.

On February 10, 1652 Biddle was released. He remained in London addressing small groups on Sundays, but he was never officially ordained. He produced a large number of tracts on different biblical topics, but principally his *A Twofold Catechism*, consisting almost entirely of Scripture verses. In his preface he speaks of "all Catechisms generally being so stuffed with the supposals and traditions of men, that the least part of them is derived from the Word of God...not one quotation amongst many being a whit to the purpose" (i.e. having any point at all).[5]

From his catechism he banned all phrases like "eternal generation of the Son," "God dying," "God made man," "mother of God." The catechism was ordered to be burnt, and he was again imprisoned along with his publisher, Richard Moore. Two days later some brethren from Poland arrived in London with tracts translated into English by Biddle and printed by Moore!

Biddle was charged with blasphemy and heresy. He escaped a capital sentence but remained in confinement. Some influential persons were bold enough to ask parliament:

whether Biddle does not, in fact, profess faith in God by Jesus Christ. Is he not like Apollos, mighty in the Scriptures? Is his crime that he believes the Scriptures according to their most

---

[4]Ibid., 125.
[5]Biddle's *A Twofold Catechism* can be read at
http://home.pacific.net.au/~amaxwell/biddle/000start.htm

obvious nearest signification, and not according to the remote and mystical interpretations?[6]

A typical argument of Biddle's is this: "He that saith Christ died, saith that Christ was not God, for God could not die. But every Christian saith that Christ died, therefore every Christian saith that Christ was not God."[7] His last days were spent writing on the personal reign of Jesus Christ on the earth.

In 1658 he was released once more. He maintained a steady contact with the Polish brethren. An observer remarked that "there is little or nothing blameworthy in him, except his opinions." Government agents pursued Biddle frequently but many were forced to admire his "strict, exemplary life, full of modesty, sobriety and forebearance, no ways contentious, altogether taken up with the great things of God revealed in the Scriptures."[8]

On June 1, 1662, he was holding a Bible study in his own home. An armed party entered the room and carried him off and imprisoned him before a Judge Brown. Five weeks later, sick with jail fever, he died, confident of his hope in the resurrection at the Second Coming. He had been unable to pay the £100 demanded as a fine. He is the father of British unitarianism.

I began with these brief sketches from the lives (and deaths) of two of the most interesting examples of dissidents to show the extraordinary antagonism which awaits any who question orthodoxy's view of the Godhead or, in the case of Sattler, other traditional doctrines. Sattler was a staunch advocate of Christians not being involved in war, a point of view recently espoused by a leading evangelical scholar in the United States.[9]

To count God as one rather than three-in-one is a risky business. The denial of popular Trinitarian notions, though less dangerous in our day, is an invitation to be labeled "cult," and to be included in the late Walter Martin's documentation of the ever-growing *Kingdom of the Cults*. It is essential for a believer in the Shema of Israel and in Jesus' affirmation of that creed to be well-informed about the doctrine of the one God. He must be expert in that teaching if he is ever to

---

[6] Alan Eyre, *The Protesters*, 129.
[7] Ibid., 130.
[8] Ibid., 130, 131.
[9] Gregory A. Boyd, *The Myth of a Christian Nation: How the Quest for Political Power Is Destroying the Church*, Zondervan, 2005.

convince anyone of its truth, especially those who have been fully exposed to "orthodox" views of God.

The Mennonites have been quick to see that converts should be given a detailed course of instruction in the history of their movement. This sense of heritage builds confidence and stability. There is a highly significant, vociferous, if often tragic heritage in the field of belief in one God, the Father, which ought to make us deeply grateful for those who lived in times of much less religious freedom. We should be conscious of their tremendous devotion to truth, often to the point of martyrdom.

For this reason *The Radical Reformation* by George Huntston Williams[10] should be central in the libraries of those espousing a "biblical unitarian" point of view. This book inspires confidence and humility, as it recalls a galaxy of dedicated Christians — those who struggled against terrible odds to preach a doctrine of God which has a firm basis in Scripture, but which is regarded as heresy by some of the mainstream.

Jesus Was Not a Trinitarian represents a Socinian view of the Son of God (after Faustus Socinus, 1539-1604).[11] A brief survey of unitarian history reveals the following as leaders in the movement which understands the Son of God as not literally preexistent, but "ideally" or "notionally" preexistent in the counsels of God. The other principal form of non-Trinitarianism is represented by the Arian position (after Bishop Arius, 250-336), which sees Jesus as preexistent but created ("There was a time when the Son was not" — Arius).[12]

---

[10]Third edition, Truman State University Press, 2000.

[11]Our Christological view does not, however, include an adherence to a Socinian view of the *atonement*. Many biblical unitarians now insist with evangelicals on the substitutionary death of Jesus for the sins of the world. Modern Socinians (in Christology) include the Church of God Abrahamic Faith, Christadelphians, and some Church of God Seventh Day members and Advent Christians. Many modern scholars of different nationalities have proposed the views we are espousing without labeling them "Socinian."

[12]Little advertised by Trinitarians is the fact that Tertullian, supposedly a stalwart supporter of orthodoxy, also stated that there was a time when the Son did not exist (*Against Hermogenes*, ch. 3). The Trinity was clearly not yet fully developed in its Nicene form.

Michael Servetus (1511-1553) is perhaps the most celebrated anti-Trinitarian. A native of Spain, anabaptist ("rebaptizer"), and "soul-sleeper,"[13] his doctrines were a constant red flag to the bull, in this case Calvin, who energetically tried to silence millenarians, soul-sleepers and anti-Trinitarians. (A little-known fact is that Luther preached a sermon in 1524 upholding the sleep of the dead.) Servetus believed that the Son of God was the biological product of God and Mary. There was no literally preexisting Son. Jesus' divinity consisted in the nature he received from God at conception. Forgotten truth was rediscovered in the Reformation period, by stages. First Servetus, later the Polish and Italian brethren led by Faustus Socinus, who arrived at a purely unitarian view (not, of course, Unitarian — capital "U" — in the contemporary sense of that word).[14] However, the Spaniard Servetus' deviation from orthodoxy on the Godhead was enough to cause his martyrdom at the hands of Calvin. His effigy was burned before he succumbed to the same fate in 1553. The theology which resulted in death for Servetus is summarized by Earl Morse Wilbur:

> What was the teaching of [Servetus'] books, that they should have so shocked the reformers?...Taking the teaching of the Bible as absolute and final authority, Servetus held that the nature of God cannot be divided, as by a doctrine of one being in three persons, inasmuch as no such doctrine is taught in the Bible, to which indeed the very terms Trinity, essence, substance, and the like as used in the Creeds are foreign, being mere inventions of men. The earlier fathers of the Church also knew nothing of them, and they were simply foisted upon the Church by the Greeks, who cared more to make men philosophers than to have them be true Christians. Equally unscriptural is the doctrine of the two natures of Christ. Servetus pours unmeasured scorn and satire on these doctrines, calling them illogical, unreasonable, contradictory, and imaginary, and he ridicules the received doctrine of the Holy Spirit. The doctrine of one God in three persons he says cannot be proved, nor even really imagined; and it raises questions which cannot be answered, and leads to countless

---

[13]I.e. the teaching that man is unconscious in death until the resurrection. The view is known as "conditional immortality."

[14]I.e. Unitarian Universalism.

heresies. Those who believe in it are fools and blind; they become in effect atheists, since they are left with no real God at all; while the doctrine of the Trinity really involves a Quarternity of four divine beings. It is the insuperable obstacle to the conversion of Jews and Mohammedans to Christianity; and such blasphemous teachings ought to be utterly uprooted from men's minds.

In place of these artificial doctrines of the creeds, Servetus draws from the Bible the following simple doctrines, and quotes many texts to prove them. Firstly, the man Jesus, of whom the gospels tell, is the Christ, anointed of God. Secondly, this man Jesus the Christ is proved by his miraculous powers and by the statements of Scripture to be literally the human Son of God, because he was miraculously begotten by him. Thirdly, this man is also "God," since he is filled with the divinity which God had granted him. Hence he is divine not by nature, as the creeds teach, but solely by God's gift. God himself is incomprehensible, and we can know him only through Christ, who is thus all in all to us. The Holy Spirit is a power of God, sent in the form of an angel or spirit to make us holy. And the only kind of Trinity in which we may rightly believe is this: that God reveals himself to man under three different aspects (*dispositiones*); for the same divinity which is manifested in the Father is also shared with his Son Jesus, and with the Spirit which dwells in us, making our bodies, as St. Paul says, "the temple of God."[15]

Anti-Trinitarianism found its fullest expression not in Spain but in Polish Socinianism[16] and Hungarian unitarianism. Many of the leaders of these movements were Italians, notably the Sozzini family, Faustus and his uncle Laelius (from whom the label "Socinian" came). Earlier and less-known pioneers who had set the scene for radical questioning of orthodoxy were Lorenzo Valla, an Italian philologist who in the 1400s raised questions about the Trinity; and a

---

[15]*Our Unitarian Heritage: An Introduction to the History of the Unitarian Movement*, Beacon Press, 1943, 61, 62. Servetus' most important work *The Restoration of Christianity* is now available in an English translation by Christopher Hoffman and Marian Hillar (Edwin Mellen Press, 2007).

[16]A noted leader was Gregory Paulus.

priest and Platonist Marsilio Ficino (d. 1499) who suggested that the *logos* of John 1:1 should be rendered not "word," but *sermo* (from which our word "sermon" is derived). He thus began a whole trend of thought which would equate the "word" with the prophetic voice of God in the Old Testament, not with an eternal second *Person*. He began thus to undermine the whole concept of the *logos* = preexisting Son as consubstantial with the Father. Where the church fathers had spoken of the "word" as an eternal Son,[17] the anti-Trinitarians of the Radical Reformation following Ficino spoke of Christ as wholly human, as the fullest and final form of the prophetic voices which had preceded him (cf. Heb. 1:1). Erasmus was also part of the anti-Trinitarian camp, and wanted to have the spurious text 1 John 5:7 removed.

In England we can single out (in addition to John Biddle mentioned earlier) a surgeon, Dr. George Van Parris, a Fleming by birth, burned at Smithfield in London on April 25th, 1557 because "he believeth that God the Father is only God, and that Christ is not very God."[18] The unitarianism produced a spate of "helpful" literature from Calvin including "A Short Instruction for to arme all-good Christian people" (i.e. against the heretics) and from Bullinger "An wholesome Antidotus or Counterpoyson" (1545) and "a most necessary and frutefull dialogue between ye seditious Libertin or rebel anabaptist and the true obedient Christian" (1551). In those days of close religious control, Bishop John Jewel reported on unitarians as follows: "We found, at the beginning of the reign of Elizabeth, a large and inauspicious crop of Arians, Anabaptists and other pests, which, I know not how, but as mushrooms spring up in the night."[19] There followed under Elizabeth I's reign the burning of two anti-Trinitarian Anabaptists, Henry Terwoort, a 35-year-old goldsmith, and John Pieters, 50, a father of nine children. Such merciful measures as strangling, suffocation or gunpowder around the neck were omitted and the two men died in unrelieved agony amidst the flames.

A notable non-Trinitarian hero was Adam Pastor, one of the clearest exponents of the unitarian view of the Godhead. He is rightly recognized as a father figure of biblical unitarianism in Europe. He

---

[17]"Son" and "eternal" are really mutually contradictory terms since one who is begotten, i.e. brought into existence, cannot be eternal.

[18]Williams, *The Radical Reformation*, 779-780.

[19]John Jewel's *Works* (1560), Cambridge, 1850, 4:1240.

had been a Roman Catholic priest before joining the Anabaptists in 1533 in Münster, Germany. Pastor held (against Menno Simons of the Mennonites) that Christ was human only, though the bearer of God's Word. Adam Pastor and a Frisian elder, Francis de Cuiper, stated at a conference in 1547 that Christ did not exist as the *Son* of God previous to his coming into the world, and was divine after his birth only in the sense that God dwelt in him. Adam Pastor was excommunicated even by some of his Anabaptist colleagues, but gained a large following calling themselves Adamites.

Pastor wrote tracts on thirteen topics including Incarnation and the Kingdom of God. The section on God is a listing of unitarian texts of the Old and New Testaments with a minimum of comment. Pastor insisted that no text showed that *the Son* existed before the Incarnation, as a member of a tri-personal Godhead. Adam Pastor was described as earnest and critical, but mild and reverent in his debates. He was to influence the Polish unitarians who later established a significant unitarian academic center, a college at Racow in Poland.

Faustus Socinus was born on December 5, 1539. His father and grandfather had been famous lawyers. His first theological essay was an explanation of the prologue to John's gospel. He maintained that Jesus was divine by office rather than Deity by nature. He wrote also on the mortality of man.[20] It was his perception of the meaning of the *logos* which led him to the truth. The word or will of God appeared in the form of flesh — a man. After his death and resurrection, Christ ascended to take his place at the right hand of God, sharing henceforth in God's power. In that sense only could Jesus be called God, as representing God, but always distinct from the one true God (John 17:3; 5:44). God, said Socinus, assigned to Christ at the ascension an adoptive deity as co-regent in the government of the world. Socinus considered Jesus to be entitled to divine adoration, in opposition to the chief spokesman for unitarianism in Transylvania, Francis David, who did not think Jesus should be worshipped. There was really no need for serious dispute on that issue.

It was this same Faustus Socinus, perhaps the most refined theologian of the Radical Reformation, who moved to Poland and helped to establish a college and printing press at Racow, as well as

---

[20]I.e. the doctrine that at death man sleeps until the resurrection and that the final punishment of the wicked is annihilation, not everlasting torture.

farms and craft industries. This organization became an institution of international repute. Many of the faculty were scholars of unquestioned learning, some of them having been originally schooled in Hebrew and Greek before becoming Anabaptists. The school drew one thousand students from all over Europe, including three hundred from families of European nobility. A Scot who visited the campus remarked, "For whereas elsewhere all was full of wars and tumult, there all was quiet, men were calm and moderate in behaviour, although they were spirited in debate and expert in language."[21] The famous Racovian Catechism makes this statement:

> Our mediator before the throne of God is a man, who was formerly promised to our fathers by the prophets, and in these latter days was born of the seed of David, and whom God, the Father, has made Lord and Christ…by whom he created the NEW world…to the end that, after the supreme God, we should believe in him, adore and invoke him, hear his voice, imitate his example, and find in him rest to our souls.[22]

In many countries this confession was banned and its owners punished, often by death. The confession contains the doctrines of adult baptism, sleep of the dead, and the Second Coming. Many passages in John's gospel are dealt with. Typical is the following:

> That a person may have had something, and consequently may have had glory, with the Father before the world was, without its being…concluded that he then actually existed…is evident from 2 Timothy 1:9, where the apostle says of believers, that grace was given to them before the world began. Besides, it is here stated [John 17:5] that Christ prayed for this glory…Christ beseeches God to give him in actual possession, with himself, the glory which he had with him, in his purposes and decrees, before the world was. For it is often said that a person has something with any one, when it is promised, or is destined for him: on this account believers are frequently said by this evangelist to have eternal life. Hence it happens that Christ does not say absolutely that he had had that glory, but that he had had it *with the Father*; as if he had said that he now prayed to have actually

[21]Eyre, *Protesters*, 109.
[22]*The Racovian Catechism*, trans. Thomas Rees, rep. Christian Educational Services, 1994, lxxiv, note.

conferred upon him that glory which had been laid up for him with the Father of old, and before the creation of the world.[23]

Having concentrated largely on the Reformation period and the century following (in which we noted John Biddle, the schoolmaster), we should now turn our attention to the earliest period of church history. Holding as a fundamental conviction (with the 15th edition of the *Encyclopedia Britannica*) that Jesus did not in any way propose to alter the strictly monotheistic faith of Israel, we are naturally keen to know how the unitarianism of the New Testament could have been disturbed.

Church history shows that the development of the "three in one" notion was a process extending over centuries, culminating in the Nicene and Chalcedonian Councils (325 and 451 AD). It is very far from the truth to suggest that the doctrine of the Trinity gained universal acceptance from the beginning of the post-New Testament era. As the Harvard theologian F. Auer says so well:

> Fourth-century Trinitarianism did not reflect accurately early Christian teaching regarding the nature of God; it was, on the contrary, a deviation from this teaching...It developed against constant unitarian opposition and was never wholly victorious. The dogma of the Trinity owes its existence to abstract speculation on the part of a small minority of scholars.[24]

The crux of the whole Trinitarian problem lies in the *logos* doctrine and its development. The "orthodox" position was based upon the understanding of *logos* as a second divine Person in the eternal Godhead. The point is obscured for contemporary readers of the Bible by the simple fact that the grammatically masculine word *logos* in Greek is referred to as "he," "him" (John 1).[25] If however *logos* were rendered "God's utterance," and "it," a quite different impression would be gained. Thus the impersonal *logos* of the prologue, i.e. God's word, wisdom and mind, becomes embodied in Jesus, the man.

"The *logos* of the prologue became Jesus; Jesus was the *logos* become flesh, but not the *logos* as such...Jesus was the *logos* in

---

[23]Ibid., 144-145.
[24]*Encyclopedia Americana*, 1956, 27:249.
[25]Eight English translations from the Greek prior to the KJV spoke of the *logos* as "it," not "him."

334 *An Introduction to Dissident Heroes*

person! He was *it* in the flesh, as [a] mortal human being." So says, correctly, a helpful German theologian.[26]

In theology's most gripping detective story, "How the *logos* became a Person, before it became a person," we are astonished to find that Justin Martyr, writing in 150 AD, contends against a Jew, Trypho, with whom he held a lengthy debate, that Jesus as Son of God preexisted his birth quite literally and was in fact the angel of Yahweh mentioned frequently in the Old Testament. Trypho the Jew protested against the inherent contradiction involved in saying that Jesus was a man, but not *really* a man. Thus he says to Justin, "When you say that this Christ existed as God before the ages, then that he submitted to be born and become man, *yet that he is not man of man*, this appears to me to be not merely paradoxical, but also foolish."[27]

The astonishing fact is that, had the Jewish argument prevailed against the philosopher Justin Martyr (supposedly representing Christianity), the Trinitarian "problem" might never have arisen. Once the idea is floated that Jesus was "around" before his birth, he must be "found" in the Old Testament. Without a shred of biblical proof, the angel of Yahweh was said to be the preexistent Jesus, and many evangelicals as well as Jehovah's Witnesses have ever since accepted the theory. It is wise to consult the New Testament on the point. In Acts 7 Stephen summarizes the history of Israel and makes specific mention of an angel of the Lord (Acts 7:30, 38), who represents the Lord God (Exod. 23:20-21). What an opportunity for Stephen to say that the angel was Jesus, preexisting! That equation he does not make; and the writer to the Hebrews took two chapters to explain that Jesus was superior to all angels. He never has been and never will be an angel. Furthermore God did *not* speak through a Son until New Testament times (Heb. 1:1-2).

With Justin the *logos* as a second divine Person became entrenched. In the ensuing centuries isolated individuals arose to challenge orthodoxy. Notable are the "dynamic monarchians." The first of these, Theodotus of Byzantium, was a man of learning. He came to Rome in 190 AD and taught that Jesus was fully a man, born of the virgin, upon whom the Spirit came at his birth. Theodotus held that Jesus became to a greater degree divine at his resurrection.

---

[26]Leonhard Goppelt, *Theology of the New Testament*, Eerdmans, 1982, 2:297, 299, emphasis added.
[27]*Dialogue with Trypho*, ch. 48.

Theodotus was promptly excommunicated by Bishop Victor of Rome. He was followed in his thinking by another Theodotus, and by Asclepiodorus and also by Artemon, but dynamic monarchianism was dying in the West.

In the East Paul of Samosata was the chief exponent of a non-preexistent Jesus. Paul was Bishop of Antioch from c. 260-272. He considered the *logos* to be an impersonal attribute of the Father, not a preexisting Son. Jesus is a uniquely inspired man. "Paul's doctrine is akin to the primitive Jewish-Christian idea of the person of Christ." So say church historians, notably Henry Chadwick in *The Early Church*.[28] Three councils considered Paul's view and the third excommunicated him. He kept his place until driven out by the Emperor Aurelian. Of Bishop Arius (father of Arianism, as distinct from Socinianism) much more is known. He contended that Jesus was pre-existent but *created* ("There was a time when he was not"). This view was thought to be unsatisfactory since it made Jesus neither God nor man. But could not exactly the same be said of the "orthodox" view which has prevailed to this day? A leading contemporary New Testament scholar, John Knox, seems to think so: "We can have the humanity without the pre-existence and we can have the pre-existence without the humanity. There is absolutely no way of having both."[29]

Before leaving the early period we should mention as representative of a Socinian school of Christology Bishop Photinus (d. 376) whom *The Catholic Encyclopedia* labels "heretic."[30] Photinian became a term to describe anyone who held Christ to be a man, who did not exist until his birth at Nazareth. Photinus' writings are lost, but he is known to us mostly through the twenty-seven anathemas of the council in 351 which condemned him. Much later in the 600s our Christology was perhaps represented by the Paulicians (possibly named after Paul of Samosata) whose leader Constantine was executed for his heretical views of the Trinity.

Of significance for the proponents of unitary monotheism in our time was the publishing in 1977 of *The Myth of God Incarnate*.[31] Though we would not subscribe to the general theological position of

[28]Penguin, 1993, 114.
[29]*The Humanity and Divinity of Christ*, Cambridge University Press, 1967, 106.
[30]Robert Appleton Co., 1911, 12:43.
[31]John Hick, ed., SCM Press, 1977.

these scholars (i.e. in eschatology, particularly), we must welcome their refreshing analysis of the doctrine of God. They seldom use the terms Trinitarian or non-Trinitarian, but they do question whether Incarnation in the traditional sense can be found in the Bible. That is just the question asked by the pioneers of return to the unitary monotheism of the Shema. It is encouraging to hear scholars say that the Trinitarian dogma "was determined *neither by scripture* nor by experience but by the Arian controversy on the doctrine of the Trinity."[32]

It is interesting to find a schoolmate of mine, at one time a well-known television theologian and Cambridge professor, writing, "God's Son is not a second co-equal person alongside God the Father but simply man 'filled' with God, united with God."[33]

The current debate in theological circles worldwide concerns eschatology and Christology. Our desire is to lead the way back to the true Jesus, and to the Gospel about the Kingdom. John A.T. Robinson, one of Britain's best-known New Testament scholars, adopted a view of Jesus which reclaims a simple unitarianism. When I told him that I was teaching in a Bible college, his immediate reaction was: "You won't last more than a few days there; a non-Trinitarian Jesus will be quite unacceptable in an American Bible college." But his own "heretical" views were orthodox in more circles than he recognized, and even in one American Bible college.[34] We might present the debate about Christology dramatically, as below.

Some "modern" theologians: "How can we present Jesus to the people today? No one will believe in a preexistent being arriving on earth at his birth."

J.A.T. Robinson: "But wait! Did anyone in the New Testament believe that anyway? No, but the early church fathers influenced by Gnosticism misunderstood the book of John, neglected the evidence of the rest of the New Testament and Old Testament, relied on a handful of difficult Pauline verses and presented a Jesus who was literally preexistent. But this is not the Jesus of the Bible."

Biblical unitarians: "But didn't we tell you so! For two thousand years you wouldn't listen and burned us to death for questioning your official dogma. Nevertheless our task is to present to the world the

---

[32]J.A.T. Robinson, *The Human Face of God*, Westminster Press, 1973, 102.
[33]Don Cupitt, *The Debate About Christ*, 28.
[34]Atlanta Bible College, formerly Oregon Bible College, Illinois, since 1939.

true Jesus, who was never a second member of an eternal Trinity. Paul, in 2 Corinthians 11:4, warned that Satan's most diabolical trick would be to replace the real Jesus with a counterfeit Jesus, and John warned in 1 John 4:2 and 2 John 7 that the confession of a Jesus who is not the fully human historical Messiah signals the spirit of antichrist."

Orthodoxy (disbelievingly): "No one is going to tell me the Church could have been wrong for nearly two thousand years on a basic doctrine."

Biblical unitarians (answering the "modern" theologians): "The arrival of Jesus as a divine being on earth will occur at the *second* coming. Jesus *is* 'preexistent' to that event because he lives after being resurrected!"

Ultimately the confusion of Jesus with the Creator seems to come perilously close to idolatry, and we may well wonder if the Living Bible is not encouraging just that in its extravagantly inaccurate paraphrase of John 1:1-3, 10: "Before anything else existed, there was Christ with God. He has always been alive and is Himself God. He created everything there is — nothing exists that He didn't make...But although He made the world, the world didn't recognize Him when He came."

Meanwhile Walter Martin says:

> Many individuals and all cults steadfastly deny the equality of Jesus Christ with God the Father, and hence, the Triune deity. However, the testimony of the Scriptures stands sure, and the above mentioned references [his "proof" texts] alone put to silence forever this blasphemous heresy, which in the power of Satan himself deceives many with its "deceitful handling of the Word of God."[35]

Another Sketch of Unitarian History

The New Schaff-Herzog Encyclopedia's article on the history of objectors to the Trinity records the cruel treatment they received from the "Christian" lands in which they lived.

When orthodox Trinitarian Christology was strongly enforced, following the church councils and the backing of imperial power under Emperor Theodosius, other views of God and Jesus subsided. A

---

[35]*The Kingdom of the Cults*, Bethany House, 2003, 107.

non-Trinitarian view of the Son of God survived amongst a group called the Paulicians in Armenia. Early British Christianity shows some evidence of unorthodox Christology, and it was widespread in Spain and found a leader in Felix of Urge of the Frankish church in 799 AD.

In Europe Poland was the home of non-Trinitarians when theologians arrived there from Italy, notably George Blandrata. After 1575 leadership was in the hands of Faustus Socinus (hence the term Socinianism). A unitarian college was founded at Racow in Poland and this institution produced a confession of faith describing their non-Trinitarian views — the Racovian Confession of 1605. There was actually a unitarian prince: John Sigismund II of Transylvania. The unitarian movement was decisively suppressed by Roman Catholic Jesuits with a decree in 1658 for the expulsion of Socinians from the realm. These believers found their way to Germany, Holland and Transylvania. In Hungary unitarians found a strong leader in Francis David, who became bishop of the unitarian churches. But in 1579 the Roman Catholic viceroy put David under the surveillance of the magistrates. He was then condemned to imprisonment for life as an innovator and blasphemer. David died in a dungeon in 1579 and the event established him as a unitarian martyr.

Though unitarians continued to have legal existence they suffered hardship. Under Austrian rule their publications were forbidden and their churches confiscated. However, a statute of 1791 relieved the pressure on these dissenters.[36]

Unitarians in Britain

Some of the English martyrs of the sixteenth century suffered for Arian[37] views, but the first noteworthy expression of the spirit and method of Unitarianism was *The Religion of Protestants a Safe Way to Salvation* (London, 1638) by William Chillingworth, and the first conspicuous application of this method with express Unitarian results was made by

---

[36]"Unitarians," *The New Schaff-Herzog Encyclopedia of Religious Knowledge,* 12:82.

[37]The term Arian was sometimes used to describe all forms of non-Trinitarian belief, i.e., both the strict Arian view of Arius and the neo-Arians of the fourth century, and the "Socinians" from the sixteenth century (and a few from earlier centuries).

John Biddle, who under the Commonwealth gathered a society in London and published his views. In 1662 he was imprisoned for the third time, and soon died of prison disease. His writings were collected and published by his disciple Thomas Firmin in 1691 (*The Faith of One God*). Although Unitarianism was excluded from the operation of the Toleration Act of 1689, while its advocates were threatened by the act of 1698 with loss of civil rights and imprisonment, Socinian and Arian views of the person of Christ found increasing favor in the course of the eighteenth century both in the Church of England and among dissenters. Noted instances of this tendency are Samuel Clarke, Nathanael Lardner, Isaac Watts [the hymn writer], and Philip Doddridge. The first chapel with the Unitarian name was founded in Essex Street, London, in 1778 by Theophilus Lindsey, who on the refusal of parliament (1772) to receive a petition for the relaxation of subscription to the Thirty-nine Articles had resigned his living in Catterick, Yorkshire. In his London Chapel he used Clarke's revision of the English liturgy. Lindsey was aided by the sympathy of Presbyterians, who had made their chapels built since 1688 free from dogmatic restrictions, and, seeking conformity with the Bible alone, had relinquished Calvinistic views and the doctrine of the Trinity. The decisive influence in this change was exercised by the eminent scientist, publicist and theologian, Joseph Priestley. As an avowed Socinian Priestley ministered to congregations in Leeds (1768-80) and Birmingham (1780-91)...He died [in Pennsylvania] in 1804...The successor of Priestley in Birmingham and of Lindsey in London (1795) was Thomas Belsham, who sought to make "the simple and proper humanity of Christ" the acknowledged Unitarian view. Another notable leader was Lant Carpenter, preacher in Bristol. In 1813 the legal disabilities of Unitarians were removed and in 1825 the British and Foreign Unitarian Association was formed by a union of Presbyterian and Baptist churches to which were later joined small Methodist groups like the "Christian brethren." By the Dissenters' Chapels Act of 1844 the possession of ancient endowments and chapels were secured. The national conference, a purely deliberative body, was founded in 1881. In 1911 there were 378 ministers, and 374 churches, of which 295 are in England [as of 1912]. The theological instruction is given in Manchester College, Oxford, and the Home Missionary College at Manchester. The Hibbert Fund, instituted by Robert Hibbert, a Jamaica planter (died 1849), has promoted scholarship and established relations with the theological liberalism of the continent. To this foundation are due the famous Hibbert lectures and the *Hibbert Journal* (since Oct., 1902). **Welsh Unitarianism** began with the Arminian revolt from Calvinism of Jenkin Jones in Llwynrhydowen in 1726. His successors adopted Arian views. There are thirty-four churches in South Wales and a college at Carmarthen. **Irish Unitarianism** began in 1726, when the presbytery of Antrim separated from the general synod in order to establish worship without subscription to creed. In 1830 the Remonstrant Synod of Ulster was formed on similar principles, and in 1835 an Association of Irish Non-Subscribing Presbyterians united these free churches. There are thirty-eight churches, chiefly in the counties of Antrim and Down. In Scotland there are seven churches, the oldest (Edinburgh) dating from 1776.[38]

Unitarianism in America

The first public confession of unitarianism began in 1785 with James Freeman of King's Chapel, the oldest Episcopal church in Boston. All reference to the deity of Christ and the Trinity was omitted from the Book of Common Prayer. In the mid-eighteenth century unitarianism flourished in the Congregational churches of eastern Massachusetts. Non-Trinitarian views prevailed at Harvard University with the eloquent preaching of Joseph Buckminster and William Ellery Channing, who produced two journals, the *Monthly Anthology* (1803) and the *Christian Disciple* (1813). Channing publicly challenged his opponents in a sermon on "Unitarian Christianity" (1819) and his *Moral Argument against Calvinism* (1820). The American Unitarian Association was formed in 1825. The first convention of churches met in New York in 1865. A

[38]Ibid., 82-83.

convention in 1894 declared "These churches accept the religion of Jesus, holding, in accordance with his teaching, that practical religion is summed up in love to God and love to man."[39] This statement would appear inoffensive, but the God in question was not the Trinity but the One God of Jesus' own creed.

Unitarianism has of course continued since the early twentieth century when the *Schaff-Herzog* article was penned. In general Unitarians have become less "biblical," meaning that they lost a grip on central biblical teachings such as the virgin birth, the resurrection and the Second Coming. The loss of these central truths is hardly likely to make nitarianism attractive to evangelicals and the fault lies in this respect with the Unitarianism which has lost its biblical basis, other than its rejection of creeds which superseded the creed of Jesus.

---

[39] Ibid., 83-84.

Chapter 12

Does Everyone Believe in the Trinity?

"It is almost impossible to draw any real conclusions even from the Gospel of John regarding the dogma of the Trinity."[1]

"In speaking of Jesus Christ, many Trinitarians call him 'God the Son.' However, the Scriptures never call him God the Son, but rather the Son of God. These two phrases are in no way interchangeable. The latter is Biblical truth, while the former is a theological invention."[2]

"On the preexistence question one can at least accept the preexistence of the eternal Word or Wisdom of God which (who?) became incarnate in Jesus. But whether any New Testament writer believed in his separate conscious existence as 'a second divine Person' is not so clear."[3]

"Christianity, in the course of the Gentile mission, had changed into another religion. The Church...had forgotten or refused to know what Jesus had actually taught."[4]

---

[1]La Due, *Trinity Guide to the Trinity*, 26. The author goes on to say that John's "Trinitarian view" inspired Ignatius and Irenaeus.
[2]Robert Carden, *One God: The Unfinished Reformation*, Grace Christian Press, 2002, 115.
[3]F.F. Bruce, letter, June 13, 1981.
[4]E.F. Scott, *The Kingdom of God in the New Testament*, 156, reflecting on how the apocalyptic Kingdom of God in the teaching of Jesus has been altered by the Church. A similar change is found in the Church's doctrine of God as Trinity.

We opened an earlier chapter by laying out the unclear thinking of many churchgoers when they contemplate who God and Jesus are. Most hold these inconsistent ideas as an unresolved logical problem: 1) "Jesus Christ is God"; 2) "God is our Heavenly Father"; 3) "Jesus Christ is not our Heavenly Father"; 4) "There are not two Gods." Yet he has never considered how to reconcile these four separate opinions of his together; it probably has not occurred to him that they are inconsistent with one another...The average Englishman has not troubled himself with the matter.[5]

The Christian "academy," which seems to have little influence on popular evangelical theology, is often candid in its admission that the Trinity as a definition of God is foreign to the first-century Christians. This opinion is widely held in so-called liberal circles, and especially since the time of the enlightenment. Evangelicals, rather than admit to a large dose of traditional thinking in their received systems, persist with very strained attempts to force the Trinity into the New Testament, and in some extreme cases even into the Hebrew Bible. The sheer contradiction found amongst writers of various schools should cause the reader to investigate as to who is telling the truth.

Popular commentary writer William Barclay expresses complete clarity when it comes to his denial that Jesus *is* Yahweh: "Nowhere does the New Testament *identify* Jesus with God."[6] John Stott, a prominent evangelical, thinks otherwise: The "transfer of God-titles and God-texts from Yahweh to Jesus...*identifies* Jesus as God." But he says also, "It is true that it is nowhere recorded in [Jesus'] teaching that he declared unambiguously, 'I am God.'"[7]

The Verdict of History

Many historians of dogma frankly admit to a post-biblical defection from New Testament teaching. Things went terribly wrong in the centuries following the death of the Apostles. The following quotations from leading experts tell their own story:

In the year 317, a new contention arose in Egypt with consequences of a pernicious nature. The subject of this fatal

---

[5]Richard Armstrong, *The Trinity and the Incarnation*, 8.
[6]*A Spiritual Autobiography*, Eerdmans, 1975, 50.
[7]*The Authentic Jesus*, Marshalls, 1985, 33, 31.

controversy which kindled such deplorable divisions throughout the Christian world, was the doctrine of three Persons in the Godhead, a doctrine which in the three preceding centuries had happily escaped the vain curiosity of human researches.[8]

When we look back through the long ages of [the doctrine of the Trinity's] reign...we shall perceive that few doctrines have produced more unmixed evil.[9]

Christological doctrine has never in practice been derived simply by way of logical inference from the statements of Scripture...The church has not usually in practice (whatever it may have claimed to be doing in theory) based its christology exclusively on the witness of the New Testament.[10]

The Greeks distorted the concept of Jesus' legal agency to ontological identity, creating an illogical set of creeds and doctrines to cause confusion and terror for later generations of Christians.[11]

Because the Trinity is such an important part of later Christian doctrine, it is striking that the term does not appear in the New Testament. Likewise, the developed concept of three coequal partners in the Godhead found in later creedal formulations cannot be clearly detected within the confines of the canon.[12]

How shall we determine the nature of the distinction between the God who became man and the God who did not become man, without destroying the unity of God, on the one hand, or interfering with Christology, on the other? Neither

---

[8]J.L. Mosheim, *Institutes of Ecclesiastical History*, New York: Harper, 1839, 1:399.

[9]Norton, *Statement of Reasons for Not Believing the Doctrines of Trinitarians,* 373-374.

[10]Maurice Wiles, *The Remaking of Christian Doctrine*, 54, 55.

[11]Professor G.W. Buchanan, from correspondence, 1994.

[12]"Trinity," *The Oxford Companion to the Bible*, Oxford University Press, 1993, 782.

the Council of Nicea, nor the Church Fathers of the [fourth] century...satisfactorily answered this question.[13]

The adoption of a non-biblical phrase at Nicea constituted a landmark in the growth of dogma; the Trinity is *true*, since the Church — the universal Church speaking by its bishops — says so, though the Bible does not!...We have a formula, but what does that formula contain? No child of the Church dare seek to answer.[14]

Some celebrated evangelical commentary is frank in its concession to unitarianism: "Only one, the Father, can absolutely be termed the 'only true God,' not at the same time Christ (who is not even in 1 John 5:20 'the true God'). Jesus, in unity with the Father, works as His commissioner (John 10:30), and is His representative (John 14:9, 10)."[15]

Professor C.K. Barrett's highly acclaimed commentary on John explains John 17:3 in an obviously unitarian sense: "The God whom to know is to have eternal life is the only being who may properly be so described; he, and it must follow, he alone is truly *theos*."[16]

Famous names in the field of Christological studies appear to grant our point that the Trinity is not a New Testament doctrine: "No responsible New Testament scholar would claim that the doctrine of the Trinity was taught by Jesus, or preached by the earliest Christians, or consciously held by any writer in the New Testament."[17]

It must be admitted by everyone who has the rudiments of an historical sense that the doctrine of the Trinity, as a doctrine, formed no part of the original message. St. Paul knew it not, and would have been unable to understand the meaning of the terms used in the theological formula on which the Church ultimately agreed.[18]

---

[13]J.A. Dorner, *History of the Development of the Doctrine of the Person of Christ*, T & T Clark, 1889, Div. I, 2:330.

[14]"Dogma, Dogmatic Theology," *Encyclopedia Britannica*, 14th edition, 1936, 7:501, 502.

[15]H.A.W. Meyer, *Commentary on the Gospel of John,* on John 17:3.

[16]*The Gospel According to St. John*, Westminster, 1978, 504.

[17]A.T. Hanson, *The Image of the Invisible God*, 87.

[18]W.R. Matthews, *God in Christian Experience*, 1930, rep. Kessinger, 2003, 180.

The propositions constitutive of the dogma of the Trinity...were not drawn directly from the New Testament, and could not be expressed in New Testament terms. They were the products of reason speculating on a revelation to faith...They were only formed through centuries of effort, only elaborated by the aid of the conceptions, and formulated in the terms of Greek and Roman metaphysics.[19]

This criticism of orthodox Christology...is not the property of a few people only...At present [1911] I do not know of a single professor of evangelical theology in Germany [who wants to reproduce the old orthodox formulae]. All learned Protestant theologians in Germany, even if they do not do so with the same emphasis, really admit unanimously that the orthodox Christology does not do justice to the truly human life of Jesus and the orthodox doctrine of the two natures in Christ cannot be retained in its traditional form. All our systematic theologians...are seeking new paths in their Christology.[20]

"Son of God" Language

Biblical studies have happily moved away from the untenable notion that Son of God is equivalent to God the Son:

The crux of the matter lies in how we understand the term "Son of God" and the questions that it poses about the relation of Jesus to the one whom he called Father...One may well ask whether the term "Son of God" is in and of itself a divine title at all. Certainly there are many instances in biblical language where it is definitely not a designation of deity. Adam is called "the son of God" in Luke's genealogy of Jesus (Luke 3:38). Hosea 11:1 (which is cited in Matt. 2:15) alludes to the nation of Israel as God's son. In Wisdom 2:18 the righteous man is called God's son. Nathan's prophecy to David contains God's promise to David's successor: "I will be his father, and he shall be my son" (2 Sam. 7:14; cf. Ps. 89:26-27). This passage also occurs in a collection of testimonies at Qumran (4QFlor 10f.), indicating

---

[19]*Encyclopedia Britannica*, 9th ed., 23:240.
[20]Friedrich Loofs, *What Is the Truth About Jesus Christ?* Charles Scribner's Sons, 1913, 202, 203.

that the messianic significance of this prophecy was a matter of continuing speculation in first-century Judaism. In Psalm 2:7 the anointed king is addressed at his installation:[21] "You are my son, today I have begotten you" (cited in Acts 13:33; Heb. 1:5; 5:5; cf. 2 Pet. 1:17). This passage is the source of the identification of Jesus with God's Son by the *Bat Qol* (voice from heaven) after his baptism (Mark 1:11; Matt. 3:17; Luke 3:22; cf. John 1:34). The voice also *identifies Jesus with the chosen servant in whom God delights* (Isa. 42:1; cf. also Matt. 12:18-21).

In the light of these passages in their context, the title "Son of God" is not in itself a designation of personal deity or an expression of metaphysical distinctions within the Godhead. Indeed, to be a "Son of God" one has to be a being who is *not* God! It is a designation for a creature indicating a special relationship with God. In particular, it denotes God's representative, God's vice-regent. It is a designation of kingship, identifying the king as God's son. Therefore, I take the application of the title "Son of God" at his baptism to be an affirmation of Jesus as God's Son-king in virtue of his anointing by the Spirit. Likewise C.F.D. Moule comments on the trial scene: "In Mark 14:61 the High Priest's words, 'Are you the Christ, the son of the Blessed One?' are presumably understood by the Evangelist as a question about a Messianic claim." The title expresses the *intimate relationship* which Jesus had through the Spirit with the Father as the Father's anointed representative, which is depicted in the Gospel narratives culminating in his death and the cry of dereliction, "My God, my God, why have you forsaken me?" (Matt. 27:46; Mark 15:34).

I believe that this is the meaning that we should attach to the term "Son of God" at the beginning of Mark's Gospel (Mark 1:1)...Nor can we read the theology of later centuries into the testimony of the centurion at the foot of the cross: "Truly this man was a son of God" (Mark 15:39; Matt. 27:54; cf. Luke 23:47 "Certainly this man was innocent!"). In my

---

[21]In Acts 13:33, Heb. 1:5, 5:5 the application of Ps. 2:7 is actually to the begetting of Jesus in Mary.

view the term "Son of God" ultimately converges on the term "image of God," which is to be understood as God's representative, the one in whom God's Spirit dwells, and who is given stewardship and authority to act on God's behalf. The designation of Jesus as "Son of God in power according to the Spirit of holiness by his resurrection from the dead" (Rom. 1:4) is a reaffirmation of that Son-kingship with divine authority, insofar as by the resurrection the Spirit has overturned the negative verdict of the Sanhedrin in condemning Jesus to death as a blasphemer who sought to lead Israel astray...

It seems to me to be a fundamental mistake to treat statements in the Fourth Gospel about the Son and his relationship with the Father as expressions of inner-Trinitarian relationships. But this kind of systematic misreading of the Fourth Gospel seems to underlie much of social Trinitarian thinking. Thus statements like "I and the Father are one" (John 10:30) and those about the mutual indwelling of Jesus and the Father (John 10:38; 14:10-11, 20; 17:21, 23) are taken to be statements about inner relations of the "persons" of the Trinity. However, the Fourth Gospel itself does not require such a reading. When read in context, the statements are *evidently statements about Jesus' relationship with the Father on earth.*

It is a common but patent misreading of the opening of John's Gospel to read it as if it said: "In the beginning was the *Son,* and the *Son* was with God, and the *Son* was God" (John 1:1). What has happened here is the substitution of *Son* for *Word* (Greek *logos*), and thereby the *Son* is made a member of the Godhead which existed from the beginning. But if we follow carefully the thought of John's Prologue, it is the *Word* that preexisted eternally with God and is God.[22]

The Trinity Without Biblical Foundation

It is customary for students of the Bible to refer to Jesus as God and to insist that belief in a Trinity of three co-equal, co-eternal

---

[22]Colin Brown, "Trinity and Incarnation," *Ex Auditu* 7, 1991, 87-89, emphasis added.

Persons in the One God is the hallmark of true faith. Many recognized Bible scholars do not think, however, that Jesus is called God, in a Trinitarian sense, in the Scriptures. Distinguished experts on the Bible, past and present, maintain that the doctrine of a tri-personal God is nowhere taught in Scripture.

A popular recent discussion of Christianity states that the doctrine of the Trinity is "unquestionably one of the most difficult Bible doctrines to understand."[23] One of the most perplexing questions facing Trinitarians is the fact that in Mark 13:32 Jesus confessed ignorance as the Son (i.e., Son of God) about the Second Coming. How can Jesus be God if he is not all-knowing? Why indeed did the Father of Jesus have to give His risen and glorified Son a revelation, if Jesus knows all things? (Rev. 1:1). Can Trinitarians provide honest answers to these questions?

In the Bible and in Jewish tradition, God knows everything including the future (Isa. 46:10; Zech. 14:7; cf. 4 Ezra 4:51, 52; 2 Bar. 21:8). Human beings and angels are not in possession of such total knowledge. Mark 13:32 demonstrably excludes Jesus from the category of absolute Deity and was therefore an embarrassment to post-biblical Christians. Subsequent attempts to explain this saying to mean that Jesus did not *make known* what in fact he really knew, have failed to make any sense of the Son of God's confessed ignorance. Saying that he spoke in his human nature, somehow suppressing what he really knew in his divine nature, merely illustrates the struggle of commentators to fit the later "God the Son" into the pages of Scripture where he does not belong.

In no text did Jesus ever say he was God. In Mark 10:18 he distinguished between himself and God who alone is absolutely good. Why if Jesus is God did he isolate his Father as the only one who is absolutely good?

The fair way to investigate the question as to who is the supreme God in the Bible is to start with that 75% of our Bibles we call the Old Testament. These were the Scriptures on which Jesus had been nourished. One very simple fact does not often receive the attention it deserves: The Old Testament describes God with *singular pronouns* many thousands of times. Singular pronouns tell us that God is a single individual.

---

[23]Ron Rhodes, *The Heart of Christianity*, Harvest House, 1996, 50.

What if you picked up a book in which the father of a family was described by the singular pronouns "I," "me" and "him" hundreds of times? If that same father then said, "Let us take a vacation" would you immediately think that the father was really *more than one person*? Or would you think that the father was inviting others to join him, a single individual, in an activity?

Amazingly when some Bible readers arrive at Genesis 1:26 and read that God said "Let us make..." they leap to the conclusion that God is more than one Person. There is no logical reason for this. Scripture describes God as "I", "He," "Him," "Me" repeatedly. When on a very rare occasion God says, "Let us..." it means that God, who is one Person, involves others with Him. How is it that Bible readers imagine "Let us..." to mean "Let us *three*..."? The verse says nothing about three members of a Godhead — nothing about a Son and Holy Spirit. Where does God ever address His own spirit?

The helpful note in the NIV Study Bible (on Gen. 1:26) points out that God involved His angels in some way with creation. Both man and angels bear a resemblance to God Himself. In a similar "let us" statement (there are only four) in Isaiah 6:8, "Who will go for us?" the address is obviously to attendant angelic beings.

From the *Word Biblical Commentary* ("From a team of international scholars, a showcase of the best in evangelical critical scholarship") comes a plain statement that the idea that Genesis 1:26 even hints at the Trinity is false:

> It is now universally admitted that this [foreshadowing of the Trinity] was not what the plural meant to the original author...When angels do appear in the OT they are frequently described as men (e.g., Gen. 18:2). And in fact the use of the singular verb "create" in 1:27 does, in fact, suggest that God worked *alone* in the creation of mankind. "Let us create man" should therefore be regarded as a divine announcement to the heavenly court, drawing the angelic host's attention to the master stroke of creation, man. As Job 38:4, 7 puts it: "When I laid the foundation of the earth...all the sons of God shouted for joy" (cf. Luke 2:13-14).[24]

---

[24]Gordon J. Wenham, *Word Biblical Commentary: Genesis 1-15,* Word Books, 1987, 27-28.

Truth-seekers should make a conscious effort not to start their investigation with the *assumption* that the Trinity is a true biblical teaching. They will begin with an open mind and look for clear evidence. Is there such evidence in the Old Testament? Many have long abandoned Genesis 1:26 as any indication of plurality in God. There is no shred of proof for the Trinity in Genesis 1:26, or in the plural form *Elohim.*

Nor is there any evidence for the Trinity in the word "one" in the famous Jewish and Christian creed (Deut. 6:4, cited by Jesus as a Christian in Mark 12:29). That most basic creed says: "Hear, O Israel! The Lord our God is one Lord." The lexicons of Hebrew tell us correctly that "one" means "one single." *Echad* is used about 970 times and there is never any doubt that it means "one," not two or more. In the central creed of Israel and of Jesus the LORD is described as "one Lord," i.e. "one single Lord." One single Lord means one Person, not three.

Opposition to the Trinity is not confined to so-called "cults." That is a public myth. Sir Isaac Newton, John Locke and John Milton have this in common: They are recognized as among the most intelligent minds of the seventeenth century. All objected strongly to the doctrine of the Trinity. These men cannot just be dismissed as ill-educated or prejudiced. They had very good reasons for what they believed and defended in writing. All three were vigorous anti-Trinitarians. So also was Thomas Jefferson, who examined the Trinitarian question carefully in the light of the Bible. How many know that Harvard University at one time expressed non-Trinitarian views? Increasing numbers of contemporary biblical scholars recognize that the Trinity is a post-biblical development.

Apparently the question about God can provoke violent emotion. It is good to be reminded that one of the cruelest episodes in church history occurred when the reformer Calvin used the strong arm of the Catholic Church to burn at the stake a brilliant linguist, physician, geographer and Bible expert, Michael Servetus.[25] The burning of others over an issue of doctrine is absolutely forbidden by the Bible

---

[25]For a fine account of this horrible cruelty in support of the Trinitarian cause, see Marian Hillar, *The Case of Michael Servetus (1511-1553): The Turning Point in the Struggle for Freedom of Conscience,* Edwin Mellen Press, 1997.

and may cause some wonder about the spirit which drives such persecuting zeal over the definition of who God is.

Review and Summary of Key Considerations

The doctrine of the Trinity depends on a very unbiblical idea: that the Son was "eternally begotten." The Trinity claims that the Son of God had no beginning. He is an eternal uncreated being. Without an "eternally begotten Son," there is no Trinity. Does the Bible support the idea that the Son of God was "begotten eternally"?

Some authorities will expect the public to swallow a considerable piece of misinformation. They will say that there is "a conversation between two members of the Godhead"[26] in Psalm 2 and Psalm 110:1. Truth-seekers should look carefully at these two passages. Psalm 2:7 reports the One God, Yahweh (the LORD) as addressing the Son, the Messiah. The Father says, *"Today* I have begotten you." To beget means to become a father of a child. "Today" obviously means today. Today is not eternity. There is no basis at all for the Trinity in Psalm 2:7. Without an "eternally begotten" Son there can be no Trinity. Psalm 2:7 contradicts the Trinity and tells us that there was a time before the begetting of the Son. Luke 1:35 tells us when the Son was begotten. It was some two thousand years ago in Palestine. When the power of God came over Mary, the Son of God came into existence as the begotten Son of the Father (see Luke 1:35; Matt. 1:20: "begotten").

Psalm 110:3 in the Septuagint version reads: "From the womb before the daystar I have begotten you." Our Old Testament reads differently, but many Hebrew manuscripts, including the Peshitta (Syriac) of the second century AD and the Hebrew text used by the church father Origen, maintain a version which agrees with the Septuagint. Is it possible that the wise men looked for a star to mark the birth of the Messiah on the basis of this prophecy in Psalm 110:3? "Before the daystar" could be taken in a spatial sense, meaning "in the presence of the star." If that is so, the magi expected to find the birthplace of the Messiah marked by a special star (Matt. 2:9).

A very fascinating repointing of some of the Hebrew manuscripts of Psalm 110:3 has occurred. By "repointing" is meant the placing of a set of new vowels with the consonants, which alters the meaning of

---

[26]Cited in Patrick Navas, *Divine Truth or Human Tradition*, 138.

the text. The Hebrew from which our Bibles are translated reads "From the womb of the morning, like dew, your youth will come to you" (NRSV). "Your youth" translates this set of Hebrew consonants: Y L D T C H. With one set of vowels this gives us "your youth." But the same consonants, with altered vowels, give us "I have begotten you."[27] That very phrase is found in all the Hebrew manuscripts of Psalm 2:7: "This day I have begotten you."

Because the Septuagint reads "From the womb before the morning star I have begotten you," this may well be the originally correct version, and if so, it provides another key reference to the begetting of the Son in history. It is certainly clear that Psalm 110 provides no information at all about an "eternally begotten Son." This is an invention of post-biblical church fathers, and it diverts attention from the historical begetting or coming into existence of the Messianic Son of God.

There is definitely no conversation between members of the Godhead in Psalm 110:1. In that Psalm the LORD speaks to "my lord." The "lord" in question is not the LORD (Yahweh) but *adoni* ("my lord"). *Adoni* in all of its 195 occurrences in the Old Testament means *not God*, but a human (or occasionally angelic) superior. There is another word for God — *Adonai* — which refers to God in all of its 449 occurrences. *Adonai* and *adoni* show us the biblical distinction between God and man. The Messiah in Psalm 110:1 is addressed by a human and not a divine title. That is why Paul wrote: "There is one God, the Father" (1 Cor. 8:6). "There is one God and one mediator between God and men, the *man* Messiah Jesus" (1 Tim. 2:5). Jesus is the Lord Messiah (Luke 2:11; Matt. 16:16) and not the Lord God.

The Evidence of Standard Authorities

The following testimonies from reputable standard authorities show that the claim that "Jesus is God" and that the Bible teaches a Trinitarian Godhead is often more an exercise in propaganda than actual fact. While much popular Christianity continues to deal harshly with non-Trinitarians, the latter can take comfort from the reflection of saner and sounder minds, both evangelical and otherwise. The

---

[27]For confirmation of these facts, see Leslie C. Allen, *Word Biblical Commentary: Psalms 101-150*, Word Books, 1983, 81.

following statements appear in the writings of distinguished experts in the field of Bible study:

"The word Trinity is not found in the Bible, and...it did not find a place formally in the theology of the church till the fourth century."[28]

The Trinity "is not directly and immediately the Word of God."[29]

"In Scripture there is as yet no single term by which the Three Divine Persons are denoted together. The word *trias* (of which the Latin *trinitas* is a translation) is first found in Theophilus of Antioch about AD 180...Afterwards it appears in its Latin form of *trinitas* in Tertullian."[30]

"Hasty conclusions cannot be drawn from usage, for [Tertullian] does not apply the words [which were later applied to Trinitarianism] to Trinitarian theology."[31]

Is the Trinity in the Old Testament?

"There is in the Old Testament no indication of interior distinctions in the Godhead; it is an anachronism to find either the doctrine of Incarnation or that of the Trinity in its pages."[32]

"Theologians today are in agreement that the Hebrew Bible does not contain a doctrine of the Trinity."[33]

"The doctrine of the Trinity is not taught in the Old Testament."[34]

The Old Testament tells us nothing explicitly or by necessary implication of a triune God who is Father, Son and Holy Spirit...*There is no evidence that any sacred writer even suspected the existence of a [Trinity] within the Godhead*...Even to see in the Old Testament suggestions or foreshadowings or "veiled signs" of the Trinity of persons, is to go beyond the words and intent of the sacred writers.[35]

[28]*The Illustrated Bible Dictionary*, 3:1597.
[29]*New Catholic Encyclopedia*, McGraw-Hill, 1967, 14:304.
[30]*The Catholic Encyclopedia*, 15:47.
[31]Michael O'Carroll, *Trinitas: A Theological Encyclopedia of the Holy Trinity*, Liturgical Press, 1987, 208.
[32]James Hastings, ed., *Encyclopædia of Religion and Ethics*, T&T Clark, 1913, 6:254.
[33]*Encyclopedia of Religion*, Macmillan, 1987, 15:54.
[34]*New Catholic Encyclopedia*, 14:306.
[35]Edmund J. Fortman, *The Triune God*, Baker, 1972, xv, 8, 9.

The Old Testament is strictly monotheistic. God is a single personal being. The idea that a Trinity is to be found there is utterly without foundation. There is no break between the Old Testament and the New. The monotheistic tradition is continued. Jesus was a Jew, trained by Jewish parents in the Old Testament scriptures. His teaching was Jewish to the core; a new gospel indeed but not a new theology...And he accepted as his own belief the great text of Jewish monotheism: Hear, O Israel, the Lord our God is one God.[36]

The Old Testament can scarcely be used as authority for the existence of distinctions within the Godhead. The use of "us" by the divine speaker (Gen. 1:26; 3:22; 11:7) is strange, but is perhaps due to His consciousness of being surrounded by other beings of a loftier order than men (Isa. 6:8).[37]

From Philo onward, Jewish commentators have generally held that the plural [Gen. 1:26: "Let us make man..."] is used because God is addressing his heavenly court, i.e., the angels (cf. Isa. 6:8)[38]...From the Epistle of Barnabas and Justin Martyr, who saw the plural as a reference to Christ, Christians have traditionally seen this verse as adumbrating the Trinity. It is now universally admitted that this was not what the plural meant to the original author.[39]

Is the Trinity in the New Testament?

"No Apostle would have dreamed of thinking that there are three divine Persons."[40]

"Theologians agree that the New Testament also does not contain an explicit doctrine of the Trinity."[41]

"The New Testament writers...give us no formal or formulated doctrine of the Trinity, no explicit teaching that in one God there are three equal divine persons...Nowhere do we find any Trinitarian

---

[36]L.L. Paine, *A Critical History of the Evolution of Trinitarianism*, 4.
[37]Hastings, *A Dictionary of the Bible*, 2:205.
[38]This is also the explanation given by the NIV Study Bible.
[39]Gordon J. Wenham, *Word Biblical Commentary: Genesis 1-15*, 27.
[40]Emil Brunner, *The Christian Doctrine of God*, Lutterworth Press, 1962, 1:226.
[41]*Encyclopedia of Religion*, 15:54.

doctrine of three distinct subjects of divine life and activity in the same Godhead."[42]

"Neither the word Trinity nor the explicit doctrine appears in the New Testament."[43]

"As far as the New Testament is concerned one does not find in it an actual doctrine of the Trinity."[44]

"The NT does not contain the developed doctrine of the Trinity."[45]

"The Bible lacks the express declaration that the Father, the Son, and the Holy Spirit are of equal essence."[46]

"An increasingly pretentious, intellectual *speculation on the Trinity* was built up on the basis of the originally straightforward triadic creedal statements...Although there are many triadic statements on Father, Son and Spirit in the New Testament, neither in John's Gospel nor in the later Apostles' Creed do we find any properly trinitarian doctrine of a God in three persons."[47]

"Jesus Christ never mentioned such a phenomenon, and nowhere in the New Testament does the word Trinity appear. The idea was only adopted by the Church three hundred years after the death of our Lord."[48]

"Primitive Christianity did not have an explicit doctrine of the Trinity such as was subsequently elaborated in the creeds."[49]

"The early Christians, however, did not at first think of applying the *Trinity* idea to their own faith. They paid their devotions to God the Father and to Jesus Christ, the Son of God, and they recognized the...Holy Spirit; but there was no thought of these three being an actual Trinity, coequal and united in one."[50]

---

[42]Fortman, *The Triune God*, xv, xvi, 16.
[43]*The New Encyclopedia Britannica*, 1985, 11:928.
[44]Bernard Lohse, *A Short History of Christian Doctrine*, Fortress Press, 1966, 38.
[45]*The New International Dictionary of New Testament Theology*, 2:84.
[46]Ibid., quoting Karl Barth.
[47]Hans Küng, *On Being a Christian,* Doubleday, 1976, 472, 473.
[48]Arthur Weigall, *The Paganism in Our Christianity*, G.P. Putnam's Sons, 1928, 198.
[49]*The New International Dictionary of New Testament Theology,* 2:84.
[50]Weigall, *The Paganism in Our Christianity*, 197.

"At first the Christian faith was not Trinitarian...It was not so in the apostolic and sub-apostolic ages, as reflected in the NT and other early Christian writings."[51]

"The formulation 'One God in three Persons' was not solidly established, certainly not fully assimilated into Christian life and its profession of faith, prior to the end of the fourth century...Among the Apostolic Fathers, there had been nothing even remotely approaching such a mentality or perspective."[52]

"Fourth-century Trinitarianism did not reflect accurately early Christian teaching regarding the nature of God; it was, on the contrary, a deviation from this teaching."[53]

"The New Testament gives no inkling of the teaching of Chalcedon. That council not only reformulated in other language the New Testament data about Jesus' constitution, but also reconceptualized it in the light of the current Greek philosophical thinking. And that reconceptualization and reformulation go well beyond the New Testament data."[54]

Does the Word *Elohim* (God) Imply That There Is More Than One Person in the Godhead?

"The fanciful idea that [*Elohim*] referred to the *trinity of persons* in the Godhead hardly finds now a supporter among scholars. It is either what grammarians call *the plural of majesty*, or it denotes the *fullness* of divine strength, the *sum of the powers* displayed by God."[55]

"It is exegesis of a mischievous, if pious, sort that would discover the doctrine [of the Trinity] in the plural form, 'Elohim.'"[56]

"*Elohim* must rather be explained as an intensive plural, denoting greatness and majesty."[57]

Early dogmaticians were of the opinion that so essential a doctrine as that of the Trinity could not have been unknown to the men of the Old Testament...*However, no modern*

[51]*Encyclopedia of Religion and Ethics*, 24:461.
[52]*New Catholic Encyclopedia*, 14:299.
[53]*Encyclopedia Americana*, 1956, 27:249.
[54]Joseph Fitzmyer, *A Christological Catechism*, 102.
[55]William Smith, *A Dictionary of the Bible* (1986), 220.
[56]*Encyclopedia of Religion and Ethics*, 24:458.
[57]*The American Journal of Semitic Language and Literature*, 1905, 21:208.

theologian...can longer maintain such a view. Only an inaccurate exegesis which overlooks the more immediate grounds of interpretation can see references to the Trinity in the plural form of the divine name *Elohim*, the use of the plural in Genesis 1:26, or such liturgical phrases of three members as the Aaronic blessing of Numbers 6:24-26 and the Trisagion of Isaiah 6:3.[58]

The plural form of the name of God, *elohim*, in the Hebrew Scriptures has often been adduced as proof of the plurality of persons in the Godhead...Such use of Scripture will not be likely to advance the interests of truth, or be profitable for doctrine...The plural of *elohim* may just as well designate a multiplicity of divine potentialities in the deity as three personal distinctions, or it may be explained as the plural of majesty and excellency. Such forms of expression are susceptible of too many explanations to be used as valid proof texts of the Trinity.[59]

Is Jesus God?

Jesus never said "I am God." He always claimed to be the Messiah, the Son of God.

"Jesus is *not God but God's representative*, and, as such, so completely and totally acts on God's behalf that he stands in God's stead before the world...The gospel [of John] clearly states that God and Jesus are not to be understood as identical persons, as in 14:28, 'the Father is greater than I.'"[60]

"Apparently Paul did not call Jesus God."[61]

"Paul habitually differentiates Christ from God."[62]

"Paul nowhere definitely equates Jesus with God."[63]

"Paul never gives to Christ the name or description of 'God.'"[64]

"When the New Testament writers speak of Jesus Christ, they do not speak of Him nor do they think of Him as God."[65]

---

[58]*The New Schaff-Herzog Encyclopedia of Religious Knowledge*, 12:18.

[59]Milton Terry, *Biblical Hermeneutics*, Zondervan, 1975, 587.

[60]Jacob Jervell, *Jesus in the Gospel of John*, Augsburg, 1984, 21.

[61]Sydney Cave, *The Doctrine of the Person of Christ*, Duckworth, 1962, 48.

[62]C.J. Cadoux, *A Pilgrim's Further Progress*, Blackwell, 1943, 40, 42.

[63]W.R. Matthews, *The Problem of Christ in the Twentieth Century*, 22.

[64]*Dictionary of the Apostolic Church*, 1:194.

"Karl Rahner [leading Roman Catholic spokesman] points out with so much emphasis that the Son in the New Testament is never described as *ho theos* [the one God]."[66]

"The clear evidence of [John is] that Jesus refuses the claim to *be* God...while vigorously denying the blasphemy of being God or his substitute."[67]

"In his post-resurrection heavenly life, Jesus is portrayed as retaining a personal individuality every bit as distinct and separate from the person of God as was his in his life on earth as the terrestrial Jesus. Alongside God and compared with God, he appears, indeed, as yet another heavenly being in God's heavenly court, just as the angels were — though as God's Son, he stands in a different category, and ranks far above them."[68]

"What, however, is said of his life and functions as the celestial Christ neither means nor implies that in divine status he stands on a par with God Himself and is fully God. On the contrary, in the New Testament picture of his heavenly person and ministry we behold a figure both separate from and *subordinate to God*."[69]

"The fact has to be faced that New Testament research over, say, the last thirty or forty years has been leading an increasing number of reputable New Testament scholars to the conclusion that Jesus...certainly never believed himself to be God."[70]

"When [first-century Christians] assigned Jesus such honorific titles as Christ, Son of Man, Son of God and Lord, these were ways of saying not that he was God but that he did God's work."[71]

"The ancients made a wrong use of [John 10:30: "I and the Father are one"] to prove that Christ is of the same essence with the Father. For Christ does not argue about the unity of substance, but about the agreement which he has with the Father."[72]

---

[65]J.M. Creed, *The Divinity of Jesus Christ*, Fontana, 1964, 122-123.
[66]A.T. Hanson, *Grace and Truth: A Study in the Doctrine of the Incarnation*, SPCK, 1975, 66.
[67]J.A.T. Robinson, *Twelve More New Testament Studies*, 175, 176.
[68]*Bulletin of the John Rylands Library*, 1967-68, 50:258.
[69]Ibid., 258, 259.
[70]Ibid., 251.
[71]Ibid., 250.
[72]John Calvin, *Commentary on John*, Vol. 1.

"The Pauline Christ who accomplishes the work of salvation is a personality who is both human and superhuman, not God, but the Son of God. Here the idea, which was to develop later, of the union of the two natures is not present."[73]

"Jesus is never identified *simpliciter* [absolutely] with God, since the early Christians were not likely to confuse Jesus with God the Father."[74]

"To be a 'Son of God' one has to be a being who is *not* God!"[75]

Is the Holy Spirit a Third Person?

It is completely misleading to read into the Bible a third Person, the Holy Spirit. The spirit of Elijah (Luke 1:17) is not a different person from Elijah. Nor is the Spirit of God a different person from the Father. The Holy Spirit is the operational presence of God, His mind and character. It is God (and in the New Testament Jesus) impacting the creation with His creative influence. It is remarkable that greetings are never sent from the Spirit and in no text in the Bible is the Spirit worshipped or addressed in prayer. Paul equates the Spirit with the risen Jesus when he says, "For this comes from the Lord who is the spirit" (2 Cor. 3:18, ESV).

The spirit of God and the mind of God are beautifully equated in 1 Corinthians 2:16 where Paul refers to "the mind of Christ," quoting from Isaiah 40:13 which refers to God's Spirit. The Hebrew text reads "spirit." Mind, heart, spirit and word are very closely associated in the Bible. Making the spirit a third Person introduced a great deal of confusion.

The following quotations speak for themselves as testimony against reading into the Bible the conclusions of post-biblical creeds.

"Although the spirit is often described in personal terms, it seems quite clear that the sacred writers [of the Hebrew Scriptures] never conceived or presented this spirit as a distinct person."[76]

"Nowhere in the Old Testament do we find any clear indication of a Third Person."[77]

---

[73]Maurice Goguel, *Jesus and the Origins of Christianity*, Harper, 1960, 109.
[74]Howard Marshall, "Jesus as Lord: The Development of the Concept," in *Eschatology and the New Testament*, Hendrickson, 1988, 144.
[75]Colin Brown, "Trinity and Incarnation," *Ex Auditu* 7, 1991, 88.
[76]Fortman, *The Triune God*, 9.
[77]*The Catholic Encyclopedia*, 15:49.

"The Jews never regarded the spirit as a person; nor is there any solid evidence that any Old Testament writer held this view...The Holy Spirit is usually presented in the synoptic gospels and in Acts as a divine force or power."[78]

"The Old Testament clearly does not envisage God's spirit as a person...God's spirit is simply God's power. If it is sometimes represented as being distinct from God, it is because the breath of Yahweh acts exteriorly...The majority of New Testament texts reveal God's spirit as *something*, not *someone*; this is especially seen in the parallelism between the spirit and the power of God."[79]

"On the whole the New Testament, like the Old, speaks of the spirit as a divine energy or power."[80]

"The third Person was asserted at a Council of Alexandria in 362...and finally by the Council of Constantinople of 381."[81]

"The grammatical basis for the Holy Spirit's personality is lacking in the New Testament, yet this is frequently, if not usually, the first line of defense of the doctrine of many evangelical writers. But if grammar cannot legitimately be used to support the Spirit's personality, then perhaps we need to reexamine the rest of our basis for this theological commitment."[82]

More on the Spirit and the Trinity

Matthew 28:19 proves only that there are the three subjects named...but it does not prove, by itself, that all the three belong necessarily to the divine nature, and possess equal divine honor...This text, taken by itself, would not prove decisively either the personality of the three subjects mentioned, or their *equality* or *divinity*.[83]

St. Paul had no doctrine of the Trinity. The Spirit of God, or Holy Spirit, was for him (apart from the identification with

---

[78]Fortman, *The Triune God*, 6, 15.

[79]*New Catholic Encyclopedia*, 14:574, 575.

[80]William E. Addis and Thomas Arnold, *A Catholic Dictionary*, 1916, rep. Kessinger, 2004, 2:810.

[81]Ibid., 2:812.

[82]"Greek Grammar and Personality of the Holy Spirit," *Bulletin for Biblical Research*, 2003, 108, 125.

[83]John McClintock and James Strong, *Cyclopedia of Biblical, Theological and Ecclesiastical Literature*, Harper, 1891, 10:552.

the Risen Christ) the energy of the Divine nature, universal in its operation, influencing the will and the intelligence of men, the source of the sevenfold gifts described in Isaiah 11:2.[84]

"There is no positive evidence that the Spirit spoken of in the Old Testament was recognized either as a mode of the divine existence, or as one of a Trinity of persons in the divine essence."[85]

"In the Old Testament the spirit is not a personal being. It is a principle of action, not a subject. It belongs properly to Yahweh alone."[86]

When the Holy Spirit is spoken of in the Johannine farewell discourse as a person, when, for example, it is said of Him, "He will not speak of Himself, but what He heareth, that will He speak: and He will show you things to come; He will take of mine, and will show it unto you" (16:13, 14), that is just a pictorial personification, such as corresponds to the representation of the Spirit as another Advocate (with the Father) in the place of Jesus; while the same evangelist in his First Epistle treats the same Spirit impersonally as *chrisma* (anointing), 1 John 2:26, 27. The Holy Spirit "hears" by means of the spiritual ears of those who have Him. He proclaims by the mouth of the prophet, precisely as He prays and cries "Abba" out of the heart of the believer (Rom. 8:15, 26).[87]

That the New Testament writers attributed a [separate] personality to the Spirit is altogether improbable. All ancient thinkers are accustomed to speak of abstractions in personal language, and forget at times that they are using metaphor. Powers and qualities are endued with separate life and are supposed to act by their own volition like personal beings. When the Spirit, therefore, is described as warning, comforting, guiding, interceding, we must be careful not to press the texts too literally. The Old Testament conception of a divine energy, taking possession of men, was so firmly established that no radical departure from it was possible and

---

[84]*Dictionary of the Apostolic Church,* 1:189.
[85]Dr. Seth Sweetser, *Bibliotheca Sacra,* Jan. 1854, 11:99.
[86]*The New Jerome Biblical Commentary,* Prentice Hall, 1990, 2:742.
[87]Willibald Beyschlag, *New Testament Theology,* 1896, rep. Kessinger, 2006, 1:279-280.

closer examination shows that no such departure was contemplated. Paul contrasts the spirit with the flesh, as something of the same order, though belonging to a higher sphere. The underlying New Testament idea, even when the Spirit is spoken of personally, is always that of a supernatural power...At the same time the conception of the Spirit as a third Person in the Godhead lay quite outside the range of the New Testament writers' speculation. They thought simply of a power from above, which manifested itself in the lives of Christian men.[88]

Belief in the Holy Spirit as a third Person in the Godhead was established long after biblical times. At Nicea in 325 the council went no further than to say that "we believe in the Holy Spirit." It is therefore impossible to establish that the Holy Spirit was believed to be a third divine Person from New Testament times onwards. Gregory of Nazianzus, Bishop of Constantinople, wrote in 380 AD: "Of the wise men among ourselves, some have conceived of him [the Holy Spirit] as an activity, some as a creature, some as God; and some have been uncertain which to call him, out of reverence for Scripture, they say, as though it did not make the matter clear either way."[89]

It is impossible on the evidence of this quotation that a doctrine of the three coequal Persons in one God existed even by the end of the fourth century. If no orthodox Trinity was established three hundred years after New Testament times, how can Protestants claim it as indispensable Christian doctrine?

"The idea of the Holy Spirit or Spirit of God was derived from Judaism. The early Christians commonly thought of it not as an individual being or person, but simply as the divine power working in the world and particularly in the Church."[90]

John 1

In none of these instances [including John 1:1] is *theos* [God] used in such a manner as to identify Jesus with him who elsewhere in the New Testament figures as *o theos*, that is, the Supreme God...If the New Testament writers believed it

[88]E.F. Scott, *The Spirit in the New Testament*, Hodder, 1923, 232, 236.
[89]Fifth Theological Oration: "On the Holy Spirit," V.
[90]Arthur McGiffert, *A History of Christian Thought*, Charles Scribner's Sons, 1954, 1:111.

vital that the faithful should confess Jesus as "God," is the
almost complete absence of just this form of confession in the
New Testament explicable?[91]

When Professor Hort produced his treatise on John 1 he noted
these important facts. "Only-begotten Son" is the right translation of
monogenes. Recent modern attempts to rid the word of the idea of
begetting fail, because the root of the word is based on the verb
ginomai which means to come into existence. The church fathers who
knew their Greek well so understood the word. In any case, everyone
in the Bible thinks of a "uniquely begotten" one as a son and all sons
are derived from the fathers. Hort insists that *monogenes theos* ("an
only begotten God") in John 1:18 (if that is the right reading which is
doubtful) describes the "highest form of *derivative* being."[92] He
admits that "the idea of an antecedent [preexisting] Fatherhood and
Sonship within the Godhead, as distinguished from the manifested
Sonship of the Incarnation...is nowhere enunciated by [John] in
express words."[93]

The Word in John 1:1

The "word" of God [in the Old Testament] is sometimes
spoken of as if *it* had an objective existence, and possessed a
native power of realizing *itself*. The "wisdom" of God in
some passages is no more an attribute of God, but *a
personification of His thought*. In Proverbs 8 "wisdom" is
God's world-plan or conception, the articulated framework of
the universe as a moral organism. Its creation is the first
movement of the divine mind outward. Being projected
outside of the mind of God, *it* becomes the subject of His own
contemplation; *it* is "with" God [cf. John 1:1: "the word was
with God," which does not mean that the word was another
person].[94]

---

[91]*Bulletin of the John Rylands Library*, 1967-68, 50:253.
[92]F.J.A. Hort, *Two Dissertations 1876*, 13.
[93]Ibid., 16. Hort thinks that the Son being "in the bosom of the Father" points
to preexistence, but this is a weak argument. It must first be shown why John
should contradict the synoptic history of Jesus as being Son only from
conception.
[94]Hastings, *A Dictionary of the Bible*, 2:205, emphasis added.

English translations of the Greek Bible before the KJV rendered John 1:3-4: "All things were made through *it,* and without *it* nothing was made that was made. In *it* was life." Similarly a number of modern German and French translations describe the word as "it," not "him." There is no reason, therefore, to think of the word as a person, until it becomes embodied in Jesus in John 1:14.[95]

Remember that "word" in the Hebrew Bible, the background to the New Testament, never meant a person in all of its 1455 occurrences. There is no indication in the Old Testament that the Messiah would be a person *before his conception.* The very opposite was taught: The Messiah would expressly *not* be Almighty God,[96] but a unique, final prophet like Moses, coming into being from a family in Israel (see Deut. 18:15-19; Acts 3:22; 7:37).

Most Bible readers engage in an interesting "switch" when they come to the opening verse of John: "In the beginning was the Word [here they suppose the meaning is, In the beginning was *the Son* of God, the second member of the Trinity], and the Word [understood as Son] was with God [God here is understood as Father]" — and what comes next? "And the Word [Son] was God [the Father]." "The Son was the Father" is obviously wrong. But to avoid this the word "God" in John 1:1 is switched by Trinitarians, in mid-sentence, from "Father" to "member of the Godhead." Surely this is most unsatisfactory and involves reading much later theology into John.

We may put the point in a similar way by substituting "Jesus" for "Word":

> John's Hebrew listeners would not have missed the connection that John was making with those first three words — identical to the words that begin the book of Genesis. In the New Testament, when you see the word "God," it refers to God the Father. We have over a thousand instances of this in the New Testament. On two occasions only for certain "god" refers to Jesus (Heb. 1:8; John 20:28).

---

[95]Leonhard Goppelt says succinctly, "The *logos* of the prologue *became* Jesus; Jesus was the *logos* become flesh, but not the *logos* as such" (*Theology of the New Testament,* 2:297, emphasis added).

[96]In Isaiah 9:6 the Messiah is to be born to Israel. No one imagined that God would be born! And the promised Son is here called "a divine hero" (*el gibbor*), not "the Almighty God" (*El Shaddai*), a title not once applied to Jesus in Scripture.

God = the Father. Applying this fact that God means the Father, the verse reads: "In the beginning was the Word, and the Word was with the Father, and the Word was the Father." Who or what is the Word? If the Word = Jesus, then it reads: "In the beginning was Jesus, and Jesus was with the Father, and Jesus was the Father." Jesus was the Father?!

If the Word = the Son, then it reads: "In the beginning was the Son, and the Son was with the Father, and the Son was the Father." The Son was the Father?!

This is *confusion.* When you *assume* that "the Word" is a person (called Jesus, or the Son), the resulting contradiction (the Son was the Father) demonstrates that *such an assumption is false.* "The word" that John wrote about was just that: the spoken word of God the Father, who is known in the Hebrew Scriptures by name as YHWH the Creator. The word in John's prologue is not a person, but rather the spoken word of the Creator, by which all was created.[97]

Only when John is misread to mean "In the beginning was the *Son*" is the monotheism of the Bible disturbed, the synoptic birth narratives contradicted, and the human Jesus replaced. If the *Son* existed in the beginning, rather than the word or promise as God's intention, then Jesus is identified with Yahweh and there are two Yahwehs and thus two Gods. But as a learned professor observed, "It was impossible for the Apostles to identify Christ with Jehovah. Psalm 110:1 and Malachi 3:1 prevented this."[98]

Dr. Colin Brown, general editor of *The New International Dictionary of New Testament Theology,* wrote: "It is a common but patent misreading of the opening of John's Gospel to read it as if it said: 'In the beginning was the *Son*, and the *Son* was with God, and the *Son* was God' (John 1:1). What has happened here is the substitution of *Son* for *Word.*"[99]

In Mark 10:18 Jesus said, "No one is good but God alone." This "crucial phrase may also be translated: '...but the one God'...This text strongly distinguishes between Jesus and God...From this text

[97]Jonathan Sjordal, "The First Verse of the Gospel of John," in Anthony Buzzard, ed., *Focus on the Kingdom,* July, 2006.
[98]R.A. Bigg, *International Critical Commentary, St. Peter,* 199.
[99]"Trinity and Incarnation: In Search of Contemporary Orthodoxy," *Ex Auditu* 7, 1991, 89.

one would never suspect that the evangelist [or Jesus!] thought of Jesus as God."[100] There is truth in this statement: "Christendom has done away with Christianity without being quite aware of it."[101]

The Massive Evidence of Statistics

There are twelve thousand occurrences of words meaning "God" in the Bible (*Elohim, Yahweh, Adonai, Theos*). Not one of these appearances of the word "God" means God in three Persons or a triune God. Thus no writer of the Bible ever spoke of a Trinitarian God. *Strong's Concordance* very misleadingly gives "the Trinity" as one definition of God (*theos*). It cites no biblical example, and there are none. That should cause the reader to pause and reflect. Is the traditional view of God really based on Scripture or does it represent a departure from the biblical creed, and the biblical creed of Jesus?

A Fall from Original Truth

Prominent modern scholars reflect on the problematic mixture of Bible and philosophy which is the legacy of most churches in our time. The remedy for the problem they highlight would be a return to the creed of Jesus himself:

> In the degree to which Christianity cut itself off from its Hebrew roots and acquired Hellenistic and Roman form, it lost its eschatological hope and surrendered its apocalyptic alternative to "this world" of violence and death. It merged into late antiquity's gnostic religion of redemption. From Justin onwards, most of the Fathers revered Plato as a "Christian before Christ" and extolled his feeling for the divine transcendence and for the values of the spiritual world. God's eternity now took the place of God's future, heaven replaced the coming Kingdom...the immortality of the soul displaced the resurrection of the body...All the Greek and Latin fathers had to fight against this contemporary Gnostic religiosity, and *most of them succumbed to it*...A Gnostic spirituality, in fact, replaces the original Jewish and Christian vitality of life reborn out of the creative God.[102]

---

[100]Raymond Brown, *Jesus: God and Man*, 6, 7.
[101]Soren Kierkegaard, *Time*, Dec. 16, 1946, 64.
[102]Jürgen Moltmann, *The Spirit of Life*, Fortress Press, 1992, 89, 90, emphasis added.

That unfortunate tendency prevails today, when the Jesus presented in church is no longer the created Son of God, created in history, but a mystical transcendent figure coequal with God. The essential Jewishness of the faith as taught by the prophets of Israel and by Jesus himself has been suppressed.

The Challenge to the Church

Professor J. Harold Ellens issued this challenge to the Church to continue the unfinished business of the Reformation and recover the creed and Christology of Jesus.

> It seems patently true that the agenda of the ecumenical councils of the Christian Church during the fourth and fifth centuries, which permanently shaped the dogmatic tradition of the Christian faith, defining the nature of divine ontology [who God is] and operational Christology, was not a biblical agenda. It was rather a special type of Hellenistic and Neo-Platonist agenda. Indeed, it proves to be a modified version of Philo's agenda of Hellenistic Judaism, mediated through the Alexandrian theologians and their Catechetical School. The objective of the agenda, like Philo's ambition, was to rationalize the tradition of biblical monotheism into Christianized Greek philosophical theology, shaped in the language, conceptual categories, and cultural context current at the time and place of those seminal conciliar theological debates, namely in terms of Philonic Middle Platonism and subsequent Neo-Platonist language, categories, and hierarchichal models of Deity.[103]

J. Harold Ellens makes our point based on the clear testimony to what the Church has done with its central figure:

> It is time, therefore, for the Christian Church to acknowledge that it has a very special type of material which constitutes its creedal tradition. It is not a creedal tradition of Biblical Theology. It is not a unique, inspired, and authoritative word from God. It is, rather, a special kind of Greek religio-philosophical mythology...It should be candidly admitted by the Church, then, that its roots are not in Jesus of

---

[103]Ellens, *Ancient Library of Alexandria and Early Christian Theological Development*, 38-39.

Nazareth...nor in the central tradition of Biblical Theology...Its roots are in Philonic Hellenistic Judaism and in the Christianized Neo-Platonism of the second through the fifth century. Since this is so, the Church should acknowledge to the world of humans seeking truth and to the world of alternate religions, that the Christian Church speaks only with its own historical and philosophical authority and appeal and with neither a divine authority nor unique revelation from Jesus Christ or from God.[104]

The complication of God through the addition of two other Persons led inevitably to the complication of the Messianic personality of Jesus. Once he became God, true monotheism was violated. The result:

Jesus Christ was now no longer a man of flesh and blood like ourselves, but a heavenly being of supernatural origin in human form. With the help of a metaphysical system taken over from Greek philosophy, christological dogma came into being, and an attempt was made to describe the person of Jesus Christ in the form of the so-called "Doctrine of the two natures." "Jesus Christ, true man and true God." So men said...From the very beginning right until the present day the Church has been tempted to stress the "divinity" of Christ so one-sidedly that his "manhood" threatened to become a mere semblance. In this way Jesus Christ was made an historical abnormality...What happened to this Christ was no longer the fate of a man but the fate of a remarkable, shadowy, fairy-tale figure, half man and half God...[Men] have woven a golden veil of pious adoration, love and superstition and spread it over the rugged contours of God's action in history.[105]

From Cambridge in recent years comes the equally impressive analysis of the disaster that occurred when the Jewish Jesus was replaced by a pre-existing eternal Son: "The consequences of this process of reinterpretation by which 'the Son of God' became identified with 'God the Son' are far-reaching indeed." Professor Geoffrey Lampe points out that when the Son was projected back on to an eternally existing pre-human Son, and when the holy spirit was

---

[104]Ibid., 39.
[105]Heinz Zahrnt, *The Historical Jesus*, Harper & Row, 1963, 29.

turned into a third "hypostasis," "the Christian concept of God then becomes inescapably tritheistic; for three 'persons' in anything like the modern sense of the word 'person' mean in fact three Gods."[106]

The effects, however, especially in popular piety, have been even more far-reaching than this. The Nicene Creed speaks of 'Jesus Christ' in person, not the Logos, as pre-existent...It is thus the Jesus of the Gospels whom the imagination of the worshipper pictures as pre-existing in heaven and descending to earth...The picture of Jesus reflected in much traditional devotion is essentially that of a superman who voluntarily descends into the world of ordinary mortals, choosing, by a deliberate act of will, to be born as man...

God the Son is conceptualized as Jesus the Son of God; the obedience of Jesus, the Servant and Son of God, the true Adam indwelt and inspired by God...is attributed to God the Son; God the Son becomes eternally the subject of Jesus' self-dedication to his Father's will, and eternally the object of the Father's love...This means in effect the abandonment of monotheism, for such a relation between God the Son and God the Father is incompatible with the requirement of monotheism that we predicate of God one mind, one will, and one single operation.[107]

Professor Lampe was a specialist in the post-biblical development of the Trinity and observed also that "the interpretation of Jesus as the pre-existent Son, and of the Son as a pre-existent Jesus, causes inconsistency and confusion." The doctrine "which follows from the identification of Jesus with a pre-existent personal divine being is ultimately incompatible with the unity of God."[108]

Equally problematic for a true monotheism and a genuinely human Messiah is the Trinitarian concept of the Son as "assuming human nature." Professor Lampe reminds us that "a person is created by his relationships with other people and especially by his interaction with his parents and family."[109] What happened then to the first-century Galilean Jew Jesus? He was lost and replaced by a

---

[106]*God as Spirit*, SCM Press, 1983, 132, 136.
[107]Ibid., 136-138.
[108]Ibid., 140, 141.
[109]Ibid., 143.

philosophical abstraction whose identity as the son of David, and thus the true and only Messiah, became irrelevant.

> The Christological concept of the pre-existent divine Son...reduces the real, socially and culturally conditioned, personality of Jesus to the metaphysical abstraction "human nature." It is this universal humanity which the Son assumed and made his own...According to this Christology, the eternal Son assumes a timeless human nature, or makes it timeless by making it his own; it is a human nature which owes nothing essential to geographical circumstances; it corresponds to nothing in the actual concrete world; Jesus Christ has not, after all, really "come in the flesh."[110]

The observant reader will note that the professor rather obviously assigns to the orthodox doctrine of Jesus the label of antichrist. It was the Apostle John who late in the New Testament period warned that any reduction of the human individual Jesus Christ to a personality not essentially human is a menace to true faith (1 John 4:2-3). The Jesus to be confessed, as distinct from other Jesuses, is the one who has truly "come in the flesh," as a fully human person. Luther set the pattern for reading into John's "theological test" the post-biblical definition of Jesus. Luther mistranslates 1 John 4:2 as "Jesus Christ coming *into* the flesh."[111] The doctrine of the Incarnation was thus imposed on John.

Professor Lampe asks in a lecture at Cambridge, "What Future for the Trinity?" "For the traditional, classical, *doctrine* of the Trinity, I am bound to reply, even within these walls of Trinity College, 'Not much.'" He reflects on the sad history of the imposition of dogma:

> "This is the Catholick Faith: which except a man believe faithfully he cannot be saved." This has been paraphrased in less dignified language: "Accept my model or I'll do you," or rather, "This is God's model: accept it or he will do you," to which a distressingly large number of Christians in the past were eager to add, "and I am ready to act as God's agent."[112]

---

[110]Ibid., 144.
[111]John wrote "in the flesh," as a human person. All other German translations render correctly "in the flesh," not "into the flesh." Luther rendered the other occurrence of "in the flesh" (*en sarki*) in 1 Tim. 3:16 correctly.
[112]*Explorations in Theology 8*, SCM Press, 1981, 31, 32.

Lampe explains how the original Messianic model of Jesus as the son of David was transformed into a different model, based on Platonic philosophy. The Logos was then equated with a preexisting Son. "But the model of a preexisting Logos/Son has always proved extraordinarily difficult — many would say impossible — to reconcile with the assertion of the genuine manhood of the historical Jesus."[113]

How the Human Son of God Was Suppressed
Adolf Harnack, prince of church historians, in his *History of Dogma* explains the shift from one understanding of Jesus to a radically different one. He calls this the "displacement or suppression of the historical Christ by the preexisting Christ, that is, the real Christ by *the imagined or fictitious Christ.*"[114] This happened through dogmatics, that is, the dogmas of the Church. As theologians fought with theologians, this development, he says, led finally to:

> the triumphant attempt to get rid of the earlier speculation about God and Christ not by going back to the original teachings but a more speculative "advance" — an advance which finally *split monotheism* and weakened it, and also made Christ unrecognizable by splitting him [i.e. into two "natures"]...When the logos Christology [i.e. the idea that Jesus *was preexistent as the Son of God*] triumphed fully, the condemnation of the teaching of strict monotheism led to the putting in place of the Gnostic two-natures teaching about Christ...This apparent enrichment of Christ amounted to an impoverishment, because it in fact obliterated the complete human personality of Christ. "Nature" took its place, but the nature of a human being without the "person" is a nobody.[115]

In his *What Is Christianity?* Harnack wrote: "Under the influence of dogma...Christ's appearance in itself, the entrance of a divine being into the world came of necessity to rank as the chief fact, as itself the real redemption." Harnack says that "with the Greeks this inevitably set an entirely *new theory* in motion." It shattered the Messianic idea. With this new view of redemption, that is, the

---

[113]Ibid., 31-34.
[114]*Lehrbuch der Dogmengeschichte*, 1:705, translation from the German mine.
[115]Ibid., 1:704-705.

entrance from a preexisting life of a person into the world, "the very existence of the Gospel was threatened by drawing away men's thoughts and interests into another direction. When we look at the history of dogma, who can deny that that is what happened?"[116]

In his *History of Dogma* Harnack points out that:

the first formulated *opposition* to the Logos Christology [i.e. that the Son preexisted his birth]...was...called forth by interest in the evangelical, the Synoptic, idea of Christ [the picture of Jesus presented by Matthew, Mark and Luke]. With this was combined the attack on the use of Platonic philosophy in Christian doctrine...The whole theological interpretation of the first two articles of the rule of faith was again gradually involved in controversy [as today still!]...

But did not the doctrine of a heavenly aeon, rendered incarnate in the Redeemer, contain another remnant of the old *Gnostic* leaven? Did not the sending forth of the Logos [i.e understood as the preexisting *Son*, rather than word] to create the world recall the emanation of the aeons? Was not ditheism [belief in two Gods] set up, if two divine beings were to be worshipped? Not only were the uncultured Christian laity driven to such criticisms...but also all those theologians who refused to give any place to Platonic philosophy in Christian dogmatics. A conflict began which lasted for more than a century...[It was not] directly a war of the theologians against the laity, for it was not laymen, but only theologians who had adopted the creed of the laity, who opposed their brethren. We must describe it as the strenuous effort of Stoic Platonism to obtain supremacy in the theology of the Church; the victory of Plato...the history of *the displacement of the historical [Christ] by the pre-existent Christ, of the Christ of reality by the [imagined Christ], in dogmatics*; finally, as the victorious attempt to substitute the mystery of the person of Christ for the person Himself, and, by means of a theological formula unintelligible to them, to put the laity with their Christian faith under guardians...When the Logos Christology obtained a complete victory, the traditional view of the Supreme deity as *one*

---

[116]*What Is Christianity?* Williams and Norgate, 1901, 185, 186.

person, and, along with this, every thought of the real and complete human personality of the Redeemer was in fact condemned as being intolerable in the Church. Its place was taken by "the nature" [of Christ], which without "the person" is simply a cipher. The defeated party had right on its side.[117]

The significance of that shift in thinking, away from the real historical Jesus, can be measured by the obvious difference between on the one hand Peter and Paul and on the other the post-biblical innovation found in 2 Clement. The biblical view is this: Jesus "was foreknown before the foundation of the world" (1 Pet. 1:20). Paul: "So also it is written, 'The *first* man, Adam, became a living soul.' The last Adam became a life-giving spirit. However, the spiritual is not first, but the natural; then the spiritual" (1 Cor. 15:45-46).

The spiritual is not first, but second. However when we arrive at the non-biblical letter 2 Clement, the order of Adam and Christ has been reversed: "Christ the Lord saved us, being *first* spirit became flesh, and thus called us." This was the cosmological view of Christ introduced by the Greeks and it changed the nature of Christianity at its heart. On that concept — namely that a spirit person preexisted the historical human Jesus — the new form of the faith was built. Monotheism in its Jewish form as affirmed by Jesus was lost. This preexistent "spirit Jesus" was "the fundamental, theological and philosophical creed on which the whole Trinitarian and Christological speculations of the Church of the successive centuries are built, and thus the root of the orthodox system of dogmatics."[118]

It was this shift, reversing the historical order of Adam and Jesus, which later caused Gnostic theologians to speak of the Son as passing through Mary "as water through a pipe."[119] When this view prevailed the identity of Jesus as the blood relative of David through Mary was jeopardized. The center of the personality of Jesus was no longer the son of David, with God as his Father, but that of a Person arriving from another sphere and being thus essentially non-human. The Church adopted here a Gnostic point of view while claiming publicly to *oppose* Gnostic views of Jesus. The Church in fact rejected the blatant forms of Gnostic Christology but was itself infected with a modified Gnosticism. Its Christology then became and has remained

---

[117]*History of Dogma*, 3:8-10, emphasis added.
[118]Ibid., 1:328.
[119]Valentinus, in Tertullian, *Against All Heresies*, ch. 4.

"crypto-Gnostic." The reversal of this tendency can be achieved by returning to Jesus' own definitions of God and of himself as Messiah.

The fatal turn of theological events, starting in the second century and coming to expression clearly in the work of Justin Martyr, has been well summed up by Professor Loofs who described the process of the early corruption of biblical Christianity:

> The Apologists ["church fathers" like Justin Martyr, ca. 100-165] laid the foundation for the *perversion/corruption* (*Verkehrung*) of Christianity into a revealed [philosophical] teaching. Specifically, their Christology affected the later development disastrously. By taking for granted the transfer of the concept of Son of God onto the preexisting Christ, they were the cause of the Christological problem of the fourth century. They caused a shift in the point of departure of Christological thinking — *away from the historical Christ* and onto the issue of preexistence. They thus shifted attention away from the historical life of Jesus, putting it into the shadow and promoting instead the Incarnation [i.e., of a preexistent Son]. They tied Christology to cosmology and could not tie it to soteriology. The Logos teaching [i.e., that God the Son preexisted literally as the Logos] is not a "higher" Christology than the customary one. It lags in fact far behind the genuine appreciation of Christ. According to their teaching it is no longer God who reveals Himself in Christ, but the Logos, the inferior God, a God who as God is subordinated to the Highest God (inferiorism or subordinationism). In addition, the suppression of economic-trinitarian ideas by metaphysical-pluralistic concepts of the divine triad (*trias*) can be traced to the Apologists.[120]

Those who are dedicated to restoring the identity of the biblical Jesus, Son of God, may take heart from the incisive words of this leading systematic theologian.

When Justin replied to Trypho the Jew's request for evidence that the Son "submitted to become man by the Virgin," Justin produced a

---

[120]Friedrich Loofs, *Leitfaden zum Studium des Dogmengeschichte* (*Manual for the Study of the History of Dogma*), 1890, Niemeyer Verlag, 1951, part 1, ch. 2, sec. 18: "Christianity as a Revealed Philosophy. The Greek Apologists," 97.

number of proof-texts.[121] Justin is one of the first of the "Apologists" to find the Son in the "us" of Genesis 1:26, to read the Son of God back on to the Old Testament angel of the Lord and to initiate a lasting image of the Son as derived from the Father before the Son's birth, as sunlight reaching the earth is related to the sun.[122] When Justin referred to the Son as "another God" he set in motion the unfortunate trend which led to the loss of Jesus' own monotheism.

Professor Bart Ehrman

In very recent times good scholarship confirms our point that the Trinitarian Son of God of church tradition bears very little resemblance to the actual Jesus of history. Bart Ehrman has encouraged the public to think about Jesus as he really was: an "apocalyptic prophet of the new millennium." Reminding us of the theological bombshell thrown at "the system" by Albert Schweitzer, Ehrman concludes that Jesus was indeed a first-century Jewish apocalypticist, announcing the Kingdom of God as a coming cosmic intervention on the part of God to correct the appalling evils of our present systems and establish peace on earth by sending Jesus back. Ehrman notes that it is "odd that scholars haven't gone out of their way to share that evidence with everyone else"[123] — evidence which not only makes Jesus intelligible in the first century but warns us against inventing him in our own imaginations or accepting him uncritically from our traditions.

Surveying the New Testament evidence Ehrman concludes that:

> Jesus stood within a long line of Jewish prophets who understood that God was soon going to intervene in this world, overthrow the forces of evil that ran it, and bring in a new kingdom in which there would be no more war, disease, catastrophe, despair, hatred, sin or death.[124]

The Gospel as Jesus preached it was indeed about the coming Kingdom of God.[125] Today that Gospel is generally not the Gospel as

---

[121]*Dialogue with Trypho*, ch. 63.

[122]Ibid., ch. 128.

[123]*Jesus: Apocalyptic Prophet of the New Millennium,* x.

[124]Ibid., 21.

[125]For an examination of the Gospel as Jesus preached it, see Anthony Buzzard, *The Coming Kingdom of the Messiah: A Solution to the Riddle of the New Testament,* Restoration Fellowship, 2002, and *Our Fathers Who*

preached in church. The difference is striking. But equally striking is the Church's very complex Jesus with "two natures," fully God and fully man, arriving on earth from an eternal prehistoric life as God, a member of a triune Deity.

Ehrman discusses the development of views concerning who Jesus was, and reminds us of the various options which did not become "orthodox," for example that it was not the *Christ* who was crucified, but *Jesus*, into whom the Christ entered at his baptism. This model which really made Jesus two different beings, producing a sort of "double-person," did not become the official line adopted by the Church and thus central to Christianity. But, says Ehrman:

> even the official line — that is, the one that ended up winning over the most adherents and so became the standard interpretation — didn't spring up out of the ground overnight. *Nor was it directly tied to the actual words and deeds of the historical Jesus.*[126]

Ehrman adds:

> It should be clear that the concerns which drove the debates over who Christ was [producing the church councils' decision to call him God] were far removed from the concerns of Jesus himself...Rather than trying to understand what a first-century Palestinian Jew might have meant in first-century Palestine, [church members today] see Jesus' words and deeds in the light of their own beliefs about him. In other words, Christians tend to interpret Jesus' life from a dogmatic, rather than a historical, perspective.[127]

Ehrman finds it ironic, as we do, that the historical evidence was often bypassed by those who constructed the later dogmatic definition of God and Jesus, those involved in "debates that Jesus had no knowledge of or interest in."[128]

The final result of the disregard for Jesus as he actually was is this:

> One of the strands of Christianity that has been consistently marginalized throughout the course of the past 1,900 years

---

Aren't in Heaven: The Forgotten Christianity of Jesus the Jew, Restoration Fellowship, 1999.
[126]Ehrman, *Jesus: Apocalyptic Prophet*, 241, emphasis added.
[127]Ibid., 242, 243.
[128]Ibid., 243.

Does Everyone Believe in the Trinity?

has been one that took the authentic words of Jesus seriously...The historical Jesus did not teach about his own divinity [Deity] or pass on to his disciples the doctrines that later came to be embodied in the Nicene creed.[129]

Jesus Was Not a Trinitarian represents that "marginalized" strand of Christianity which struggles to retain the words of Jesus himself. Our point is that the centrally important declaration of Jesus that God is a single Person is amongst those precious and instructive words that the Church has set aside and labeled "Jewish." But Jesus was a Jew and we must relate to him within that context, lest we fall for "another Jesus."

The Challenge to Honesty

Tom Harpur recalls a conversation with a seasoned church member who observed that he understood "precious little, if anything" of the creeds recited in church. Harpur then complains:

In fact, very few preachers can give a reasonable account of either the doctrine of the Trinity or the doctrine of the Incarnation, that is, that Jesus was truly human and yet fully God. They repeat formulae that were worked out, with much quarreling and bitterness, in the fourth and fifth centuries...These formulae...raise an insurmountable barrier for many who might otherwise become disciples of Jesus in our day...You simply cannot find the doctrine of the Trinity set out anywhere in the Bible...As a pious Jew, [Paul] would have been shocked and offended by such an idea.[130]

Harpur's research leads him to believe that "very few clerics ever pass on what they have learned in theological school about contemporary scholarship on the Bible...Surely it is time for greater honesty from the pulpit." He notes also the alarming fact that "the great majority of regular churchgoers are, for all practical purposes, tritheists."[131] Might not this situation attract the sort of criticism from Jesus that called forth his startling warning that it is possible to "replace God's commands with [our] own man-made teachings"? (Matt. 15:9, NLT).

---

[129]Ibid., 243.
[130]Harpur, *For Christ's Sake,* 10-11.
[131]Ibid., 11, 12.

Jesus the Son of David and of God

The New Testament opens with a definitive headline about Jesus. "This is the genealogical table [*genesis*] of Jesus Christ, the son of David" (Matt. 1:1). The wise men from the east came to worship him "who was born King of the Jews" (Matt. 2:2) and to find "the ruler who will shepherd Israel" whose birthplace was Bethlehem (Matt. 2:6). Mary bore a child after becoming pregnant supernaturally. Only when a tsunami of Greek philosophical speculation overwhelmed the biblical story was Jesus promoted to the status of God the Son, rivaling the God of Israel. With this fateful move the Church threw away the Jewish framework within which the biblical story is set and within which it alone makes sense.

No one opening a New Testament and reading the matchless story of the origin of Jesus will be misled into thinking that "God was born," or that as a Roman Catholic priest said on television, "God came to Mary and said, 'Will you please be my mother?'" Nor, as Max Lucado wrote, quoted by Dr. Charles Swindoll, that "Mary changed God's diaper."[132] God's actual story is incomparably more noble and challenging to our chaotic world. It is the account of what the One God of Israel accomplished and will accomplish in His promised unique Son, Israel's Messiah, descendant of David and Savior of the world. Surely it is time for the New Testament's witness to that extraordinary promised son of David to be taken with the utmost seriousness, as the real story to be believed by believers.

The Jesus of popular piety and tradition does not clearly match the biblical Jesus who worshipped the One God of Israel. We are to avoid a "fairytale" pseudo-Savior who has usurped the position of God's Messiah. Crowning our concerted effort to return to the Jesus of history will be the reemergence of the unitarian theology of Jesus and the Bible, that God is one single Person, the Father.

---

[132] *Jesus: When God Became a Man,* 10.

Epilogue

A Future for Monotheism

"For a Jew the word God could mean one Person only…The use of the word God for Jesus would have seemed to have been an infringement of monotheism, whereas by calling Jesus Lord they confessed that he was associated with his Father in the exercise of authority."[1]

"In my view Christianity should be much more tightly focused upon Jesus' words than it usually has been in the past…The real Jesus is a much more interesting and religiously relevant figure than the divine Christ of later faith and he has the advantage of having actually lived."[2]

"In the teaching of Jesus Christ God is preeminently the Father."[3]

"Forget the pseudo-orthodox attempts to make Jesus of Nazareth conscious of being the second Person of the Trinity…The word Messiah had of course nothing to do with Trinitarian or incarnational theology."[4]

The Original Jesus
The original Jesus was a Jew who recited and affirmed as the center of true theology the unitarian creed of Israel. Attempts to expand that creed, *on the basis of the Bible*, into a Trinitarian one

---

[1]D.E.H. Whiteley, *The Theology of St. Paul*, Blackwell, 1980, 106.
[2]Don Cupitt, *The Debate About Christ*, 138.
[3]"God," *International Standard Bible Encyclopedia*, 1983 ed., 2:1261.
[4]N.T. Wright, "The Historical Jesus and Christian Thought," *Sewanee Theological Review* 39, 1996.

have failed, as historians and many Bible experts recognize. The creed of Jesus must on no account be modified. To do so is to risk compromise with paganism.

The original Jesus is not only a confirmed unitarian, underlining the creed of Israel. He himself is the one whose "genesis" or origin (Matt. 1:1, 18) is spelled out for us in the clearest terms in Matthew's and Luke's opening chapters. Jesus is the Son of God who is rooted in a miraculous human history (Luke 1:35) and specifically by divine promise in the history of Israel. He is the "Jesus Christ" who came "in the flesh" (not *"into* the flesh," as mistranslated by Luther[5]), that is to say as an originally human, historical person, a member of the human race. This is John's yardstick for our grasp of the true spirit (1 John 4:1-6).

The original Jesus is not a *pre*-historical person. That would not fit the profile of the son of David promised as Messiah by the Hebrew Bible. Once his history is moved out of history and outside time and space, the faith loses its anchor in history and in fact. We are then left adrift on the stormy seas of speculation and fantasy.

The very same timelessness and spacelessness which in *later* theology was applied to Jesus' origin has adversely and confusingly affected Jesus' very Hebrew view of the future. Our destiny is not to disappear as souls to heaven, but to govern a renewed society on a renewed earth over which the returned Messiah will preside (Matt. 5:5; Rev. 5:10, etc.). The "end of the world" in the Bible is in fact not the end of the space-time universe. It is (as properly translated from the Greek) "the end of the [present] age."[6] Jesus announced that the age of the Kingdom of God fully manifested would follow the end of this age. The new age of the Kingdom is positively not beyond space and time!

Both the beginning of God's story of salvation in the historical Messiah born in Bethlehem and the end of God's story promising a restored earth have become confused in the churchgoer's mind, and the Bible becomes a difficult book to read with pleasure, because our traditional story is not that of the Bible writers.

---

[5]"In das Fleisch gekommen" (1 John 4:2; 2 John 7). Other German versions corrected the mistake by translating the Greek *en sarki* "im Fleisch."
[6]Jesus was asked about this future end of the present era of history and the arrival of the Kingdom of God with the Messiah's return in Matt. 24:3.

"Orthodoxy" not only disturbs the biblical picture of Jesus as the human Messiah. It defines the Gospel in a way which excludes Jesus as the model evangelist whose task was to preach the Gospel about the Kingdom of God (Mark 1:14, 15; Luke 4:43). In the Great Commission (Matt. 28:19, 20) the task of taking the very same Gospel of the Kingdom to the world was conferred by Jesus on the Church until his return (see also Matt. 24:14).

Astonishingly, leading evangelicals, while claiming the Bible as their authority, set themselves in direct opposition to Jesus' commission to announce the Kingdom of God as the Gospel. In *1001 Bible Questions Answered* two leading evangelicals wrote, "We are convinced that this [the belief that Jesus commissioned the Church to preach the Gospel of the Kingdom] is an error. It would be a strange thing to find the Church's commission in the Kingdom Gospel."[7] An amazing assault on Scripture and the Messiah's teaching is revealed by these authors' confident assertion, reflected widely in evangelical literature:

> I have long been convinced, and have taught that the Great Commission of Matthew 28:19, 20 is primarily applicable to the Kingdom rather than to the Church. If this were kept in mind we should not fall into confusion regarding our marching orders, which are found in Acts 1:8, with details in the Epistles to the Churches. The Matthew commission [i.e. the command to preach the Kingdom of God Gospel as Jesus always did] will come into force for the Jewish Remnant after the Church is caught away.[8]

Then this staggering rejection of the teaching of Jesus:

> Mark's gospel, like Matthew's and Luke's, is primarily a kingdom book, and I am satisfied that none of them contains the Church's marching orders — not even the so-called "Great Commission" of Matthew 28:18-20...To be sure, we are to preach the gospel to every creature but what gospel? The only gospel known to the synoptics was the gospel of the kingdom. Our gospel of the grace of God is found among the four evangelists only in John.[9]

---

[7]Pettingill and Torrey, *1001 Bible Questions Answered*, 120.
[8]Ibid., 127.
[9]Ibid., 113. Note that for Paul the Gospel of grace is synonymous with the Gospel of the Kingdom (Acts 20:24, 25) and the whole notion of two saving

The loss of the Gospel as the Jewish Jesus preached it (Heb. 2:3) goes hand in hand with the Church's rejection of his unitarian creed.

According to the prophets of Israel one day the whole world will indeed recognize the God of Israel as the one true God: "And the Lord will be king over all the earth; in that day there will be one Lord and His name one" (Zech. 14:9). Jesus will be acknowledged too, not as Almighty God, but as the unique servant of that one God. He will be recognized for who he truly is, "the Son of God, the Messiah" (Matt. 16:16), and "the man Messiah Jesus" (1 Tim. 2:5), the mediator between the One God and mankind to whom all judgment has been delegated: "The Father judges no one, but has given all judgment to the Son" (John 5:22).

1 Timothy 2:5, defining the One God as the Father, distinct from the man Messiah Jesus, if believed, could in an instant revolutionize two thousand years of distorted theology and enable us to return to our Jewish roots in Jesus. No other testimony is really needed when once the words of Paul's creed are grasped: "There is one God and one mediator between God and men, the man Messiah Jesus." Could not the creed of Jesus and Paul provide a rallying point, at least a center of intense conversation, between millions of Jews and a billion Christians, and of course more than a billion Muslims?

Liberal Christians are very much aware of the early loss of the Jewish creed from the faith, but they do not regard this defection from the Bible as very serious, holding a low view of Scripture. Evangelicals however regard the Bible as authoritative and have so far been unwilling to face the difference between their creed and that of Jesus. In fact they are the ones who have shown the most ingenuity in attempting the hopeless task of finding the Trinity in the Bible, even in the Old Testament. By cobbling together their case using a small number of verses, taken out of the overall biblical context, they try to turn the New Testament writers into Trinitarians or at least struggling to become Trinitarians!

In practice Trinitarian proof texts are taken almost exclusively from John and Paul with some help from Hebrews. But the doctrine

---

gospels is utterly foreign to the NT. For a similar systematic departure from the Gospel as Jesus preached it, see the article "Gospel" in *Unger's Bible Dictionary*, and in scores of evangelical tracts which do not invite the convert to obey Jesus' command in Mark 1:14, 15 to repent and believe the Gospel of the Kingdom.

of God must be established across the whole range of Scripture, certainly not neglecting the Old Testament in which the New is rooted. The fact that Jesus' creed was not a Trinitarian creed does not seem to disturb or deter evangelicals. This is because of the enormous emphasis they place on the death of Jesus rather than on his teaching. Many evangelicals seem to view Paul as the founder of the faith they recognize as Christian and forget that Jesus was the original preacher of the Gospel and that the Apostles describe as the greatest peril of all the failure to hear and heed the words of Jesus (Heb. 2:3; 1 Tim. 6:3; 2 John 7-9; 1 John 5:20). Being Christlike should surely include believing the same creed as Jesus.

The problem requiring resolution is simply this: Jesus must be taken seriously in the matter of defining God. The sacred birth narratives of Matthew and Luke were designed as definitive accounts of the supernatural origin of Jesus as descendant of David and Son of God. That picture should have guaranteed that the human Messiah remain at the center of Christian faith.

However, under the distorting influence of a post-biblical philosophical theology from the Greek world, John and Paul were made to support that later creed. They were found to be the most susceptible of "interpretation" in support of that later "revised" view of God and Jesus. But they have been made to say what they did not intend. The post-biblical creeds have simply been read into them and not out of them. They have thus been made to disturb the cardinal unitarian creed of Jesus, something they never intended. John and Paul have been turned into servants of a creed they did not recognize. They should be read in harmony with the Hebrew Bible and synoptic and Acts accounts of Jesus which preserve, as the primary data about his person, his descent from King David and his supernatural status as Son of God, not God Himself. Only then will the God of Jesus be honored as the single unrivaled God of the universe.

Appendix 1
On John 20:28: What Did Thomas
Say in Hebrew?

CLIFFORD HUBERT DUROUSSEAU, PHD (CAND.)

The book by Dan Brown, *The Da Vinci Code* (2003), which has sold over forty million copies to date, and the recently released movie version (May 19, 2006), which will be seen by at least an equal number of people, has focused attention upon Mary of Magdala (Mary Magdalene), who appears in John 20:1-18 and is credited by the narrative as being the first person to whom Jesus appeared after his execution by Pontius Pilate on the charge of claiming to be "The King of the Jews."[1] The phenomenal bestselling novel has also focused attention upon Constantine and the first ecumenical council held at Nicea (modern-day Iznik, Turkey), where, drawing heavily upon the fourth Gospel, the Christian bishops defined God and Jesus in this way: "I believe in one God, the Father Almighty, Maker of heaven and earth, and in one Lord Jesus Christ, the only-begotten Son, begotten of the Father before all worlds; God of God, Light of Light, true God of true God, begotten, not made, of one substance [ὁμοούσιον] with the Father, by Whom all things were made: who for us men and our salvation came down from heaven."[2]

There are two more apparitions in this first conclusion of the fourth Gospel: one to ten of the original twelve apostles on the evening of the same day (John 20:19-23), Thomas being absent, and

---

[1] According to Paul, Peter (whom he calls by his Hebrew nickname Kepha) was the first person to whom Jesus appeared (1 Cor. 15:5). According to *The Gospel According to the Hebrews*, which was used by the Ebionites, fragments of which still survive in patristic citations, James (Ya'akov), the brother of Jesus, was the first.

[2] See "Nicene Creed" and "Ecumenical council" at Wikipedia.com; also "Seven Ecumenical Councils" and "Iznik (Nicaea)" at allaboutturkey.com. For an enlightening account of this important turning point in the history of Christianity, when the Church became the pawn of a pagan emperor of the Roman Empire and the Trinitarians defeated the Arians, read *When Jesus Became God: The Struggle to Define Christianity During the Last Days of Rome* by the Jewish scholar Richard Rubenstein (Harvest Books, 2000).

one eight days later, at which time he was present (20:26-29). These two episodes have given to Thomas a paradoxical fame. On the one hand, for his skepticism after being told by the ten that they had seen the Lord (20:25), he is known as Doubting Thomas (and all who like him doubt the resurrection of Jesus are called Doubting Thomases).[3] "Thomas, called...'Twin,' who was one of the twelve, was not with them when Jesus came. So the other disciples said to him, 'We have seen the Lord,' but he answered, 'Unless I can see the holes that the nails made in his hands and can put my finger into the holes they made, and unless I can put my hand into his side, I refuse to believe'" (New Jerusalem Bible).

On the other hand, for the fragmentary statement he makes eight days later (ὁ κύριός μου καὶ ὁ θεός μου, John 20:28), Thomas is considered the apostle who made a "confession" greater than that of Peter in the Synoptics ("You are the Messiah," Mark 8:29 and parallels, New American Bible).[4]

> Eight days later the disciples were in the house again and Thomas was with them. The doors were closed, but Jesus came and stood among them. "Peace be with you," he said. Then he spoke to Thomas, "Put your finger here, look, here

---

[3]See 1 Corinthians 15, where Paul employs an apostolic creed and the Aristotelian syllogism in an attempt to persuade the Corinthian "Doubting Thomases," who said, "There is no resurrection of the dead."

[4]The fourth Gospel reports a different saying of Peter according to most recent translations, based as they are upon better manuscript evidence than earlier translations: "and we believe [and] we have come to know that you are the Holy One of God" (John 6:69). According to the Greek text of the Nestle-Aland 27th edition of the fourth Gospel, John the Baptist is the first to call Jesus "the Son of God," that is, the Messiah (1:34). And he is followed in turn by Andrew: "We have found the Messiah! (which is translated Anointed)" (1:41, NAB); Philip: "We have found him of whom Moses wrote in the Law, and the Prophets, Jesus, son of Joseph, of Nazareth!"(1:45); and Nathanael: "Rabbi, you are the Son of God; you are the King of Israel!" On 1:41, the New American Bible notes: "the Hebrew word masiah, 'anointed one'...appears in Greek as the transliterated messias only here and in John 4:25." And on 1:49, the NAB states: "this title is used in the Old Testament, among other ways, as a title of adoption for the Davidic king (2 Sam 7:14; Psalm 2:7; 89:27), and thus here with King of Israel, in a messianic sense. For the evangelist, Son of God also points to Jesus' divinity (cf. John 20:28)."

are my hands. Give me your hand, put it into my side. Do not
be unbelieving anymore but believe." Thomas replied, "My
[l]ord and my God!" Jesus said to him: "You believe because
you [have seen] me. Blessed are those who have not seen and
yet believe" (20:26-29).

Was Thomas by his exclamation giving utterance to a more
profound revelation than Peter at Caesarea Philippi? Did the early
Jewish believers teach that "Jesus is LORD and God" (John 20:28)
rather than "Lord and Messiah" (Acts 2:36)? Is that a correct
interpretation of what Thomas uttered? Is that how we are to
understand what we are told he said here in the fourth Gospel?

Trinitarians commonly consider the fragmentary statement of
Thomas (John 20:28) the strongest proof in the New Testament that
"Jesus is God" — a formulation which, apparently no one seems to be
aware, constitutes Eutychianism or Monophysitism, a view
anathematized by the fifth ecumenical council, the Council of
Chalcedon (553 CE). See, for example, Raymond Brown's comment
in his magisterial *Anchor Bible* commentary where he calls it "the
supreme christological pronouncement of the Fourth Gospel,"[5] and in
his more recent *Introduction to New Testament Christology* he says in
the essay in the appendix "Did New Testament Christians Call Jesus
God?": "This is the clearest example in the NT of the use of 'God' for
Jesus."[6] Rudolf Bultmann writes of John 20:28: "the only passage in
which Jesus is undoubtedly designated or, more exactly, addressed as
God."[7]

More than a century before these two, Adam Clarke in his
commentary on the Bible (famous for its rejection of the doctrine of
the eternal generation of the Son) had this to say about the famous
fragment of Thomas: "Thomas was the first who gave the title 'God'
to Jesus, and, by this glorious confession, made amends for his former
obstinate incredulity."

Even much earlier still, in the third century Novatian in his
Treatise Concerning the Trinity twice used John 20:28 as proof that
it is correct to believe that "Jesus is God." In Chapter XIII, he writes:

---

[5]*The Gospel According to John (xiii-xxi)*, Doubleday, 1970, 1047.
[6]*An Introduction to New Testament Christology*, Paulist Press, 1994, 188.
[7]Rudolf Bultmann, "The Christological Confession of the World Council of
Churches," in his *Essays Philosophical and Theological*, SCM Press, 1955.

And if, whereas it is the portion of no man to come from heaven, He descended by coming from heaven; and if, whereas this word can be true of no man, "I and the Father are one," Christ alone declared this word out of the consciousness of His divinity; and if, finally, the Apostle Thomas, instructed in all the proofs and conditions of Christ's divinity, says in reply to Christ, "My Lord and my God"; and if, besides, the Apostle Paul says, "Whose are the fathers, and of whom Christ came according to the flesh, who is over all, God blessed for evermore," writing in his epistles; and if the same apostle declares that he was ordained "an apostle not by men, nor of man, but by Jesus Christ"; and if the same contends that he learned the Gospel not from men or by man, but received it from Jesus Christ, reasonably Christ is God. Therefore, in this respect, one of two things must needs be established. For since it is evident that all things were made by Christ, He is either before all things, since all things were by Him, and so He is justly God; or because He is man He is subsequent to all things, and justly nothing was made by Him. But we cannot say that nothing was made by Him, when we observe it written that all things were made by Him. He is not therefore subsequent to all things; that is, He is not man only, who is subsequent to all things, but God also, since God is prior to all things. For He is before all things, because all things are by Him, while if He were only man, nothing would be by Him; or if all things were by Him, He would not be man only, because if He were only man, all things would not be by Him; nay, nothing would be by Him. What, then, do they reply? That nothing is by Him, so that He is man only? How then are all things by Him? Therefore He is not man only, but God also, since all things are by Him; so that we reasonably ought to understand that Christ is not man only, who is subsequent to all things, but God also, since by Him all things were made.

And in Chapter XXX, where he seeks to show that "Jesus is LORD and God," he writes:

And let us therefore believe this, since it is most faithful that Jesus Christ the Son of God is our Lord and God; because "in the beginning was the Word, and the Word was with God, and God was the Word. The same was in the beginning with God." And, "The Word was made flesh, and dwelt in us." And, "My Lord and my God." And, "Whose are the fathers, and of whom according to the flesh Christ came, who is over all, God blessed for evermore." What, then, shall we say? Does Scripture set before us two Gods? How, then, does it say that "God is one"? Or is not Christ God also? How, then, is it said to Christ, "My Lord and my God"? Unless, therefore, we hold all this with fitting veneration and lawful argument, we shall reasonably be thought to have furnished a scandal to the heretics, not assuredly by the fault of the heavenly Scriptures, which never deceive; but by the presumption of human error, whereby they have chosen to be heretics. And in the first place, we must turn the attack against them who undertake to make against us the charge of saying that there are two Gods. It is written, and they cannot deny it, that "there is one Lord." What, then, do they think of Christ? — that He is Lord, or that He is not Lord at all? But they do not doubt absolutely that He is Lord; therefore, if their reasoning be true, here are already two Lords. How, then, is it true according to the Scriptures, there is one Lord? And Christ is called the "one Master." Nevertheless we read that the Apostle Paul also is a master. Then, according to this, our Master is not one, for from these things we conclude that there are two masters. How, then, according to the Scriptures, is "one our Master, even Christ"? In the Scriptures there is one "called good, even God"; but in the same Scriptures Christ is also asserted to be good. There is not, then, if they rightly conclude, one good, but even two good. How, then, according to the scriptural faith, is there said to be only one good? But if they do not think that it can by any means interfere with the truth that there is one Lord, that Christ also is Lord, nor with the truth that one is our Master, that Paul also is our master, or with the truth that one is good, that Christ also is called good; on the same reasoning, let them understand that, from the fact that God is one, no obstruction arises to the truth that Christ also is declared to be God.

The confusion caused by interpreting the fragmentary statement of Thomas as a proof that it is correct to assert that "Jesus is LORD and God" is evident here. The Hebrew Scriptures teach that "Yahweh is one" (Deut. 6:4). Jews recite the Shema in prayer every day, hanging it on the doorposts of their homes (mezuzah) and binding it to the head and hand (tefillin). This statement of God's Oneness constitutes the first words a Jewish child is taught to say, and the last words uttered before a Jew dies. Jesus taught the Shema (Mark 12:29; see p. 410).[8] If one asserts that John 20:28 proves that "Jesus is LORD and God," one is then placed on the horns of a dilemma and faced with an apparent contradiction, as Novatian above pointed out and sought to resolve.

The purpose of this article is to present considerations which show that the exclamation of Thomas in John 20:28 has been misinterpreted because it has been read out of context and because the underlying Hebrew words for "lord" and "God,"[9] which would have been known and, I argue, spoken by Thomas in such a situation, are universally overlooked. The words will also be discussed in Aramaic, though such a term for the language spoken by the Jews in that time is not used in the Greek New Testament, and David Flusser, the eminent Jewish scholar who wrote a book on Jesus and the article on him in *Encyclopedia Judaica*, argued that Jesus and his disciples spoke Hebrew.[10]

By the early half of the 20th century, modern scholars reached a nearly unanimous opinion that Aramaic became a

---

[8]The parallel accounts in Matthew (22:37) and Luke (10:27) omit the first line of the Shema, which Mark has. And Luke places the scene much earlier than Mark and Matthew.

[9]See John 5:1; 20:16; 19:13, 17, 20; Rev. 9:11, 16:16 = seven texts; in addition, John 1:41; 4:25; compare Acts 21:40; Acts 22:6; also Acts 26:14.

[10]*Encyclopedia Judaica*, 10:10, Jerusalem, 1971. See also now the article by one of his students at the Jerusalem School of Synoptic Research at Hebrew University, Dr. Shmuel Safrai, "Spoken Languages in the Time of Jesus," at JerusalemPerspective.com, where he says, "Hebrew was the primary language spoken in the land of Israel in the time of Jesus." This echoes what had been suggested by Hebrew University professor M.H. Segal as early as 1909 when he argued that Mishnaic Hebrew showed the characteristics of a living language, and that the Jewish people in the land of Israel at the time of Jesus used Hebrew as their primary written and spoken language (see M.H. Segal, "Mishnaic Hebrew and Its Relation to Biblical Hebrew and to Aramaic," *Jewish Quarterly Review,* Old Series 20 (1908-1909), 647-737; also Segal, *A Grammar of Mishnaic Hebrew*, Oxford, 1927).

spoken language in the land of Israel by the start of Israel's Hellenistic Period in the 4th century BCE, and thus Hebrew ceased to function as a spoken language around the same time. However, during the latter half of the 20th century, accumulating archeological evidence and especially linguistic analysis of the Dead Sea Scrolls has qualified the previous consensus. Alongside Aramaic, Hebrew also flourished as a living spoken language. Hebrew flourished until near the end of the Roman Period, when it continued on as a literary language [in] the Byzantine Period in the 4th century CE...

Although the survival of Hebrew as a spoken language until the Byzantine Period is well-known among Hebrew linguists, there remains a lag in awareness among some historians who do not necessarily keep up-to-speed with linguistic research and rely on outdated scholarship. Nevertheless, the vigor of Hebrew is slowly but surely making its way through the academic literature. *The Hebrew of the Dead Sea Scrolls* distinguishes the Dead Sea Scrolls Hebrew from the various dialects of Biblical Hebrew it evolved out of: "This book presents the specific features of DSS Hebrew, emphasizing deviations from classical BH." *The Oxford Dictionary of the Christian Church* that once said in 1958 in its first edition, Hebrew "ceased to be a spoken language around the fourth century BC," now says in 1997 in its third edition, Hebrew "continued to be used as a spoken and written language in the New Testament period." *An Introductory Grammar of Rabbinic Hebrew* says, "It is generally believed that the Dead Sea Scrolls, specifically the Copper Scroll and also the Bar Kokhba letters, have furnished clear evidence of the popular character of MH [Mishnaic Hebrew]." And so on. Israeli scholars now tend to take it for granted that Hebrew as a spoken language is a feature of Israel's Roman Period.[11]

---

[11]"Hebrew Language" at Wikipedia.org. It is universally agreed that Jesus and the twelve used the Hebrew Scriptures in their teaching in the land of Israel (see Matt. 5:17-18, where Jesus says, "Do not imagine that I have come to abolish the Law or the Prophets...In truth I tell you, till heaven and earth disappear, not one [*yod*] and [*qots*] is to disappear" and 23:35: "and so you will draw down on yourselves the blood of every upright person that has

ὁ κύριος **in John 20**

First, then, does anyone learned in the Scriptures maintain that John 20:28 teaches that Jesus is LORD and God, Yahweh and Elohim, like his Father and God? Yes. Raymond Brown, the most distinguished Roman Catholic biblical scholar of the 20th century in the United States, in his landmark commentary in *The Anchor Bible, The Gospel According to John*, says, "It is Thomas who makes clear that one may address Jesus in the same language in which Israel addressed Yahweh,"[12] thereby justifying prayer to Jesus as well as to God the Father Himself, though Jesus himself taught his disciples to pray to the Father alone.[13] In *Introduction to New Testament Christology*, Brown writes:

> Here Jesus is addressed as "God" (a nominative form with definite article, which functions as a vocative). The scene is designed to serve as a climax to the Gospel: As the resurrected Jesus stands before the disciples, one of their number at last gives expression to an adequate faith in Jesus. He does this by applying to Jesus the Greek (Septuagint) equivalent of two terms applied to the God of the OT (κύριος, "Lord," rendering *YHWH*, and θεός, "God," rendering *Elohim*)...In three reasonably clear instances in the NT [Heb. 1:8-9; John 1:1; 20:28] and in five instances that have probability [John 1:18; 1 John 5:20; Rom. 9:5; Tit. 2:13; 2 Pet. 1:1] Jesus is called ["]God.["]The use of "God" for Jesus that is attested in the early 2nd century [in the seven authentic letters of Ignatius of Antioch] was a continuation of a usage that had begun in NT times. There is no reason to be surprised at this. "Jesus is Lord" was evidently a popular confessional formula in NT times, and in this formula Christians gave Jesus the title κύριος which was the Septuagint translation for *YHWH*. If Jesus could be given this title, why could he not be called "God" (θεός), which the

---

been shed on earth, from the blood of Abel the holy to the blood of Zechariah son of Barachiah," where the Hebrew Bible, its text and canon, are alluded to by Jesus. It is to be noted in passing here that the mistake of Matthew, "Zechariah son of Barachiah," is corrected in Luke 11:51).

[12]*Gospel According to John*, 1047.

[13]John 15:15; 16:23; see also the Matthean and Lukan forms of the prayer he gave to the apostles, Matt. 6:9-13; Luke 11:2-4.

Septuagint often used to translate *Elohim*? The two Hebrew
terms had become relatively interchangeable, and indeed
YHWH was the more sacred term.[14]
In a footnote he adds:
> The earliest major preserved copies of the Septuagint were
> copied by Christians in the 4th and 5th centuries AD. We are
> not certain about how consistently earlier copies and other
> Greek translations circulating in NT times used κύριος for
> *YHWH*. I make no claim that all "high christology"
> appearances of κύριος for Jesus in the NT consciously
> reflected a translation of *YHWH*. Yet in general the NT
> authors were aware that Jesus was being given a title which in
> Greek was used to refer to the God of Israel.

Where, I ask, is this clearly so indicated in the NT? Where, in
particular, in the fourth Gospel?

Now, that the words ὁ κύριός μου are not equivalent to "my
YHWH"[15] the context shows.[16] Mary of Magdala calls Jesus ὁ κύριος
three times earlier, in verses 2, 13, and 18:
> It was very early on the first day of the week and still dark,
> when Mary of Magdala came to the tomb. She saw that the
> stone had been moved away from the tomb and came running to
> Simon Peter and the other disciple, the one whom Jesus loved.
> "They have taken the Lord [τὸν κύριον] out of the tomb," she
> said, "and we don't know where they have put him"...But Mary
> was standing outside near the tomb, weeping. Then, as she
> wept, she stooped to look inside, and saw two angels in white
> sitting where the body of Jesus had been, one at the head, the
> other at the feet. They said "Woman, why are you weeping?"
> "They have taken my [l]ord [τὸν κύριόν μου] away," she
> replied, "and I don't know where they have put him"...So Mary
> of Magdala told the disciples, "I have seen the Lord [τὸν
> κύριον]," and that he had said these things to her.

---

[14]*Introduction to New Testament Christology*, 188-189.
[15]YHWH occurs some 7000 times in the Hebrew Bible but never with a
possessive pronoun, that is, never as "my YHWH" — *A.B.*
[16]See David Bivin, "'Jehovah' — A Christian Misunderstanding," at
JerusalemPerspective.com

In verse 15, she addresses the man whom she thinks is the gardener as κύριε ("sir"): "Supposing him to be the gardener, she said, 'Sir [κύριε], if you have taken him away tell me where you have put him, and I will go and remove him.'" And in verse 20b the author says, "The disciples were filled with joy when they saw the Lord [τὸν κύριον]." Later, in verse 25, "They said to him that they had seen the Lord [τὸν κύριον]."

Who will argue, or has argued, that in the six uses of the term ὁ κύριος in this section of the narrative it means YHWH? In verses 18, 20, and 25, the term τὸν κύριον ("the Lord") refers to Jesus in the resurrected state. It does not mean YHWH in those places. Why should it mean so now in the mouth of Thomas at 20:28?

Totally, then, there are seven occurrences of the word ὁ κύριος in the Johannine resurrection narrative in John 20. Four times it is used by Mary (vv. 2, 13, 15, and 18), once by the author (v. 20), once by the ten (v. 25), and once by Thomas (v. 28). In neither of the first four instances does the term signify YHWH, nor in the next two; in particular, in the three places where it refers to Jesus in the resurrected state (vv. 18, 20, and 25) it is not equivalent to YHWH. What is there in the text to suggest that in the seventh use by Thomas at 20:28 ὁ κύριός μου = the impossible "my YHWH"?

The verses that follow, when carefully considered, reinforce this. Observe that Thomas is not given a benediction by Jesus for the statement. He does not say, "Blessed are you, Thomas ['Twin']! For flesh and blood have not revealed this to you, but my Father in heaven." Rather, he is gently rebuked. "You believe [that I have been raised from the dead] because you [have seen]. Blessed are those who have not seen but believed" (John 20:29). Moreover, the author himself does not claim that the statement by Thomas is a proof that "Jesus is LORD and God." He indicates immediately afterwards that this story and all the others in the book were written for the purpose of proving that *the Messiah, the Son of God, is Jesus*:[17] "There were many other signs that Jesus worked in the sight of the disciples, but

---

[17]So the Greek should be rendered in English, as D.A. Carson pointed out in a major article in the *Journal of Biblical Literature* a few years ago: "The Purpose of the Fourth Gospel: John 20:31 Reconsidered," *JBL* 106/4, 1987, 639-651; see now his recent commentary on *The Gospel According to John*, Apollos, 1991.

they are not recorded in this book. These are recorded so that you might believe that *the Messiah, the Son of God, is Jesus*, and that believing this you might have life through his name" (John 20:30-31, my translation). So the author himself gives us his intention in writing the story of Thomas. It is not given to prove that "Jesus is LORD and God," Yahweh and Elohim, like his Father and his God, but that *the Messiah, the Son of God, is Jesus*.

After all, eight days earlier, Mary had claimed that Jesus had appeared to her and had told her to tell the eleven that he had a Father and a God, and that his Father and his God was their Father and their God. "Jesus said to her, 'Do not cling to me because I have not yet ascended to the Father. But go and find my brothers, and tell them: I am ascending to my Father and your Father, to my God and your God'" (20:17). Was Thomas with the other ten when Mary came with this message? If so, how could he now contradict what Jesus said by calling him YHWH?

And a little before this, Jesus had prayed, in the presence of the eleven, this way in part: "And eternal life is this: to know you, the only true God, and Jesus Christ whom you have sent" (17:3). He and Thomas had even spoken with each other at this same time in this way: "Thomas said, 'Lord, we do not know where you are going, so how can we know the way?' Jesus said: 'I am the Way...Truth and Life. No one can come to the Father except through me. If you know me, you will know my Father too. From this moment you know him and have seen him'" (14:5-7).

Jesus explains what he means when he says, "From this moment you know him and have seen him" in the immediately succeeding conversation with Philip:

> Philip said, "Lord, show us the Father and then we shall be satisfied." Jesus said to him, "Have I been so long with you, Philip, and you still do not know me? Anyone who has seen me has seen the Father, so how can you say, 'Show us the Father'? Do you not believe that I am in the Father and the Father is in me? What I say to you I do not speak of my own accord: it is the Father, [who is] in me, who is doing the works. You must believe me when I say that I am in the Father and the Father is in me; or at least believe it on the evidence of these works...for the Father is greater than I" (14:8-11, 28).

"The Father is greater than I," "the Father is *in* me," "*in* me," "the Father is *in* me." These words of Jesus are overlooked by those who take John 20:28 out of context, or, if considered, they are not understood correctly. Six times the Johannine Jesus says "the Father is *in* me" (10:38; 14:10-11; 17:21 and 23). This was taught also by Paul in 2 Corinthians 5:19: "God was *in* Christ." (It should be carefully noted that "God" in the Greek here is anarthrous, articleless, as is "God" in John 1:1c.) And Colossians 2:9 states, "*In* him dwells the fullness of the godhead bodily" (AV).

We can go further back. Jesus declares publicly at one point (John 12:44-50) the well-nigh same statement that he made to Thomas and Philip: "Whoever believes in me believes not in me but in the one who sent me, and whoever sees me sees the one who sent me" (12:45).

Does this mean that Jesus was claiming to be God? No, it means exactly what it says: Jesus was claiming to represent his Father and God. The fourth Gospel (12:49; 14:9) expands the teaching of Paul in 2 Corinthians 2:4 that Jesus is "the image of God." And in Colossians 1:15, Jesus is called "the image of the invisible God." The author of Hebrews says of him, as the New Jerusalem Bible puts it, "He is the reflection of God's glory[18] and bears the impress of God's own being [*hypostasis*]" (Heb. 1:3; compare Wisdom of Solomon 7:26: "For she [Wisdom] is a reflection of the eternal light, untarnished mirror of God's active power, and *image of his goodness*.")

In the fourth Gospel, as in the Synoptics, Jesus calls himself "the son of man." Thirteen times in the first thirteen chapters this term, which has sparked much interest and discussion among modern biblical scholars since the end of the nineteenth century, occurs (eleven times in the mouth of Jesus and twice in the mouth of "the Jews"); and, even plainly, one time in the fourth Gospel, Jesus calls himself a man: "As it is, you want to kill me, a man who has told you the truth as I have heard it from God" (8:40).

He does not claim to be God, whom, as we have seen, he calls "the only true God" (17:3). He says in another place that God is "the one God" (5:44). If, then, God is "the one God," as Jesus taught, then Jesus cannot be that God. And if God is "the only true God," as Jesus prayed, then Jesus cannot be that only true God or "true God of true

---

[18] See the Nicene-Constantinopolitan Creed: "Light of Light."

God," as the Nicene-Constantinopolitan Creed formulated in the fourth century CE puts it, basing this on an erroneous reading of 1 John 5:20.

ὁ κύριος and ὁ θεός in John 21

If the material in the appended second conclusion of the book, John 21, is considered, in connection with an attempt to correctly comprehend John 20:28, though this has never been done to my knowledge, it can be seen that even there ὁ κύριος ("the Lord") does not connote YHWH. In this appendix or second conclusion, there are seven more verses where ὁ κύριος ("the Lord" in the nominative case) or κύριε ("Lord" in the vocative case) occurs. In 21:7 it appears twice (once in the mouth of the anonymous disciple whom Jesus loved, and once by the author): "The disciple whom Jesus loved said to Peter, 'It is the Lord' (ὁ κύριος). At these words 'It is the Lord,' (ὁ κύριος), Simon Peter tied his outer garment round him (for he had nothing on) and jumped into the water."

Again it is used by the author in 21:12: "Jesus said to them, 'Come and have breakfast.' None of the disciples was bold enough to ask, 'Who are you?' They knew quite well it was the Lord (ὁ κύριος)."

And three times in the mouth of Peter in verses 15, 16, and 17 it appears again.

> When they had eaten, Jesus said to Simon Peter, "Simon, son of John, do you love me more than these others do?" He answered, "Yes, Lord (κύριε), you know that I love you." Jesus said to him, "Feed my lambs." A second time he said to him, "Simon, son of John, do you love me?" He replied, "Yes, Lord (κύριε), you know I love you." Jesus said to him, "Look after my sheep." Then he said to him a third time, "Simon, son of John, do you love me?" Peter was hurt that he asked him a third time, "Do you love me?" and said, "Lord (κύριε), you know everything; you know I love you." Jesus said to him, "Feed my sheep. In all truth I tell you, when you were young you put on your own belt and walked where you like, but when you grow old you will stretch out your hands, and somebody will put a belt around you and take you where you would rather not go." In these words he indicated the

kind of death by which Peter would give glory to God (20:15-19).[19]

In 21:20, κύριε ("Lord") appears in the mouth of the anonymous disciple again: "Peter turned and saw the disciple Jesus loved following them — the one who had leant back close to his chest at the supper and said to him, 'Lord (κύριε), who is it that will betray you?'"

And, lastly, again in the mouth of Peter in 21:21: "Seeing him, Peter said to Jesus, 'What about him, Lord (κύριε)?'"

Totally, then, there are eight occurrences of κύριος ("Lord") in these seven verses: five are in the vocative (κύριε) and three in the nominative case (ὁ κύριος). In none of these instances after the exclamation of Thomas at 20:28 can it be construed to mean YHWH, even though the term refers to Jesus in the resurrected state. Is this not strange if Thomas really called Jesus LORD and God? Why is this so-called confession not reinforced and amplified in the immediately following second conclusion or appendix?

The Exclamation of Thomas in Hebrew (and Aramaic)

It appears that it has never been noticed in the history of the interpretation of the fourth Gospel that in the original language that Thomas and Jesus spoke, Hebrew (John 20:16; Acts 26:14),[20] the fragment of Thomas at 20:28 would have been:

Adoni ve Eli! (אֲדֹנִי וְ אֵלִי) and not *Adonai ve Eli* (אֲדֹנָי וְ אֵלִי)

If we translate this expression into Aramaic, Thomas answered and said to him:

Mari ve Elahi! (מָרִאי וְ אֱלָהִי)

---

[19] Notice that the only occurrence of the word "God" in John 21 appears here (v. 19), and it refers to God the Father, not to Jesus. The supposedly momentous declaration of Thomas at 20:28 is not amplified and reinforced, and the author takes no notice of it, even though Thomas is listed at the beginning of this section as being among the seven disciples present when this apparition of Jesus is alleged to have occurred (John 21:2). John 21 makes no mention of it, nor does the text allude in any way to it, as one can see is the case likewise immediately afterwards in Acts, the record of the preaching of Peter, apostle and leader of the Jewish believers (the Nazarenes), and Paul, apostle to the Gentiles.

[20] See Brenton Minge, "Jesus Spoke Hebrew: Busting the Aramaic Myth" at sharesong.org/JESUSSPOKEHEBREW.htm

In neither case is Jesus being equated with YHWH in the first title (*Adoni* in Hebrew and *Mari* in Aramaic). And the second title (*Eli* in Hebrew and *Elahi* in Aramaic) must be read in the light of what Jesus taught at 10:33-38, where he claimed to be "Son of God," not God, and that God "the Father is in me" (10:38), and he said that this was not blasphemy because the Jews themselves are called "gods" (*elohim*) in the Hebrew Scriptures. This is, indeed, not blasphemy, and this is not making them equal to YHWH. Neither is it the case here that Thomas is blaspheming or making Jesus YHWH or equal to YHWH. We do not say, "How can this man talk like that? He is being blasphemous" (Mark 2:6). And Jesus does not say, "Why do you call me God? There is no one who is God but one — God." We do well to remember here what he said to the young man who had addressed him in the Gospel of Mark as "Good master": "Why do you call me good? No one is good but one — God" (Mark 10:18; see p. 411). Observe, moreover, that:

(1) It is Thomas who makes this statement, not Jesus. If Jesus is called "God" in John 20:28, it is Thomas who calls him so. No other Gospel bears witness to this. This climactic incident and saying is not corroborated by the Synoptics, that is to say, by neither the inauthentic longer ending of Mark (16:9-20), nor Matthew 28:1-20, nor Luke 24:1-53. *The traditional Chalcedonian Trinitarian interpretation of John 20:28 as a proof-text for the teaching that Jesus is a divinity, a deity, the second Person of the Trinity is euhemerism.* The Holy Qur'an, the scriptures which are sacred to Islam and which are as strongly monotheistic as the Hebrew Bible of Judaism, have this to say (and who can gainsay it?): "They surely disbelieve who say: Lo! Allah is the Messiah, son of Mary. The Messiah (himself) said: O Children of Israel, worship Allah, my Lord and your Lord" (The Qu'ran, Surah 5:72a).

(2) Even more precisely, it is the author who reports this who makes Thomas say so. If Jesus is called "God," it is John who makes him so (compare Acts 2:36, where it is said that God made Jesus "Lord and Messiah"). If Jesus is called "God," it is John who lifts up very highly or super-exalts Jesus, and it is John who through the mouth of Thomas gives him the name "God" (compare the so-called Christ hymn at Phil. 2:5-11, where it is said that it is God who "super-exalted" Jesus, God who gave him the name "Lord").

(3) If Jesus is truly called "God" by Thomas, why is it no one calls Thomas "the brother of God," or Peter, or John, or any of the other Apostles, as Mary came to be called "the mother of God" (*theotokos*)? After all, Jesus himself called them his brothers, did he not? "Go and find *my brothers* [see also Matt. 28:20; Heb. 2:11-13] and tell them: I am ascending to my Father and your Father, to my God and your God" (20:17). It must be conceded that "In the *Liturgy of St James,* the brother of Jesus is raised to the dignity of *the brother of the [true] God (Adelphotheos)*."[21] But "the *Liturgy of St James* as it presently exists has been brought into conformity with developed Trinitarian Christianity and Eastern Orthodoxy...Forming the historical basis of the Liturgy of Antioch, it is still the principal liturgy of the Syriac Orthodox Church and Syrian Catholic Church in communion with Rome in Syriac and, in the ancient Indian Orthodox Church, the Syro-Malankara Catholic Church in translations into Malayalam, Hindi and English."[22]

(4) Jesus did not call himself LORD and God in the fourth Gospel. He only sanctioned being called Lord and Master. He said to the twelve the night before he died, "You call me *Master* and *Lord*, and rightly; so I am. If I then, *the Lord* and *Master*, have washed your feet, you must wash each other's feet" (John 13:13). And in John 20 Mary of Magdala calls him *the Lord* (vv. 2 and 18), *my [l]ord* (v. 15), and, in Hebrew, *Rabbouni* ("my Master," v. 16).[23] As Julian wrote in 363 CE:

> At any rate neither Paul nor Matthew nor Luke nor Mark ventured to call Jesus God. But the worthy John, since he perceived that a great number of people in many of the towns of Greece and Italy had already been infected by this disease, and because he heard, I suppose, that even the tombs of Peter and Paul were being worshipped — secretly, it is true, but still he did hear this — he, I say, was the first to venture to call Jesus God" (*Contra Galilaeos*).

---

[21]Philip Schaff, *History of the Christian Church*, chapter 4, section 29 as quoted in "James the Just" at Wikipedia.com.
[22]"Liturgy of St James" at Wikipedia.com.
[23]Observe that "Rabbouni" is transcribed in the preceding sentence with an "o" as it is in the koine Greek of the New Testament. Also, note that this is a Hebrew word. See the note in the New American Bible: "a Hebrew or Aramaic word."

But, what about John 1:1?

John 1:1-3, 10b ("In the beginning was the word and the word was with God and the word was God...and the world was made by him") is the statement of the author of the fourth Gospel (compare 1 Cor. 7:10: "I, Paul, say this, not the Lord") and is a midrash of Proverbs 8:22 ("Yahweh created me the beginning...") and Genesis 1:1 after the manner of the anonymous author of Hebrews 1:2 and 1:8-12, where "the Son" (Jesus) is called "God" on the basis of the Septuagint version of Psalm 44:7-8 (45:6-7).[24] Further, "the Son" is called "Lord" on the basis of Psalm 101:25-27 LXX (102:25-27), a psalm originally addressed to YHWH (see the Hebrew text), and he is credited with the creation of the world.[25] As the aforementioned Julian writes concerning this verse:

---

[24]Which, by the way, is a mistranslation of the Hebrew: see *The Tanakh,* New Jewish Society Publication Version; also Raymond Brown, *Introduction to New Testament Christology,* 186, footnote 269: "Actually, the Septuagint reading is a misunderstanding of the Hebrew (Masoretic) text of the psalm." [However the New Testament validates the Septuagint, so that "Thy throne, O God" remains an acceptable translation — *A.B.*]
[25]The exegetical key to John 1:1-3, 10b and Hebrews 1:2 and 1:8-12 — passages which have baffled everyone for centuries now — I have recently discovered here in Istanbul in the 2nd-century work by Irenaeus called *The Proof of the Apostolic Preaching,* 43-55, where there is an exegesis of Genesis 1:1 *mistranslated* from a *corrupt* Hebrew text (*Baresith bara Elowin basan benuam samenthares,* "In the beginning, the Son, God, established then the heaven and the earth"); Genesis 19:24; Psalm 44:7-8 LXX (45:6-7); Psalm 109:1, 3 LXX (110:1, 3); Proverbs 8:22; Isaiah 7:14; 9:6 based on the Septuagint and where these verses are used to prove that Jesus is LORD and God and that he created the world ("So then the Father is Lord and the Son is Lord, and the Father is God and the Son is God; for that which is begotten of God is God") — argumentation very similar to which can be found in Justin Martyr's *Dialogue with Trypho* (see Demetrios Christ Trakatellis, *The Pre-Existence of Christ in Justin Martyr: An Exegetical Study with Reference to the Humiliation and Exaltation Christology,* Harvard Dissertation Series 8, Missoula, Montana: Scholars Press, 1976; consult also Günther Reim, "Jesus as God in the Fourth Gospel: The Old Testament Background," *New Testament Studies* 30, 1984, 58-60, for a brief analysis of Justin Martyr's use of Psalm 44:7-8 LXX as a proof-text for showing that Jesus is "God.") Irenaeus was a student of Polycarp, who was a student of John the Apostle at Ephesus in Asia Minor or present-day Turkey (see his work at tertullian.org/fathers). This work by Irenaeus was discovered in December

But that Moses believed in one God, the God of Israel, he says in Deuteronomy: "So that thou mightest know that the Lord thy God he is one God; and there is none else beside him." And moreover he says besides, "And lay it to thine heart that this the Lord thy God is God in the heaven above and upon the earth beneath, and there is none else." And again, "Hear, O Israel: the Lord our God is one Lord." And again, "See that I am and there is no God save me." These then are the words of Moses when he insists that there is only one God. But perhaps the Galilaeans will reply: "But we do not assert that there are two gods or three." But I will show that they do assert this also, and I call John to witness, who says: "In the beginning was the Word, and the Word was with God and the Word was God." You see that the Word is said to be with God? Now whether this is he who was born of Mary or someone else — that I may answer Photinus at the same time — this now makes no difference; indeed I leave the dispute to you; but it is enough to bring forward the evidence that he says "with God," and "in the beginning." How then does this agree with the teachings of Moses? (*Contra Galilaeos*).

1904 in the Church of the Blessed Virgin at Eriwan in Armenia by Dr. Karapet Ter-Mekerttshian, one of the most learned scholars of the Armenian clergy. It was edited by him with the translation into German in collaboration with Dr. Erwand Ter-Minassiantz in 1907 in *Texte und Untersuchungen* (xxxi. 1). Dr. Adolf Harnack added a brief dissertation and some notes. In 1912 Dr. Simon Weber of the Faculty of Catholic Theology in the University of Frieburg in Breisgau published another translation with the help of some Armenian scholars. Dr. J. Armitage Robinson, Dean of Wells, published a translation in English in 1920. Eusebius in his *Ecclesiastical History* mentions that Irenaeus, in addition to his great work *Against Heresies*, had written *In Demonstration of the Apostolic Preaching* (bk. 5, ch. 26). As Dr. Robinson remarks, "This work was entirely lost sight of: no one seems ever to have quoted a word of it." After its discovery and translation in the early part of the 20th century, it has not been generally known. It was placed online by Roger Pearse of Ipswich, United Kingdom in 2003. I happened to discover it this week, June 14, 2006 while doing research for this article.

What about John 1:18?

John 1:18 reads this way in the Jerusalem Bible (1966) and the New Jerusalem Bible (1985): "No one has ever seen God; it is the only Son, who is close to the Father's heart, who has made him known." The translators have twice rejected the text recently introduced in the latter part of the twentieth century by other major translations. And rightly so, as I see it. Shall it be thought credible that a text which calls Jesus "God" would have disappeared for 1,500 years and no Christian knew about it? Shall a text which the New Revised Standard, the Bible endorsed by the World Council of Churches and favored by the Society of Biblical Literature, has just included in 1989, though it was well known when the Revised Version was made at the end of the nineteenth century — shall this awkward-sounding Gnostic and Arian-like text be now considered along with John 20:28 as one of the strongest proof-texts for the euhemeristic teaching that Jesus who was called "the Messiah" was/is also God? Call me a Doubting Thomas, if you will, on this one, but I cannot accept it. Neither does the eminent textual critic and New Testament scholar, Bart Ehrman (see his book *The Orthodox Corruption of Scripture* for a penetrating and illuminating discussion).

What about John 3:13?

John 3:13 ("No one has gone up to heaven except the one who came down from heaven, the Son of man, who is in heaven"), which the Tome of Damasus (382 CE) used as a proof-text to teach that Christians were bound to believe that Jesus was in heaven with God the Father while he lived on earth, is a corrupt text and all recent major translations of the New Testament omit the relative clause at the end "who is in heaven," which is found in the King James Version, the Douay-Rheims-Challoner Bible, and even in the New American Bible (1970, first edition).

What about John 8:58?

John 8:58 ("Before Abraham was, I am [he]") has been mistranslated for centuries (see now the New American Bible: "Before Abraham was, I AM"). The Jerusalem Bible (1966) translated the *ego eimi* of the Greek as "I Am," but changed this to the still incorrect "I am" in the New Jerusalem Bible (1985).[26]

What about John 10:30?

John 10:30 ("I and the Father are one") has been misinterpreted. Trinitarians misread the *en* ("one"), which is neuter in the Greek, as *eis*, a masculine form. John Calvin in his commentary on the Bible says this concerning this verse: "The ancients greatly perverted this passage, when they would prove from it that Christ is identically of the same nature (or consubstantial) with the Father, for Christ speaks not concerning an unity of substance, but of the mutual agreement between the Father and himself, to wit, affirming that whatsoever he does would be sanctioned by the power of the Father."

(5) **If Jesus is indeed called "God" here,** in the sense which Chalcedonian Trinitarians take it, why is it that he himself appears to John on the island of Patmos and claims in the very first verse that God has given him a revelation to show unto his servants "things which must soon take place" (Rev. 1:1)? In Revelation 5:1-14, we are even shown the vision of the exact time when Jesus received from "him who sits on the throne" the knowledge of these things of the future which he did not know before and which he commanded John to write on the Lord's Day while he was on the isle of Patmos in the Aegean Sea:

> I saw in the right hand of the One sitting on the throne there was a scroll that was written on back and front and was sealed with seven seals. Then I saw a powerful angel who called with a loud voice, "Who is worthy to open the scroll and break its seals?" But there was no one, in heaven or on the earth or under the earth, who was able to open the scroll and read it. I wept bitterly because no one could be found to open the scroll and read it, but one of the elders said to me, "Do not weep. Look, the Lion of the tribe of Judah, the Root of David, has triumphed, and so he will open the scroll and its seven seals." Then I saw, in the middle of the throne with its four living creatures and the circle of the elders, a Lamb that

---

[26]See Anthony Buzzard and Charles Hunting, *The Doctrine of the Trinity: Christianity's Self-Inflicted Wound*, University Press of America, 1998, 218-223. For John 3:13, see Ibid., 205-210.

seemed to have been sacrificed; it had seven horns, and it had seven eyes, which are the seven spirits that God has sent out over the whole world. The Lamb came forward to take the scroll from the right hand of the One sitting on the throne; when he took it, the four living creatures prostrated themselves before him and with them the twenty-four elders; each one of them was holding a harp and had a golden bowl full of incense which are the prayers of the saints. They sang a new hymn: "You are worthy to take the scroll and to break its seals, because you were sacrificed and with your blood you bought people for God of every race, language, people and nation and made them a line of kings and priests for God, to rule the world."

In my vision, I heard the sound of an immense number of angels gathered round the throne and the living creatures and the elders; there were ten thousand times ten thousand of them and thousands upon thousands, loudly chanting: "Worthy is the Lamb that was sacrificed to receive power, riches, wisdom, strength, honor, glory and blessing." Then I heard all the living things in creation — everything that lives in heaven, and on earth, and under the earth, and in the sea, crying: "To the One seated on the throne and to the Lamb be all the praise, honor, glory and power, for ever and ever." And the four living creatures said, "Amen"; and the elders prostrated themselves to worship.

(6) **And, yet again, if Jesus is indeed called "God" by Thomas at John 20:28** in a sense different from that in Psalm 82:6 in the Hebrew Bible, why is it that Jesus himself still calls God "my Father" and "my God" when he descends from heaven and speaks with John on the island of Patmos, just as he did when he spoke to Mary of Magdala in the garden in Jerusalem after he rose from the dead according to John 20:17? Observe the use of "my Father" (three times) and "my God" (five times) in these words of Jesus:

"To anyone who proves victorious, and keeps working for me until the end, I will give the authority over the nations which I myself have been given by **my Father**, to rule them with an iron scepter and shatter them like so many pots. And I will give such a person the Morning Star. Let anyone who can hear, listen to what the Spirit is saying to the churches" (Rev. 2:27; at 2:7 many manuscripts read,

"Let anyone who can hear listen to what the Spirit is saying to the churches: those who prove victorious I will feed from the tree of life, which is in the paradise of **my God**.")

"So far I have failed to notice anything in your behavior that **my God** could possibly call perfect. Remember how you first heard the message. Hold on to that. Repent!" (Rev. 3:2b).

"Anyone who proves victorious will be dressed, like these, in white robes; I shall not blot that name out of the book of life, but acknowledge it in the presence of **my Father** and his angels" (Rev. 3:5).

"Anyone who proves victorious I will make a pillar in the sanctuary of **my God**, and it will stay there for ever; I will inscribe on it the name of **my God** and the name of the city of **my God**, the new Jerusalem which is coming down from **my God** in heaven, and my own new name as well" (Rev. 3:12).

"Write to the angel of the church of Laodicea and say, 'Here is the message of the Amen, the trustworthy, the true witness, the beginning of the creation of God...'" (Rev. 3:14, my translation; see Prov. 8:22 in the Hebrew Bible, and the commentary on it in *Bereshit Rabbah*).

"Anyone who proves victorious I will allow to share my throne, just as I myself have overcome and have taken my seat with **my Father** on his throne" (Rev. 3:21).

(7) If Jesus is indeed to be called "God" in the Chalcedonian sense because of John 20:28, how is it that John also in the epistolary prescript of the same book, Revelation of Jesus Christ, speaks of Jesus as having a God and a Father?

> John, to the seven churches of Asia: grace and peace to you from him who is, who was, and who is to come, from the seven spirits who are before his throne, and from Jesus Christ, the faithful witness, the first-born from the dead, the highest of earthly kings. He loves us and has washed away our sins with his blood, and made us a Kingdom of Priests to serve **his God and Father**; to him, then, be glory and power for ever and ever. Amen.

(8) The last book of the New Testament is more properly and fully called Revelation of Jesus Christ (Rev. 1:1). This whole book of 22 chapters consists of information about the future which Jesus claims to have received in heaven from his God and his Father after his ascension and which clearly he did not know before — a fact which ill accords with Chalcedonian Trinitarianism.

(9) Jesus never says in the body of the fourth Gospel that his name is The Word — this is the late first-century ascription of the author of the prologue (John 1:1, 14).[27]

(10) Likewise, Jesus never says that he is the only-begotten/only son of God in the fourth Gospel (see the New American Bible and the New Revised Standard Version of John 3:16 and 18, where these words are those of the author of the fourth Gospel and not the words of Jesus).[28]

The Reason for the Confusion over "Lord" and "LORD"

The Greek Septuagint and the New Testament authors who used Greek and quoted from it did not distinguish between the term κύριος when it referred to Yahweh and κύριος when it referred to a human being, as the Masoretic text of the Hebrew Bible does.[29] Therefore, all, Trinitarians especially, have been confused when they come to John 20:28, as we see in R. Brown's statement in the introduction above. (I call this *the blind spot in fourth Gospel scholarship* — alas, but one of several.) **But Thomas and Jesus knew the difference between *Adoni* and *Adonai*** (with kametz). This is the key which unlocks the mystery which has surrounded this otherwise puzzling statement of Thomas in the fourth Gospel. If we retrovert the fragment into Hebrew (John 20:16) or Aramaic, we see that what

---

[27]John says that all things came into existence through the word, through "it," as all translations of the prologue before Rheims-Douay and KJV read — A.B.

[28]But nevertheless very much part of Scripture and thus authoritative—A.B.

[29]The confusion this has caused in the minds of Gentile Christians can be seen in the manuscript tradition at John 12:41; Acts 10:36b ("He is the God who is Lord of all," Hippolytus, *Against Noetus,* 13); 13:48; 15:40; 20:28 and 32; Rom. 10:16-17; 14:10-11; 1 Cor. 2:16; 10:9 (the RSV reads "the Lord"; the NRSV reads "Christ"; the NJB reads "the Lord"; the NAB reads "Christ"); 1 Pet. 3:14-15; 5:1 (p 72 reads "suffering of God"; all other versions read "suffering of Christ"); 2 Pet. 1:2 (most mss. read "May grace and peace be multiplied to you in the knowledge of God and our Lord Jesus"; p 72 deletes the "and" and reads "God our Lord Jesus"); Jude 4 and 5 (the Vulgate and Douay-Rheims read "Jesus"; p 72 reads "God Christ"; all other versions read "the Lord"); and Rev. 1:8 (the KJV reads "the Lord"; all modern versions "the Lord God").

Thomas says harmonizes with the three uses of κύριος referring to Jesus in the resurrected state which precede his statement (John 20:18, 20 and 25) and the eight uses that follow afterwards in the seven verses in the second conclusion or appendix (John 21:7, 12, 15, 16, 17, 20 and 21). If it was indeed Jesus that he addressed, and not the Father in Jesus, as it has been and can be more precisely read, he did not say the equivalent of "my YHWH!" but rather he said, "*Adoni ve Eli*" ("my lord and my God!")

This is certainly what Peter taught about 40 days later at the Feast of Weeks (Shavuoth) or Pentecost when he quoted Psalm 110:1 from the Hebrew Scriptures ("YHWH said to *adoni*, 'Sit at my right hand'") and then concluded, "For this reason the whole House of Israel can be certain that the Lord [*Adon/Mar*] and Messiah [*Meshicha*] whom God [*Elohim*] has made is this Jesus whom you crucified" (Acts 2:36).

As Geza Vermes, the famous Jewish scholar at Oxford University, states in his recent book *The Changing Faces of Jesus*:

> It is well known that the Jews employed "Lord" as a synonym for God in their religious language. The various divine names, the sacrosanct and unpronounced YHWH ("Jehovah"), as well as the Hebrew *Adon* ("Lord") and *Adonay* or the Aramaic *Mar* ("Lord") are all translated into Greek by the same word, *Kurios* ("Lord"). We can be sure that Jews, whatever language they spoke, had no difficulty in distinguishing a divine "Lord" from a human one. The hurdle which Hellenized Gentile Christians, like the members of the church of John, had to leap was considerably higher.[30]

Conclusion

John Calvin, a Chalcedonian Trinitarian and a leading light of the Reformation, pointed out that the Church Fathers had made a wrong use of John 10:30. And Sir Anthony Buzzard in his book *The Doctrine of the Trinity: Christianity's Self-Inflicted Wound* has pointed out how John 8:58 has been misread. It should now be pointed out that John 20:28 as a proof-text that Jesus is YHWH is likewise a misreading. It is an exegetical fallacy that should be abandoned as have many, but not yet all, of the "proofs" of the Trinity

---

[30]Geza Vermes, *The Changing Faces of Jesus*, Penguin, 2002, 39.

from the Hebrew Bible used by Chalcedonian Trinitarians, such as Genesis 1:1 and 26; 16:9 (the angel of Yahweh as pre-incarnate Christ); 18:1ff (the three men who visit Abraham — one of whom is called Yahweh, and the other two "angels"); 19:24 ("The LORD rained fire and brimstone on Sodom and Gomorrah from the LORD from heaven," KJV); Exodus 4:2ff (the angel of Yahweh at the burning bush on Horeb, "the mountain of God," in Sinai who reveals to Moses his name, Exod. 3:14-15); the angel of great counsel (Isaiah 9:6, LXX); the Word of God (the Johannine name of Jesus at Rev. 19:11); the personification of Wisdom as a Lady in Proverbs 8 = the so-called pre-incarnate Christ! So also "the Son of God" (KJV) — "a most unfortunate translation" (Adam Clarke) — in the fiery furnace in Babylon with the three Jewish friends of Daniel (Daniel 3:25) = Jesus! Concerning this notorious translation error, the Jerusalem Talmud reports one of the rabbis as saying, "When Nebuchadnezzar spoke of 'the Son of God' (Dan. iii. 25), an angel came and smote him on the face, saying, 'Does God have a son?'" (Yer. Shab. vi. 8d). Note also the false capital "L" on "lord" in Daniel 12:8 (KJV).

Summary

In fourteen instances (six in John 20 before 20:28 and eight in the appendix John 21 after 20:28) the word ὁ κύριος does not mean YHWH. This contextual evidence, therefore, indicates quite plainly that the two-millennia-old construal of ὁ κύριός μου at John 20:28 as equivalent to "my YHWH" is not correct. And the *theos* in ὁ θεός μου should be read as having the same metaphorical signification as it does in Psalm 82:6, as Jesus taught in the body of the fourth Gospel (John 10:34-36). This reading of both terms in the exclamation of Thomas, ὁ κύριός μου καὶ ὁ θεός μου (John 20:28) is further confirmed when the underlying Hebrew, the original language of the saying, is considered. The use of θεός in the prologue (1:1) is a statement from the author, not Jesus, and is similar to its use by the anonymous author of Hebrews, where at 1:8-12 the titles "God" (ὁ θεός, 1:8) and "Lord" (κύριε, 1:10) are applied to "the Son" (1:1ff) by means of quotations from Psalm 44:7-8 (45:6-7) and Psalm 101:25-27 (102:25-27) in the Septuagint, the Greek version of the Hebrew Bible, and where the creation of the (new) world is credited to him. Irenaeus in his *Proof of the Apostolic Preaching* does the same, using Psalm 44:7-8, and adding a *mistranslation* of a *corrupt*

Hebrew text of Genesis 1:1 (*Baresith bara Elowin basan benuam samenthares*: "In the beginning, the Son, God, established then the heaven and the earth"). But these three texts — Psalm 44:7-8, Psalm 101:25-27, and Genesis 1:1— in the version of the Greek and Hebrew Scriptures used by Irenaeus do not correspond to the Masoretic text of the Hebrew Bible.

God and Lord
The Only God There Is

"The command that brings Israel into being is the Shema. It is read aloud in the form, *Shema Israel Adonai Eloheynu Adonai Echad* (Deuteronomy 6:4). Translated word for word, that means, 'Hear, O Israel, my [LORD] our God my [LORD] One.' The words sound strange, but they hold the all-important key that unlocks the Jewish understanding of God. *'Adonai'* means 'my [LORD]'[31] but that word does not actually appear in the Hebrew text. Written in the text are the four letters YHWH (known, from the Greek for 'four-lettered,' as the Tetragrammaton). YHWH was the name revealed by God to Moses, but because it shared in the holiness of God, it was pronounced by no one except the high priest on the Day of Atonement. Many Jews prefer to say instead *haShem*, the Name, translating it perhaps as 'the Eternal'; and wherever the letters YHWH occur in the text of scripture, the vowels of Adonai are inserted, to remind the reader not to try to pronounce the name, but to say instead Adonai. That is why, in English translations of what Christians call the Old Testament, the name of God is translated as 'the LORD.' Older translations made a mistaken attempt to transliterate the name, putting the vowels of Adonai into YHWH and producing the impossible form, Jehovah. In academic scholarship, it has become conventional to represent this name of God as Yahweh. Already, therefore, this reveals something important about the self-revelation of God: God's holiness extends even to God's name, which must be treated with due reverence. The word *eloheynu* is the word *elohim*, God, with a pronoun added to its end, so that it means 'our God.' So the sentence means 'Yahweh is our God, Yahweh is One'; or 'Yahweh our God, Yahweh is One'; or 'Yahweh is our God, Yahweh alone.'"[32]

---

[31]*Adonai* is far more probably "the LORD" — A.B.
[32]John Bowker, *GOD: A Brief History*, DK Publishers, 2003, 178.

Note on Matthew 19:17 and Parallels[33]

It is often claimed that the text of the New Testament can be reconstructed from quotations of the early Church Fathers. As an example — Matthew 19:17/Mark 10:18/Luke 18:19:

- JUSTIN, an early Church Father, writing in 140-160, writes in his Dialogue 101.2: "One is good, my Father in the heavens." This very early quotation is not what we read in the Bible today.
- EPHREM: Commentary on the Diatessaron, XV.9, in both the original Syriac and the Armenian (2 manuscripts) reads: "One is good, the/my Father who [is] in the heaven." Ephrem died in 373, and the Syriac manuscript of the Commentary is fifth century.
- TATIAN, about 172, composed the Diatessaron (the Gospel harmony upon which Ephrem was commenting), on the basis of the Gospel texts current then. And this citation agrees precisely with Justin's.
- IRENAEUS: Haer. V.7.25 (pre-185): "One is good, the/my Father in the heavens." Another second century source confirming the "wrong" version of Matthew 19:17.
- HIPPOLYTUS: Haer. V.7.25 (pre-222): "One is good, the/my Father in the heavens." Another early Christian Father has the "wrong" version.
- CLEMENT OF ALEXANDRIA: Strom. V.10.63 (composed c. 207): "One is good, the/my Father."
- PSEUDO-CLEMENTINE HOMILIES: XVI.3.4 about 260 AD. "For one is good, the/my Father in the heavens."
- VETUS LATINA MS c (apud Matthew, fifth century): "Unus est bonus, pater." This is the second most ancient manuscript and it also has "Father."
- VETUS LATINA MS d (apud Luke, fifth century): "Nemo bonus nisi unus Deus pater." "Father" again.

The Douay-Rheims-Challoner Version and the King James Version (1611) read that "no one is good except God alone." This was changed from the older "no one is good except the Father" so as to conform with the evolving idea that Jesus was also God, just like the

---

[33]From "New Testament Alterations" at http://essenes.net/gop31nt.htm — with minor corrections.

Father. The saying in Matthew has been changed yet again recently in all major modern translations to read "Why do you ask me about what is good?" And the man who talks to Jesus does not address him as "Good Master" but as simply "Master"!

The Confusion over "Lord" in a Recent Papal Document

In "Apostolic Letter **Dies Domini** of the Holy Father John Paul II to the Bishops, Clergy and Faithful of the Catholic Church on Keeping the Lord's Day Holy" we find the following: "And when Christians spoke of the 'Lord's Day,' they did so giving this term the full sense of the Easter proclamation: 'Jesus Christ is Lord' (Phil. 2:11; cf. Acts 2:36; 1 Cor. 12:3). Thus Christ was given the same title which the Septuagint used to translate what in the revelation of the Old Testament was the unutterable name of God: YHWH." The word "lord," however, in Acts 2:26 refers to a human being, for it is the conclusion drawn from the quotation of Psalm 110:1 ("YHWH said to *adoni*") by Kepha (Peter) on the day of Pentecost. And in the Hebrew Bible, from which Kepha quoted, there is a distinction made between the two persons in the opening of that psalm. **YHWH** (elsewhere *Adonai*) refers to the Lord God and **adoni** refers to the Messiah. The Septuagint gives both of these personages the title "lord" and thus leads to the common confusion witnessed in the pope's letter and seen in Raymond Brown's *An Introduction to New Testament Christology*.

As a concluding aside, be it noted that such a confusion occurs also throughout the notes of the New Jerusalem Bible, the most popular Bible among Catholics in Europe (see, for example, 1691e: "So he is the Messiah awaited, but he will be 'Lord,' a title which the OT meticulously reserved for God." See also earlier 1689x. Likewise, 1801x: "The Christians style themselves 'those who invoke the name of the Lord,' 9:14, 21; 22:16; 1 Co 1:2; 2Tm 2:22; the title 'Lord' indicates no longer Yahweh but Jesus.")

Appendix 2
Where Jewish Opposition Breaks Down

Jewish opponents of Christ are mistaken when they deny that the historical Jesus can qualify to be the Messiah of Israel. Bruce James says these are the requirements of the Messiah:

(1) He must be Jewish (see Deut. 17:15; Num. 24:17)
(2) He must be descended from Judah (Gen. 49:10) and Solomon (numerous places, but see 1 Chron. 22:9-10)
(3) With the coming of the Messiah will be the physical ingathering of Judah from the four corners of the earth (Isa. 11:12; 27:12-13)
(4) Also with the coming of the Messiah will be the reestablishment of the Holy Temple (Mic. 4:1)
(5) In addition the Messianic age will be one of worldwide peace (Isa. 2:4; 11:6; Mic. 4:3); and, finally,
(6) In the Messianic age the entire world will believe in G-d (Isa. 11:9; 40:5; Zeph. 3:9).[1]

The New Testament unanimously expects points three to six to be realized at the return of Jesus to inaugurate the Kingdom of God, that prospect being the heart of Jesus' own saving Gospel of the Kingdom (Luke 4:43, etc., as it was also of Paul, Acts 19:8; 28:23, 31).

As to the descent of Jesus from Judah, Jews object that genealogically Jesus is disqualified from being Messiah. The work done by Lord Arthur Hervey, a British clergyman, in his *The Genealogies of Our Lord and Savior Jesus Christ*[2] demonstrates the lineal descent of Jesus from David and a very reasonable way of harmonizing the genealogical tables provided by Matthew and Luke. These two different genealogical records of Jesus point to his descent legally from Solomon (Matt. 1:6-7) and biologically from Nathan (Luke 3:31), another son of David. Examples of a double genealogy for the same person are known elsewhere in Scripture.

---

[1]Bruce James (Baruch Gershom), "Why Can't a Jew Believe in Jesus?" http://judaism.about.com/od/jewishviewofjesus/a/jesus_onegod.htm
[2]Macmillan, 1853, rep. Kessinger, 2007. A useful summary of Hervey's work is found in Smith's *Concise Dictionary of the Bible*, John Murray, 1865, under "Genealogy of Jesus Christ," 283-285.

There is a clear reason why Matthew traces the line of Joseph back to Solomon, son of David while Luke traces the lineage of Jesus to another son of David, Nathan. The Old Testament records that the natural descendant of Solomon, King Jehoiachin,[3] was disqualified because of his sin from ever providing a Davidic descendant as heir to the throne: "None of his offspring will prosper; none will sit on the throne of David or rule any more in Judah" (Jer. 22:30).

When the line from Solomon was disqualifed in Jehoiachin, a legal substitute was provided from another Davidic line. Shealtiel (Salathiel) and Zerubbabel were adopted from the Nathan line (Luke 3:27) into the Solomon line (Matt. 1:12) to provide the necessary legal heirs. These two as blood relatives of David through Nathan were themselves genuine heirs to the royal throne. Lord Hervey argues that eventually the two lines from Nathan and Solomon met in Matthan (Matt. 1:15; Matthat in Luke 3:24), who is the grandfather of both Joseph and Mary.

The right of Jesus to the throne of David is found in the fact that Jacob, son of Matthan, gave his daughter Mary in marriage to his nephew Joseph. Thus Mary and Joseph were first cousins and both, through the "legal" line back to Solomon and the natural blood line traced to Nathan, members of the royal Davidic family. Jesus thus inherited a legal right to the Messianic throne through Joseph and a right by virtue of lineal descent through Mary, who was like Joseph descended from Nathan, son of David. Matthew records the legal line of Joseph back through Solomon, whose blood line expired in Jehoiachin. Joseph was in fact son-in-law of Jacob, but is listed as his son (Matt. 1:16) because he was a legal heir to the throne.[4]

By his marriage to Mary, whose legal and blood lines are also traced back to David, Joseph provides Jesus with his legal right to the throne, while his blood relationship to David is secured through

---

[3]He is called also Jeconiah and Coniah. For the expiry of his line, see Jer. 22:28-30.

[4]Legal sonship is granted to Zerubbabel who is said to be son of Shealtiel. He was in fact the nephew of Shealtiel and his father was Pedaiah, Shealtiel's brother (1 Chron. 3:16-19). Hervey identifies the Hananiah of 1 Chron. 3:19 with Joanan of Luke 3:27, and Hodaviah of 1 Chron. 3:24 with Luke's Joda (3:26) and Matthew's Abihud (1:13). The plausibility of these identifications may be examined by comparing Ezra 3:9, Neh. 11:9, Ezra 2:40 and 1 Chron. 9:7.

Mary. Jesus is indeed heir to the throne of David. He is the one promised in Psalm 132:11: "The Lord has sworn to David a truth from which He will not turn back: 'Of the fruit of your body I will set one upon the throne.'"

Satisfying the Criteria: The Genealogy Problem
Jewish objections run as follows:
Even if Christians could establish that (a) Jesus existed and (b) Jesus was Jewish, they would have trouble proving that (c) Jesus was descended from Judah and Solomon. Both of the detailed genealogies in Matthew and Luke trace Joseph's lineage to King David, albeit differently since Matthew 1:16 says that a fellow named Jacob was Joseph's father, and Luke 3:23 tells us that Joseph was the son of Eli. (It seems that that family had a lot of problems determining fatherhood.) But these genealogies are bogus because Matthew tells us that Joseph wasn't the father of Jesus, but Mary was still a virgin even after he was conceived through the "Holy Spirit"! Matt. 1:18. Since we know that genealogy runs from the father (Num. 1:18; 2:2), Jesus cannot claim descent from Judah.[5]

These problems are solved on the thesis of Lord Hervey's scheme outlined above. The biblical text implies that Mary had children with Joseph, after her firstborn Son was produced by miracle (Matt. 1:25; Mark 6:3).

No Messianic Era?
"Even still, Christians still have a problem because they still can't establish points 3, 4, 5, or 6 above. Saying that those events will happen in a second coming is circular at best and contradicts Revelation 22:20 ('Yes, I am coming quickly')."[6]

The promise of an early return of Jesus to set up the Kingdom is common to all our New Testament writings. The prophets of Israel centuries before even the birth of Jesus declared that the "day of the Lord is at hand" (Isa. 13:6).[7] Jesus takes up the same prophetic

---

[5]Bruce James (Baruch Gershom), "Why Can't a Jew Believe in Jesus?" http://judaism.about.com/od/jewishviewofjesus/a/jesus_onegod.htm
[6]Ibid.
[7]The idea that Jesus predicted his return within one generation is mistaken. His reference to "this generation [which] will not pass until all these things

warning, using exactly the same language, with his urgent call to repentance "because the Kingdom of God is at hand" (Mark 1:15). Since none of us knows how long we may live, the call to repentance in view of the impending Kingdom is always of the greatest urgency. The New Testament speaks also of a long period of time elapsing between the comings of Jesus (Matt. 25:19; Luke 20:9). A universal presentation of the Gospel of the Kingdom is foreseen as a necessary warning before Jesus comes back. "This Gospel of the Kingdom will be preached in the whole world and *then* the end will come" (Matt. 24:14).

Christianity in its biblical form is in no sense inconsistent or contradictory. It presents its Savior as the legal descendant of David through Nathan and Solomon. The end of the line in Matthew is very probably that of Mary whose husband Joseph appears as the legal male descendant. Luke records the ancestors of Joseph, who was "as was supposed" by the public, the father of Jesus (Luke 3:23), from Nathan, son of David (Luke 3:31).

The important point to note in Hervey's work is that Shealtiel and Zerubbabel appear in both lists. This is because the line from Solomon failed in Jehoiachin. He was barred from ever having his descendants as lawful heirs to the Davidic throne. Shealtiel son of Neri (Luke 3:27) was thus moved from the Nathan line to provide a "legal" rather than biological descendant for the Solomon line. It remains entirely plausible that Mary and Joseph were cousins sharing a common grandfather in Matthat (Matthan).[8] Jesus is then related by blood to David through Mary, who is a descendant of David via Nathan. Jacob (Matt. 1:16) would then be the father-in-law of Joseph, the husband of Mary, and the father of Mary.

---

have happened" (Mark 13:30) points to the evil society which will prevail right up to his return. *Genea* has a broader meaning than a period of time limited to 70 years (see for example Luke 16:8, "kind"; cf. Prov. 30:11-14; Ps. 24:6). In Acts 1:7, Jesus could well have said, "I told you I am coming back within a few years," if he had indeed ever said such a thing. Rather he explained that no one knows when the Second Coming will occur (Mark 13:32). "*This* generation" certainly did not point to a future limited period, now nearly two thousand years removed from Jesus.

[8]Smith's *Concise Dictionary of the Bible* notes that Matthan, grandfather of Joseph, is probably identical with Matthat (285, 527).

Jesus fits the identity of the promised son of David. His Father is God and he is the biological son of David (Rom. 1:3). At his first coming he proclaimed the Gospel of the Kingdom and his own Messiahship amidst a turmoil of opposition from established religion. He promised to return to execute that part of the divine program for which he was destined — to rule the world successfully from the restored throne of his father David in the restored Eden of the Kingdom of God (cf. Acts 1:6).[9] The New Testament begins by defining Jesus as the son of David (Matt. 1:1) and ends by praying for the return of that same "descendant of David, the bright morning star" (Rev. 22:16). Belief in Jesus as the Son of God is equivalent to belief in him as the supernaturally begotten descendant of David.

---

[9]For a full account of the Messianic program, see Anthony Buzzard, *Our Fathers Who Aren't in Heaven*, Restoration Fellowship, 1995, and *The Coming Kingdom of the Messiah: A Solution to the Riddle of the New Testament*, Restoration Fellowship, 2002.

Appendix 3
Hebrews 1:10

Hebrews 1:10 says of the Son of God that he laid the foundation of the heaven and the earth.

There are three "proof texts" addressed to the Son in Hebrews 1:8-13. There is no hint in the text that they refer to someone other than the Son. Verse 8 begins, "But of the Son He [God] says..." Then follow three different quotes. The series ends in verse 13 with a proof that Jesus was not an angel: "But to which of the angels did He [God] ever say..." Psalm 110:1 is then quoted as referring to the Son, Jesus.

Much of chapter 1 of Hebrews compares the Son of God with angels, showing that the Son was never an angel and is superior to them. This proves that the Son cannot be God! It is not necessary to prove God superior to the angels. It is obvious. Equally clear is the fact that the Son cannot be an angel or archangel as maintained by Jehovah's Witnesses. Both angels and archangels are angels! Jesus was never an angel, because high priests are "chosen from among men" (Heb. 5:1). And holy angels are immortal (Luke 20:36), which would make the death of Jesus the Son impossible.

What then of Hebrews 1:10? In what sense is the Son the founder of the heavens and earth? How can this be since Jesus nowhere claimed to be the Creator and it was not Jesus, but God who rested on the seventh day (Heb. 4:4)? "God [not Jesus] made them male and female" (Mark 10:6) and "The Lord God [not Jesus] formed man of dust from the ground" (Gen. 2:7). Fifty texts say that God, the Father, created the heavens and the earth. Luke 1:35, Matthew 1:18, 20 and 1 John 5:18 (not KJV) say that the Son *did not exist* until he was created/begotten in Mary. Was Jesus both six months younger than John the Baptist and billions of years older? Was Jesus thirty years old when he began his public ministry and yet really billions plus thirty years old? What part of Jesus was thirty and what part was billions of years old? Jesus cannot be so divided up, split in two. Mary bore a human being. She did not bear an angel. She did not bear GOD. She did not bear "impersonal human nature," as Trinitarian theory says. Mary bore a lineal, biological son of David. Otherwise Jesus does not qualify to be the Messiah.

God cannot be begotten, and the Son of God was begotten. The immortal God (1 Tim. 6:16) cannot die. The Son of God died. God cannot be tempted (James 1:13), yet the Son of God was tempted. Not to observe these category differences is to throw away precious biblical instruction.

Hebrews 1:1-2 says that God did *not* speak through a Son in the Old Testament times. Verse 2 also says that God made the ages *through* Jesus. This could refer to future ages, or it may refer to Jesus being the reason for God's creation of everything. Hebrews 1:5, quoting the prophecy of Psalm 2:7, speaks of the *coming into existence* of Jesus, the Son: *"Today* I have begotten you." The same verse speaks of 2 Samuel 7:14's promise, given a thousand years before Jesus' birth, that God *"will be* a Father to him and he *will be* a Son."* That promise was given to David and it referred to the Messiah who was to come. The beginning of Messiah's existence is the moment when God becomes the Father of the Messiah. Acts 13:33 refers also to the beginning of Jesus' existence, his raising up (not raising up *again* as wrongly translated in the KJV), and verse 34 to his resurrection. The same beginning of the Son is exactly what we find in Luke 1:35 and Matthew 1:20 ("that which is begotten in her is from the holy spirit").

Isaiah 44:24 says that God, unaccompanied, unaided, created the Genesis heavens and earth. He was entirely alone. "Who was with me?" At the time of the Genesis creation there was no Son with Him (cf. Heb. 1:1-2).

God did not speak in a Son until the New Testament. So then, who said, "Let there be light"? It would be a flat contradiction of Hebrews 1:1-2 to say it was the Son. The God of the Old Testament is quite distinct from His unique Son. The latter had his *genesis* in Matthew 1:18 ("the genesis of Jesus was as follows"). The Bible becomes a book of incomprehensible riddles if God can have a Son before He brought him into existence! Luke 1:35 describes how the Son of God *came to exist.* He was begotten. To beget in the Bible and in English is a word which of all words denotes a before and after. Therefore the Son had a beginning. There was a time before he was begotten, before he was. If he already existed, these testimonies in Matthew 1 and Luke 1 are nonsense. Mary bore a human being, not God or an angel. Human mothers bear humans. Mary certainly did not just bear "human nature," and "human nature" as Mary's son would not be the descendant of David and thus not the Messiah.

The notion that the Son of God was in fact God would make a charade out of his whole struggle in obedience to God and on our behalf as Savior and model. The whole point of a High Priest is that he must be "selected from among men" (Heb. 5:1). He is the "man Messiah Jesus" in contrast to his Father (1 Tim. 2:5). The Father in John 17:3 is "the only one who is God." If God is the only one who is God, no one else is God except the Father, which is exactly what Paul declared when rehearsing the creed in 1 Corinthians 8: "There is no God except the one God the Father" (combining vv. 4 and 6).

If the Son were God, there would be two Gods. To call Jesus God and the Father God is not monotheism, however much the label may be applied. The Bible never uses "God" to mean a triune or biune God.

In Hebrews 1:10, there is a complication *due to the fact that the writer quotes Psalm 102 from the Greek version (LXX) and not the Hebrew version.* The LXX has a different sense entirely in Psalm 102:23-25. It introduces thoughts not found in the Hebrew text. The LXX says, "He [God] answered him [the suppliant]…Tell me [God speaking to the suppliant]…Thou, lord [God addressing *someone else* called 'lord']." But the Hebrew text has "He [God] *weakened* me…I [the suppliant] say, 'O my God…'"

Thus the LXX introduces a second lord who is addressed by God: "At the beginning you founded the earth, and the heavens are the work of your hands" (v. 25). The writer to the Hebrews had open before him the LXX and not the Hebrew (rather as today someone might quote the NIV instead of the KJV). F.F. Bruce in the *New International Commentary* on Hebrews explains:

> In the Septuagint text the person to whom these words ["of old you laid the foundation of the earth"] are spoken is addressed explicitly as "Lord"; and it is God who addresses him thus. Whereas in the Hebrew text the suppliant is the speaker from the beginning to the end of the psalm, in the Greek text his prayer comes to an end with v. 22, and the next words read as follows: "He [God] answered him [the suppliant] in the way of his strength: 'Declare to me the shortness of my days: Bring me not up in the midst of my days. Thy [the suppliant's] years are throughout all

generations. Thou, Lord [the suppliant, viewed here as the Messiah by Hebrews], in the beginning didst lay the foundation of the earth.'"[1] This is God's answer to the suppliant; he bids him acknowledge the shortness of God's set time (for the restoration of Jerusalem, as in v. 13) and not summon him [God] to act when that set time has only half expired, while he [God] assures him [the suppliant] that he and his servants' children will be preserved forever...

Bacon suggested that the Hebrew, as well as the Greek, text of this psalm formed a basis for messianic eschatology, especially its reference to the "shortness" of God's days, i.e., of the period destined to elapse before the consummation of his purpose [the arrival of the yet future Messianic Kingdom on earth]; he found here the OT background of Matt. 24:22, Mark 13:20 and *Ep. Barn.* 4.3 ("as Enoch says, 'For to this end the Master [God] has cut short the times and the days, that his Beloved [Jesus] should make haste and come to his inheritance'")...

But to whom (a Christian reader of the Septuagint might well ask) could God speak in words like these? And whom

---

[1] The reason for the completely different translations, between Greek and Hebrew, is the Hebrew vowel points. The sense can be altered if the vowel points are changed, and sometimes it is not clear which of the possible senses is the right one. Thus the Hebrew takes *innah* to mean "He [God] afflicted" (v. 23) but the LXX repoints the same Hebrew consonants as *anah* which means "He [God] answered [him]." So then in the LXX God is answering the one praying and addressing that person as "lord." The LXX adds "lord" in v. 25. Next the Hebrew has *omar eli* ("I say, 'O my God,'" v. 24). But the LXX reads these consonants as *emor elai* ("Say to me," v. 23b; i.e. the person praying is commanded by God to tell God). The idea is that God is asked to cut short the days which have to elapse before the Kingdom comes (cf. Matt. 24:22). Ps. 102 is largely about the age to come and the restoration of Israel in the future Kingdom and so was entirely appropriate as a proof text for Hebrews 1 in regard to what the Son is destined to do in the future, indeed his role in the new, not the Genesis creation. This sense is reversed when it is made to support the unbiblical idea that Jesus was the Creator in Genesis!

would God himself address as "Lord," as the maker [or founder] of earth and heaven?[2]

Reading the LXX the Hebrews writer sees an obvious reference to the new heavens and earth of the *future* Kingdom and he sees God addressing the Messianic Lord in connection with the prophecies of the rest of Psalm 102 which speak of "the generation to come" (v. 18) and of the set time for Yahweh to build up Zion and appear in His glory.

The important article by B.W. Bacon (alluded to by Bruce above) stresses the fact that "The word 'lord' is wholly absent from the Hebrew [and English] text of Psalm 102:25." But it appears in the LXX cited by Hebrews.

[With the translation in the LXX "he answered him"] the whole passage down to the end of the psalm becomes *the answer* of Yahweh to the suppliant who accordingly appears to be addressed as *Kurie* [lord] and creator of heaven and earth...Instead of understanding the verse as a complaint of the psalmist at the shortness of his days which are cut off in the midst, *LXX and the Vulgate understand the utterance to be Yahweh's answer* to the psalmist's plea that he will intervene to save Zion, because "it is time to have pity on her, yea, the set time is come" (v. 13). He is bidden acknowledge (or prescribe?) the shortness of Yahweh's set time, and not to summon him when it is but half expired. On the other hand he [the Messianic lord] is promised that his own endurance shall be perpetual with the children of his servants.[3]

This is exactly the point, and it can only be made clear when we see that 1) the Hebrews writer is reading the LXX, not the Hebrew text, and finding there a wonderful prophecy of the age to come (Kingdom, restoration of Israel) which fits his context exactly and that 2) there is a Messianic Lord addressed *by* Yahweh and invited to initiate a founding of the heaven and earth, the new political order in Palestine, exactly as said in Isaiah 51:16. This is precisely the message the Hebrews writer wants to convey about the superiority of Jesus over angels. Jesus is the founder of that coming new Kingdom

---

[2]F.F. Bruce, *The Epistle to the Hebrews* (*New International Commentary on the New Testament*), Eerdmans, 1990, 62-63.
[3]B.W. Bacon, "Heb. 1:10-12 and the Septuagint Rendering of Ps. 102:23," *Zeitschrift für die Neutestamentliche Wissenschaft* 3, 1902, 280-285.

order. The Hebrews writer in 2:5 tells us expressly that it is about "the inhabited earth of the future that we are speaking."

This is really not so difficult when this difference in the LXX is explained. Both Psalm 102 and Hebrews 2:5 and indeed the whole of Hebrews 1 refer to the new order of things initiated by Jesus and it would not matter whether we think of the new order as initiated at the ascension ("All authority in heaven and earth has been given to me," Matt. 28:18), or at the second coming.

Psalm 102 is all about the coming age of the Kingdom and the restoration of Jerusalem in the millennium (see vv. 13-22). The writer looks forward to the restoration of the city when God appears in His glory (v. 16). The Psalm is written for the "generation to come" (v. 18) and a newly created people of the future Kingdom on earth. Hebrews is speaking not of the Genesis creation but the "economy to come" (2:5).

Isaiah 51:16 confirms this explanation. It speaks of an agent of God in whom God puts His words and whom He uses "to plant the heavens and earth." The *Word Biblical Commentary* says:

> That makes no sense if it refers to the original [Genesis] creation...In the other instances God acts alone, using no agent. Here the one he has hidden in the shadow of his hand is his agent. *Heavens* and *land* here must refer metaphorically to the totality of order in Palestine, *heavens* meaning the broader overarching structure of the Empire, while *land* is the political order in Palestine itself.[4]

Thus both in Psalm 102 (LXX) and in Isaiah the Messiah is the agent whom God will use to establish the new political order of the age to come. Hebrews 1:10 is a prophecy, written in the past tense (as customarily prophecies are), but referring to the "inhabited earth of the future about which we are speaking" (Heb. 2:5). That is the concern in Hebrews 1:10. Jesus is the "father of the age to come" (Isa. 9:6, LXX).

Finally, in Hebrews 9:11 the writer speaks of "the good things to come" as the things "not of *this* creation." By this he means that the things to come are of the new, future creation (see Heb. 2:5). That creation is under way since Jesus was exalted to the right hand of God where he is now co-creator, under the Father, of the new creation, and

---

[4]*Word Biblical Commentary: Isaiah 34-66,* Word Books, 1987, 212.

has "all authority in heaven and earth" (Matt. 28:18). Even the millennial age of the future will be replaced by a further renewed heaven and earth (Rev. 20:11; 21:1).

Once again, eschatology is the great factor in revealing the truth. God has a new creation in Jesus and we are to be new creatures in Christ (2 Cor. 5:17). The world is going to be reborn and it will come under the supervision of Jesus and his followers (Matt. 19:28, etc.) We must resist the temptation to be looking backwards to Genesis when the whole book of Hebrews bids us look forward to the "inhabited earth of the future" (Heb. 2:5). Note that in several places Hebrews speaks of the eternal redemption, inheritance, covenant, judgment, salvation and spirit "of the age [to come]" (*aionios*). *Aionios* refers to the Kingdom age to come and not just to eternity. Christians receive now the "holy spirit of the promise" (Eph. 1:13, NJB).

Bibliography

Alford, Henry. *The Greek Testament*. Rivingtons, 1859.

Allen, Leslie C. *Word Biblical Commentary: Psalms 101-150*. Word Books, 1983.

Anderson, Hugh. *The Gospel of Mark (The New Century Bible Commentary)*. Eerdmans, 1981.

Armstrong, Karen. *The Battle for God*. Ballantine Books, 2001.

————. *The Great Transformation*. Alfred A. Knopf, 2006.

————. *A History of God*. Gramercy Books, 2004.

Armstrong, Richard A. *The Trinity and the Incarnation*. 1904, rep. Kessinger, 2005.

Bacon, B.W. "Heb. 1:10-12 and the Septuagint Rendering of Ps. 102:23." *Zeitschrift für die Neutestamentliche Wissenschaft* 3, 1902. 280-285.

Barclay, William. *The Gospel of Mark*, Westminster John Knox, 1975.

————. *A Spiritual Autobiography*. Eerdmans, 1975.

Barrett, C.K. *Essays on John*. SPCK, 1982.

————. *The Gospel According to St. John*. Westminster, 1978.

Barzun, Jacques. *From Dawn to Decadence*. HarperCollins, 2000.

Bateman, Herbert. "Psalm 110:1 and the New Testament." *Bibliotheca Sacra* 149, Oct-Dec., 1992.

Bauckham, Richard. *God Crucified: Monotheism and Christology in the New Testament*. Eerdmans, 1999.

BeDuhn, Jason David. *Truth in Translation: Accuracy and Bias in English Translations of the New Testament*. University Press of America, 2003.

Beisner, E. Calvin. *God in Three Persons*. Tyndale House, 1984.

Beyschlag, Willibald. *New Testament Theology*, 1896. Rep. Kessinger, 2006.

Bigg, Charles. *1 Peter, International Critical Commentary*. T&T Clark, 1910.

Blanchard, John. *Does God Believe in Atheists?* Evangelical Press, 2000.

Boice, J.M. *The Sovereign God*. Intervarsity Press, 1978.

Borg, Marcus and N.T. Wright. *The Meaning of Jesus: Two Visions*. HarperCollins, 2000.

Bowker, John. *God: A Brief History*. DK Publishers, 2003.

Bowman, J.W. *The Intention of Jesus*. SCM Press, 1945.

Boyd, Gregory A. *The Myth of a Christian Nation: How the Quest for Political Power Is Destroying the Church*. Zondervan, 2005.

————. *Oneness Pentecostals and the Trinity*. Baker, 1992.

Brown, Colin. "Towards a Contemporary Orthodoxy." *Ex Auditu* 7, 1991. 83-100.

Brown, Dan. *The Da Vinci Code*. Doubleday, 2003.

Brown, Harold O.J. *Heresies: Heresy and Orthodoxy in the History of the Church*. Hendrickson, 1998.

Brown, Michael L. *Answering Jewish Objections to Jesus*, Baker Books, 2000, 2:10.

Brown, Raymond. *The Birth of the Messiah*. Geoffrey Chapman, 1977.

———. *The Gospel According to John*. Doubleday, 1970.

———. *An Introduction to New Testament Christology*. Paulist Press, 1994.

———. *Jesus: God and Man*. MacMillan, 1967.

Bruce, F.F. *Canon of Scripture*. Intervarsity Press, 1988.

———. *Commentary on the Greek Text of the Acts of the Apostles*. Eerdmans, 1975.

———. *The Epistle to the Hebrews (New International Commentary on the New Testament)*. Eerdmans, 1990.

———. *The Gospel and Epistles of John*. Eerdmans, 1994.

———. *Jesus: Lord and Savior*. Intervarsity Press, 1986.

Bruce, F.F. et al. *The Origin of the Bible*. Tyndale House, 2003.

Brunner, Emil. *The Christian Doctrine of God*. Lutterworth Press, 1962.

Bultmann, Rudolf. "The Christological Confession of the World Council of Churches." In *Essays Philosophical and Theological*. SCM Press, 1955.

Buswell, J.O. *A Systematic Theology of the Christian Religion*. Zondervan, 1962.

Buzzard, Anthony. *The Coming Kingdom of the Messiah: A Solution to the Riddle of the New Testament*. Restoration Fellowship, 2002.

———. *Our Fathers Who Aren't in Heaven: The Forgotten Christianity of Jesus the Jew*. Restoration Fellowship, 1999.

——— and Charles Hunting. *The Doctrine of the Trinity: Christianity's Self-Inflicted Wound*. University Press of America, 1998.

Cadoux, C.J. *A Pilgrim's Further Progress*. Blackwell, 1943.

Caird, C.B. "The Development of Christ in the New Testament." In *Christ for Us Today*, 66-80. SCM Press, 1968.

Carden, Robert. *One God: The Unfinished Reformation*. Grace Christian Press, 2002.

Carroll, Lewis. *Through the Looking-Glass*. HarperCollins, 2003.

Carson, D.A. *The Gospel According to John*. Apollos, 1991.

———. "The Purpose of the Fourth Gospel: John 20:31 Reconsidered," *Journal of Biblical Literature* 106/4, 1987: 639-651.

Casey, Maurice. *From Jewish Prophet to Gentile God*. Westminster/John Knox Press, 1991.

Cave, Sydney. *The Doctrine of the Person of Christ*. Duckworth, 1962.

Chadwick, Henry. *The Early Church*. Penguin, 1993.

Chapman, Colin. *The Case for Christianity*. Eerdmans, 1981.

Clark, William. *Catechism of the Catholic Church*. German ed. Oldenbourg, 1993.

Cole, R. Alan. *Mark (Tyndale New Testament Commentaries)*. Eerdmans, 1983.

Cooper, David. *The Messiah: His Redemptive Career*. Biblical Research Society, 1938.

Creed, J.M. *The Divinity of Jesus Christ*. Fontana, 1964.

Cullmann, Oscar. *The Christology of the New Testament*. SCM Press, 1963.

Cupitt, Don. *The Debate About Christ*. SCM Press, 1979.

Davies, W.D. *Invitation to the New Testament*. SPCK, 1983.

Demmitt, Greg. "The Christologies of Barton Stone and Alexander Campbell, and their Disagreement Concerning the Preexistence of Christ." *A Journal from the Radical Reformation* 12:2.

Dorner, J.A. *History of the Development of the Doctrine of the Person of Christ*. T & T Clark, 1889.

Dunn, James D.G. *Christology in the Making*. Eerdmans, 1996.

———. *The Theology of Paul the Apostle*. Eerdmans, 1998.

———. *Unity and Diversity in the New Testament*. SCM Press, 1977.

Ehrman, Bart D. *Jesus: Apocalyptic Prophet of the New Millennium*. Oxford University Press, 1999.

———. *The Orthodox Corruption of Scripture*. Oxford University Press, 1993.

———. *Truth and Fiction in The Da Vinci Code*. Oxford University Press, 2004.

Ellens, J. Harold. *The Ancient Library of Alexandria and Early Christian Theological Development*. Institute for Antiquity and Christianity, 1993.

Erickson, Millard J. *God in Three Persons*. Baker Books, 1995.

———. *Making Sense of the Trinity*. Baker Books, 2000.

Evans, Craig A. *Word Biblical Commentary: Mark 8:27-16:20*. Thomas Nelson, 2001.

Eyre, Alan. *The Protesters*. The Christadelphian, 1975.

Farrar, F.W. *The Bible: Its Meaning and Supremacy*. Longmans, Green and Co., 1897.

———. *The Gospel According to St. Luke. The Cambridge Bible for Schools and Colleges*. Cambridge University Press, 1902.

Fitzmyer, Joseph. *A Christological Catechism*. Paulist Press, 1991.

———. *The Gospel According to Luke I-IX (Anchor Bible)*. Doubleday, 1981.

Flusser, David. *Jesus*. Magnes Press, 1997.

Ford, Desmond. *The Abomination of Desolation in Biblical Eschatology*. University Press of America, 1979.

Fortman, Edmund J. *The Triune God*. Baker, 1972.

Franklin, Eric. *Christ the Lord*. Westminster Press, 1975.

Godet, Frederic. *Commentary on St. Luke's Gospel*. I.K. Funk & Co., 1881.

Goguel, Maurice. *Jesus and the Origins of Christianity*. Harper, 1960.

Goldstone, Lawrence and Nancy. *Out of the Flames: The Remarkable Story of a Fearless Scholar, a Fatal Heresy and One of the Rarest Books in the World.* Broadway Books, 2003.

Goppelt, Leonhard. *Theology of the New Testament.* Eerdmans, 1982.

Goudge, H.L. "The Calling of the Jews." In *Judaism and Christianity*, ed. Lev Gillet, J.B. Shears & Sons, 1939. 45-56.

Green, Michael. *Evangelism Now and Then.* Intervarsity Press, 1979.

Grensted, L.W. *The Person of Christ.* Nisbet & Co., 1933.

Grillmeier, Aloys. *Christ in Christian Tradition.* Westminster John Knox Press, 1975.

Grisar, Hartmann. *Martin Luther: His Life and Work.* Newman Press, 1930.

Hamilton, H.F. *The People of God: An Inquiry into Christian Origins.* Oxford University Press, 1912.

Hanson, A.T. *Grace and Truth: A Study in the Doctrine of the Incarnation.* SPCK, 1975.

————. *The Image of the Invisible God.* SCM Press, 1982.

Hanson, R.P.C. "The Doctrine of the Trinity Achieved in 381." *Scottish Journal of Theology* 36, (1983): 41-57.

Harnack, Adolf. *History of Dogma.* Dover Publications, 1961.

————. *Lehrbuch der Dogmengeschichte.* Wissenschaftliche Buchgesellschaft, 1983.

————. *What Is Christianity?* Williams and Norgate, 1901.

Harpur, Tom. *For Christ's Sake.* Beacon Press, 1987.

Harris, Murray J. *Jesus as God: The New Testament Use of Theos in Reference to Jesus.* Baker, 1992.

Harvey, Anthony. *Jesus and the Constraints of History.* Duckworth, 1982.

Hervey, Arthur. *The Genealogies of Our Lord and Savior Jesus Christ.* Macmillan, 1853. Rep. Kessinger, 2007.

Hick, John, ed. *The Myth of God Incarnate.* SCM Press, 1977.

Hiers, Richard. *Jesus and the Future.* John Knox Press, 1981.

Hillar, Marian. *The Case of Michael Servetus (1511-1553): The Turning Point in the Struggle for Freedom of Conscience.* Edwin Mellen Press, 1997.

————, trans. *The Restoration of Christianity: An English Translation of Christianismi Restitutio by Michael Servetus.* Edwin Mellen Press, 2007.

Hinchliff, Peter. "Christology and Tradition." In *God Incarnate, Story and Belief*, ed. A.E. Harvey. SPCK, 1981.

Hodgson, Leonard. *Christian Faith and Practice.* Blackwell, 1952.

————. *The Doctrine of the Trinity.* Charles Scribner's Sons, 1944.

Holt, Brian. *Jesus: God or the Son of God?* TellWay, 2002.

Hort, F.J.A. *Two Dissertations 1876.* rep. Kessinger, 2004.

Hunt, Dave. *The Berean Call.* Dec., 2006.

Hurtado, Larry. *Lord Jesus Christ: Devotion to Jesus in Earliest Christianity.* Eerdmans, 2003.

Jervell, Jacob. *Jesus in the Gospel of John.* Augsburg, 1984.

Jocz, Jacob. *The Jewish People and Jesus Christ.* SPCK, 1962.

Johnson, Luke Timothy. *The Creed: What Christians Believe and Why It Matters.* Doubleday, 2003.

Kaiser, Christopher B. *The Doctrine of God: A Historical Survey.* Crossways, 1982.

Kaylor, R. David. *Jesus, the Prophet: His Vision of the Kingdom of God on Earth.* Westminster John Knox Press, 1994.

Killian, Lindsey and Emily Palik. *The God of the Hebrew Bible and His Relationship to Jesus.* Association for Christian Development, 2005.

Kirkpatrick, A.F. *The Book of Psalms (XC-CL). The Cambridge Bible for Schools and Colleges.* Cambridge University Press, 1901.

Knox, John. *The Humanity and Divinity of Christ.* Cambridge University Press, 1967.

Kopecek, Thomas. *A History of Neo-Arianism.* Philadelphia Patristic Foundation, 1979.

Küng, Hans. *On Being a Christian.* Doubleday, 1976.

Kuschel, Karl-Josef. *Born Before All Time? The Dispute over Christ's Origin.* Crossroad, 1992.

La Due, William J. *The Trinity Guide to the Trinity.* Trinity Press International, 2003.

Ladd, George. *A Theology of the New Testament.* Eerdmans, 1974.

Lampe, Geoffrey. *Explorations in Theology 8.* SCM Press, 1981.

———. *God as Spirit.* SCM Press, 1983.

Lawson, John. *Introduction to Christian Doctrine.* Francis Asbury, 1980.

Lebreton, Jules. *History of the Dogma of the Trinity.* Benziger Brothers, 1939.

Lewis, C.S. *Christian Reflections.* Eerdmans, 1995.

———. *Mere Christianity.* HarperCollins, 2001.

Little, Spence. *The Deity of Christ.* Covenant Publishing, 1956.

Lohse, Bernard. *A Short History of Christian Doctrine.* Fortress Press, 1966.

Loofs, Friedrich. *Leitfaden zum Studium des Dogmengeschichte (Manual for the Study of the History of Dogma),* 1890. Niemeyer Verlag, 1951.

———. *What Is the Truth About Jesus Christ?* Charles Scribner's Sons, 1913.

MacArthur, John. *The MacArthur New Testament Commentary: Hebrews.* Moody, 1983.

MacCulloch, Diarmaid. *The Reformation.* Penguin, 2003.

Mackey, James. *The Christian Experience of God as Trinity.* SCM Press, 1983.

Macleod, Donald. *The Person of Christ.* Intervarsity Press, 1998.

Major, H.D.A., T.W. Manson and C.J. Wright. *The Mission and Message of Jesus*. E.P Dutton and Co., 1953.

Marshall, Howard. *Acts, Tyndale Commentaries*. Eerdmans, 1980.

———. "Jesus as Lord: The Development of the Concept." In *Eschatology and the New Testament*. Hendrickson, 1988.

Martin, Walter. *The Kingdom of the Cults*. Bethany House, 2003.

Matthews, W.R. *God in Christian Experience*, 1930, rep. Kessinger, 2003.

———. *The Problem of Christ in the Twentieth Century*. Oxford University Press, 1950.

McGiffert, Arthur. *A History of Christian Thought*. Charles Scribner's Sons, 1954.

McGrath, Alister. *Christian Theology: An Introduction*. Blackwell, 2006.

Meier, John P. *A Marginal Jew: Rethinking the Historical Jesus*. Doubleday, 1994.

Metzger, Bruce. *A Textual Commentary on the Greek New Testament*. United Bible Societies, 1971.

Meyer, H.A.W. *Commentary on the Gospel of John*. Funk and Wagnall, 1884.

Milton, John. "On the Son of God and the Holy Spirit." Rep. in *A Journal from the Radical Reformation* 5:2 (1996): 44-64.

Moltmann, Jürgen. *The Spirit of Life*. Fortress Press, 1992.

Morey, Robert. *The Trinity: Evidence and Issues*. World Publishing, 1996.

Morgan, Campbell. *Notes on Psalms*. Fleming Revell, 1947.

Morgridge, Charles. *The True Believer's Defence Against Charges Preferred for not Believing in the Deity of Christ*, 1837. Rep. Christian Educational Services, 1994.

Morris, Leon. *The Gospel According to John (New International Commentary on the New Testament)*. Eerdmans, 1995.

Mosheim, J.L. *Institutes of Ecclesiastical History*. Harper, 1839.

Mounce, William D. *Word Biblical Commentary: Pastoral Epistles*. Thomas Nelson, 2000.

Navas, Patrick. *Divine Truth or Human Tradition*. Authorhouse, 2007.

Newman, John Henry. *Select Treatises of St. Athanasius*. James Parker and Co., 1877.

Nicoll, W. Robertson. *Expositor's Greek Commentary*. Eerdmans, 1967.

Nolan, Albert. *Jesus Before Christianity*. Orbis Books, 1992.

Norton, Andrews. *A Statement of Reasons for Not Believing the Doctrines of Trinitarians*, 1833. Rep. University of Michigan, 2005.

O'Carroll, Michael. *Trinitas: A Theological Encyclopedia of the Holy Trinity*. Liturgical Press, 1987.

Oehler, Gustav. *The Theology of the Old Testament*. Funk & Wagnalls, 1893.

Ohlig, Karl-Heinz. *One or Three? From the Father of Jesus to the Trinity.* Peter Lang, 2003.

Olson, Roger and Christopher Hall. *The Trinity*, Eerdmans, 2002.

Olyott, Stuart. *The Three Are One.* Evangelical Press, 1979.

Orr, James. *The Virgin Birth of Christ.* Charles Scribner's Sons, 1912.

Otto, Rudolf. *The Kingdom of God and the Son of Man.* Lutterworth Press, 1943.

Packer, J.I. *Knowing God.* Intervarsity Press, 1998.

Paine, L.L. *A Critical History of the Evolution of Trinitarianism.* Houghton Mifflin and Co., 1900.

Pannenberg, Wolfhart. *Jesus — God and Man.* Westminster Press, 1968.

Parker, Samuel. *A Free and Impartial Censure of the Platonick Philosophie.* Oxford, 1667.

Peake, Arthur S., ed. *Peake's Commentary on the Bible.* Thomas Nelson and Sons, 1919.

Peters, George N.H. *The Theocratic Kingdom of Our Lord and Savior.* rep. Kregel, 1952.

Pettingill, William and R.A. Torrey. *1001 Bible Questions Answered.* Inspirational Press, 1997.

Pfeiffer, Charles F. and Everett F. Harrison, eds. *The Wycliffe Bible Commentary.* Moody Bible Institute, 1990.

Purves, George T. "The Influence of Paganism on Post-Apostolic Christianity." Rep. in *A Journal from the Radical Reformation* 8:2, 1999, 25-50.

Quick, Oliver. *Doctrines of the Creed.* Nisbet, 1938.

Rahner, Karl. *Theological Investigations.* Helicon, 1963.

Rees, Thomas, trans. *The Racovian Catechism*, rep. Christian Educational Services, 1994.

Reim, Günther. "Jesus as God in the Fourth Gospel: The Old Testament Background." *New Testament Studies* 30, 1984: 58-60.

Réville, Albert. *History of the Dogma of the Deity of Jesus Christ.* Philip Green, 1905.

Rhodes, Ron. *The Heart of Christianity.* Harvest House, 1996.

———. *Reasoning from the Scriptures with the Jehovah's Witnesses.* Harvest House, 1993.

Robinson, John A.T. "The Fourth Gospel and the Church's Doctrine of the Trinity." In *Twelve More New Testament Studies.* SCM Press, 1984.

———. *The Human Face of God.* Westminster Press, 1973.

———. *The Priority of John.* SCM Press, 1985.

Rowley, H.H. *The Unity of the Bible.* Living Age, 1957.

Rubenstein, Richard. *When Jesus Became God: The Struggle to Define Christianity During the Last Days of Rome.* Harvest Books, 2000.

Sanders, E.P. and Margaret Davies. *Studying the Synoptic Gospels.* SCM Press, 1991.

Schaeffer, Edith. *Christianity Is Jewish.* Tyndale House, 1975.

Schrodt, Paul. *The Problem of the Beginning of Dogma in Recent Theology.* Peter Lang, 1978.

Schweizer, Eduard. *The Good News According to Mark.* John Knox Press, 1970.

Scott, E.F. *The Kingdom of God in the New Testament.* Macmillan, 1931.

————. *The Spirit in the New Testament.* Hodder, 1923.

Segal, M.H. *A Grammar of Mishnaic Hebrew.* Oxford, 1927.

————. "Mishnaic Hebrew and Its Relation to Biblical Hebrew and to Aramaic." *Jewish Quarterly Review,* Old Series 20 (1908-1909): 647-737.

Showers, Renald and George Zeller. *The Eternal Sonship of Christ: A Timely Defense of This Vital Biblical Doctrine.* Loizeaux Brothers, 1993.

Snaith, Norman. *Distinctive Ideas of the Old Testament.* Epworth Press, 1944.

Snobelen, Stephen. "'God of gods and Lord of lords': The Theology of Isaac Newton's *General Scholium* to the *Principia.*" *Osiris* 16, 2001.

Southern, Randy. *The World's Easiest Guide to Understanding God.* Northfield, 2003.

Spurgeon, Charles. *The Treasury of David.* Baker Book House, 1983.

Stott, John. *The Authentic Jesus.* Marshalls, 1985.

Strobel, Lee. *The Case for Christ.* Zondervan, 1998.

Swindoll, Charles. *Jesus: When God Became a Man.* W Publishing Group, 1993.

Swindoll, Charles and Roy Zuck, eds. *Understanding Christian Theology.* Thomas Nelson, 2003.

Terry, Milton. *Biblical Hermeneutics.* Zondervan, 1975.

Toon, Peter. *Our Triune God.* Victor Books, 1996.

Townsend, James. "C.S. Lewis's Theology: Somewhere Between Ransom and Reepicheep." *Journal of the Grace Evangelical Society* 13:24 (spring 2000).

Trakatellis, Demetrios Christ. *The Pre-Existence of Christ in Justin Martyr: An Exegetical Study with Reference to the Humiliation and Exaltation Christology,* Harvard Dissertation Series 8, Missoula, Montana: Scholars Press, 1976;

Treffry, Richard. *An Inquiry into the Doctrine of the Eternal Sonship of Our Lord Jesus Christ.* John Mason, 1837.

Turner, Nigel. *Grammatical Insights into the New Testament.* T & T Clark, 1965.

Van Buren, Paul. *A Theology of the Jewish-Christian Reality.* Harper & Row, 1983.

Vermes, Geza. *The Changing Faces of Jesus*. Penguin, 2002.

Wachtel, Bill. "Christian Monotheism: Reality or Illusion." *The Restitution Herald*, April, 1985.

Wainwright, Arthur. *The Trinity in the New Testament*. SPCK, 1980.

Walvoord, John and Roy Zuck, eds. *The Bible Knowledge Commentary*. Victor, 1983.

Watts, John D.W. *Word Biblical Commentary: Isaiah 34-66*. Word Books, 1987.

Weigall, Arthur. *The Paganism in Our Christianity*. G.P. Putnam's Sons, 1928.

Wendt, H.H. *System Der Christlichen Lehre*. Vandenhoeck and Ruprecht, 1906.

———. *Teaching of Jesus*. T&T Clark, 1892.

Wenham, Gordon J. *Word Biblical Commentary: Genesis 1-15*. Word Books, 1987.

Werner, Martin. *The Formation of Christian Dogma*, Harper, 1957.

Whale, J.S. *Christian Doctrine*. Cambridge University Press, 1952.

Whidden, Woodrow, Jerry Moon and John Reeve. *The Trinity*. Review and Herald, 2002.

White, James. *The Forgotten Trinity*. Bethany House, 1998.

Whiteley, D. E. H. *The Theology of St. Paul* Blackwell, 1980.

Wilbur, Earl Morse. *Our Unitarian Heritage: An Introduction to the History of the Unitarian Movement*, Beacon Press, 1943.

Wiles, Maurice. *The Remaking of Christian Doctrine*. SCM Press, 1974.

Williams, George Huntston. *The Radical Reformation*. 3rd edition. Truman State University Press, 2000.

Wilson, Ian. *Jesus: The Evidence*. Harper & Row, 1984.

Wilson, John. *Unitarian Principles Confirmed by Trinitarian Testimonies*. Rep. University of Michigan, 2005.

Wilson, Marvin. *Our Father Abraham: Jewish Roots of the Christian Faith*. Eerdmans, 1989.

Wise, Michael, Martin Abegg, Jr., and Edward Cook. *The Dead Sea Scrolls: A New Translation*. HarperCollins, 1999.

Wright, N.T. "The Historical Jesus and Christian Thought." *Sewanee Theological Review* 39, 1996.

———. *Jesus and the Victory of God*. Augsburg Fortress, 1997.

Zahrnt, Heinz. *The Historical Jesus*. Harper & Row, 1963.

Hey, John, 71, 253n1
Hezekiah, 137, 164n39, 168
Hibbert Journal, 340
Hibbert, Robert, 340
Hick, John, 146
Hiers, Richard, 1n2, 61
Hilary of Poitiers, 18, 276
Hillar, Marian, 329n15, 351n25
Hillel, 97
hiphil, 266
Hippolytus, 407n29, 411
ho theos (o theos), 31n2, 32, 103–5,
    109, 140, 359
Hodgson, Leonard, 54–55, 55n37,
    56, 263, 300–301
Holy Spirit
    God distinct from, 104, 109–10,
        112
    status of, 152, 228n4, 233, 272,
        360–63
    words of, 130
    worship not offered to, 139
homoousios, 265n27
Hort, F.J.A., 115n6, 364, 364nn92–
    93
Hosea, 119, 346
Hungarian unitarianism, 329
Hunt, Dave, 223–24
Hunting, Charles F., 404n26, 408
Hurd, Bishop, 72
Hurtado, Larry, 140n34, 166
hypostases (hypostasis), 18, 47, 88,
    110, 320n30, 370, 396
    See also substance
        (philosophical)

idolatry, 51, 84, 90, 100, 109n44,
    196, 253, 296, 337
Ignatius of Antioch, 112, 133, 204–
    5n23, 297, 342n1, 392
Immanuel, 186n74

Incarnation doctrine
    biblical support lacking, 120,
        142, 165, 187, 213–14,
        268n34, 279, 354, 364
    as corruption of the text, 67,
        258n10, 298, 306n7, 324,
        371, 375
    illogicality of, 200–208, 270,
        272, 278, 284, 378
    Jesus viewed as active in Old
        Testament, 126n12, 132–
        35, 334, 376, 409
    mistranslations and, 165, 257–58,
        371
    preexistence problem and, 208,
        220, 223–25, 278, 284,
        306n7, 331
    two natures problem and, 231–
        32, 258
    See also preexistence
        Christology; two natures
        doctrine
inferiorism, 375
Irenaeus, 111–12, 270n1, 342n1,
    401 2n25, 409–11
Irish Unitarianism, 340
Islam, 2n6, 20, 42, 58, 62, 101,
    197, 243, 300, 399
Ithiel, 186n74

Jacob, 416
James (Jesus' half-brother), 49,
    292, 315, 385n1
James, Bruce, 321–22, 413, 415n5
Jeconiah, 414n4
Jefferson, Thomas, 351
Jehoiachin, 414, 416
Jehovah's Witnesses, 18n9, 159,
    207, 334, 418
Jeremiah, 285n77